D1318038

NEW JERSEY POLITICS AND GOVERNMENT

*Politics and Governments
of the American States*

General Editor

John Kincaid
U. S. Advisory Commission on
Intergovernmental Relations
and the University of North Texas

Founding Editor

Daniel Elazar
Temple University

Editorial Advisory Board

Thad L. Beyle
University of North Carolina
at Chapel Hill

Diane D. Blair
University of Arkansas

Ellis Katz
Temple University

Charles Press
Michigan State University

Stephen L. Schechter
Russell Sage College

Published by the University of
Nebraska Press in association
with the Center for the Study
of Federalism.

BARBARA G. SALMORE & STEPHEN A. SALMORE

New Jersey Politics and Government

SUBURBAN POLITICS COMES OF AGE

UNIVERSITY OF NEBRASKA PRESS

LINCOLN & LONDON

© 1993 by the
University of Nebraska Press
All rights reserved
Manufactured in the
United States of America

The paper in this book
meets the minimum requirements of
American National Standard
for Information Sciences—Permanence of
Paper for Printed Library Materials,
ANSI Z39.48-1964.

Library of Congress Cataloging-in-Publication Data
Salmore, Barbara G., 1942–
New Jersey politics and government:
suburban politics comes of age /
Barbara G. Salmore & Stephen A. Salmore.
p.   cm.—(Politics and governments
of the American states)
Includes bibliographical references and index.
ISBN 0-8032-4208-5.—ISBN 0-8032-9195-7 (pbk.)
1. New Jersey—Politics and government.
I. Salmore, Stephen A.
II. Title.   III. Series.
JK3516.s35   1993
320.9749—dc20
93–16836   CIP

For our daughter, Elizabeth Hiatt Salmore,
a native New Jerseyan, suburban through and through.

Other volumes in the series Politics and Governments of the American States:

CONTENTS

TABLES, MAP, AND FIGURES

Acknowledgments

Although, like many residents of New Jersey, both authors of this book were born in New York City, we have been privileged to be observers, participants in, and analysts of New Jersey politics all of our adult lives. Our greatest debts are to the countless members of the state's political community who have observed, participated, and analyzed along with us. Without the insights so many of them shared over so many years, this book truly could not have been written. Some demand special mention.

Former Governor Thomas H. Kean deserves our first thanks. Generous with his time and knowledge, he was also a careful reader of the entire manuscript, without ever trying to influence our assessments in any way.

In the past few years, Stephen Salmore has served as a political consultant to numerous candidates and officeholders. In many of these campaigns, he has worked with Dave Murray, a Republican political consultant, and learned a great deal about campaigns and politics from him. He is also particularly grateful for the learning opportunities provided by Bob Franks as Republican Party Chairman and Chuck Haytaian as leader of the Assembly Republicans.

New Jersey's statehouse press corps is rich in talent. During the time we worked on this volume, we learned a great deal from Michael Aron and Kent Manahan of New Jersey Network, David Blomquist of *The Record* of Hackensack, Jim Goodman of the *Trenton Times*, Sal Paolantonio and Dick Pohlman of the *Philadelphia Inquirer*, Joe Sullivan and Wayne King of the *New York Times*, and David Wald of the *Newark Star–Ledger*.

Democratic consultants Barry Brendel, Don Herche, and Steve DeMicco (a former executive director of the party) have also been our friends and teachers, as has the bipartisan lobbying team of Roger Bodman, Harold Hodes, and Jim McQueeney. It has been a special pleasure to learn from former students who are now active participants in New Jersey politics, especially Drew alumni Lysa Israel and Larry Purpuro, and Rutgers alumni Gregg Edwards, and Bill Palatucci.

A number of experts gave us the benefit of their wisdom on individual subjects and what we wrote about them. We acknowledge with thanks the assistance of Ross Baker, Andrew Baron, Stanley Friedelbaum, Frederick Hermann, Peggi Howard, Perry Leavell, Maureen Moakley, Alan Rosenthal, Douglas Simon, Carl Van Horn, Christy Van Horn, and Paul Wice. Fred Hermann and Steven Kimmelman at the Election Law Enforcement Commission and Ken Dautrich of the *Star–Ledger*/Eagleton Poll responded to special requests for data with graciousness and alacrity. We also benefited from numerous and thoughtful comments by Daniel Elazar, Russell Harrison, and Steven Schechter, who read the manuscript for the University of Nebraska Press.

Aside from the authors, no one spent as much time with this book as did series editor John Kincaid. His painstaking reading and helpful suggestions have affected almost every page and we cannot sufficiently express our gratitude for his contribution. We also thank Neal Riemer for bringing John Kincaid and the authors together.

Grants of released time and administrative support from our employers, Drew University and the Eagleton Institute of Politics at Rutgers University, were essential for getting us started on our work. Paolo Cucchi, Dean of the College of Liberal Arts at Drew, played a particularly significant role in the evolution of this book. Kathleen McFadden prepared the final manuscript and the index with the meticulous care and intelligence that characterizes all of her work. She also has a wonderful sense of humor, which she often needed during this process. Joanne Pfeiffer of the Eagleton Institute was also very helpful in various stages of this project.

The Eagleton Institute has long been a place where practitioners and scholars gather to discuss and study New Jersey politics. In a reflection of this commitment, since 1975 Eagleton has sponsored three edited volumes on New Jersey politics and government. This book can be considered an extension of that series. Since it is not an edited volume, it reflects the opinions and idiosyncrasies of its authors. We are, however, a bipartisan team that moves comfortably between applied and academic studies of state politics.

JOHN KINCAID

Series Preface

The purpose of this series is to provide intelligent and interesting books on the politics and governments of the fifty American states, books that are of value not only to the student of government but also to general citizens who want greater insight into the past and present civic life of their own states and of other states in the federal union. The role of the states in governing America is among the least known of all the 83,217 governments in the United States. The national media focus attention on the federal government in Washington, D.C., and local media focus attention on local government. Meanwhile, except when there is a scandal or a proposed tax increase, the workings of state government remain something of a mystery to many citizens—out of sight, out of mind.

In many respects, however, the states have been, and continue to be, the most important governments in the American political system. They are the main building blocks and chief organizing governments of the whole system. The states are the constituent governments of the federal union, and it is through the states that citizens gain representation in the national government. The national government is one of limited, delegated powers; all other powers are possessed by the states and their citizens. At the same time, the states are the empowering governments for the nation's 83,166 local governments—counties, municipalities, townships, school districts, and special districts. As such, states provide for one of the most essential and ancient elements of freedom and democracy, the right of local self–government.

Although for many citizens the most visible aspects of state government are state universities, some of which are the most prestigious in the world, and state highway patrol officers, with their radar guns and handy ticket books, state governments provide for nearly all domestic public services. Whether elements of those services are enacted or partly funded by the federal government and actually carried out by local governments, it is state government that has the ultimate responsibility for ensuring that Americans are well served by all their governments. In so doing, all the American states are more democratic, more prosperous, and better governed than most of the world's nation–states.

This is a particularly timely period in which to publish a series of books on the governments and politics of each of the fifty states. Once viewed as the "fallen arches" of the federal system, states today are increasingly seen as energetic, innovative, and fiscally responsible. Some states, of course, perform better than others, but that is to be expected in a federal system. Each state is unique in its own right. It is our hope that this series will shed light on the public life of each state and that, taken together, the books will contribute to a better, more informed understanding of the states themselves and of their often pivotal roles in the world's first and oldest continental–sized federal democracy.

DANIEL J. ELAZAR

Introduction

The more than continental stretch of the American domain is given form and character as a federal union of 50 different states whose institutions order the American landscape. The existence of these states made possible the emergence of a continental nation where liberty, not despotism, reigns and self–government is the first principle of order. The great American republic was born in its states as its very name signifies. America's first founding was repeated on thirteen separate occasions over 125 years, from Virginia in 1607 to Georgia in 1732, each giving birth to a colony which became a self–governing commonwealth. Its revolution and second founding was made by those commonwealths, now states, acting in congress, and its constitution was written together and adopted separately. As the American tide rolled westward from the Atlantic coast, it absorbed new territories by organizing 37 more states over the next 169 years.

Most of the American states are larger and better developed than most of the world's nations. Each has its own story, each is a polity with its own uniqueness. The American states exist because they are civil societies. They were first given political form and then acquired their other characteristics. Each has its own constitution, its own political culture, its own relationship to the federal union and to its section. These in turn have given each its own law and history; the longer that history, the more distinctive the state.

It is in and through the states, no less than the nation, that the great themes of American life play themselves out. The advancing frontier and the continuing experience of Americans as a frontier people, the drama of American ethnic blending, the tragedy of slavery and racial discrimination, the political struggle for expanding the right to vote—all found, and find, their expression in the states.

The changing character of government, from an all–embracing concern with every aspect of civil and religious behavior to a limited concern with maintaining law and order to a concern with providing the social benefits of the contemporary welfare state, has been felt in the states even more than in the federal government. Some states began as commonwealths devoted to establishing model societies based on a religiously–informed vision (Massachusetts, Connecticut, Rhode Island). At the other end of the spectrum, Hawaii is a transformed pagan monarchy. At least three were independent for a significant period of time (Hawaii, Texas, and Vermont). Others were created from nothing by hardly more than a stroke of the pen (the Dakotas, Idaho, Nevada). Several are permanently bilingual (California, Louisiana, and New Mexico). Each has its own landscape and geographic configuration which time and history transform into a specific geo–historical location. In short, the diversity of the American people is expressed in no small measure through their states, the politics and government of each of which have their own fascination.

New Jersey Politics and Government is the eighth book in the Center for the Study of federalism and University of Nebraska Press series—State Politics and Government. The aim of the series is to provide books on the politics and government of the individual states of the United States that will appeal to three audiences: political scientists, their students, and the wider public in each state. Each volume in the series examines the specific character of one of the fifty states, looking at the state as a polity—its political culture, traditions and practices, constituencies and interest groups, constitutional and institutional frameworks.

Each book in the series reviews the political development of the state to demonstrate how the state's political institutions and characteristics have evolved from the first settlement to the present, presenting the state in the context of the nation and section of which it is a part, and reviewing the roles and relations of the state vis–a–vis its sister states and the federal government. The state's constitutional history, its traditions of constitution–making and constitutional change, are examined and related to the workings of the state's political institutions and processes. State–local relations, local government, and community politics are studied. Finally, each volume reviews the state's policy concerns and their implementation from the budgetary process to particular substantive policies. Each book concludes by summarizing the principal themes and findings to draw conclusions about the current state of the state, its continuing traditions, and emerging issues. Each volume also contains a bibliographic survey of the existing literature on the state and a guide to the use of that literature and state government documents in learning more about the state and political system.

Although the books in the series are not expected to be uniform, they do focus on the common themes of federalism, constitutionalism, political culture, and the continuing American frontier, to provide a framework within which to consider the institutions, routines, and processes of state government and politics.

Federalism

Both the greatest conflicts of American history and the day–to–day operations of American government are closely intertwined with American federalism—the form of American government (in the eighteenth century sense of the term, which includes both structure and process). American federalism has been characterized by several basic tensions. One is between state sovereignty—the view that in a proper federal system, authority and power over most domestic affairs should be in the hands of the states—and national supremacy—the view that the federal government has a significant role to play in domestic matters affecting the national interest. The other tension is between dual federalism—the idea that a federal system functions best when the federal government and the states function as separately as possible, each in its own sphere—and cooperative federalism—the view that federalism works best when the federal government and the states, while preserving their own institutions, cooperate closely on the implementation of joint or shared programs.

New Jersey's relationship with the federal government has been strongly influenced by the fact that New Jersey was one of the original thirteen states, whose origins antedate the United States of America. While New Jersey was not a conventional colony, having developed in two parts that united under a common government relatively late, still, there was a political tradition in the Garden State—indeed, one of extreme localism, reflecting the state's very localistic origins—that antedated union. Moreover, since active intergovernmental collaboration prior to the twentieth century rested so heavily on the use of the public domain, the kind of tradition of federal involvement which evolved in the public land states did not affect the original thirteen, which did not begin to feel the hand of the federal government in massive ways until the New Deal.

Because New Jersey itself was in many respects a product of the American Revolution, from the first it had a positive attitude toward Union. At the same time, its antebellum Democratic leanings led it to explore the possibility of neutrality or even secession during the civil War and it was the last state above the Mason–Dixon line to eliminate slavery within its boundaries. In the end, however, it participated fully in the struggle for Union, although it must be said without any special distinction.

While never a major beneficiary of federal aid, the state has benefitted from direct federal activities. As the state has acquired more sense of self, its institutions have been mobilized to advance common state interests in Washington. Indeed, the links between members of its Congressional delegation for New Jersey interests considerably preceded popular recognition of those interests. Thus New Jersey is institutionally alert to the realities of American federalism and has done well to mobilize its Congressional delegation and governmental institutions to secure the assistance it has sought from federal sources, even as it has struggled to forge its own identity as a state.

Constitutionalism

Representatives of the Connecticut River valley towns of Hartford, Windsor, and Wethersfield met in January 1639 to draft a constitution. That document, the Fundamental Orders, established a federal union to be known as Connecticut and inaugurated the American practice of constitution–making as a popular act and responsibility, ushering in the era of modern constitutionalism. The American constitutional tradition grows out of the Whig understanding that civil societies are founded by political covenant, entered into by the first founders and reaffirmed by subsequent generations, through which the powers of government are delineated and limited and the rights of the constituting members clearly proclaimed in such a way as to provide moral and practical restraints on governmental institutions. That constitutional tradition was modified by the federalists, who accepted its fundamental principals but strengthened the institutional framework designed to provide energy in government while maintaining the checks and balances they saw as needed to preserve liberty and republican government. At the same time, they turned nonbinding declarations of rights into enforceable constitutional articles.

American state constitutions reflect a melding of these two traditions. Under the U.S. Constitution, each state is free to adopt its own constitution, provided that it establishes a republican form of government. Some states have adopted highly succinct constitutions like the Vermont Constitution of 1793 with 6,600 words that is still in effect with only 52 amendments. Others are just the opposite, for example, Georgia's Ninth Constitution, adopted in 1976, which has 583,000 words.

State constitutions are potentially far more comprehensive than the federal constitution, which is one of limited, delegated powers. Because states are plenary governments, they automatically possess all powers not specifically denied them by the U.S. Constitution or their citizens. Consequently, a state constitution must be explicit about limiting and defining the scope of governmental powers, especially on behalf of individual liberty. So state constitutions normally include an explicit declaration of rights, almost invariably broader than the first ten amendments to the U.S. Constitution.

The detailed specificity of state constitutions affects the way they shape each state's governmental system and patterns of political behavior. Unlike the open–endedness and ambiguity of many portions of the U.S. constitution, which allow for considerable interpretative development, state organs, including state supreme courts, generally hew closely to the letter of their constitutions because they must. This means that formal change of the constitutional document occurs more frequently through constitutional amendment whether initiated by the legislature, special constitutional commissions, constitutional conventions, or direct action by the voters, and, in a number of states, the periodic writing of new constitutions. As a result, state constitutions have come to reflect quite explicitly the changing conceptions of government which have developed over the course of American history.

Overall, six different state constitutional patterns have developed. One is the commonwealth pattern, developed in New England, which emphasizes Whig ideas of the constitution as a philosophic document designed first and foremost to set a direction for civil society and to express and institutionalize a theory of republican government. A second is the constitutional pattern of the commercial republic. The constitutions fitting this pattern reflect a series of compromises required by the conflict of many strong ethnic groups and commercial interests generated by the flow of heterogeneous streams of migrants into particular states and the early development of large commercial and industrial cities in those states.

The third is that found in the South and which can be described as the southern contractual pattern. Southern state constitutions are used as instruments to set explicit terms governing the relationship between polity and society, such as those which protected slavery or racial segregation, or those which sought to diffuse the formal allocation of authority in order to accommodate the swings between oligarchy and factionalism characteristic of southern state politics. Of all the southern states, only Louisiana stands somewhat outside this pattern, since its legal system was founded on the French civil code. Its constitutions have been codes—long, highly–explicit documents that form a pattern in and of themselves.

A fifth pattern is that found frequently in the less populated states of the Far West, where the state constitution is first and foremost a frame of government explicitly reflecting the republican and democratic principles dominant in the nation in the late nineteenth century, but emphasizing the structure of state government and the distribution of powers within that structure in a direct, business–like manner. Finally, the two newest states, Alaska and Hawaii, have adopted constitutions following the managerial pattern developed and promoted by twentieth century constitutional reform movements in the United States. Those constitutions are characterized by conciseness, broad grants of power to the executive branch, and relatively few structural restrictions on the legislature. They emphasize natural resource conservation and social legislation.

What is particularly noteworthy about New Jersey's constitutional history is its earlier emphasis on keeping state government weak and maximizing local self–government and control, followed by a constitutional reversal in 1947 and subsequently. New Jersey's present constitution was the first of the post–World War II state constitutions and was long considered a model for other states to emulate. As such, it has been one of the most influential state constitutions, comparable to the great Revolutionary Era constitutions of Virginia and Massachusetts. State constitution makers followed the New Jersey model for a full generation after its adoption in the Garden State.

The New Jersey Constitution of 1947 was the first to be structured around twentieth century managerial ideas. As such it brought a new thrust in structure in American constitutional development, one which spread as rapidly as the public would allow it to spread to become the dominant model for postwar advocates of constitutional change until it reached its apotheosis in Alaska and Hawaii. Since the 1970s, it has run into a series of challenges regarding the relationship between managerialism and democratic self–government. In the meantime, in New Jersey, that constitution made possible the development of strong state government and much internal centralization, although it took a full generation before the habits and traditions of localism were overcome. The New Jersey constitution also provided for a strong and constitutionally active state supreme court which also has had great impact on state constitutional law and on the role of the state courts in developing constitutional law in the United States.

The Continuing American Frontier

For Americans, the very word frontier conjures up the images of the rural–land frontier of yesteryear—of explorers and mountain men, of cowboys and Indians, of brave pioneers pushing their way west in the face of natural obstacles. Later, Americans' picture of the frontier was expanded to include the inventors, the railroad builders, and the captains of industry who created the urban–industrial frontier. Recently television has begun to celebrate the entrepreneurial ventures of the automobile and oil industries, portraying the magnates of those industries and their families in the same larger–than–life frame as once was done for the heroes of that first frontier.

As is so often the case, the media responsible for determining and catering to popular taste tell us a great deal about ourselves. The United States was founded with a rural–land frontier that persisted until World War I, more or less, spreading farms, ranches, mines, and towns across the land. Early in the nineteenth century, the rural–land frontier generated the urban frontier based on industrial development. The creation of new wealth through industrialization transformed cities from mere regional service centers into generators of wealth in their own right. That frontier persisted for more than 100 years as a major force in American society as a whole and perhaps another 60 years as a major force in various parts of the country. The population movements and attendant growth on the urban–industrial frontier brought about the effective settlement of the United States in freestanding cities from coast to coast.

Between the world wars, the urban–industrial frontier gave birth in turn to a third frontier stage, one based on the new technologies of electronic communications, the internal combustion engine, the airplane, synthetics, and petro–chemicals. These new technologies transformed every aspect of life and turned urbanization into metropolitanization. This third frontier stage generated a third settlement of the United States, this time in metropolitan regions from coast to coast, involving a mass migration of tens of millions of Americans in search of opportunity on the suburban frontier.

In the 1970s, the first, post–World War II generation came to a close. Many Americans were speaking of the "limits of growth." Yet despite that anti–frontier rhetoric, there was every sign that a fourth frontier stage was beginning in the form of the rurban or citybelt–cybernetic, frontier generated by the metropolitan–technological frontier just as the latter had been generated by its predecessor.

The rurban–cybernetic frontier first emerged in the Northeast, as did its predecessors, as the Atlantic Coast metropolitan regions merged into one another to form a six–hundred–mile–long megalopolis (the usage is Jean Gottman's)—a matrix of urban and suburban settlements in which the older central cities came to yield importance if not prominence to smaller ones. It was a sign of the times that the computer was conceived at MIT in Cambridge and developed at IBM in White Plains, two medium–sized cities in the megalopolis that have become special centers in their own right. This in itself is a reflection of the two primary characteristics of the new frontier. The new locus of settlement is in medium–sized and small cities and in the rural interstices of the megalopolis.

The spreading use of computer technology is the most direct manifestation of the cybernetic tools that make such citybelts possible. In 1979 the newspapers in the Northeast published frequent reports of the revival of the small cities of the first industrial revolution, particularly in New England, as the new frontier engulfed them. Countrywide, the media focused on the shifting of population growth into rural areas. Both phenomena are as much a product of direct dialing as they are of the older American longing for small town or country living. Both reflect the urbanization of the American way of life no matter what lifestyle is practiced, or where.

Although the Northeast was first, the new rurban–cybernetic frontier, like its predecessors, is finding its true form in the South and West, where these citybelt matrices are not being built on the collapse of earlier forms, but are developing as an original form. The present sunbelt frontier—strung out along the Gulf Coast, the southwestern desert, and the fringes of the California mountains—is classically megalopolitan in citybelt form and cybernetic with its aerospace–related industries and sunbelt living made possible by air conditioning and the new telecommunications.

The continuing American frontier has all the characteristics of a chain reaction. In a land of great opportunity, each frontier, once opened, has generated its successor and, in turn, has been replaced by it. Each frontier has created a new America with new opportunities, new patterns of settlement, new occupations, new challenges, and new problems. As a result, the central political problem of growth is not simply how to handle the physical changes brought by each frontier, real as they are. It is how to accommodate newness, population turnover, and transience as a way of life. That is the American frontier situation.

Since the opening of the metropolitan–technological frontier, New Jersey has been on its cutting edge. Indeed, as that frontier became pervasive and transformed American society, it also made New Jersey the heart of the American "Main Street," replacing Manhattan in that role. There is an intricate relationship here which the book brings to our attention, as what Samuel Lubell referred to as "the Old Tenement Trail" led out from New York City and Philadelphia.

The spread of suburban settlement through most of the Garden State strengthened New Jersey's already strong localism and further weakened its sense of self as transplanted New Yorkers and Pennsylvanians looking for more advantageous places of residence continued to see themselves as New Yorkers or Philadelphians. However, as metropolitanization spread throughout the state, a new generation was born and raised in the state, the children of those first settlers, those first metropolitan frontiersmen. As that new generation came of age, it was responsible for the awakening of New Jersey's sense of self, for the strengthening of state government to provide services that local government was perceived as not being able to provide or to provide well, and in general responding to what has been considered a more progressive attitude toward the state's needs.

At the same time, New Jersey passed through its original suburban frontier stage, when the new settlers continued to commute to work in the neighboring states. Then business and industrial enterprises came into the state to be where the people who were employed in them were. As on earlier frontiers, the people were the pioneers and only after they had settled in were more cautious, established enterprises attracted to follow them. Their coming, in turn, gave the state more of a "Main Street" character, even to the point where national conventions began to be held in hotels along the New Jersey Turnpike rather than in crowded, expensive New York City. Indeed, the construction of that turnpike was a major turning point—the buckle in the megalopolitan belt that stretched from southern New Hampshire to northern Virginia—it immediately became, in fact, the Main Street, stimulating industrial, commercial and recreational growth along its corridor.

While New Jersey's first suburban settlements simply extended the circles around New York and Philadelphia, as suburbanization continued New Jersey passed easily into the rurban–cybernetic frontier. Most of its second phase "suburban" settlement was really in the form of rurban citybelts—people who worked in the state and did not see their towns attached to either of the traditional central cities or to any new ones. Thus New Jersey was among the first states to move onto the rurban–cybernetic frontier. This was reflected practically and symbolically in the election of Frank Lautenberg to the U.S. Senate. Lautenberg had made his fortune building up one of the first great data processing firms in the United States and was a perfect symbol of the new New Jersey. New Jersey promises to continue as one major expression of the rurban–cybernetic frontier, at least through this generation, consolidating a favorable self–image, activist state government, and its new place in American society and economy, all because of these frontiers.

The Persistence of Sectionalism

Sectionalism—the expression of social, economic, and especially political differences along geographic lines—is part and parcel of american political life. The more or less permanent political ties that link groups of contiguous states together as sections reflect the ways in which local conditions and differences in political culture modify the impact of the frontier. This overall sectional pattern reflects the interaction of the three basic factors. The original sections were produced by the variations in the impact of the rural–land frontier on different geographic segments of the country. They, in turn, have been modified by the pressures generated by the first and subsequent frontier stages. As a result, sectionalism is not the same as regionalism. The latter is essentially a phenomenon—often transient—that brings adjacent state, substate, or interstate areas together because of immediate and specific common interests. The sections are not homogeneous socioeconomic units sharing a common character across state lines, but complex entities combining highly diverse states and communities with common political interests that generally complement one another socially and economically.

For example, New England is a section bound by the tightest of social and historical ties even though the differences between the states of lower and upper New England are quite noticeable even to the casual observer. The six New England states consciously seek to cooperate with one another in numerous ways. Their cooperative efforts have been sufficiently institutionalized to create a veritable confederation within the larger American Union. It is through such acts of political will that sectionalism best manifests itself.

Intrasectional conflicts often exist but they do not detract from the long–term sectional community of interest. More important for our purposes, certain common sectional bonds give the states of each section a special relationship to national politics. This is particularly true in connection with those specific political issues that are of sectional importance, such as the race issue in the South, the problems of the megalopolis in the Northeast, and the problems of agriculture and agribusiness in the Northwest.

The nation's sectional alignments are rooted in the three great historical, cultural, and economic spheres into which the country is divided: the greater Northeast, the greater South, and the greater West. Following state lines, the greater Northeast includes all those states north of the Ohio and Potomac rivers and east of Lake Michigan. The greater South includes the states below that line but east of the Mississippi plus Missouri, Arkansas, Louisiana, Oklahoma, and Texas. All the rest of the states compose the greater West. Within that framework, there are eight sections: New England, Middle Atlantic, Near West, Upper South, Lower South, Western South, Northwest, and Far West.

From the New Deal years through the 1960s, Americans' understanding of sectionalism was submerged by their concern with urban–oriented socioeconomic categories, such as the struggle between labor and management or between the haves and have–nots in the big cities. Even the racial issue, once the hallmark of the greater South, began to be perceived in nonsectional terms as a result of black immigration northward. This is not to say that sectionalism ceased to exist as a vital force, only that it was little noted in those years.

Beginning in the 1970s, however, there was a resurgence of sectional feeling as economic social cleavages increasingly came to follow sectional lines. The sunbelt–frostbelt contribution is the prime example of this new sectionalism. "Sunbelt" is the new code word for the Lower South, Western South, and Far West; "frostbelt" is the code word for the New England, Middle Atlantic, and Great Lakes (Near Western) states. Sectionalism promises to be a major force in national politics, closely linked to the rurban–cybernetic frontier.

A perennial problem of the states, hardly less important than that of direct federal–state relationships, is how to bend sectional and regional demands to fit their own needs for self–maintenance as political systems. One of the ways in which the states are able to overcome this problem is through the use of their formal political institutions, since no problems can be handled governmentally without making use of those formal institutions.

Some would argue that the use of formal political institutions to deflect sectional patterns on behalf of the states is "artificial" interference with the "natural" flow of the nation's social and economic system. Partisans of the states would respond not only by questioning the naturalness of a socioeconomic system that was created by people who migrated freely across the landscape as individuals in search of opportunity, but by arguing that the history of civilization is the record of man's efforts to harness his environment by means of his inventions, all artificial in the literal and real sense of the term. It need not be pointed out that political institutions are among the foremost of those inventions.

New Jersey is one of the Middle Atlantic states, the section that is least sectionally conscious while being extraordinarily well–defined as a section. Because the Middle Atlantic states have been at the very heart of the American enterprise at least since the mid–nineteenth century when they replaced New England in that capacity, Middle Atlantic states have tended to identify their aspirations and beliefs with those of the United States as a whole, to the discomfort and even anger of Americans from other sections. Because of that easy if mistaken self–perception, Middle Atlantic staters themselves have not thought in terms of sectional differences, being too unaware of the rest of the country to be conscious of them or at least of their legitimacy.

As New Jersey inherits New York's mantle as the Empire State, it also must share that mantle with other states such as California, Texas, and Florida. This, indeed may lead to the fostering of a sense of sectional identity. It certainly has led to a sectional reality which in fact was always present.

The Vital Role of Political Culture

The United States as a whole shares a general political culture that is rooted in two contrasting conceptions of the American political order that can be traced back to the earliest settlement of the country. In the first, the polity is conceived as a marketplace in which the primary public relationships are products of bargaining among individuals and groups acting out of self–interest. In the second, the political order is conceived to be a commonwealth—a polity in which the whole people have an undivided interest—in which the citizens cooperate in an effort to create and maintain the best government in order to implement certain shared moral principles. These two conceptions have exercised an influence on government and politics throughout American history, sometimes in conflict and sometimes complementing each other.

The national political culture is a synthesis of three major political subcultures. All three are of nationwide proportions, having spread, in the course of time, from coast to coast. At the same time each subculture is strongly tied to specific sections of the country, reflecting the streams and currents of migration that have carried people of different origins and backgrounds across the continent in more or less orderly patterns. Considering their central characteristics, the three may be called *individualistic, moralistic*, and *traditionalistic*. Each of the three reflects its own particular synthesis of the marketplace and the commonwealth.

The *individualistic political culture* emphasized the democratic order as a marketplace in which government is instituted for strictly utilitarian reasons, to handle those functions demanded by the people it is created to serve. Beyond the commitment to an open market, a government need not have any direct concern with questions of the good society, except insofar as it may be used to advance some common view formulated outside the political arena just as it serves other functions. Since the individualistic political culture emphasized the centrality of private concerns, it places a premium on limiting community intervention—whether governmental or nongovernmental—into private activities to the minimum necessary to keep the marketplace in proper working order.

The character of political participation in the individualistic political culture reflects this outlook. Politics is just another means by which individuals may improve themselves socially and economically. In this sense politics is a business like any other, competing for talent and offering rewards to those who take it up as a career. Those individuals who choose political careers may rise by providing the governmental services demanded of them and, in return, may expect to be adequately compensated for their efforts. Interpretations of officeholders' obligations under this arrangement vary. Where the norms are high, such people are expected to provide high–quality public services in return for appropriate rewards. In other cases, an officeholder's primary responsibility is to serve himself and those who have supported him directly, favoring them even at the expense of the public.

Political life within the individualistic political culture is based on a system of mutual obligations rooted in personal relationships. In the United States, political parties serve as the vehicles for maintaining the obligational network. Party regularity is indispensable in the individualistic political culture because it is the means for coordinating individual enterprise in the political arena and is the one way of preventing individualism in politics from running wild. Such a political culture encourages the maintenance of a party system that is competitive, but not overly so, in the pursuit of office.

Since the individualistic political culture eschews ideological concerns in its business conception of politics, both politicians and citizens look upon political activity as a specialized one, essentially the province of professionals, of minimum and passing concern to the lay public, and with no place for amateurs to play an active role. Furthermore, there is a strong tendency among the public to believe that politics is a dirty—if necessary—business, better left to those who are willing to soil themselves by engaging in it. In practice, then, where the individualistic political culture is dominant, there is likely to be an easy attitude toward the limits of the professionals' perquisites. Since a fair amount of corruption is expected in the normal course of things, there is relatively little popular excitement when any is found, unless it is of an extraordinary character. It is as if the public is willing to pay a surcharge for services rendered and rebels only when it feels the surcharge has become too heavy. (Of course the judgments as to what is normal and what is extraordinary are themselves subjective and culturally conditioned.)

Public officials, committed to giving the public what it wants, normally will initiate new programs only when they perceive an overwhelming public demand for them to act. The individualistic political culture is ambivalent about the place of bureaucracy in the political order. Bureaucratic methods of operation fly in the face of the favor system, yet organizational efficiency can be used by those seeking to master the market.

To the extent that the marketplace provides the model for public relationships in American civil society, all Americans share some of the attitudes that are of first importance in the individualistic political culture. At the same time, substantial segments of the American people operate politically within the framework of two political cultures.

New Jersey is one of the strongest bastions of the individualistic political culture among American states. While from earliest times when Puritans and New England Yankees settled in northeastern New Jersey and Southerners in south Jersey, that part of the state geographically below the Mason–Dixon line, there have been pockets of moralistic and traditionalistic political culture, the overwhelmingly predominant culture in the state has been individualistic. That political culture was further strengthened by the arrival of the mass immigration from Ireland, southern and eastern Europe, and later Afro–Americans from the South, Hispanics, and Asians, all of whom fit in neatly to the individualistic political culture.

The sources of that political culture, of course, were in the original settlers from New York and Pennsylvania. The patterns they established were merely adapted later on and continued to be dominant during the years of the mass immigration. In many places, New Jersey's individualistic political culture is expressed at its lowest level through urban political machines, boss rule, and extensive corruption. The passage of time and the Americanization of immigrants has weakened if not eliminated boss rule in most parts of the state.

The individualistic political culture should not be perceived only in its lowest forms. The people living in the state's loveliest suburban communities for the most part share that same culture, only in more acceptable ways. Indeed, standards of political behavior have been rising throughout the state as they have been rising throughout the United States, especially in the areas of governmental honesty and efficiency and the definition of what constitutes scandalous behavior, but this has not changed the individualistic character of New Jersey's political culture which is deeply embedded in every part of the state.

Summing Up

New Jersey, long the butt of comedians' jokes and a public attitude which the closer one was to the state, the more one saw it as "nowhere," is now emerging from a long period of being an appendage to New York City and Philadelphia and the victim of their scorn, to become a powerful and important state in its own right. One of the ten largest states in the Union in terms of its population, increasingly it is the Main Street of the Northeast, which still means in many respects being the Main Street of the country as a whole or certainly one of them. Today its citizens are beginning to understand New Jersey's new reality, to appreciate it, and to develop a greater sense of pride in their state. This, in turn, has led state government to become a much greater factor in the lives of its citizens, a transformation made possible by New Jersey's influential postwar constitution, which has not only put its stamp on the Garden State but has influenced many others as well.

All of this has been brought about by New Jersey's position on the continuing American frontier, its place on the cutting edge first of the metropolitan–technological and then the rurban–cybernetic frontier stages. New Jersey promises to remain a frontier state, at least into the next generation, which will only enhance the trends discussed here. Thus New Jersey is likely to become much more visible as a state and as a place to its own residents and to the United States as a whole.

NEW JERSEY POLITICS AND GOVERNMENT

CHAPTER ONE

Prologue

Countin' the cars on the New Jersey Turnpike....they've all gone to look for America....

—Paul Simon[1]

In 1923, Ernest Gruening edited a delightful guide for armchair travelers, *These United States*. Edmund Wilson, Jr.—distinguished literary critic and native of Red Bank, New Jersey—contributed the essay entitled "New Jersey: The Slave of Two Cities." He offered the following thesis: "It is precisely its suburban function which gives New Jersey such character as it has. It is precisely a place where people do not live to develop a society of their own but where they merely pass or sojourn on their way to do something else. Its distinction among eastern states is that it has attained no independent life, that it is the doormat, the servant, and the picnic–ground of the social organisms that drain it." [2]

In 1971, Gruening wrote a new preface to a reprint of his 1923 work. It was important, he told a new generation of readers, to know "a different America." He offered but one caveat: "I doubt that Edmund Wilson, Jr....would find much to change in his 'New Jersey, the Slave of Two Cities.'"[3]

Gruening reflected a common view of New Jersey, but one already becoming out–of–date. Twenty years later, it is almost entirely wrong. It is not that New Jersey is no longer a suburban state. It is that the United States has become a suburban society, and in so becoming, has enabled New Jersey to develop a society of its own.

A current New Jersey resident, Yogi Berra, once remarked, "You can observe a lot just by looking." New Jersey looks different than it did in 1923, or even in 1971. To be sure, there are still pockets of "the cramped smudgy life of industry" Wilson described. Parts of the southern Pinelands are still "desolate wilderness." And certainly a journey to Princeton still means that "one seems to have at last reached a place where no one cares what is happening in New York."[4] Yet old Paterson silk mills are now artists' lofts, retirement communities encroach on the Pinelands, and many New Jerseyans all over the state no longer care what is happening in New York.

Today, the symbols of change are everywhere. Among the places George Washington slept is eighteenth–century Liberty Hall, ancestral home of William Livingston, New Jersey's first governor, and of Thomas Kean, its 48th governor. Liberty Hall will soon become a museum, its grounds given over to luxury apartments and offices. The stately Chalfonte–Haddon Hall Hotel "on the boardwalk in Atlantic City" has become the Resorts International Casino Hotel, the first legal gambling salon on the East Coast. A Newark synagogue, built at the turn of the century, is now a Pentecostal church. Hoboken's Irish saloons have been replaced by restaurants serving young professionals who have renovated the city's brownstones and commute to Wall Street. A glittering sports and entertainment complex is built atop the northern Meadowlands' swampy landfills.

A traveler seeking contemporary New Jersey should visit Toms River, seat of Ocean County.[5] In 1950, the population of Toms River was 7,000, and Ocean County, with 50,000 people, was the second poorest and second most sparsely populated county in the state. In 1955, the Garden State Parkway opened, and "for the first time, everybody in North Jersey could get to the shore without spending half the day in the car. And everybody did."[6] Some stayed to buy the development houses being built a few miles away in Toms River. By 1970, its population had grown to 43,000, Ocean County's to over 200,000, and the huge Ocean County Mall opened in 1972. Echoing Edmund Wilson, Joe McGinniss wrote: "A suburb, in fact, was what Toms River was becoming. The only peculiar thing was that there wasn't any 'urb.' Toms River was 60 miles from anywhere, not part of the social or cultural or economic orbit of either New York or Philadelphia. It was a town with no connection to anyplace else."[7]

On this last point, McGinniss was wrong. Toms River was connected to all the other rapidly suburbanizing places in Ocean County. During the 1970s, as McGinniss himself noted, Ocean County's population grew at the rate of one person every four minutes. Only Orange County, California, grew as fast. By 1990, there were 76,000 people in Toms River, and 437,000 in Ocean County. During the 1980s, Ocean was the fastest growing county in the state. In the state, as in the nation, the population was moving south and west.

Many of Ocean County's new residents left New Jersey's cities. The "Big Six"—Camden, Elizabeth, Jersey City, Newark, Paterson, and Trenton—were home to one in four New Jerseyans in 1950, but only one in 12 in 1990. Newark's losses were especially dramatic. The nation's sixteenth largest city in 1905, Newark's population fell by 16 percent during the 1980s, dropping below 300,000 for the first time in the century. Superhighways, office parks, single–family homes, and shopping malls had created Toms River. The nation's Newarks were "places built for another kind of world."[8]

Overall, New Jersey's population during the 1980s grew by about 5 percent, to 7.8 million, but the state's minority population increased by over 30 percent. The sort of middle–class whites who were leaving the cities and moving to Toms River made up less than 1 percent of the net increase. It was, rather, African Americans, Hispanics, Pacific Islanders, Indians, other Asians, West Indians, and a dozen other nationality and ethnic groups that helped New Jersey grow.

African Americans, almost a million strong, comprised New Jersey's largest minority group, but the 12 percent increase in their numbers during the 1980s was overshadowed by spectacular increases in other groups. The Hispanic population grew by a half, to 740,000. Proportionally, New Jerseyans of Asian extraction were the fastest–growing group, increasing by over 160 percent to about 273,000 in 1990.

These new arrivals allowed some cities, such as Camden and Elizabeth, to hold their own during the 1980s, but New Jersey's minority citizens were moving to the suburbs too. Bergen—composed entirely of 70 suburban towns—narrowly overtook Essex—dominated by Newark—as the state's most popu-lous county. Bergen actually lost 20,000 people between 1980 and 1990, but its 54,000 Asian residents, the heaviest concentration in any county, helped compensate for the outflow. The newest of the shopping malls dotting Bergen was Edgewater's Yaohan Plaza, where the video rental shop specialized in Japanese–language films. It was the first large Asian specialty mall outside California.

Many of Bergen's Asians and other émigrés were professionals who worked for 1,400 foreign subsidiaries doing business in the state. Concentrated in high–technology fields like consumer electronics and pharmaceuticals, these firms were the leading edge of an economic transformation that began in the 1970s and gained steam in the 1980s. Between 1983 and 1987, New Jersey created more than 100,000 jobs per year, more than twice the state's long–term average. In 1950, New Jersey's jobs were evenly divided between the industrial and service sectors. By 1990, the service sector dominated by a three–to–one ratio.

North Jersey offered half as many jobs as New York City did in 1950, but by 1990 it was closing in on parity. The new white–collar occupations were higher paying than the factory jobs they replaced, and this was soon reflected in New

Jerseyans' income. Per capita income growth tracked the national average through the 1960s and 1970s but exceeded it substantially during the 1980s. It made New Jersey's always relatively well–off population on average the second wealthiest in the nation. There were new demands on their personal income, however. Median single–family home prices in the state, which were at the national average in 1970, were a third higher than the average in 1990.

Growth and development had other costs, too. New Jersey's students scored twelfth highest, and highest among large states, on 1990's national mathematics tests—skills critical to jobs in the state's new high–tech economy. But the range of scores was among the widest in the nation. Students in urban schools were most likely to do poorly. Yet Paterson textile mills, Jersey City railyards, Trenton pottery factories, and Camden assembly plants that might once have employed the less educated were almost all gone. Commuters to suburban office parks suffered some of the worst traffic congestion anywhere. Combating air and water pollution and disposing of the state's garbage as open space dwindled became leading public questions. As they entered the 1990s, New Jerseyans recognized that growth at the pace of the 1980s was unlikely, and might "even be undesirable in view of the environmental consequences."[9]

POLITICS AND GOVERNMENT IN THE "NEW" NEW JERSEY

The issues that drive New Jersey politics today, and that have transformed its politics and government, grow directly out of the population dispersion that began after World War II, but reached dramatic new heights during the 1980s. More than any other populous American state, New Jersey politics then and now has been dominated by those generally unfriendly to cities—rural interests before 1970 and suburban ones thereafter. Aside from that, state politics and government have been almost entirely reshaped since 1970, and that transformation is at the center of virtually every chapter of this book.

Chapters 2 and 3 offer an overview of New Jersey's political history and the forces that shaped it. Edmund Wilson's biting portrait describes a conservative, parochial state that seemed to have no function but to serve New York City and Philadelphia. What identity New Jersey citizens had was with their own towns—more of them per square mile than anywhere else in the country. This was a potent recipe for strong home rule, strong local political machines, and weak statewide institutions. This New Jersey grew more slowly than its neighbors and resisted social and political innovation.

The catalysts for the changes that became widely apparent in the 1970s and dominant in the 1980s were largely external—a postwar population boom fueled by federal highway and housing policies and U.S. Supreme Court decisions ending legislative malapportionment. These forces destroyed the "unholy alliance" of Republican rural–based machines and Democratic urban ones that dominated New Jersey politics for 150 years. The partners' only common interest was maintaining each's individual power base. As they disappeared, a new political system could emerge.

Chapters 4 and 5 describe the volatile, candidate–centered elections that replaced party–dominated contests and were increasingly decided by politically independent suburbanites. Chapter 6 details an interest–group universe that changed correspondingly as new interests appeared along with the scattering population and increasingly complex economy, and were no longer brokered or aggregated by political parties.

A state's constitution sets out its government's structures, limits, powers, and also its aspirations. New Jersey's first two constitutions, of 1776 and 1844, were, like its citizens, already somewhat behind the times when they were promulgated. In contrast, the current constitution of 1947 anticipated the future. It was written by New Jersey's "moralistic" reform element, never dominant but always present. New Jersey's three constitutions and the political forces that produced them are described in chapter 7.

After actively fighting it for years, the political traditionalists agreed to the 1947 constitutional convention because, in line with their usual mode of thinking, they believed they could extract parochial advantage as the price of cooperation. The urban Democrats indeed got concessions on local railroad taxes, and the southern Republicans retained control of the state Agriculture Department, and both won continuation of the malapportioned state senate that was the foundation of their power. The traditionalists won their battles but did not realize they had lost the war.

Out of the constitutional convention emerged state executive and judicial institutions that were among the most powerful and far–reaching in the nation. Within twenty years, the federal courts would dismantle the traditionalists' base in the legislature. Railroads and agriculture became afterthoughts in the wake of the developers and the superhighways. Suburbanization moved people out of the cities and transformed the countryside, and both elements of the uneasy alliance thus lost power in the voting booth.

For a brief period, the legislature, which had ruled politics and policy since New Jersey became a state, was so weakened as to be almost irrelevant. However, a new breed of independent and entrepreneurial legislators soon gave it the capacity and resources to deal, as an equal partner, with the governor and the courts. Chapters 8 through 11 trace the development of the state's political institutions.

All these changes in state government—one might almost say the creation of a genuine state government—also brought vast changes in other relationships within and without the state. As service in Washington became more important to talented politicians than a stint in the legislature or county and municipal government, New Jersey's delegation became more distinguished and active. New Jersey adopted a far more confident and assertive posture toward New York City and Philadelphia. Bewildered local officials found themselves caught between the Scylla of new state aid and the Charybdis of new state mandates. Chapters 12 and 13 describe Trenton's uneasy new relationships to New York City and to New Jersey's 567 municipalities and 21 counties.

Massive alterations in government bring massive alterations in public policy, and so they have in New Jersey. As stronger state institutions developed, bent on forceful intervention in the state's life, New Jersey became one of the last states to adopt broad–based taxes. So intense was public aversion to an income tax that only the state supreme court, backed by the governor, could mandate its passage in 1976.

When Trenton proved that the modest new tax actually lowered local property taxes (at least temporarily), New Jerseyans gave it grudging acquiescence. Hikes in the broad–based taxes as the economy took off in the early 1980s produced undreamed of revenue, and the state budget quadrupled over 15 years. The evolution of state taxing and spending, a metaphor for the contest between state and local forces, is described in chapter 14.

Expenditures for public education consume nearly a third of the state budget, and New Jersey has ranked first or second in spending for elementary and secondary education among the states for some years (although somewhat lower when spending is related to per capita income). Despite that, the state's proportional fiscal contribution is still below the 50–state average, and local property taxes in New Jersey remain among the highest in the nation.

Nowhere else is the state's home rule tradition more apparent than in the realm of public education. Almost all New Jersey municipalities have their own elementary schools, and high schools of barely 500 students are the rule rather than the exception. Arguments for curricular enrichment or economies of scale pall when they mean eliminating the institution most central to the identity of New Jersey's towns; where high school football is practically a ritual, reinforced by the historic absence of major professional or even collegiate competition in the state.

New Jerseyans are barely inclined to redistribute their school tax dollars outside their own communities, much less to redistribute their children. Battles over public education—who should control it and how to fund it—

have devoured more debate time in New Jersey in the last two decades than even the tax system to which they are intimately connected. Chapter 15 tells this long–running tale.

If there is anything about which residents agree, it is that their quality of life is threatened. The cars they drive to their suburban jobs bring air pollution and traffic gridlock. Stormwater runoff from land paved over for development, illegal dumping, and overburdened municipal sewage systems pollute too many streams and rivers and threaten the beaches New Jerseyans prize. New Jerseyans will thus do almost anything to protect the environment, remaining open space, and natural wonders—except welcome restrictions on how they use their own property or on the way their own towns develop. Trenton's increasing ventures into environmental, transportation, and land–use regulation, and the response from citizens and local governments, are the subjects of chapter 16.

The 1980s were good years for many Americans and nowhere more than in New Jersey. Americans regained confidence about their place in the world, and New Jerseyans, for perhaps the first time, gained confidence about their place in the nation. As the 1990s opened, the nation recognized challenges lying ahead. Providing quality education, protecting the quality of life, and continuing to accommodate to a multicultural society while sustaining growth and opportunity were likely to become central domestic issues as the United States moved inexorably toward becoming a nation of suburbs.

America's most suburban state is, for those who know it, a continuously fascinating place, whose astonishing complexity and diversity can never be fathomed by those who race down the Turnpike. New Jersey is a place more Americans should get to know, because of what it may tell them about their own future.

Foundations: New Jersey, 1600–1900

It was Alexander Hamilton who discovered the uses of New Jersey.
—Lincoln Steffens[1]

When children study the American Revolution, they read about its opening and closing chapters in Massachusetts and Virginia, and they tour Lexington, Concord, Philadelphia, and Yorktown. But few travel to New Jersey, aptly called "the cockpit of the Revolution." All Americans count Massachusetts's Paul Revere a hero. Few know of New Jersey's Nathaniel Scudder. Scudder rode all night on July 1, 1776, to warn the provincial Congress that the Sandy Hook militia had spotted an approaching British naval fleet. The provincial Congress alerted the Continental Congress sitting in Philadelphia, which proclaimed the Declaration of Independence three days later.

It was across New Jersey that George Washington was thrown back from New York to Pennsylvania, and fought the battles of New Brunswick, Monmouth, and Princeton. It was in Morristown and Somerville that the ragtag revolutionary army spent three bitter winters, and at the Battle of Monmouth that Molly Pitcher became immortal. The tide of the war turned when Washington crossed the Delaware River and captured the Hessian garrison at Trenton. The man who would be the nation's first president wrote his farewell address to his troops in a house in Rocky Hill.

In this early history are significant clues to what New Jersey would become, and in critical respects remain, for centuries thereafter. As it was for the revolutionary armies New Jersey was long "a region that one traverses to go somewhere else, a kind of suburb and No Man's Land between New York and Philadelphia."[2] The immense consequences of New Jersey's location between two of the nation's most important cities led to revolutionary–era characterizations of New Jersey as a "valley between two mountains of conceit" and a "cask tapped at both ends." New Jersey's most famous governor, Woodrow Wilson, would complain more than a century later, "We have always been inconvenienced by New York on the one hand and Philadelphia on the other."[3]

Location contributed powerfully to the lack of a clear state identity, and other factors reinforced it. One was the almost immediate division of the original British royal land grant into East Jersey and West Jersey. Throughout the colonial period, the once–divided province maintained two capitals at which the provincial legislature met alternately—Perth Amboy in the east and Burlington in the west. The counties that West Jersey comprised would still be threatening to secede two centuries later.[4]

Ethnic and religious diversity complicated the initial regional cleavage. By the early eighteenth century, there were Dutch settlements in Bergen and Middlesex, Scots in Perth Amboy and Freehold, and Germans in Hunterdon. Puritans from New England settled in the north. Some of them founded Newark after fleeing Connecticut when that colony extended the franchise to persons of other faiths. Quakers lived along the Delaware River. Presbyterians dominated Princeton and its college, while the Dutch Reformed church founded New Jersey's other colonial college, Queen's College (later Rutgers), at New Brunswick. Later waves of immigration made the New Jersey of 1910 the state with the fifth highest proportion of foreign–born residents.

Domination by larger neighbors, parochialism, and social cleavages fostered suspicion of centralized authority. The state's earliest political "parties" were East Jersey versus West Jersey factions. By 1800, the contending parties had adopted county conventions as nominating bodies. The counties would remain the state's most powerful political units for almost two centuries, and some of America's hardiest political machines blossomed there.

The first state constitution of 1776 assigned virtually all powers to a legislature dominated by county interests, and made the governor little more than a figurehead. In this respect, New Jersey was little different from the other original states, but weak state government had incredible persistence in New Jersey. The second constitution of 1844, in force until 1947, still limited the governor to one three–year term, gave the "chief executive" almost no appointment powers not shared with the legislature and only the weakest of vetoes. None of these officials had much to do in any case; counties and localities raised almost all the money for the limited public purposes citizens saw fit to support.[5] In 1960, New Jersey was still one of only three states without a broad–based state sales or income tax.

It also took a long time for New Jersey to accept its role in the federal union. The local militia's tendency to melt away during the War of Independence led General Washington to write in exasperation, "The conduct of the Jerseys has been most infamous."[6] During the Civil War, draft riots in New York overshadowed similar events in Newark. New Jersey was the only northern state to deny a plurality of its popular vote to Abraham Lincoln in 1860 and 1864, and that era's momentous amendments to the U.S. Constitution were, variously, rejected or rescinded by the state's legislature.

Thus, the keys to understanding New Jersey's politics from the earliest days forward lie in how profoundly its location and social and political fragmentation worked against identity with state or nation. This chapter describes how these factors shaped the state's early politics. The next chapter carries the story through most of the twentieth century. As they will show, for almost 200 years, the lineaments of New Jersey's politics, government, and policy remained almost frozen. The cast of characters changed; the drama's basic plot did not.

COLONIAL NEW JERSEY

New Jersey's original inhabitants, the Leni–Lenape Indians, were the first to repel an invasion from New York. In 1618, Dutch settlers ventured across the Hudson River to establish a trading station but were driven back to Manhattan by 1643. When the British gained control of the area about two decades later, King Charles II gave to his brother, James, Duke of York, all the lands between the Connecticut and Delaware rivers. They were named Albania, after James's Scottish title, Duke of Albany. Fortunately, this appellation was short–lived. Like so many after him, James focused his attention on the northeastern portion of the territory and gave the region between the Hudson and the Delaware to Lord John Berkeley and Sir George Carteret. A map error led the new owners to believe they had acquired an island; thus they named the tract after Carteret's native island of Jersey.

Before the end of the century, Berkeley had sold the western portion to a group of Quakers headed by William Penn. The Quakers' proprietorship was also brief. After buying East Jersey from Carteret's widow in 1680, the Quakers rapidly sold it off in sections and within a few years, also transferred West Jersey to a society of London merchants. East and West Jersey formally became one colony in 1702, but the ostensibly unified colony retained two capitals until after the revolutionary war.

Queen Anne showed no more interest in the colony than had the earlier Stuarts. In 1703, she appointed Lord Cornbury royal governor of New York— and as an afterthought, also governor of New Jersey. Perhaps this was because there was so little to govern. Only 10,000 souls lived in the entire province (7,500 in the east and 2,500 in the west), as compared with the 20,000 residents of New York City and the 15,000 in Philadelphia. After much agitation by the colonial assembly, Lewis Morris was named New Jersey's first separate governor in 1738. Although Morris had acquired 3,500 acres in the colony and went on to a distinguished career in New Jersey, the family manor, Morrisania, was located in what it is now the New York City borough of the Bronx. His grandson and namesake was one of New York's signatories of the Declaration of Independence.

New Jersey's early inhabitants were overwhelmingly rural, living on small farms in East Jersey and larger ones in the West. Among those laboring on the farms were indentured servants and African slaves—8,000 of them as early as 1760. The duke of York, president of the Royal Africa Company, had directed Governor Cornbury to oversee "a constant and sufficient supply of merchantable negroes, at moderate rates."[7] Aside from good farmland, the colony had few resources to diversify its economy. A small iron–mining industry centered in the northwestern hills quickly failed for lack of timber to drive the furnaces and forges.[8]

Location was New Jersey's most valuable resource. Consequently, the first regular transportation services in North America became an early bulwark of the economy. "Jersey wagons" first ran on old Indian trails from Burlington to Philadelphia in 1733, from New Brunswick to Trenton in 1738, and from South Amboy to Bordentown in 1740. At the end of each route, ferries transported travelers across the Hudson, Raritan, and Delaware rivers. By 1765, New Jersey had more roads than any other colony, and almost all of them led to the two important cities on its borders.

Jerseyans' discontent with British rule stemmed primarily from their relations with New York and Philadelphia. With no important seaport of its own, the colony's trade passed through these cities, draining New Jersey of cash. Tensions rose when the British banned the colony from issuing paper money. Debtors stormed the Monmouth County Courthouse and clashed with creditors in Newark riots.

Rebellious sentiments were strongest among the Baptists and Presbyterians, who were headquartered at the Presbyterian College of New Jersey at Princeton. Opposing them were the West Jersey Quakers, who condemned war as against the Gospel and civil harmony. The Anglican and Dutch Reformed communities were divided. Even the most vociferous objectors were somewhat leery of independence, for they saw the British Parliament as their protector from domination by New York.

Ignoring pleas from their last colonial governor (Benjamin Franklin's illegitimate offspring, William), New Jersey's delegates to the First Continental Congress in early 1775 supported a boycott of British goods and other resolutions hostile to Britain. Rebels dominated the Provincial Congress meeting in Trenton in May. The Presbyterians successfully intimidated Tory sympathizers from casting ballots for the Congress's members. Despite virtually universal male suffrage, two–thirds of the eligible electors did not vote. The Provincial

Congress sent four Presbyterians and a Baptist to the Second Continental Congress in Philadelphia, including Princeton's John Witherspoon, the president of the college. When war broke out, the Provincial Congress ordered William Franklin deported to Connecticut as a prisoner of war.

Historians estimate that at least a third and perhaps half the population was active or covert Tories when the war came to New Jersey. The Presbyterians maintained their leadership role, distributing political preferments and appointments to the Continental army. The rebels selected William Livingston of Liberty Hall in Essex County as their first provincial governor. Livingston ordered mass arrests of Tory sympathizers and their deportation to the colony's interior.

Linking New England and New York with the South, New Jersey felt the full force of the independence struggle and was the site of four major battles and more than ninety smaller ones. Washington spent a quarter of his generalship in New Jersey. His armies crossed the colony four times, spending the winters of 1778 in Somerville and 1777 and 1779 in Morristown. After bidding farewell to his troops in Rocky Hill in 1783, Washington met with the independent nation's first Congress at the College of New Jersey's Nassau Hall.

Between the Revolutionary and Civil Wars:
"The State of the Camden and Amboy"

After independence, New Jersey continued to languish in the shadow of New York and Philadelphia. Between 1790 and 1820, the population barely more than doubled, from about 95,000 to 227,500. In comparison, by 1820, New York State boasted a million inhabitants. In 1830, there were 242,000 residents of New York City and 80,000 in Philadelphia; Newark, New Jersey's largest city, had only 11,000 people.

Thanks largely to Alexander Hamilton and his associates, promising urban locales in the northern part of the state remained under the control of New Yorkers. Hamilton sought to achieve his dream of great industrial cities by founding the Society for Useful Manufactures at the Great Falls of Paterson and drawing the charter for the Associates of the Jersey Company at the site of what is now Jersey City.

The Society for Useful Manufactures was given a "perpetual monopoly" on manufacturing activities in Paterson in 1791 and acted as its effective government until 1830. The 1831 Paterson city charter gave its government minimum powers and the Society tax–free status. When the City of Jersey was chartered in 1838, rights to the valuable Hudson River waterfront remained with the Jersey Company. Until the state government signed a treaty with New York State in

1833, New Jersey had no rights to use the waters of the Hudson.

Just as all New Jersey roads led to New York, waterborne transportation was also dominated at first by its powerful neighbor. In 1807, the New York legislature granted a monopoly on steamboat transportation between the two states to inventor Robert Fulton and his partners. Thomas Gibbons, a Georgia entrepreneur who had moved to Elizabethtown, challenged the New Yorkers' monopoly with one granted him by the United States Congress. His rival boat, piloted by New Brunswick's Cornelius Vanderbilt, "puffed about New York Harbor" flying a streamer proclaiming, "New Jersey must be free!"[9] The dispute led to a landmark U.S. Supreme Court case, *Gibbons v. Ogden*, which affirmed the federal government's authority to regulate traffic on navigable waterways under the interstate commerce power. Daniel Webster argued the case for the victorious Gibbons.[10]

The century's most important form of transportation did boast local ownership. In 1811, the state legislature had rejected as "visionary" the petition of Hoboken's John Stevens to build a rail line. The persistent Stevens family was finally granted a charter for the Camden and Amboy Railroad in 1830. In return for a thirty-year monopoly of a route between the Hudson and Delaware rivers, forbidding any competing line "between the cities of New-York and Philadel-phia," the Stevens gave the state 1,000 shares in the railroad and a guarantee that the annual dividends would never fall below $30,000.[11]

This suited both the corporation and the state very well. The railroad's monopoly permitted it to charge outrageous rates to hapless travelers between New York and Philadelphia. The Camden and Amboy's second-class fare was $2.50, at a time when a dollar was the average laborer's weekly wage. As Horace Greeley noted in his *New York Tribune*, the Camden and Amboy's fare from New York to Philadelphia was four times higher than the fares in the competitive Albany–to–New York market. The benefit to the state was that transit levies, imposed on out–of–state travelers rather than on the company, "neatly eliminated the need for statewide taxes."[12] In 1850, Trenton's entire operating fund totalled only $128,600, and the transit tax alone contributed $86,000, with other railroad taxes making up most of the rest.[13]

With so much literally riding on this mutually beneficial relationship, the Camden and Amboy was quick to involve itself in politics. Duane Lockard notes that "railroads from Maine to California played an important role in state politics during the nineteenth century, but in no state was that role assumed earlier or more pervasively than in New Jersey."[14]

The Federalist party in New Jersey was formed in 1789 to contest the first congressional elections. It remained an important force, never garnering less than 48 percent of the vote through 1814 when, as elsewhere, it effectively disappeared. New York Federalists, migrating across the Hudson River as they lost control of New York City to the Democrats of Tammany Hall, were an important element of the party's support. In 1798, the Federalists controlled the New Jersey legislature by a margin of thirty–eight to twelve.

In reaction to the Alien and Sedition Acts, followers of Thomas Jefferson formed the Democratic–Republican party in 1798 and elected three of the state's five at–large U.S. congressmen. The heavy concentration of their support in the northern counties of Sussex, Essex, and Morris, however, hampered the Jeffersonians' progress. It permitted them to win statewide victories such as the at–large congressional elections, but only a small minority in the Trenton legislature.

Early voting in New Jersey was as enthusiastic, widespread, and corrupt as elsewhere. A 1790 law forbade voters to come to the polls with any "Weapons of War, or Staves, or Bludgeons." Most polling places were in taverns, producing the scenes described in the September 27, 1804, edition of the *New Brunswick Guardian*: "Lo! a voter brimful of freedom and grog, marching up to the election box, guided by two or three staunch patriots, lest the honest soul should mistake, lose his way, or be surprised by the other party and lost."[15] The state's 1776 constitution briefly permitted truly universal suffrage for "all inhabitants...of full age," including women and blacks. After women hustled to the polls made the difference in a fierce fight between Newark and Elizabethtown over the location of the Essex County Courthouse, an 1807 law confined the franchise to free, white, property–owning males.[16]

From 1828 until the Civil War, state politics settled into close contests between the Jacksonian Democrats and the Whigs. Both parties had well–organized get–out–the–vote operations, centered in the several counties. Election rules designed to benefit one party or the other changed often, as the alliances traded legislative majorities in Trenton. Until an 1842 federal law required U.S. representatives to be chosen from congressional districts, whichever party was dominant opposed such district elections and favored statewide at–large choices. Similarly, the Whigs favored stricter taxpayer and citizenship qualifications and closing the polls at sunset, while the Democrats, with greater support among immigrants and the lower classes, pushed for fewer restrictions on the franchise and extended polling hours.

State politics meant legislative politics; the 1776 constitution made the governor "a convenience occasionally employed by the legislature to carry out a mandate it did not see fit to direct to some other officer or body."[17] Chosen annually by the legislature, and with no appointment or veto powers, the governor was more a judicial than an executive official. He served as the presiding officer of the legislative upper house, which acted as the highest court. New Jersey's governors of the first half of the century thus held a mostly honorific position and were usually members of prominent families.

About the time the Camden and Amboy Railroad was established, New Jersey politics became "democratized" in a number of ways that led the railroad to involve itself ever more heavily in political activities. Immigrants, especially from Ireland, were flooding into the northern part of the state and swelling the Democrats' ranks. A new constitution in 1844 made the governorship an elective office and removed property qualifications for the franchise.

Although inspired to some degree by the national fervor for Jacksonian democracy, the new constitution hardly constituted a revolution. The governor, while gaining modest appointment and veto powers, was limited to one three-year term—an election schedule that also effectively insulated state politics from national politics. Members of the legislature's upper house continued to be elected one from each county, and it selected or ratified all officers of the executive branch, save the governor and state auditor. Assemblymen were elected for terms of only one year, their nominations firmly in the hands of county party organizations. Although Dorothea Dix led a successful campaign for a state mental hospital in 1848, and a state normal school was established to train teachers in 1855, the government's largest operation was a prison, whose keeper was appointed by the legislature. Moreover, the white Protestants still leading the Democratic party were suspicious of strong, central government in state or nation. The 1844 constitution banned the creation of any state debt in excess of $100,000 without a public referendum. This provision made it almost impossible for the state to take over the Camden and Amboy by purchasing it.

It was thus to the Democrats that the railroad entrusted its fate. State elections became contests between its supporters and opponents. The railroad's local agents mobilized the Democratic faithful, often paying them for their votes; it "extended if not practically introduced" the role of money in elections.[18] Great electoral exertions were necessary because after 1840, "New Jersey was at all times a doubtful state."[19]

Starting in 1852, New Jersey endorsed every Democratic presidential candidate for the next four decades, except for split electoral votes in 1860 and 1872. Twelve of the fifteen governors in this period were also Democrats, but victory margins in all these races never reached 54 percent. With the railroad dominating the Democratic party, "New Jersey became known as the state of the Camden and Amboy, and that is what she was, and as such she was execrated and ridiculed throughout the Union."[20]

THE CIVIL WAR AND AFTER: "NEW JERSEY:
THE TRAITOR STATE"

Just as many New Jerseyans had opposed the War of Independence, many sympathized with the southern cause as the United States moved toward civil war. New Jersey was, in 1804, the last northern state to pass a law gradually abolishing slavery. Slavery was outlawed completely in 1846, but the 1844 constitutional convention ignored freed slaves' demand for the franchise.[21] South Jersey Quakers, however, were key participants in the "Underground Railroad" which sheltered escaping slaves. Three principal routes and nine smaller ones ran into New Jersey from Maryland and Delaware.[22] New Jerseyans' chief concerns, rather than slavery, were the economic links to the Confederacy and especially, the principle of states' rights—a sore point in New Jersey since colonial times. Although a still overwhelmingly rural state in 1860, among New Jersey's 600,000 residents were 56,000 factory workers, ranking it sixth among the 33 states in industrial production. Industry depended heavily on southern markets; a popular contemporary saying was that "the south walks on Newark shoe leather." A budding tourist industry relied on southern visitors; Cape May, on the South Jersey shore below the Mason–Dixon line, hosted many visitors from Maryland and Virginia. The college at Princeton drew over a third of its students from the Confederacy.[23]

Even more powerful than these economic concerns was the widespread sympathy for the states' rights argument. Support for the Democratic position on states' rights was so great that the nascent New Jersey Republican party chose to call itself the "Opposition Party" throughout the Civil War era. Despite tapping New Jerseyan William L. Dayton as his runningmate, John Fremont ran a poor second to the Democrats' James Buchanan in the 1856 presidential election and barely outpolled the American party's Millard Fillmore, candidate of the nativist "Know–Nothings." Buchanan's runaway New Jersey victory was more than triple that of the greatest victor in the previous three presidential elections, despite the three–way race.

In the same year though, a coalition of Republicans and Know–Nothings gave a razor–thin victory to the Opposition Party gubernatorial candidate, as they did again in 1859. This latter governor, Charles Olden of Princeton, was almost singlehandedly responsible for persuading New Jersey not to secede. The state's critical balancing act between north and south also was evident when the U.S. House of Representatives in 1860 chose a first–term Republican congressman from New Jersey as its compromise candidate for Speaker of the House.

Although the Republican loss in New Jersey's presidential balloting was narrower in 1860 than 1856, with the war looming, New Jersey continued to deny Abraham Lincoln's Republican electors a complete victory and repeated this choice in 1864. Mixed feelings about the war were evident throughout the conflict. Although Brigadier General Philip Kearny became a hero who could rightly brag, "I can make my men follow me to Hell," the secretary of war ordered the arrest of another New Jersey officer, Peace Democrat Colonel James Wall. Outrage over Wall's arrest carried a Democrat to a landslide win in the 1862 gubernatorial contest, and Wall himself to a seat in the U.S. Senate in an 1863 special election.

That year was the height of the Peace Democrats' influence. In March, both houses of the Democratic–dominated legislature passed resolutions opposing the Emancipation Proclamation and the Thirteenth Amendment to the U.S. Constitution and urged peace talks with the Confederacy. In July, draft riots broke out in Newark. Vast numbers of draftees sought to purchase substitutes; of the 6,981 men drafted in March 1864, only 380 actually served.[24]

In the years following, Republicans and Democrats traded control of the governorship and the legislature. A total Republican takeover in 1865 led to the legislature finally ratifying the Thirteenth Amendment and also the Fourteenth; when the Democrats prevailed in the 1867 legislative elections, they rescinded the Fourteenth Amendment's ratification and in 1870, refused to ratify the Fifteenth Amendment. When a Republican majority replaced them later that year, the legislature reversed course on ratification once again. The state constitution's own white–suffrage provision remained in place until 1875.

If the Civil War brought acrimony, it also brought growth. The population rose by 50 percent during the 1860s, reaching 906,000 in 1870 and 1 million in 1875. Its geographic distribution changed markedly. Before the war, the largely rural populace was divided evenly among the state's counties. By 1880, two–thirds of the 21 counties still did not have a community as large as 10,000, and only 9 of the state's 270 municipalities were that large. However, almost three–quarters of all New Jerseyans lived in eight cities along the Camden and Amboy line snaking from the northeast to the southwest between Jersey City and Camden.

The factories whose numbers more than doubled between 1870 and 1900 were located in these railroad–oriented cities. Newark, with 72,000 residents in 1860, grew to 137,000 a decade later, and Jersey City mushroomed from 29,000 to 121,000 people. In contrast, areas farthest from the railroad and New York or Philadelphia were often more thinly settled than at the time of the Revolution.

Politics now reflected the political aftermath of the war and the demographic and economic changes. A crucial event occurred in 1871, when the Camden and Amboy leased all of its property and rights–of–way to the Pennsylvania

Railroad, destroying the "local ownership" justification for its monopoly in the New York–Philadelphia corridor. The *New York Herald* editorialized, "The halo of New Jersey's glory has left her. Her Ichabod hath departed. The Camden and Amboy Road, the pride of the state and the ruler of her Legislature, has been ceded to Pennsylvania."[25]

By 1873, a Republican–dominated legislature ended the Pennsylvania Railroad's monopoly, and other lines expanded or were built. Between 1870 and 1880, trackage in New Jersey increased from 1,125 miles to 1,684; eventually there would be 2,500 miles of track in a state that only extended 166 miles from north to south and 57 miles from east to west. Industrial and urban growth exploded as the railroads reached every corner of the state.

Three competing lines along the Atlantic coast turned the Jersey Shore town of Atlantic City into the nation's premier middle–class vacation resort. A wealthier clientele summered in Long Branch, the "summer White House" of presidents from Grant through Garfield–who died there some months after an attack by an assassin. The extensive rail lines swelled the ranks of New York and Philadelphia commuters who went home to "bedroom suburbs" in New Jersey.

Most affected by the rail explosion was Hudson County, and especially its largest municipality, Jersey City. Across the Hudson River from Manhattan, Jersey City had suffered indignities from transportation companies and the government in Trenton from its earliest days. After the state finally won the right to use the Hudson waters, it gave a private company rights to much of the city's waterfront. The state courts denied Jersey City the right to run a ferry line competing with the Jersey Company, and the city's lack of control over its own waterfront was reaffirmed by the legislature in a new city charter in 1851.

Shortly thereafter, the Jersey Company sold its waterfront rights to a local railroad, which transferred them to the Camden and Amboy in 1867. Another part of the waterfront was acquired by the Jersey Central Railroad, which in 1868, over the loud and futile protests of local residents, made it suitable for rail construction by importing New York City garbage to fill in the mud flats extending 1000 feet into the river. Mayor Orestes Cleveland vainly protested that his city was: "hedged round about, cut up and run over by the great monopolies; her commercial facilities cut off; her natural energies crushed; her public spirit smothered; her growth retarded; the very air she breathes as a city dealt out to her in small quantities by one or the other of these gorged institutions that have no souls and no eye for anything that does not fill up and protect their own plethoric purses."[26]

The insult to Jersey City did not end there. By 1870 it was the terminus of several railroads and was known as "the gateway to the West." Rail lines owned almost a third of all city property–declared by Trenton exempt from local taxes. Altogether, a quarter of the state's real property was railroad–owned and tax–exempt.

More indignities were to come. Hudson County, anchored by Jersey City, was the source of much of the state's Democratic vote and contributed massively to narrow Democratic gubernatorial victories in every election between 1873 and 1892. The Republican stronghold was the legislature, where rural counties retained dominance of the upper house through the proviso that each county be represented by one senator.

Republican domination of the assembly, however, was less secure. In 1871, when the GOP gained complete control of the legislature, it was especially unprincipled in its treatment of Hudson County and its heavily Irish Catholic population. The county was gerrymandered into six tiny assembly districts containing most Protestant voters and one huge, oddly shaped district taking in most of Jersey City. Dubbed the Horseshoe, it contained most of the Democrats and Roman Catholics in the county.

Not content with exempting much of the city's wealth from taxation and weakening its role in state politics, the final Republican coup was ending Jersey City's self–government with a so–called "ripper" law. In reaction to the 1870 Democratic legislature's appointment of a state–controlled police commission for Republican Newark, the 1871 Republican legislature stripped Democratic Jersey City of all public functions and appointed a series of state commissions to handle all governance matters. The low point of the "Ring" controlling Jersey City was reached when the state–appointed city treasurer (named Alexander Hamilton) absconded to Mexico with the city's funds. Finally in 1876, the state's highest court returned governance to the city's residents after a constitutional amendment prohibited legislative regulation of the internal affairs of municipalities.

Before the Civil War, state politics had revolved around the Democratic supporters and Republican opponents of the Camden and Amboy. Now, with many competitor lines appearing, the railroads collectively continued to run state politics. There were enough lines—35 different ones by 1900–to bankroll and control every political organization in the state. William J. Sewall, the undisputed Republican boss and U.S. senator for the last three decades of the nineteenth century, was a Pennsylvania employee who "held court" in the railroad's Camden office.[27]

His Democratic counterpart from 1870 to 1897, Secretary of State Henry Kelsey, masterminded the election of railroad vice–president George McClellan (former Union general and Democratic presidential candidate) to the governorship in 1877. McClellan's predecessor, Joseph

D. Bedle, became counsel to the Jersey Central upon leaving office. The Democratic boss of Middlesex County was an agent of the Lehigh Valley Railroad. An especially close 1880 gubernatorial election, which the Democrats won by less than 700 votes, was a battle between candidates representing the Pennsylvania and the Jersey Central railroads.

With most gubernatorial elections decided by less than 2 percent, the larger railroads found it prudent to have agents in both parties. Along with the Protestant and Republican Sewall of South Jersey, the Pennsylvania was also allied with the Catholic and Democratic Essex County boss, James Smith of Newark, elected U.S. senator in 1892. Even the Democratic leader of beleaguered Hudson County controlled local railroads and utilities within the county in the 1890s. With increasing use of gas, electricity, and motorized public transportation, public utilities like Elizabeth Gas and Light and the Public Service Corporation played a role similar to that of the railroads—seeking exclusive and perpetual franchises from the legislature and placing their agents inside state government.

As the nineteenth century wore on, state government remained weak and undeveloped. There was no governor's mansion in Trenton, and many chief executives continued to work in New York City. Journalist William Sackett nicely captured the flavor of the period: " 'Governor's Day' [Tuesday]...was marked by 'Cabinet meetings,' at which the Department heads laid before the Governor the things they had done—or rather had not done—during the week past for the public weal, and the programmes for the week ahead were laid out. And they all flitted out of town into seclusion again until the next week's gathering was due."[28]

Gradually, however, state government took on more responsibilities, particularly in education. When an 1871 legislative act compelled all municipalities to offer a nine–month school term and prohibited tuition charges, New Jersey became one of the last two states to guarantee free public education.[29] An 1875 constitutional amendment reinforced the commitment by calling for a "thorough and efficient" public school system for all children between the ages of five and eighteen.

These initiatives eventually required the state to raise more revenue, because total reliance on the local property tax to finance public schools increasingly beggared municipalities—especially those where more and more railroad property was exempt from local levies. By an 1880 estimate, New Jersey was nineteenth among the states in population but fifth in its burden of public debt. In neighboring New York City, local tax rates were under 1 percent of assessed valuation, whereas in Jersey City, they were almost 3 percent.[30]

New Jersey was fortuitously saved once again from tapping residents' pocketbooks for state purposes by the push in much of the rest of the country for antitrust legislation. In 1889, the legislature allowed companies to hold stock in other companies—commonly known as "holding corporations" or "trusts." Only West Virginia and Delaware had similar laws, and New Jersey's proximity to Wall Street got it most of the business. One Jersey City office building near the ferry landing was the official "headquarters" for more than 1,500 companies. The price to corporations for this favored treatment was a state tax of twenty cents on each thousand dollars of capitalization.

Thus, for example, when the U.S. Supreme Court dissolved the Rockefellers' Standard Oil Trust in 1892, the company quickly reincorporated in New Jersey and was able to achieve domination of the domestic oil industry. Standard Oil's example was followed by many others, leading the former "State of the Camden and Amboy" to be called the "Mother of the Trusts," the "business Tenderloin of the United States," and "the Traitor State." In giving New Jersey this last appellation, muckraker Lincoln Steffens wrote: "Every loyal citizen of the United States owes New Jersey a grudge. The State is corrupt; so are certain other states....The offense that commands our special attention, however, and lifts this state into national distinction is this; New Jersey is selling out the rest of us....our sister State was not prompted by any abstract consideration of right and wisdom. New Jersey sold us out for money....And she gets her revenue. Her citizens pay no direct State tax. The corporations pay all the expenses of the State, and more."[31] Steffens's final observation captured what most New Jerseyans saw as ample justification for friendliness to the trusts. The $292,000 earned for the state by the capitalization tax in its first year rose to $707,000 by 1896.

New Jersey's politics in the 25 years after the Civil War show how the state tracked national events and how it diverged. As was true nationally, both major political parties were dominated by their conservative, business–oriented wings. The state's Republicans had opposed the GOP's abolitionists during the Civil War era and were favorably inclined to the "captains of industry" who dominated the party after the war.

New Jersey Democrats also identified with their party's conservative wing. The Populist movement of the 1880s onward, later absorbed by the Democratic Party and personified by three–time presidential candidate William Jennings Bryan, never made headway in New Jersey. Prosperous farmers, many of them Quakers, did not share the Populists' discontent. Agricultural interests became less important in the late nineteenth century anyway, as industry and urban areas boomed. Some Democrats, especially the party elite, were business people;

many of the rest were urban, Catholic, immigrant laborers—unlikely to be attracted by the fundamentalist Protestant Populists in the nation's hinterlands who agitated against liquor and lenient immigration policies.[32]

New Jersey Republicans thus became more amenable to the national direction of their party in the late nineteenth century; New Jersey Democrats were comfortable with the "Gold Democrat" wing headed by Grover Cleveland and considerably less so with the Bryan wing. The conservatism of both parties' adherents thus made state politics countercyclical to national trends until almost the end of the century. National politics from 1860 through 1892 was competitive with a Republican tilt; New Jersey politics was competitive with a Democratic tilt.

Scholars who study late nineteenth–century voting behavior debate its nature and meaning. Walter Dean Burnham characterizes it as a time of intense participation, high turnout, and issue–based partisanship. Others ascribe the turnout to corruption and vote–buying and the strong partisanship to patronage jobs and party–prepared ballots that made split–ticket voting difficult.[33] New Jersey provides some evidence for both interpretations.

Turnout was high, averaging close to 90 percent in presidential elections and only about 10 percent lower in the usually off–year triennial gubernatorial contests. On the other hand, an 1883 legislative commission estimated that a fifth to a quarter of the vote was for sale. With annual assembly elections as well as other frequent state and national contests, these citizens could rely on payment for their ballots as a "regular source of income."[34]

THE BIRTH OF A NEW POLITICAL ORDER

The national election of 1896, which presaged the almost unbroken domination of the conservatives in both parties for the next three decades, was a watershed election in New Jersey as well. The Republicans began a long string of victories in state and federal elections, and major changes occurred in the leadership of both parties, even though there were few significant policy differences between them.

Democratic governors elected in 1889 and 1892 had some reform instincts, but this was not true of their partisans in the legislature, many of whom were supported financially by increasingly influential racetrack owners and gamblers. The 1893 legislature passed a set of notorious laws legalizing betting at a rapidly growing number of tracks. When Democratic Governor George Werts vetoed this legislation, his fellow partisans in the legislature led the way in overriding it.

Along with other related scandals, these events led voters to hand the Democrats a massive defeat in 1895, and the Republicans elected their first governor in nine terms and 27 years. The new Republican legislature overturned the condemned Democratic legislation and amended the state constitution to prohibit bookmaking, pari–mutuel betting, and lotteries.

The defeat of the "Ring" that had reigned in Trenton for three decades left the Democrats mired in factionalism. The divisions were not ideological, because the party had no "reform" wing. There were, rather, loyalties to different local bosses in the northern counties producing most of the Democratic vote. The two principal figures were Robert "Little Bob" Davis of Hudson County and James C. Smith of Essex.

Instead of making common cause, Davis and Smith fought over preferments such as choosing the U.S. senator the legislature would elect in 1892. Smith was successful in getting himself named over Hudson County's candidate, popular, governor Leon Abbett, who was leaving office. Abbett's bitterness, and his death soon thereafter, intensified the enmity between the Democratic factions.[35]

On the Republican side in the later 1890s, party boss William J. Sewall of the Pennsylvania Railroad expanded his links to other sections of the state's corporate elite, especially after corporate leaders became more important in financing the operations of state government. At his behest, the legislature elected to the U.S. Senate John F. Dryden, president of the Prudential Insurance Company, and John F. Kean, president of Elizabeth Gas and Light. Sewall himself went to the Senate three times.

Not forgetting his own employer, Sewall also arranged the appointment of the Pennsylvania Railroad's chief legislative lobbyist as the state commissioner of banking and insurance in 1895. Yet divisiveness also came to the newly triumphant GOP. Sewall died in 1901, just as progressivism was emerging in the party nationally. As elsewhere, the New Jersey Republicans splintered—along both ideological and geographic lines.[36] The business–oriented, conservative faction, however, generally prevailed.

Officeholders in both parties were engaged in less genteel corruption or impropriety. Walter Edge, later an outstanding Republican governor, was a young state senate journal clerk in 1898. His memoirs describe an exciting legislative investigation of local Democratic officials in Hudson County, "including grand jury packing by the sheriff to protect what were alleged to be Democratic–sponsored vice–rings; but this died quickly when the opposition suggested an inquiry into Republican activities in Camden County where conditions appeared to be at least as bad."[37]

Most New Jerseyans were more than willing to trade off the state's unsavory reputation—at least as the "mother of the trusts," if not as a gambling den—for the financial benefits. At his inaugural in 1905, Governor Edward C. Stokes spoke for many when he declared: "Of the entire income of the state, not a penny was contributed directly by the people....The state is caring for the blind, the feeble–minded and the insane, supporting our prisoners and reformatories, educating the younger generations, developing a magnificent road system, maintaining the state government and courts of justice, all of which would be a burden on the taxpayer except for our present fiscal policy."[38]

Still, voices began to be heard and would gather force, protesting a system that supported the small Trenton government handsomely but favored huge and powerful employers over their employees and utility cartels over municipal governments. As Stokes made his pronouncement, a young Irish Catholic resident of the Jersey City Horseshoe was beginning a career in Hudson County Democratic politics. About fifty miles southwest, a Virginia minister's son had recently assumed the presidency of the renamed Princeton University. The first of these men was Frank Hague. The second was Woodrow Wilson. Together, they would embody the conflicting strains in New Jersey's political culture for the next half–century.

INDIVIDUALISM AND MORALISM IN NEW JERSEY POLITICS

Daniel J. Elazar has described the dominant patterns of political culture variously evident in the American states.[39] A state's political culture determines (1) the dominant perceptions of what politics is and what the role of government should be, (2) the kinds of people who choose to enter political life, and (3) the way government is practiced. The initial dominant culture of particular states results from early immigration and settlement patterns, and modifies only slowly. Later arrivals are more apt to adopt the prevailing culture than to change it.

The initial political culture of New Jersey adheres closely to a model Elazar calls "individualistic." In the individualistic political culture, politics is perceived as utilitarian. It centers on private concerns and advancement—individual and group patronage and preferments rather than communal notions of a common good and policies that support it. It is rooted in personal relationships organized through political parties. Its practitioners are professionals to whom is left the sometimes unsavory business of allocating individual and group rewards. A certain amount of public corruption is thus "expected": "The public is willing to pay a surcharge for services rendered and only rebels when it feels the surcharge has become too heavy."[40] The states most likely to exhibit this culture were settled early by immigrant groups most concerned with individual freedom and advancement.

Standing in direct contrast to the individualistic model is a "moralistic" one. In the moralistic culture, government is an instrument of the common good and may be used to regulate or intervene in the private sphere when necessary for the public weal. Since politics is the sphere of all concerned citizens, it is more likely to be practiced by amateurs, and corruption is less tolerated.

New Jersey's early settlers were precisely those Elazar identifies as most concerned with individual opportunity—primarily from Britain and the Germanic states. Later immigrants—from Ireland, Italy, and Eastern Europe— "soon adopted...individualistic attitudes and goals which brought them into the [individualistic] culture."[41] Cohesive, localist, political parties quickly arose to "divide the spoils," and professional politicians made that task a life's work.[42] Only the most egregious corruption received notice, and resulting rebellion and reform were likely to be transitory and superficial.

As the period described in this chapter drew to an end, the moralistic impulses that were arising nationally, symbolized by the Progressive movement, washed over New Jersey. New residents migrating from areas where moralism was dominant could harness a period of particularly strong feeling that the "corruption surcharge" was too high. Early in the twentieth century, Woodrow Wilson would emerge as a leader of the moralistic crusade, first in his adopted state and later in the nation. Although Wilson's extraordinary governorship would leave lasting marks on New Jersey, it was Frank Hague, the embodiment of the individualistic culture that still dominated, who would have much the stronger effect on the state's politics for the next half–century.

CHAPTER THREE

"The Statesman and the Boss"[1]

How the hell do I know whether he'll make a good governor?...he will
make a good candidate, and that is the only thing that interests me.[2]
—"Little Bob" Davis, Democratic machine leader, on Woodrow Wilson's
gubernatorial nomination, 1910.

If the reform side of him is twice as efficient as reform ever was, the
Tammany side is twice as efficient as Tammany ever was.[3]

—journalist's assessment of Jersey City Mayor Frank Hague

Two towering figures, Woodrow Wilson and Frank Hague, symbolize divergent strains in New Jersey's politics in the first half of the twentieth century. The early part of the period saw the state's first political reform movement. By the 1920s, its force was spent, but it would reemerge five decades later. The later part of the era was a period of archetypical, county–machine–dominated government, not seriously challenged until the 1970s. Vestiges of it still remain.

To comprehend this period, one must begin again with demography. The state's population almost doubled between 1890 and 1915. New Jersey ranked eighteenth among the states in population in 1890; tenth in 1910. Nineteenth–century settlement patterns were further reinforced. In the first decades of the next century, nearly two–thirds of municipalities had fewer than 2,000 residents, but 75 percent of the population was concentrated in seven of the 21 counties—six in the New York City metropolitan area and one bordering Philadelphia.[4]

Two of the northern counties—Hudson and Essex—each contained about a fifth of the state's residents in 1910. Half of Hudson's were in Jersey City, and two–thirds of those in Essex lived in the state's largest city, Newark. The county next in population, Passaic, was less than half the size of Hudson or Essex, just as its largest city, Paterson, was similarly dwarfed by Newark and Jersey City.

New Jersey's cities were not very large and would never get much larger. Newark's population was 347,000 in 1910, and Jersey City's was 268,000.

The citizens of Camden, on the Philadelphia border, numbered only 95,000. Thanks to the dominance of New York and Philadelphia, New Jersey was already assuming a suburban character. As Edmund Wilson observed in 1923, these metropolises kept New Jersey's "minor cities from rising above their flatness and drabness. They are content to leave to New York and Philadelphia ambition, liveliness and brilliance."[5]

By the late nineteenth century, immigrants from other countries and other states had begun to flood into New Jersey, another trend that intensified in the succeeding decades. In 1920, almost a quarter of the state's 3 million inhabitants was foreign–born, and another fifth had been born in another state—the highest proportion of nonnatives in any state save Delaware.[6]

Foreign–born immigrants were not evenly distributed but rather concentrated in the New York–area counties. Hudson County's peculiar geography produced the classic ethnic neighborhood in its purest form. Its Irish, German, Slavic, and Italian communities were clearly delineated by their churches, saloons, and local shops but often further separated by the ubiquitous railroad tracks.

Geography also ensured that Hudson County would not develop spacious suburbs. The Meadowlands, a vast marsh to its west, forced development into a narrow strip along the Hudson River. Upwardly mobile citizens seeking suburban homes thus went north to Bergen, south to Middlesex and Monmouth, or west across the wetlands into Essex.[7] Hudson's residents remained newer, poorer immigrants or those who did not want to leave old, ethnic neighborhoods.

Neither the suburban commuters nor the insular ethnics felt much identity with the state. Thus, New Jersey's politics remained local, parochial, and based in county organizations. Indeed, one might say there was no state politics to speak of. Political attention always focuses on where public money is raised or distributed. In the New Jersey of the early 1900s, Trenton continued to raise its modest budget almost entirely from the corporations and the railroads and to spend it on the penal system and skeletal social services.

In contrast, localities raised and spent four times as much, almost all of it coming from the highly visible local property tax and going to visible services such as roads and public schools. State government's 2,900 employees in fiscal year 1916 to 1917 were not nearly so rich a source of patronage jobs as were counties and municipalities. Still, the price exacted by Trenton, especially in Hudson County, made possible a surge of reform. Its exemplar became Woodrow Wilson.

THE STATESMAN: WOODROW WILSON AND
NEW JERSEY PROGRESSIVISM

In the early 1900s, New Jersey was "one of the last strongholds of an industrial–feudal order that was the object of violent attack by progressive leaders throughout the country."[8] As a Hudson progressive who became an intimate of Woodrow Wilson described it, "Every election was, in its last analysis, a solemn referendum upon the question as to which corporate interest should control legislation—whether the Pennsylvania Railroad, whose mastermind was the Republican leader of the state, U.S. Senator Sewall, or the Public Service interests, whose votaries and friends were [Democratic] Senator Smith of New Jersey and Milan Ross, Sr., of Middlesex County."[9] Consequently, a small band of reformers could be found in both parties, for neither was hospitable enough to attract them as a group.

The first major reform victory occurred in beleaguered Jersey City. Because of its Democratic machine's close ties to local railroads and utilities, reform initially found its home in the Republican party. In the 1901 mayoral election, a young Irish reformer, Mark N. Fagan, assisted by Maine native and recent party convert George L. Record, swept to victory on a platform demanding "equal taxation" of the railroads.

For five years, the reformers won important battles, moving on from the railroad issue to an attack on the tax preferences and perpetual franchises of the public utilities. Fagan was reelected in 1903, and with other Republican reformers, notably in Essex County, launched the "New Idea" movement, with a standard progressive platform. Led by Everett Colby, the Essex reformers defeated the Republican regulars in the 1905 state primaries for delegates to county party conventions.[10]

By 1907, however, the Republican New Idea movement had disintegrated. To Fagan's disappointment, Progressive Republican President Theodore Roosevelt refused to withdraw federal patronage from the Republican regulars, although he had similarly helped Wisconsin's Robert La Follette and New York's Charles Evans Hughes.

Fagan lost the mayoralty in 1905 when his financial support of the public schools and lax enforcement of Sunday blue laws led the Jersey City Catholic hierarchy to withdraw its support. Abandoning their co–religionist, the church supported his Democratic German–Protestant opponent, Otto Wittpen. The movement's other major leader, Colby, declined to run for governor in 1905 and lost a bid for the state senate to an Essex Democratic progressive. With the Republican party back in the hands of the regulars, the reform–minded shifted their attention to the Democrats.

Some Hudson Democratic reformers, such as Joseph P. Tumulty, gained election to the legislature. They achieved some further success, including passage of the direct primary for local elections in 1907 and the institution of civil service hiring for state government and for municipalities at their option. New Jersey's reformers emphasized the aspects of the progressive agenda related to bossism and corruption. More radical ideas that made headway in progressive strongholds in the West—woman suffrage, initiative, referendum, recall, and direct election of U.S. senators—received scant attention in New Jersey.[11]

The reformers had less success in electing statewide candidates. Trenton Mayor Frank Katzenbach made the Democrats' best gubernatorial showing since 1892 when he garnered 47 percent of the vote in 1907, but the Republicans had won five straight gubernatorial elections since 1895, and control of the state legislature also gave them command of U.S. Senate elections. With Republican legislators electing U.S. Senate candidates until direct Senate elections began in 1913, Democratic Senate candidates were sacrificial lambs. Democratic reformers were thus sometimes able to nominate the party's candidates for an office of little interest to the conservative regulars.

The preeminent political role of the counties made even the reformers center their attention there. As Lincoln Steffens wrote of the New Jersey progressives in 1906, "such citizenship as they have is mean, narrow, local. Jersey, in the minds of the average Jerseyman is a group of counties, and his concern, if he worries at all, is with the petty evils of his own sordid surroundings."[12]

Thus, when it came time for the Democrats to select a U.S. Senate candidate who would face certain defeat in 1908, the progressives backed one of their own, and paid little attention to the candidate touted by the regulars, Woodrow Wilson.

The Virginia–born Wilson had been president of Princeton University since 1902, arriving there as a professor in 1890 when it was still the College of New Jersey. So far as the reformers knew, Wilson was just an articulate version of the typical regular. He opposed regulation of the trusts, labor legislation, and other favorite progressive themes, calling them "confused thinking and impossible points of law."[13] A strong supporter of the Cleveland wing of the party, Wilson refused to let William Jennings Bryan speak at Princeton and declined to appear with him anywhere.[14]

Tiring of battles with the university's faculty and trustees, Wilson began to think about a political career—but in national politics rather than state government. Like so many of New Jersey's outstanding citizens, there was no evidence "that he concerned himself one whit about New Jersey politics before 1907."[15]

An early champion and confidant of Wilson's was journalist George Harvey, a power in the Cleveland wing of the party. Harvey's association with New Jersey dated from 1883, when he became New Jersey bureau chief of Joseph Pulitzer's influential Democratic organ, the New York *World.*

By 1899, Harvey had bought the *North American Review* and become editor of *Harper's Weekly*, but he summered at an estate in the Jersey Shore town of Deal, maintained interest in New Jersey Democratic politics, and a friendship with James Smith, leader of the Essex County Democratic organization.[16] Smith was president of a Newark bank, publisher of the *Newark Evening Star*, a friend of Public Service, and had served as U.S. senator from 1892 to 1898. His nephew, James R. Nugent, was state party chairman.

Harvey urged Wilson to seek the Democratic Senate nomination to gain credibility for a presidential run in 1912 and offered to intercede with the Smith–Nugent faction, which had little interest in who got the "empty" designation. Wilson permitted his name to go forward but did not seem to have his heart in the enterprise. Hudson Progressive Joseph Tumulty, who proposed the eventual designee, described events in the legislative nominating session: "The speech nominating Woodrow Wilson...was the shortest on record. It was delivered by one of the Smith–Nugent men from Essex County....No applause greeted the name of the man he nominated. It seemed as if the college professor had no friends in the Legislature except the man who had put his name forward."[17]

Wilson eventually withdrew his name, but his failure to endorse the Progressives' nominee seemed further proof that Wilson was not one of them. Tumulty was thus unenthused when the Princetonian surfaced again as a gubernatorial candidate in 1910: "We suspected that the 'Old Gang' was up to its old trick of foisting upon the Democrats of the state a tool...who, under the name of the Democratic party would do the bidding of the corporate interests which had, under both the 'regular' organizations, Democratic and Republican, found in New Jersey their most nutritious pastures." At a strategy meeting (held, typically, in a New York City club), Tumulty and the other "Young Turks" pledged their "undying opposition" to Wilson's candidacy.[18]

Unknown to them, however, Wilson had become converted to the Progressive agenda between 1908 and 1910, and more convinced that he wanted to seek national office. The governorship became a means to that end. As he wrote to a friend and Princeton trustee, David B. Jones on June 27, 1910, "The question of my nomination for the governorship of New Jersey is the mere preliminary of a plan to nominate me in 1912 for the presidency....Last evening I dined with Colonel Watterson of the Louisville Courrier [sic] Journal, Colonel [George] Harvey, of Harper's Weekly, and James Smith, the reputed Democratic boss of New Jersey....Whatever one may think of Colonel Watterson, there can be no doubt of his immense political influence....before the evening was over [Watterson] said that, if New Jersey would make me Governor, he would agree to take off his coat and work for my nomination in 1912. The opportunity really seems most unusual."[19]

With Harvey's advice to stay out of the party's internecine battles and his own sharp political instincts, Wilson at first steered a cautious course. He declined to take any public position on contentious issues like regulation of the utilities, direct U.S. Senate elections, or workmen's compensation. To an intermediary, John Maynard Harlan, he wrote on June 23, 1910, "I would be perfectly willing to assure Mr. Smith that I would not, if elected Governor, set about 'fighting and breaking down the existing Democratic organization.'"[20] This confirmed Progressive opinion that Wilson was the regulars' cats–paw. The *Trenton Evening Times* editorialized that his failure to answer the questions directed to all the candidates was "conclusive proof of his hypocrisy."[21]

Still, most of the regulars were also suspicious. At the June meeting of the state committee, 20 of the 21 county leaders, including Smith's nephew, Nugent, favored Frank Katzenbach, the 1907 nominee. But Wilson had the most crucial party leaders, Smith and "Little Bob" Davis of Jersey City, in his corner. Smith, who had sent three sons to Princeton, liked the idea of being a president–maker and backing a winner who could deliver state and then federal patronage. Davis favored Wilson because he could ensure the defeat of Otto Wittpen, Davis's local nemesis and another gubernatorial hopeful. Smith and Davis prevailed, and so, on September 15, 1910, the unwilling delegates assembled in Trenton to make their nomination: "They were arriving all day....to renew old friendships with men they had not seen in years, to smoke awful convention cigars and to talk and talk and talk....'Frank's entitled to it and he's going to have it!' is a declaration I heard over and over again. And a disquieting question I heard, too, many times: Where does Wilson come in? Do you ever see him...."[22]

Wilson's acceptance speech to the distrustful convention delegates truly began the reform era. He proclaimed his independence from the bosses, voiced strong support for equal taxation of corporations, and advocated a regulatory public utilities commission. All around him, Joe Tumulty heard the cry, "Thank God, at last, a leader has come!"[23]

As the campaign went on, Wilson's criticisms of the "bosses" of his own party became even more trenchant. The campaign's turning point was provided by Republican Progressive George L. Record, who had labored in the trenches of reform since the days of the Fagan mayoralty in Jersey City. In his Jersey City newspaper column, Record challenged Wilson to a debate on progressivism. Wilson declined to debate a noncandidate but said he would answer questions in writing. Record then addressed 19 probing questions to Wilson.

Wilson's responses, published in most of the state's newspapers in the last week of October, determined the election's outcome. In answer to Record's query, "Do you admit that the boss system exists as I have described it?" Wilson replied, "Of course I admit it. Its existence is notorious. I have made it my business for many years to observe and understand that system, and I hate it as thoroughly as I understand it. You are quite right in saying that the system is bipartisan."

When Record asked how "such Democratic leaders as Smith, Nugent and Davis" differed from a number of Republicans, including the last three governors, Wilson responded, "They differ from the others in this, that they are in control of the government of the State, while the others are not and cannot be if the present Democratic ticket is elected."[24] Record concluded, "That letter will elect Wilson governor," and historian Arthur Link has compared its importance to the Lincoln–Douglas debates.[25] Wilson's 54 percent margin was the most decisive win for a New Jersey Democrat since the institution of an elected governor and equal to the best Republican performances. So great was his victory that the assembly also passed into Democratic hands for the first time since 1893.

Once in office, the former professor fulfilled his campaign promises, mostly in the extraordinary 1911 legislative session. Wilson achieved passage of the direct primary for all offices, establishment of a regulatory public utilities commission, and workman's compensation legislation. From a political standpoint, however, the most stunning event was the opportunity to elect a Democratic U.S. senator—an event beyond the Democrats' "wildest dreams or vain imaginings."[26]

It was here that Wilson's mettle was truly tested. Boss Smith was staggered by the governor's legislative agenda, but his most important personal agenda was to return to the U.S. Senate, from which he had been swept after the Democratic legislative debacle in the 1890s. Support of Smith would give the lie to everything Wilson had pledged. The situation was further complicated by the results of a preferential primary, which would give the nomination to a perennial candidate and buffoon, the "farmer–orator" James Martine. Martine had run unsuccessfully eleven times for various state and federal offices. His selection by the small number who bothered to vote in the preferential primary underscored the Democrats' disbelief that they could actually be in a position to select the next U.S. senator.

Many thought Wilson's best strategy was to stay out of the race and claim it was the legislature's problem. However, the new governor defended the hapless Martine against both Smith and the Republican incumbent, utility magnate and former gubernatorial candidate John Kean. In a statement to the *Trenton True American*, on December 24, 1910, Wilson observed, "So far as the voters of the state are concerned and the state's essential interests, there is no reason why a change should be made from Mr. John Kean to Mr. James Smith, Jr. They are believed to stand for the same influence and to represent the same group of selfish interests.... If Mr. Smith is sent back to the United States Senate, the Democratic party and State itself is once more delivered into the hands of the very influence from which it had struggled to set itself free."[27]

The governor–elect's conversion to reform was genuine, but he also had in mind the effect of the Senate election on the national future of his party and his own prospects in 1912. As Wilson wrote George Harvey on November 15, 1910, "ridiculous though it undoubtedly is,—I think we shall have to stand with Mr. Martine. After all that has been said and done, we shall be stultified if we do not." Addressing the larger issue, he continued, "It is a national as well as a State question. If the independent Republicans who in this state voted for me are not to be attracted to us they will assuredly turn again to Mr. Roosevelt, and the chance of a generation will be lost to the Democracy: the chance...through new leaders...to constitute the ruling party of the country for the next generation."[28]

When the new legislature turned its attention to the choice for Senate, Martine received 40 votes on the first ballot (one short of the number needed for election) and Smith only ten. With the outcome clear, Smith released his supporters, and Wilson exulted to a friend, Mary A. Hulbert, "My victory was overwhelmingly complete."[29] It only remained to remove Nugent as party chairman. A drunken encounter with members of the New Jersey National Guard at a shore restaurant contributed to Nugent's demise. Raising his glass, Nugent told the appalled officers, "I propose a toast to the governor of New Jersey, the commander–in–chief of the Militia, an ingrate and a liar. Do I drink alone?"[30]

To keep his chairmanship, Nugent refused to convene the state committee, which then held a rump meeting in Asbury Park in August. Nugent arrived at the conclave with a "strong–arm mob of petty gangsters from New York" and "kidnapped" a committee member to deny the group a quorum. When another member arrived to reestablish the quorum, the committee promptly voted to remove the Essex boss.[31]

After the brilliant successes of 1911, Wilson's momentum slowed. In the legislative elections at the end of the year, the Republicans recaptured control of the assembly, despite the governor's plea that the election be seen as a referendum on his record. In large measure, he was thwarted by his nominal partisans, Smith and Nugent. The bosses sat out the election in their Essex County redoubt. The Essex vote was barely half that of 1910 and resulted in a complete Republican victory there.

Wilson became increasingly preoccupied with his presidential quest, leaving the state for long periods and making little effort to conciliate the legislature's Republican majority. Although he carried New Jersey in the three–way presidential contest of 1912, his 41 percent share of the vote was down thirteen points from his gubernatorial showing only two years earlier, and slightly behind his national performance.

In March 1912, Wilson resigned the governorship to take up his new duties in Washington. He took with him Joe Tumulty, the progressive Democrats' most effective political tactician. Two and a half years, as dazzling as they were, could not obliterate the state's traditional political patterns: "New Jersey did not have Wilson long enough."[32] With the Progressives' commander gone, the regulars reasserted themselves.

Political energy quickly passed from Trenton back to the county satraps. Hudson's "Little Bob" Davis had died in 1911, leaving the Smith–Nugent Essex organization even more dominant in the party's perennial internal struggles. However, Hudson County would soon produce a new leader whose skills and staying power would far surpass those of Wilson.

THE BOSS: FRANK HAGUE AND THE "GIBRALTAR OF DEMOCRACY"

Woodrow Wilson began public life as a sympathizer of the regulars and then blazed an extraordinary career as a reformer. Frank Hague, the state's other legendary political figure, followed precisely the opposite path. He rose to prominence as a purported reformer and spent a long career as the apotheosis of the regulars.

In 1875, the year Jersey City rid itself of the "ripper" laws giving Trenton Republicans control of its government, Hague was born in Jersey City's Irish Catholic Horseshoe. The Horseshoe's political life was organized around its saloons, and Hague got his start in politics when one of the saloonkeepers backed his run for constable in 1896.

Hague rose steadily through the Hudson Democratic organization, becoming a deputy sheriff in 1898, a precinct leader in 1901, and a ward leader in 1906. He was 36 when Davis died in 1911 and became an important warlord among the factions that emerged thereafter. By 1916, Hague was able to name two county freeholders, the county surrogate, and two members of the state assembly.[33] In that year he was elected Jersey City's commissioner of public safety, giving him command of the police and fire departments. This post had rich political payoffs—control of many patronage jobs and the very public employees charged with "enforcing" election laws.

Political reform movements often produce outcomes opposite to what the reformers wish. New Jersey in this period provides an example. Hague achieved power by using some of the Progressives' most cherished policies for his own ends—in particular the direct primary and government reorganization schemes aimed, like the primary, at sapping the strength of party bosses and their allies.[34]

After a series of half-measures, New Jersey fully adopted the direct primary with passage of the Geran Act in 1911. Its intended consequence was clear: to take nominations out of the hands of party organizations and give them to "the people." The reality, however, especially in the Democratic party, was to increase the power of organizations in the populous counties that were able to dominate primaries because of their large numbers of voters.

Malapportionment made it difficult to end Republican legislative control, especially in the senate, whose 21 members each represented one county, regardless of population size. On the other hand, the large populations of the few reliable Democratic counties made it possible for Democrats to prevail in gubernatorial elections—at least after political independents and Republicans with reformist tendencies learned with Wilson the habit of voting for mildly progressive Democratic candidates.

As long as the Smith–Nugent regulars dominated the Essex County Democracy, such candidates were likely to come from Hudson County, and about half the Hudson vote came from Jersey City. Thus, Hudson and Jersey City became the key players in Democratic gubernatorial politics just at the time Hague's influence in the Hudson organization was growing.

Municipal reform was another Progressive idea that Hague turned to his own purposes. The 1913 Walsh Act permitted municipalities to adopt commission–style government, and Jersey City chose to do so. This form of government, entailing election of commissioners who head specific administrative departments and are accountable for their performance, gave Hague control over the most politically sensitive and useful organ of city government—the police.

Similar reorganization schemes for state government were also transformed into a source of power for the Hudson organization. By the time Wilson became governor, state boards and commissions were proliferating. Their members, appointed by the legislature, were a fertile source of patronage for county party leaders. When Wilson appointed a commission to study reorganization in 1912, his legislative message inquired quizzically, "Why should every oyster bed have a commission of its own?"[35]

Although it would be another 35 years before Trenton's administrative quagmire was overhauled by a new constitution, a number of agencies were consolidated between 1915 and 1920, with appointment powers given to the governor. These became additional patronage resources for the county leaders to whom Democratic governors owed their election—and most of these leaders, like Frank Hague, were in Hudson County.

Finally, external events also aided Hague in unanticipated ways. The traditional opponents of Hudson's Irish Catholic politicians were German Protestants. The outbreak of World War I damaged the political careers of German–American politicians. Even the national movement for Prohibition was a boon for the politicians then in power. Prohibition, or its selective enforcement in Hudson County, closed down saloons that were the organizational hubs for the opposition.

All these things came together for Hague in the years between 1917 and 1920. In 1917, Hague was elected Jersey City's mayor, which began his preeminence in the Hudson County organization. He consolidated his power over the state party when the Smith–Nugent machine was defeated decisively in the 1919 gubernatorial election, and progressive Republicans took control in Essex.

In the 1919 Democratic gubernatorial primary, Nugent was opposed by Hudson's Edward I. Edwards, a Progressive who had been the Democrats' U.S. Senate candidate in 1908 when Woodrow Wilson first considered entering state politics. Edwards defeated Nugent by a margin of about 14,000 votes. Nugent won Essex by 13,000 votes, but thanks to Hague, he lost Hudson by 25,000. Edwards went on to a narrow win in the general election. A beneficiary of enhanced gubernatorial patronage, he gifted Hague with the power to name the president of the state civil service commission, a third of the members of the public utilities commission, the state highway engineer, and the members of the Hudson County tax board and board of elections. Hague's success in this election also gave him a role in the national party. He led New Jersey's delegation to the 1920 Democratic national convention and became the state's national party committeeman, a position he held for almost 30 years. The 1922 Democratic gubernatorial victor, George S. Silzer, added to Hague's authority the appointment of the county prosecutor and many judicial nominations.[36]

The 1919 and 1922 elections solidified Hague's domination of state politics. Through 1940, the partisan vote in the rest of the state was balanced closely enough that massive Democratic majorities in Hudson (which earned it the sobriquet "the Gibraltar of Democracy") could produce a Democratic gubernatorial victory most of the time.

Between 1916 and 1940, Democrats won six of the nine gubernatorial contests, and their victories were usually attributable to Hudson landslides. For example, Silzer in 1922 won by 46,000 votes statewide, and by 80,000 in Hudson. His successor, Hudson County's A. Harry Moore, ran 38,000 votes ahead of his Republican opponent statewide and an astonishing 103,000 votes ahead in his home bailiwick. Moore would go on to win twice more in nonconsecutive contests in 1931 and 1937 and still holds the state record for years of service—nine—in the elected governorship.[37]

Not only did Hague produce victories for Democratic governors, but he put Republicans in his thrall as well. The Hudson "dictator" was perfectly willing to collude with Republicans to secure his home base and maintain control of Hudson's patronage. In 1916, Hague assured the election of Republican Walter E. Edge because Edge's opponent was Hague's Hudson archenemy, Otto Wittpen. The Democratic majority in Hudson, as compared with the previous election, was cut by almost two–thirds: "Organization Democrats were not urged to vote Republican in that election; they simply were urged not to vote."[38]

Edge returned the favor. One of his major goals was improved transportation links to New York and especially, given his South Jersey home base, Philadelphia. Northern New Jersey was then connected directly to New York City only by rail links. Pedestrians and automobiles still traveled on ferries, as they did to Philadelphia. To win approval of a bridge to Philadelphia that North Jersey had long opposed, Edge paired the South Jersey project with a vehicular tunnel to New York, conveniently entering the state in Jersey City. The two proposals were submitted to the legislature simultaneously and passed with Hudson's backing.

The 1928 and 1934 elections also demonstrated Hague's ability to profit from inevitable Republican victories. As in 1916, the Democrats were hard–pressed in the 1928 gubernatorial race because of the flood of Republican presidential voters. Hague therefore backed the most "cooperative" Republican, Morgan S. Larsen of Middlesex County, who won the general election. A 1929 inquiry established that 22,000 Hudson Democrats participated in the Republican gubernatorial primary.

In 1934, Hague faced the prospect of an extraordinarily popular Republican gubernatorial candidate, Harold G. Hoffman of normally Democratic Middlesex County. As a Middlesex Democratic paper editorialized, "We were opposed to his election but....He swept through the District even in strong Democratic sections with an ease that made one fairly gasp for breath."[39] The charismatic Hoffman had the same effect statewide. He won office in the only federal midterm election year in history that the sitting President's party (and not Hoffman's) has ever gained congressional seats and despite an 80,000 vote plurality in Hudson for his opponent.

However, it was not long before Hoffman, too, found himself in the debt of the Hudson County boss. Like the rest of the nation, New Jersey faced a staggering Depression–era welfare burden. True to their heritage, voters remained adamantly opposed to a revenue–producing statewide tax. To meet a $2–million–per– month relief bill, much of which emanated from Jersey City, the governor proposed a statewide sales tax. Hoffman managed to guide it through the assembly by a 31–to–27 margin, although outraged voters obtained its repeal four months later. Only 11 of Hoffman's Republican colleagues supported it; the other twenty votes came from Hague–controlled Democrats. Immediately after the vote, Hoffman named the Democratic assembly minority leader to the state's highest court and other Hudson figures to many boards and commissions.

Hague's patronage resources were not limited to New Jersey. Although a firm supporter of his Irish Catholic co–religionist Al Smith in both 1928 and 1932, Hague was willing to back Franklin D. Roosevelt just as strongly in exchange for New Jersey's share of federal patronage. Smith won a 61 percent to 39 percent victory over Roosevelt in New Jersey's 1932 presidential primary. Yet once Roosevelt defeated Smith (and Hague's second choice, John Nance Garner) at the Democratic national convention, the mayor produced one of the largest turnouts in history for Roosevelt's kick–off campaign rally. It was held at Governor Moore's summer home in Sea Girt in August.[40]

Hague gifted Roosevelt with a 118,000–vote margin in Hudson County in November, enabling the Democrat to carry New Jersey by 38,000 votes. Roosevelt carried the state all four times he ran, but only in 1936 could he have done so without Hudson County. It was Hague and Chicago boss Ed Kelly who were largely responsible for Roosevelt's unprecedented third–term nomination in 1940.

Hague himself had suffered near electoral defeat in 1929, when the ungrateful Republican governor Larsen launched a legislative probe of political corruption in Hudson County and Hague's personal finances. Although Hague had never earned more than $8,000 a year, an investigating committee discovered $393,000 in transactions by dummy corporations connected to Hague that handled real estate and bank stock. When the mayor refused to answer the committee's questions, he was arrested for contempt. A Hague–selected justice quickly granted him habeas corpus, and the state's highest court, also populated with his designees, upheld the writ.

Fortuitously, the onset of the Great Depression revived the mayor's popularity. New Deal relief programs gave Hague access "to huge amounts of *legal* money and jobs."[41] His affronted constituents forgot their moral scruples in their need for Hague's patronage. By 1939, one out of every twenty Hudson County adults depended on it for his or her livelihood.[42]

Yet by 1940, the mayor's statewide power was slipping, and cities had begun the population decline from which they would never recover. In the 1940s, New Jersey gained 700,000 people, most of them suburban commuters to New York and Philadelphia. The last "Hague governor," Charles Edison (son of inventor Thomas), elected in the first year of the decade, was a reform–minded New Deal official whom FDR imposed on the county boss. One of Edison's first official acts was to disconnect Hague's private telephone line to the governor's office.[43]

The next gubernatorial election, in 1943, was won by Republican Walter E. Edge, who after years in the U.S. Senate, diplomatic service, and retirement, returned to the office to which he had been elected in 1916. A 97,000 vote Democratic plurality in Hudson was now offset by an almost identical advantage for Edge out of the Essex and Bergen suburbs.

Hague's decline through the 1940s was only gradual, however. Although unable to prevent Republican gubernatorial victories for Edge or his successor, Alfred Driscoll, in 1947, the mayor extracted the same sort of concessions he had exacted from Edge back in 1916. The signal New Jersey political battle of the 1940s, described in detail in chapter 7, was the struggle for a new constitution to replace the antiquated 1844 state charter. It was Hague's last major victory.

For the mayor, the important matters in the constitutional campaign were protecting the judicial patronage that kept him free of investigation and obtaining concessions on railroad taxes, still a major issue in Hudson County. Edge, who pledged in 1943 to end Republican cooperation with Hague, could not be budged. Their combat over the constitution in 1944 overshadowed all other political happenings: "The presidential duel between Roosevelt and Dewey was a matter of secondary importance."[44]

To win this final victory, Hague reached into the primal psyches of his supporters. He began with extensive newspaper advertising, claiming the new constitution's tax provisions were a front for lower railroad taxes and the opening wedge for a state income tax, and that the new charter also threatened the tenure and pensions of public employees. The fatal blow, however, was Hague's charge in the last days before the election that the document was anti–Catholic.

Rumors spread that church property would be taxed under the new constitution and priests forced to reveal the secrets of the confessional. The Newark archdiocese ordered all priests to speak against the constitution the Sunday before the election. Despite formation of a group of prominent Catholic laity (such as a U.S. senator and the editor of the *Trenton Times*) to combat the hysterical rumors, Hague's denunciation of the referendum as a tool of the railroads and the Protestant Republicans was primarily responsible for the 54 percent to 46 percent defeat of the proposed constitution.[45]

Governor Driscoll, Edge's successor, took a more pragmatic approach to the Hudson leader. He first negotiated a change in railroad taxes that produced a $5 million annual windfall for Jersey City and then supported constitutional revision that would leave much of the county court system intact. Finally, instead of a Republican–dominated legislature sitting as a convention, as proposed in 1944, Driscoll suggested a bipartisan elected body.

Hague's reversal of position was dramatic. He told his followers, "I cannot too strongly urge all of you to support it on election day....With this new constitution, we forgive everyone—because we won."[46] This time, the constitutional convention referendum passed easily. In response to cries of a sellout, Driscoll remarked with considerable foresight that "equal treatment...would remove one of the major issues on which Hague has flourished—that he was Hudson's only savior."[47]

Driscoll's characterization of Hague explains how a man called a "dictator" and an "American fascist" maintained power for over three decades. No amount of electoral chicanery can yield margins like the 111,000–to–7,000 victory he achieved in 1937. Governor Edge wrote in 1948 of his long–time antagonist, "He is a cold, calculating and ruthless political boss, but he is at the same time an able administrator with strong humanitarian qualities, and Jersey City is in many ways a well–managed municipality."[48]

Where one stood on Hague depended on where one sat. From a "good government" perspective, Hague was a loathsome creature, ruling through criminality and intimidation. His control of civil service regulatory bodies made the "merit system" a sham, as Hague dismissed opponents on grounds of "economic necessity" or "job abolition." Willingness to pay the organizational "mace" of from 3 to as much as 40 percent of the annual take from patronage jobs and contracts, was the chief qualification for their award. Hague's command of the criminal justice system allowed him to seek or quash criminal indictments as he pleased.[49] Supervision of the police had many uses. At election time, "It was relatively easy for Hague's people manning the polls to erase ballots, change ballots, destroy ballots, miscount ballots—while Hague–controlled policemen looked the other way or pressured inspection officials to stand aside.... [a state election superintendent said of the 1925 gubernatorial election] 'we know it is futile to arrest anyone belonging to the Democrat organization in Hudson County on Election Day. The accuser usually finds himself in jail as the arrested party by the time he gets to the station house....' "[50] The police were on the job for the mayor every day of the year, protecting businesses, legal and illegal, that enriched the machine and its leader and intimidating those that did not. Jersey City became the illegal betting capital of the nation. Illicit wagering on races at every major track in the U.S. and Canada earned the city the title of the "Horse Bourse."[51] Famed gangster Joseph "Newsboy" Moriarity operated a $10 million a year numbers racket under police protection. Friendly mobsters and cooperative AFL unions controlled the Jersey City waterfront, while CIO organizers were called "Communists" and driven out.[52]

By conservative estimate, these varied activities brought in $1 million to $1.5 million per year for the Hudson Democrats, and the constabulary received its share. A study of police forces in U.S. cities of similar size found that the average Jersey City police salary was 65 percent higher than its closest competitor.[53]

Yet from the perspective of the mayor's Catholic and working–class constituents, Hague was a savior. Christmas turkeys, coal for winter heating, and summer picnics for thousands of children accompanied the patronage employment. New Deal money built Hague's proudest monument, the 2,000–bed Jersey City Medical Center. Offering free care to residents, it was then the third largest hospital in the world. Hague's stinginess regarding public education did not concern those who sent their children to parochial schools. If garbage collection still depended on horse–drawn carts into the 1940s, failure to mechanize preserved many jobs.

Illegal betting was "clean graft;" the mayor, who neither smoked nor drank, was diligent in keeping drugs and prostitution out of Jersey City; and women were barred from public taprooms. Yet this most traditional of men gave women political opportunities long before they were available elsewhere. Hudson women served in the state assembly and county governing body from the early 1920s, and U.S. Representative Mary T. Norton was sent to Washington for 13 terms beginning in 1925.[54]

Hague embodied the resentment of Catholics and workers toward Protestants and corporations. His crusade against these enemies began in 1917, when the new mayor announced he was raising municipal taxes on Standard Oil from $1 million to $14 million, on the Public Service Corporation from $3 million to $30 million, and on the railroads from $67 million to $160 million. The State Board of Taxation's cancellation of this edict was seen as proof of Hague's charge that Republican Governor Edge and his board were "the tools of the interests."

Detractors were appalled when Hague made his famous pronouncement, "I am the law." His supporters put it in context—Hague made the remark when he gave jobs to young delinquents without legal working papers, a plan the mayor regarded as more effective rehabilitation than a term in reform school.[55]

When critics demanded "reform" of the Hague organization, Hudsonites recalled that "reform was often a code word for Protestant hegemony and Catholic disenfranchisement."[56] It was this world view that Hague used in his shameful attack on the constitutional referendum. As Thomas Fleming has observed of the sectarianism of the 1870s, "only by grasping its persistence as a motive force can the political and social history of the state for the next several decades be understood."[57]

In 1947, Hague, who spent increasing time at his homes in New York City and Florida, resigned the mayoralty he had held for 30 years and installed his nephew, Frank Hague Eggers, in his place. He still retained his seat on the Democratic National Committee, control of federal patronage, and selection of county officials and the 1949 Democratic gubernatorial nominee. Yet Hague's political life was ending. Returning war veterans with a broader view of the world recoiled from machine politics, high tax rates, and declining public services.

Other ethnic groups—Italians and eastern Europeans—were now a majority in Jersey City. They became restive at their exclusion from the organization's upper echelons when Hague continued his traditional practice of awarding city council nominations to four Irish Catholics and a token Protestant.

John V. Kenny, the most senior of Hague's ward leaders (known as the "Twelve Apostles"), resented being passed over in favor of the mayor's nephew. He allied himself with Poles and Italians and ran as a "reform" opponent against Eggers in 1949. The torchlight parade celebrating the Kenny ticket's victory "resembled nothing less than the liberation of Paris five years earlier."[58] A tightly controlled Hudson County organization was dying. Discipline disintegrated as 51 county freeholder candidates contested a few seats in 1950.

Hague, who finally resigned the last of his positions after the 1949 rout, and whose allies lost local Hudson battles thereafter, died in his New York City apartment in 1956 at the age of 81. His mausoleum still dominates Jersey City's Holy Name Cemetery. Hague was unable to build a strong statewide Democratic organization and had little interest in doing so. His departure accelerated political change and made development of a statewide Democratic party possible for the first time.

The Democrats were aided by one of the state's frequent political scandals. In the spring of 1953, the Republican state chairman testified that gamblers had made large contributions to Governor Driscoll's reelection campaign. There were also allegations that the governor had personally collected "protection money." Driscoll forcefully denied the charges, and the alleged go-between was tried and acquitted. Still, the damage was done, and Democrat Robert Meyner of Warren County, candidate of the party's anti–Hague forces, coasted to victory in 1953, even as the Republicans maintained control of both houses of the legislature.[59]

Warren County was a Democratic stronghold, but it was small, largely rural, and on the banks of the Delaware River, far from ethnic and boss–controlled Hudson and Middlesex. Meyner distributed patronage to counties where Democrats were traditionally weak, but whose local leaders had backed his campaign. The traditional bosses' displeasure was an overall plus for the governor, contributing to an image that pleased many voters. As a writer for state's leading newspaper, the *Newark Evening News*, commented on January 20, 1958: "He came to terms with party bosses, while preserving a reputation for independence. He has so thinned out his image that he won over the progressive concerned with human welfare and the conservative concerned with property. His youthful energy delighted the young, his marriage [while in office] enchanted the romantic, his concern about the aged, the disabled, the underpaid and underprivileged touched the public conscience."[60]

The 1947 constitution made Meyner the first Democratic governor who could run for reelection. He achieved a resounding victory in 1957 over well–known financier and Republican state senator Malcolm Forbes, and the Democrats gained control of the assembly for the first time since 1937. They would remain dominant or highly competitive in state politics thereafter, although New Jersey continued to tilt Republican in presidential elections.

The Republicans' own long–standing factionalism also helped the Democrats. One of its sources was regional competition between the party's northern and southern wings, usually led by Essex and Atlantic counties, respectively. A second was ideological disagreement between the GOP's progressives and regulars. This intense feud resulted in two relatively centralized and competing sources of Republican campaign funds for candidates representing the party's two wings.[61]

Finally, because legislative control (especially of the state senate) was so crucial to the Republicans' power base, its county party leaders, unlike the Democrats, regularly sought legislative election. The Republican analogue to Frank Hague was Atlantic County Senator Frank "Hap" Farley, who served for thirty years between 1941 and 1972. Through control over other Republican senators from small southern counties, Farley dominated the legislature. Like Hague, the patronage–minded Farley had little desire or ability to build a statewide party.

It might thus appear that Meyner's governorship ushered in a new political era. The new constitution created one of the strongest state executives in the country. Governors could now run for two four–year terms, they were the only statewide elected officials, they appointed all high–level officials to a greatly reduced number of more powerful cabinet departments and courts, and they had a variety of strong veto powers.

Further, although Meyner's first victory and that of his successor, Richard J. Hughes, depended on the Hudson County vote, both won easily without Hudson in their second races, as did a later Democratic governor, Brendan Byrne (1974 to 1982), in both his contests. The Hudson organization was no longer essential to Democrats' statewide success, and it had also degenerated into factionalism. After Kenney, no Jersey City mayor of the next fifty years would complete two terms in succession.

On the other hand, although party organizations now counted for less in general elections, until the 1970s they remained central to nomination contests. Governor Byrne, a superior court judge whose primary victory was assured when a wiretapped mobster called him a man who "couldn't be bought," has admitted he would not have sought office in 1973 without Hudson county's endorsement.[62] The same was true of his predecessor, Richard Hughes. William T. Cahill (1970 to 1974), the lone Republican victor between 1949 and 1981, and a man loath to deal with Republican county leaders, was denied renomination when those leaders withdrew their support.

County organizations also continued as arbiters of governors' legislative success well into the 1960s. In the senate, malapportionment favoring the smaller Republican counties meant that Meyner and Hughes faced a Republican senate dominated by "Hap" Farley for fourteen of the sixteen years they served. For many years, the Republicans required eleven votes (a majority of the entire senate) in their caucus before any bill would be released. Thus, as the writer of an editorial in the National Municipal Review pointed out, in 1950 when there were 14 Republicans in the senate, only four Republican senators representing 3 percent of the state's population could hold a proposal hostage. The Review asked rhetorically, "What is the essential difference between the Russian system and the New Jersey system?"[63]

Even a partisan majority was no guarantee of gubernatorial success. In 1945, a second attempt to revise the 1844 constitution failed because of the opposition of Essex Republican leader Arthur T. Vanderbilt to elements of his own governor's proposal. Comparing Vanderbilt to Hague, Governor Edge later wrote of this impasse, "Vanderbilt, in a benevolent way, was as absolute a political boss in the Republican Party as Hague was in the Democratic organization. While these two men used their power to different ends...his control over the thirteen Essex legislators was just as absolute....For the second year in succession,

New Jersey had lost the opportunity to modernize its archaic constitution."[64]

New gubernatorial powers in the revised charter still did not give the governor reliable control over county–controlled legislators. Meyner met regularly "with his political cabinet of Democratic county leaders when the Legislature [was] in session to decide on the action to be taken on major legislative policy questions." Their periodic rebellion suggested that "no New Jersey political party can ever be more than a confederation of county organizations, more or less held together by the glue of patronage."[65]

Emboldened by a 1965 landslide victory and the 20th century's first Democratic legislative majorities in both houses, Meyner's successor, Governor Hughes, proposed the abidingly unthinkable, a state income tax. The urgent need for more state aid, especially for hard–pressed cities, was all the more evident because of the recent major riot in Newark. The tax went down to defeat when the Essex Democratic leader withdrew his support. Republican Governor Cahill received almost no backing from his party's legislative majorities for a similar proposal in the next administration.[66] Although county leaders were more likely to attend to parochial issues affecting their own powers and patronage resources than to broader public policy, these instances demonstrate the power they could exert when they so chose.

Yet internal forces already threatened the dominance of the county party organizations–especially the decline of the cities and the growth of middle class suburbs. Between 1940 and 1960, New Jersey's population swelled by almost half—from about four million to six million residents. Only California grew faster. Almost all of the population increase was in the suburbs.

Counties that doubled in size in this period included Bergen and Morris in the north, Middlesex and Somerset in the central part of the state, Monmouth and Ocean along the shore, and Burlington and Gloucester in the south. In contrast, Hudson's population declined, and Essex only held steady. By 1970, the "Big Six" cities (Camden, Elizabeth, Jersey City, Newark, Paterson, and Trenton) had lost half their total population of 1930 and contributed but 11 percent to the statewide vote.[67]

Many of the new suburban residents had little interest in state politics. Large numbers worked in New York and Philadelphia, and their political information came from sources in those cities. New Jersey and Delaware were (and remain) the only states without their own network television stations.[68] Residents thus listened to out–of–state "local news" on television, as did over half of those who used radio as a major source of political information.

Of the ten largest circulation newspapers, four were published in New York or Philadelphia. New Jersey–based papers were locally oriented, serving small central cities and their surrounding areas, or covering sprawling suburbs. The leading Newark papers circulated fairly widely but served only a limited number of readers in the northern half of the state. Although they did reach much of the narrow political elite, they could not reflect or shape public opinion.

Thus, New Jersey residents remained notoriously ignorant, apathetic, and cynical about state politics. In October 1973, more residents in the northern part of the state could name a candidate in New York City's mayoral election than could identify a New Jersey gubernatorial candidate [69].

We cannot know when this archaic system would have fallen of its own weight, for its end came from an external source—the U.S. Supreme Court's 1964 decision in *Reynolds v. Sims*. Noting that the Supreme Court's mandate of "one person, one vote," was flagrantly violated in the state senate, the New Jersey Supreme Court enjoined further legislative elections and called for an interim election plan and constitutional revision. It further rejected an attempt to retain a county–based senate using weighted voting.

In 1966, a constitutional convention created a forty–member senate and an eighty–member assembly, whose districts were to be composed of "contiguous territory, as nearly compact and equal in the number of their inhabitants as possible." Another state supreme court decision in 1972 specifically directed that county boundaries be ignored in the drawing of district lines in favor of more attention to population equality and contiguity.[70] In thus destroying the county organizations' control over legislative nominations, the court did much to destroy their overall political role.

Other developments completed the job by ending much of the county organizations' influence on gubernatorial nominations as well.[71] By the early 1970s, campaign finance reform was on the national agenda because of the Watergate scandal, and its appeal was strengthened in New Jersey by scandals in the Cahill administration. Governor Byrne, the "man who couldn't be bought," took advantage of the climate and pushed through the first public finance scheme for gubernatorial elections in the United States. Not only did the state provide proportionally more generous public funding than the federal program for presidential contests, but as with the federal plan, money was funneled through candidate committees rather than party organizations.

Byrne himself was the first beneficiary of these developments. In 1977, county leaders withdrew their support of his renomination and ran five different county organization candidates against him in the Democratic primary. Byrne conducted the first statewide campaign heavily dependent on television. His victory, with 28 percent of the vote in a large field of candidates, and his subsequent landslide general election win truly ushered in New Jersey's modern political era. Individual candidates' appeal, television, and money replaced the county organizations as the driving forces in campaigns.[72]

The 1977 gubernatorial election was a genuinely pivotal event, for the content of Byrne's campaign was just as significant as its conduct. In 1973, the state supreme court had overturned the state's public school funding formula based on the local property tax. For three years, the governor and legislature wrangled over the issue. Faced with an injunction shutting down all the public schools in the state, the legislature in 1976 finally passed a statewide income tax.

Yet it was the governor whom voters held chiefly responsible for the income tax. The tax legislation was the major reason that Byrne's approval ratings at the start of the 1977 campaign plummeted to 19 percent. Byrne made his reelection quest a referendum on the need for the income tax. Byrne's opponent could not make a persuasive case that New Jersey could get by without it. The voters demonstrated their respect, if not affection, for the governor by giving him a fourteen–point victory margin.[73] The revenues the income tax generated for state projects went far in making a state politics possible for the first time in New Jersey.

With the end of county party domination, the rise of candidate–centered politics, and an assured flow of money for state initiatives, a genuinely new era for New Jersey politics and policy began in 1977. The new era produced an ironic twist of fate. Governor Byrne was succeeded in 1982 by a Republican who neither sought nor received many county endorsements. He expressed concerns about the role of money in politics and business's social responsibilities, courted and won Hudson County Democratic voters, and significantly expanded the reach and role of state government.[74] One can only wonder what New Jersey's first governor, William Livingston (1776 to 1790), and its Old Guard Republican senators John Kean, (1898 to 1910) and Hamilton Fish Kean (1928 to 1934), would make of their descendant—New Jersey's leading political figure of the 1980s and its two–term governor, Thomas H. Kean.

CHAPTER FOUR

Contemporary Political Patterns

I have eaten everything from sauerbraten to pirogies to tacos, because New Jersey has only about ten fewer ethnic groups than the UN has countries.
—Former Governor Thomas H. Kean[1]

In addition to the number of family members who have served New Jersey in high political office, two–term governor Tom Kean holds another record. Kean was elected by first the smallest and then the largest margins in the history of the elected governorship. In 1981, he won by fewer than 2,000 votes of approximately 2.3 million cast. Four years later, 70 percent of New Jersey voters chose the incumbent.

Split–ticket voting and alternating close and landslide elections are now common everywhere, but New Jersey practices the politics of volatility in one of its more extreme forms. At the same time voters gave Republican President Ronald Reagan a landslide victory in 1984, they awarded an even larger margin to Democratic Senator Bill Bradley. Republican George Bush's comfortable win in 1988 accompanied a similar outcome for Democratic Senator Frank Lautenberg.

This electorate also awarded Governor Brendan Byrne a 1977 victory margin of 14 percent, which almost matched the proportion of citizens rating him favorably at the start of that campaign. The 67 percent of the vote that Byrne received in 1973 set the record Kean eclipsed in 1985. Thus New Jersey voters, within twelve years, went from awarding that record to a Democrat to exceeding it for a Republican.

CONTEMPORARY POLITICS: CHANGE AND CONTINUITY

Although New Jersey is often described as a "typical" northern industrial state, California may be the more apt comparison. Like California, nineteenth–century New Jersey was dominated by the railroads. Their Progressive governors, Woodrow Wilson and Charles Evans Hughes, opposed each other for the presidency in 1916. Both states are strongly demarcated by a north–south split, and have endless beaches threatened by environmental pollution. Today they anchor bicoastal centers of high technology and are leading exemplars of media–based, celebrity–infested politics. Their highways are the most choked with traffic, and their auto insurance problems among the worst in the nation. Culturally polyglot, middle class, independent, suburban voters, many recently arrived from somewhere else, decide their elections.

There are important differences. California went directly from railroad dependency to volatile independence, encouraged by a deeper and more thoroughgoing Progressive heritage. New Jersey made a long stop between corporation–dominated politics and suburban, media–based politics. Its traditional party machines were the symbol of the breed for almost a century. New Jersey also differs from California in its ideological coloration. California often produces representatives of the left wing of the Democratic party and the far–right fringes of the GOP, but both New Jersey parties are dominated by raging moderates. These two differences are not unconnected.

New Jersey's Democrats were never prominent in the ascendant Roosevelt "liberal" wing of their party, when "liberal" had a principally economic definition. Frank Hague, New Jersey Democrats' long–time leader, had a strong antipathy to the labor unions that were a major force among Democratic liberals. New Jersey's many small cities, located from one end of the state to the other, also did not inspire the kind of upstate–downstate, liberal–conservative, Democratic–Republican split of California, Illinois, or New York.

Even the ethnic and religious hostilities separating New Jersey's Democrats and Republicans for a century began to fade as Catholic and Democratic urban dwellers started moving to the suburbs fifty years ago. Hudson County remained an ethnic enclave; Monmouth County—"Jersey City South"—did not. The reform–minded "amateur democrats" who blossomed in New York, Illinois, and California in the 1950s had no counterpart in New Jersey.

The only New Jersey organization of liberal Democratic reformers, ever, was the short–lived New Democratic Coalition (NDC). It grew out of the 1960s' civil rights and antiwar movements and culminated in the 1968 presidential campaigns of Eugene McCarthy and Robert Kennedy. The New Jersey chapter self–destructed in 1969 on the shoals of disagreement between purists and pragmatists. Purists insisted that the 1969 Democratic gubernatorial nominee support a state income tax. Their preferred candidate, antiwar Democrat Henry Helstoski, lost the Democratic gubernatorial primary to former Governor Robert

Meyner, who refused to take such a pledge. Disputes over whether the group should support Meyner, remain neutral, or support Republican William Cahill to "teach the Democrats a lesson" effectively ended the organized NDC.[2]

By the 1960s, New Jersey was poised to become what California already was. The old–style party system remained in place, continuing to dominate state politics because there was no way for the new independent–leaning suburban majority to communicate or for politicians to reach them. They read local newspapers or the Philadelphia and New York press and listened to out–of–state radio stations and watched out–of–state television stations.

The United States and New Jersey supreme courts finally smashed the old political structure based on county party organizations with the reapportionment decisions described in chapter 3. With that external blow, a new system could finally begin to emerge. But the traditional underpinnings did not entirely disappear, and their demographic and geographic vestiges in some respects still remain.

DEMOGRAPHY

The state's politics is rooted in its demography. New Jersey has always been a "multicultural" state. Early Dutch, British, and German settlers were joined in the mid–1800s by the Irish, and shortly thereafter by, among others, large numbers of Italians, Poles, Hungarians, and European Jews.[3] The Jewish population of slightly over 5 percent is proportionally second only to New York, and Catholics, making up over two–fifths of the state's residents, are the fourth highest Catholic population share in the nation.

Ethnic and Religious Patterns

In this century, new groupings have joined the older ones. The 5 percent of the population that was black in 1940 has proportionally tripled in the past fifty years and is the fourteenth largest among the 50 states.[4] Numerous Hispanics, especially Puerto Ricans and Cubans, are among the more recent arrivals, and New Jersey ranks sixth in the U.S. in its proportion of Hispanics. The Newark primary metropolitan statistical area alone is home to 423,000 African Americans and 188,000 Hispanics.

During the 1980s, 266,000 international immigrants entered New Jersey. They accounted for one in twelve of all legal immigrants arriving in the United States.[5] Over two–thirds of the new residents came from India, the Caribbean, and Central and South America. The Newark and Jersey City primary metropolitan statistical areas are both among the top twenty intended destinations declared by immigrants. Between 1980 and 1990, New Jerseyans reporting they spoke a language other than English at home grew from 1.1 million to 1.4 million, or almost a fifth of the entire population.

Like earlier immigrants, many newer ones have settled in urban areas. A quarter of the residents of Hudson County are still foreign born, as they were early in the century, compared to 1 or 2 percent in the more rural counties of the northwest. According to the 1990 census, almost 970,000 New Jerseyans were foreign born, an increase of 27 percent in a decade.[6]

African Americans, the largest minority group, are concentrated in particular areas. Atlantic, Camden, Cumberland, Essex, Salem, and Union counties all have populations that are more than 15 percent black, while the far northwestern counties and Ocean County along the shore are less than 3 percent black. In 1950, Newark, at 17 percent, had the largest proportion of black residents. Now, more than half of Newark, Camden, and Trenton residents are black. Elizabeth and Plainfield in Union County, Paterson in Passaic County, and Atlantic City in Atlantic County also have large black populations. However, there are also heavily black rural areas in Cumberland and Salem, dating back to their days as stops on the Underground Railroad.

To date, voters have chosen statewide officeholders from the earlier arriving ethnic groups. New Jersey did not elect an Irish Catholic to the governorship until the 1960s and did not choose one of Southern European extraction until 1989. Its first Jewish senator, Frank Lautenberg, was thought by many to be a German Protestant. No African American was elected to the U.S. House until 1988.

In local politics (see chapter 13), New Jersey's "tribalism" still holds sway. Hudson County's local races involve mortal combat between Irish, Italian, Polish, African–American, and Cuban candidates, among others. An Italian Republican in the western "Hunt Country" has told us that its WASP Republican establishment finds him unacceptable as county chairman. Statewide candidates can rise above ascriptive identifications. Republican Governor Kean, for example, won a majority of the black vote in 1985 and defeated Democratic opponent Peter Shapiro among Shapiro's Jewish co–religionists. Yet, when one looks at their base areas of strength, there are still significant differences in the demographic makeup of New Jersey's parties.

Bases of the Partisan Vote

We define the "partisan base vote" as the vote in those municipalities that supported candidates of the party defeated in statewide elections in the 1970s and 1980s. In other words, the Republican base consists of municipalities consistently carried by the Republicans' losing gubernatorial and senatorial candidates from 1973 through 1988, while the Democrats' base is those municipalities carried by their losing presidential candidates from 1976 through 1988. Localities with mixed records are "swing" areas. In this period, the Republican base vote remained stable at about 43 percent. The Democratic base vote dropped from 44 percent to 41 percent, and the "swing" vote rose at the Democrats' expense from 13 to 16 percent. The rather even partisan base vote and the growing number of swing areas account for New Jersey's political volatility.

The most staunchly partisan demographic groups are self–identified blacks, Germans, and English. The first is strongly Democratic, and the other two are almost as strongly Republican. Among primarily Catholic ethnic groups, the Irish have moved the most toward the Republican party. Italians and Poles are most likely to be "swing" or split–ticket voters but are more likely than the Irish to wind up in the Democratic column. The highest income areas are the most dependably Republican and the lowest income areas most dependably Democratic.[7]

Geographically, the Republican base has grown in counties with concentrations of its demographic loyalists—Warren and Hunterdon in the northwest and Monmouth, Ocean, and part of Burlington in the south. It has decreased in the most urban portions of Bergen, Essex, Passaic, and Union counties, where the minority vote has increased. Changes in the Democratic base are mirror images of the Republican changes. Democratic strength has grown in areas with large black and Jewish populations.

Areas where the Democratic base is dropping show two different patterns. One inclines voters toward the Republican side, and one moves them toward the "swing" category. Democratic declines in the shore counties—Hunterdon, Warren, and Burlington—represent even weaker performances in traditional Republican areas with growing populations. Most of their new residents come from groups favorably disposed to Republicans, and thus these rapidly growing areas have become even more strongly Republican. In contrast are the declines in Democratic strength in portions of Middlesex, Monmouth, and Union counties. There, Democrats have lost base support in suburban towns—but the older, less wealthy suburbs in these counties. These towns often have large Southern and Eastern European ethnic populations that are shedding traditional Democratic loyalties but are not yet reliably Republican voters either.

To further complicate matters, net shifts in voting within occupational groups over the past two decades show trends in the opposite direction from the current base. A majority of professionals, managers, and white collar workers is still in the Republican camp, but since the 1970s have been trending toward the Democrats. A majority of skilled and unskilled blue collar workers is in the Democratic base, but they have been shifting toward the Republicans. Thus, New Jersey has more than its share of both "limousine liberals" moving Democratic and "lunchbucket conservatives" flirting with the Republicans.

Suburbanization and Population Change

The U.S. Census Bureau classifies every New Jerseyan as an urban dweller. Population density is slightly over a thousand per mile—the highest in the United States. It is three times higher than the average for the Northeast; fifteen times higher than the average for the entire nation. Thus, the fifth smallest American state geographically has the ninth largest population. Yet these figures mask broad internal variations. The density in Essex is 6,000 per mile and an astonishing 12,000 in Hudson. On the other hand, some southern and western counties have fewer than 300 people per square mile.

New Jersey is overwhelmingly suburban rather than urban. Only Newark and Jersey City have populations over 200,000. Smaller cities like Elizabeth, Trenton, and Paterson are not much larger than suburban townships such as Edison and Woodbridge in Middlesex County, Hamilton in Mercer County, Brick in Ocean County, or Cherry Hill in Camden County. These suburban townships have no identifiable "downtowns" or other traditional urban features. Even more New Jerseyans live in prototypical small towns in the northern half of the state, which merge into each other in a seamless web. All these suburbanites meet not downtown, but in vast shopping malls along the major highways.

The Appalachian foothills of the northwest and the southern Pine Barrens were, traditionally, the New Jersey of sparse population and unspoiled natural beauty. Thanks to protective legislation in the 1970s and 1980s, the Pine Barrens—with great stands of forest, blueberry and cranberry bogs, and grassy wetlands—will remain one of the most ecologically pristine areas in the entire Boston–Washington corridor.

Although the Delaware Water Gap, a magnificent 1,200 foot gorge through the Kittatinny Mountains, and other scenic places in the northwest retain their grandeur, newer interstate highways have brought them "closer" to population centers. Each year, as one travels west toward the Delaware River, shopping malls, research parks, and condominium developments march further into the "country," replacing scattered lakeside summer cottages.

Another recent change is a marked shift in the age distribution of the state's people. Between 1970 and 1980, there were large numerical declines among the youngest residents (those up to 14 years of age) and the group most likely to be their parents (aged 35 to 49) and an even larger increase, of almost a quarter, in residents over the age of 65. In the following decade, the younger age cohorts continued to decline, while the oldest cohort went up another fifth in size.[8]

The Economy

A transformation of the occupational structure has also had important effects on politics. Superficially, the New Jersey of 1989 resembled that of 1969, with high incomes and low unemployment. But in 1969, manufacturing employment was at its peak. Over the next five years, inflation–adjusted family income dropped, unemployment more than doubled, and 185,000 manufacturing jobs disappeared. An analyst observed in 1977, "The question of what new industry will arise to replace what is lost is the number one developmental question."[9]

The answer was an explosion of service jobs. Although manufacturing jobs continued to decline three times faster than the national rate, the creation of almost 600,000 jobs in the service sector during the 1980s brought virtually full employment. Jobs in hotels, real estate, legal services, and business services increased by a third to a half. Employment grew by 146 percent in the securities and commodities industry, as Wall Street moved "back–office" jobs across the Hudson. Urban, black, and teenage unemployment dropped by half between 1982 and 1989. At the end of the 1980s, New Jersey's per capita income of $24,683, compared to a national average of $17,596, was second highest among the states. Over the decade, its rate of job creation ranked 18th among the fifty states and fourth among the eleven most industrialized states.

New Jersey's superheated economy cooled considerably during the recession of the early 1990s, which hit the Northeast the hardest. By mid–1992, the state had lost 280,000 jobs, almost half the increase during the 1980s. Urban counties like Union, Essex, and Passaic saw their entire employment gain during the decade wiped out, and Bergen and Hudson lost about half their gain. Still, economic diversity helped the state as a whole withstand recession better than in earlier years.[10]

Economic climates affect population growth, as vibrant economies act as a magnet for mobile workers. During the 1980s, New Jersey's population increased far less than many states in the South and West, but much more than the other large northeastern states of Massachusetts, New York, and Pennsylvania. As in the nation at large, the 1990 census found New Jerseyans moving south (especially into southern Middlesex and Ocean Counties) and west (especially into Somerset and Hunterdon Counties).

Rutgers University demographers have aptly described the engines of New Jersey's economic growth as the "New Jersey Sunbelt," "Trans–Hudson Manhattan," "Trans–Delaware Philadelphia," "Retirement City," and "Las Vegas East."

The New Jersey Sunbelt is concentrated along newer east–west interstate highways and houses many research and communications firms. Especially numerous are installations of AT&T, which has its international headquarters in Somerset County and is the state's largest employer. There are also Sunbelt outposts in the "Route 1 corridor" centered around Princeton and in Monmouth County along the Garden State Parkway.

Bergen and Hudson counties in the north (Trans–Hudson Manhattan) and Camden and Burlington counties in the south (Trans–Delaware Philadelphia) also harbor many firms that have relocated closer to their managers' suburban homes, where space is cheaper and corporate taxes lower. Once grimy Hudson County towns like Hoboken and parts of Jersey City have become trendy yuppie havens.

What was farmland in southern Middlesex, southern Monmouth, Atlantic, Cape May, and Ocean counties is now Retirement City, the largest concentration of planned retirement communities outside Arizona and Florida. Within five years of its inception in the mid–1970s, the take from legalized gambling in Atlantic City—Las Vegas East—surpassed that of Las Vegas, and the industry added 30,000 new jobs. "In the face of these developments, New Jersey's always undistinguished cities have been left as monuments to advanced industrialization ....New Jersey has long been known as the most urban of states. Today this is a misnomer, given the location of its growth zones....Indeed, there are few states of equivalent size within which major cities play so small a role."[11]

Joel Garreau has called the kind of new growth zones that characterize New Jersey "Edge Cities." Edge Cities have at least 5 million square feet of office space, 600,000 square feet of retail space, more workers than residents, and were largely residential or rural less than 30 years ago. Garreau counts 10 Edge Cities in New Jersey, second only to California's 26. They represent a "third wave" of suburban migration–a movement of corporate employers to the suburbs that has followed the earlier movement of first people and then retailers.[12]

The Geography of the New Jersey Vote

Population distribution and the new economic structure interact with the traditional political focus on counties and recent developments like the power of incumbency to produce New Jersey's geographic voting patterns. These patterns vary considerably for different political offices.

In the years between the departure of Franklin Roosevelt and the arrival of

Ronald Reagan, presidential voting in New Jersey showed considerable stability. Republican strength was greatest in the rural northwestern reaches of Hunterdon, Morris, and Sussex counties and along the southern portions of the shore, in Ocean and Atlantic counties. The Democrats did best in Camden and Cumberland, the counties bordering Pennsylvania and Delaware; in heavily urban Essex and Hudson counties near New York City; and in the state capital's county of Mercer, with its many government workers. The parties alternated presidential victories through 1964. Republicans won every election thereafter, through 1988, although the 1968 and 1976 contests were relatively close, as they were nationally. In 1992, Bill Clinton became the first Democratic presidential candidate to carry New Jersey in 28 years, although he received less than a majority of the vote in the three–candidate contest.

On average, GOP presidential candidates have run about three points ahead of their national showings, as George Bush did in 1992. However, the relative partisan rankings of the counties are almost unchanged since 1948. At the presidential level, almost all of the state has shifted fairly evenly in a Republican direction. Strongly Republican counties have become even more Republican; strongly Democratic ones less so. Between 1948 and 1976, the average Democratic presidential vote in the banner Democratic counties was over 50 percent. In the three presidential contests between 1980 and 1988, it dropped below 50 percent in all except Essex. There, the black population of 37 percent, more than twice that of any other county, produced a Democratic increase.

A very different pattern characterizes contests for the U.S. senate. In postwar Senate elections through the mid–1970s, the Senate vote closely tracked the presidential vote. The statewide average for the period was only about 2 percent more Democratic for Senate races than presidential ones. In all of the Senate races in that 28 year period, candidates or current issues resulted in only two counties swinging more than 5 percent in their average partisan division in presidential as opposed to Senate contests.

In contrast, in the four Senate and three presidential races between 1978 and 1988, the state voted an average of 16 percent more Democratic in the Senate elections. Only five of the 21 counties had an average presidential–Senate partisan swing under 15 percent. Even Essex, the most strongly Democratic county in this later period, had an 11 percent deviation favoring the Senate candidates.

The separation of voters' presidential and Senate choices is seen most directly when elections are concurrent. In 1984, Bill Bradley ran 25 points ahead of Democratic presidential candidate Walter Mondale statewide and at least 20 percent ahead in every county. In 1988, Frank Lautenberg ran 11 points ahead of Michael Dukakis statewide and at least 9 percent ahead in every county.

Table 1: Presidential-House Split-Ticket Voting by County, 1948-1988

Year	Percentage of voters Splitting Tickets
1948	3.0
1952	4.0
1956	7.3
1960	3.7
1964	11.9
1968	7.1
1972	11.5
1976	10.5
1980	12.3
1984	13.0
1988	14.5

Source: County level election results.

A vast academic literature documents the increased importance of incumbency in voters' choices from 1970 to 1990.[13] In New Jersey, the media situation, coupled with the disruption of political recruitment by county party organizations, created conditions especially made–to–order for incumbent success. Incumbency is the major reason Democrats have continuously maintained the majority of New Jersey's House delegation which they achieved in 1964.

Congressional redistricting had an unusually strong impact on the House delegation in 1992, when three senior Democrats unexpectedly announced their retirements—the result of a unique combination of factors. These included the state's loss of a seat, court orders to draw "majority–minority" districts, House members' final opportunity to keep unspent campaign funds for personal use, and the sour atmosphere surrounding Congress.[14]

When House seats open in New Jersey, the common pattern is a narrow first victory followed by large reelection margins. Although perhaps half the state's congressional districts seem on their face to be "safe" for one party and several others highly competitive, strong candidates and effective use of incumbency can overwhelm these nominal patterns. Republican Chris Smith's mostly Mercer district, for example, was considered a Democratic stronghold until he defeated a scandal–tarred Democratic incumbent in 1980; Smith has won easily ever since.

Another way to illustrate the incumbency effect in House elections and the propensity of the state's voters to split their tickets is to look at the difference between presidential and congressional voting patterns (see table 1).

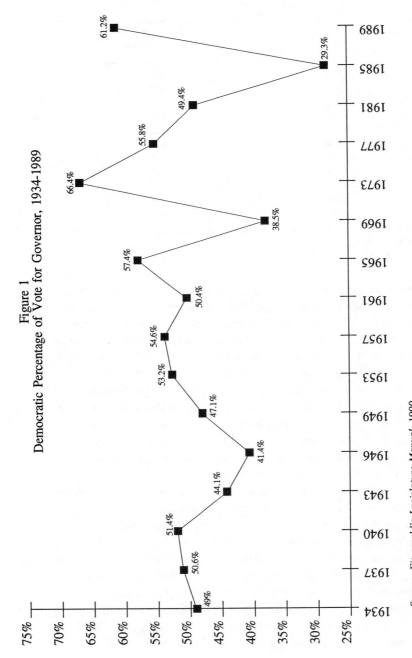

Figure 1
Democratic Percentage of Vote for Governor, 1934-1989

Source: Fitzgerald's Legislature Manual, 1990

Before 1972, split–ticket voting for president and Congress was rare, except on occasions such as 1956 and 1964. Then, large numbers of partisans crossing over to vote for an exceptionally popular presidential candidate (or against an exceptionally unpopular candidate of their own party) returned home to vote for the rest of the ticket. Beginning in 1972, however, heavy split–ticket voting became the norm. The shifts shown here are a conservative estimate, since more precise measures that would show even higher levels of split partisan choices (such as individual–level survey data on votes for all offices) are not available.

In contrast to the increasing Republicanism of New Jerseyans in presidential contests, growing Democratic strength in Senate races, and incumbents' strength in House races, recent gubernatorial contests show wild gyrations.

In considering the patterns in the gubernatorial vote seen in figure 4–1, two points must be borne in mind. First, the governorship is the only elected state office. New Jersey does not have the elected lieutenant governors, attorneys general, or high–ranking judges who launch gubernatorial bids in other states after gaining public recognition in their runs for other office. It is also difficult for ranking state legislators to build recognition and organizational support because of a tradition, broken only in the most recent years, of rotation of the legislative leadership in the legislature after each election. These attributes give incumbent governors an extra leg up, since their opponents are generally unknown; they also mean that open seat races generally feature candidates who are unfamiliar to the public.[15]

The 1947 constitution allowed New Jersey governors to run for two consecutive terms for the first time in the state's history. As of 1992, all of the six incumbents who could do so sought renomination, and the five who were successful all won reelection.[16] The seven governors since 1947 came to office from careers in the state legislature (three), the state judiciary (two), and Congress (two). All of their opponents in the eleven elections between 1949 and 1989 came from either the Congress or the state legislature, with the exceptions of one county executive, one appointed state official and one federal cabinet official.

Conspicuously missing, as compared with other states, are the occupants of other statewide elective offices which New Jersey does not have, and "amateur" business executives.[17] The many New Jerseyans in the latter category tend to be oriented to New York, Philadelphia, the nation, or the world, rather than to Trenton. Well–known financier Malcolm Forbes ran for the governorship in the 1950s but had previously "served his time" in the state legislature. Political neophytes like Senators Bradley and Lautenberg tend instead to run for the U.S. Senate, where there is less competition and interest from those who focus on the governor's chair.

A second focus in analyzing New Jersey gubernatorial elections is the traditional role of powerful county party organizations that cared little about federal races with no patronage payoffs. Governors, unable to succeed themselves before 1949, could not build personal organizations.

On the Democratic side, even after the demise of the Hague organization, Hudson County's support was usually essential for Democratic candidates, especially in the nomination phase. Hudson's control of the nominating phase explains why there were no significant Democratic primary battles for the governorship between 1933 and 1946. On the Republican side, nomination contests were frequently competitions between candidates of the strong county organizations in South Jersey and those of the north and west. General election duels took place between the urban Democratic counties and the suburban and rural Republican ones. Thus, there was a stronger regional cast to gubernatorial elections than those for other offices.

Television, court reapportionment decisions, and the end of the party–line primary slate in 1978 have not succeeded in erasing the stronger regional flavor of gubernatorial elections, particularly those with no incumbent. Public financing of governors' races, which began in 1977, puts a fairly tight cap on campaign expenditures. This prevents gubernatorial candidates, particularly in the nomination phase, from getting well known outside their home regions through television, the way that Senate candidates do. The nomination phase budget allows for, at most, two or three weeks of heavy buys in the Philadelphia and New York TV media markets during the primary season— not nearly enough for candidates to paint detailed positive pictures of themselves, or negative ones of their opponents.

"Free" TV coverage, in the guise of news reports and interview appearances, is limited by competition for airtime from New York City and Philadelphia politicians. Despite taking place in odd–numbered "off–years," the governor's contest always competes for news coverage in the more heavily populated northern part of the state with the usually more "colorful" and "entertaining" mayor's race in New York City.

Thus, while county party organizations are now far less important than they were, gubernatorial candidates' own organizations and recognition levels still have regional bases, and the common mode of electoral analysis is still geographical. This can be seen clearly in the structure and outcomes of the open seat governors' races in 1981 and 1989.

Camden–area Congressman Jim Florio was the Democratic candidate in both of these contests. Florio won the 1981 primary with 26 percent of the vote by piling up huge margins in seven South Jersey counties. Fully 60 percent of his statewide vote came from these counties, more than a quarter of it from Camden alone, which gave him over 80 percent of its vote. There were thirteen candidates in the Democratic field, five of whom garnered more than 10 percent. The potential counterweights to Florio's southern juggernaut, Essex and Hudson, divided their votes among multiple "hometown" candidates, and Florio was thus able to run second in these counties, as well as in vote–rich Middlesex and Mercer, which also had their "own" candidates.

When Florio lost to Tom Kean by a hair's breadth in 1981 and passed on the chance to run against the popular incumbent in 1985, he was quickly assumed to be the Democrats' leading contender for 1989. The 1985 Democratic nominee, Peter Shapiro, had a mortifying showing of 30 percent, followed by a subsequent loss in the Essex County Executive race. That took him out of the running for 1989. The only other serious contender, the state senate president, withdrew early.[18] This time, as the Democrats' heir apparent, Florio drew only two weak primary opponents and won two–thirds of the Democratic primary vote.

On the Republican side, both Kean, the 1981 nominee, and Representative Jim Courter, the 1989 standard–bearer, constructed regional bases that won them each about 30 percent of the primary vote in fairly large fields. Almost six out of ten of Kean's votes came from his home county of Essex; the shore counties of Monmouth and Ocean; the most heavily populated northwestern county, Morris; and the largest county, Bergen. Kean ran first in all but Bergen, where he was a close second. Less than a third of the total Republican primary vote was enough in a contest in which there were six candidates who got more than 10 percent.

The 1989 primary winner, Courter, began with a strong base in his meander-ing congressional district, which took in parts of seven counties, including all or most of the northwestern Republican bastions of Morris, Somerset, Warren, and Sussex. This gave him a recognition level the four other serious candidates (Kean's former attorney general, the assembly majority leader, and state senators from Atlantic and Bergen counties) could not match. By adding first–place showings in Monmouth and Ocean to his base and running respectably in Bergen, Courter constructed a Northwest–Shore axis similar to Kean's and won an only slightly smaller proportion of the vote.

With the exception of Florio's large Democratic primary victory in 1989, the three other nominations in these two contests were won with a distinct minority of the primary vote. There have been no calls for the imposition of a runoff system that would increase voters' knowledge about candidates and provide more decisive judgments.

In the 1981 and 1989 general elections, the distribution of the candidates' votes also had a regional coloring, despite the fact that Florio lost narrowly in 1981 and won in a landslide in 1989. In 1981, Florio led by two to one in Camden and Gloucester, the southern counties comprising his congressional district, and had a similar margin in the flagship Democratic county of Hudson. Kean had large leads in the Republican redoubts of Hunterdon, Morris, Somerset, and Warren and did well in the shore counties of Atlantic and Ocean. Florio's narrow loss resulted from anemic wins in traditionally Democratic Middlesex and Mercer. The weakening ability of those county Democratic organizations to "deliver" in governors' races and Kean's own skills in cutting into the Democratic base gave him his victory.[19]

In 1989, Florio piled up similar margins in Camden, Gloucester, and Hudson. Unlike 1981, he achieved large majorities in Mercer and Middlesex and also carried Republican Ocean and Monmouth comfortably and Somerset narrowly. Despite losing by the third largest margin in the history of state gubernatorial contests, Courter still won the northwestern Republican counties of Morris, Warren, Hunterdon, and Sussex.

Kean's 1985 landslide and Florio's large 1989 victory indicate that few counties are impregnable for the local "minority party" candidate, even in governor's races. However, regionalism still makes some more difficult than others. Any Democrat will find the far northwestern counties very tough going, and any Republican will still have major obstacles in Camden, Essex, and Hudson. Among the "safe" counties, the Republican shore areas present more opportunities for a Democrat than does the northwest. Middlesex, Passaic, and Union counties, although usually Democratic territory, are more promising turf for a Republican than are the historic Democratic bastions of Hudson, Essex, and Camden.

If gubernatorial elections still reflect old regional partisan lines more than federal elections do, one might expect that contests for the state legislature would be even more likely to show these patterns. To some extent they do, although even at this level the candidate–centered campaign has taken hold and incumbency has become a significant factor.

In postwar legislative elections prior to the mid–1970s, the "usual suspects" were arrayed in familiar patterns. The shore counties and most of the northwest fell firmly in the Republican column; the "railroad counties" constituting the spine between New York and Philadelphia, led by Hudson, were the areas of Democratic strength. From the mid–1970s to 1991, there was a Democratic trend. Five counties moved from the competitive or Democratic to Democratic or strong Democratic categories, and four more shifted from Republican categories into the competitive range. The only countertrend was in the northwest, with Sussex becoming even more strongly Republican and Warren moving almost all the way from Democratic to strong Republican.

To some extent, these changes reflected underlying shifts in partisan strength. Increased Democratic voting in Atlantic, Camden, and Essex was a product of growing black populations. Bergen gained a large number of liberal Manhattanites who have moved to huge apartment complexes on the Palisades with spectacular views of the New York skyline and easy access to the city. The Republican shift in Warren (the one northwestern county that was historically Democratic) results from the declining vote share of the county's single urban center of Phillipsburg (hometown of former Governor Meyner) and the growth of exurban development in that county. More important for legislative races than underlying partisan changes, however, is the impact of gubernatorial elections in the later period, magnified by the effects of *Reynolds v. Sims*.

Most of the earlier period just described consists of years when county organizations controlled nominations and practiced rotation in office. In the later period, districts crossed county lines, and legislative candidates had to construct personal organizations. With county organizations less of a factor, the legislative vote began more strongly to reflect gubernatorial landslides and somewhat later, the effects of incumbency.

We can demonstrate this by looking at the statistical relationship between the gubernatorial vote and the assembly vote since 1969. Between 1969 and 1981, there was a consistent relationship between the governor's vote and the total vote for his party's assembly candidates. For every 1 percent of the vote over 50 percent the governor received, the total assembly vote over 50 percent for his party increased by 1/2 percent. Each one–point increase in the statewide partisan assembly vote resulted in three additional legislative seats. For example, Governor Byrne's 67 percent landslide in 1973 produced a total Democratic assembly vote of 58 percent, and the Democrats captured 66 of the 80 assembly seats. Many independents and Republicans who chose the Democratic gubernatorial candidate chose Democratic assembly candidates as well.

In contrast, the Kean and Florio landslide victories of 1985 and 1989 illustrated the continued but declining power of gubernatorial coattails in assembly voting. Kean's 70 percent share of the vote should, in accord with past voting patterns, have resulted in 60 percent of the assembly vote for his party and 70 seats. Instead, Republican assembly candidates received 57.5 percent of the total vote and only 50 seats. By the previously established formula, 57.5 percent of the vote should have produced 62 or 63 seats rather than 50.[20] In 1989, Florio's 62 percent share should have produced 56 percent of the total assembly vote for the Democrats, and 58 seats; the Democrats won only 53 percent of the vote and 44 seats.

Kean and Florio were unable to give assembly candidates as much of a lift in the 1980s as Byrne had in 1973 because of the increasing effect of incumbency over time. In 1973, the overall incumbent success rate in the assembly was 71 percent; in 1985, that figure rose ten points. In 1973, on average, incumbency added slightly less than 4 percent to the average legislator's vote; in 1985, it added about 12 percent. An exit poll for New Jersey Public Television in 1985 revealed that 28 percent of all voters that year split their tickets—31 percent of those voting Republican for governor, and 22 percent of those voting Democratic.

In the early 1970s, Neal Peirce, writing of New Jerseyans' fondness for incumbents, noted, "Only state legislators, more faceless and thus nameless to the general public, tend to get shunted in and out of office rapidly in Jersey. It may be that those fickle suburban voters, once they get the name of an officeholder in their heads, simply vote the familiar until some cataclysmic event propels them to change their habits."[21] In the case of legislators, at the time Peirce wrote, being on the wrong side of a gubernatorial landslide was a sufficiently "cataclysmic event" to get them dislodged from office. By the 1980s, they were well on their way to achieving the incumbency effects pioneered by their legislative brethren in the U.S. House.

The prisms of census data and election returns explain many aspects of New Jersey's politics. But its volatility can only be fully understood when one also understands the attitudes and opinions of its voters. That is our next subject.

CHAPTER FIVE

Voters, Elections, and Parties

In a sense the campaign was only twelve and a half minutes long, the cumulative time of both sides' television spots.
— analysis of the 1988 New Jersey U.S. senate campaign[1]

In an era of "negative political campaigns," those in New Jersey are state of the art. Consider the campaign strategy of Governor Jim Florio. In the 1989 gubernatorial contest, Florio was opposed by another congressman, Republican Jim Courter. Experts predicted a close race. Thanks to his two previous tries for the governorship, more than 90 percent of voters knew Florio's name as early as June. More than 70 percent also recognized Courter's name. However, name recognition was the extent of many voters' knowledge. In September, more than half the electorate said they knew little else or nothing about both candidates. Only about a fifth knew that either was a member of the state's congressional delegation.[2]

Although Florio had the early edge, both sides assumed voters would quickly learn about Courter. He also had some advantages. The 1989 electorate contained more self–identified Republicans than when Florio lost the governor's contest by less than 2,000 votes in 1981. Just as George Bush had pledged to continue the Reagan presidency, Courter was expected to wrap himself in popular Republican Governor Tom Kean's mantle.

Florio's TV commercials aired first and began with a devastating attack on his opponent. Along with high auto insurance rates, New Jersey voters were most worried about the environment. The first Florio ad in mid–September depicted what was described as barrels of toxic waste (actually home heating oil, left by a "midnight dumper") on a property owned by Courter and his brother. It correctly reported that the state Department of Environmental Protection had cited the Courters for not removing the barrels. The ad's announcer also noted that environmental groups rated Florio's voting record as the best in the congressional delegation and Courter's as the worst. The announcer said, "Imagine. It's almost unbelievable. A candidate for governor with toxic–waste barrels on his own property."

Courter's response was slow and uncertain. His discomfort was intensified because his first TV ad featured a medal he had received from the Sierra Club for an environmental vote. The group's state affiliate announced that the medal was a token given to more than 200 members of Congress, and that the Sierra Club strongly endorsed Florio. Voters began to form the opinion that Courter not only had questionable environmental credentials, but that he was not a trustworthy or credible person.

Those suspicions had begun during the summer, when Courter waited two days to comment on *Webster v. Reproductive Health Services*, the U.S. Supreme Court ruling opening the door to state regulation of abortion. Courter seemed to shift abruptly from a strong "pro–life" position to a more "pro–choice" stance. Contradictory comments about gay rights reinforced the bumbling image. The more Courter denied previous statements, the more the press highlighted them. Reservations about the Republican candidate's character became the campaign's driving force. A contest expected to be a cliff–hanger ended with Florio winning 61 percent of the vote, the third largest gubernatorial landslide in the state's history.

The campaign illustrated New Jersey voters' most pronounced qualities— prickly sensitivities about the state and its politicians' motivations, pragmatism and independence, low levels of knowledge about candidates, a resulting tendency to make judgments based on candidates' personal qualities, and late voting decisions producing volatile election outcomes. This chapter examines how New Jersey's political culture and climate of opinion affect its voters, candidates, election campaigns, and political parties.

THE CONTEXT OF PUBLIC OPINION

Almost all New Jersey political contests begin with an electorate that knows little about the candidates. Voters watch television news and read newspapers emanating from New York and Philadelphia or New Jersey dailies that emphasize local news. Historically beset by "New Jersey jokes," citizens have recently become prouder of their state and begun to identify more with it, but an inferiority complex lingers on. A long tradition of political corruption also inclines New Jerseyans to be cynical about politicians and wont to profess partisan independence at a higher rate than elsewhere. The decline of the county party organizations and their patronage jobs further bolsters the trend to political independence.

When the economy is healthy, the now dominant suburban and educated middle class is concerned less with economic issues than with "quality–of–life" issues–environmental degradation, congestion, and overdevelopment (see chapter 16). In fact, New Jersey's environmental problems are perceived in part as economic problems. Waste washing up on beaches threatens the tourist industry along the shore. Gridlocked traffic may make companies think twice about relocating or expanding in New Jersey. This is the context in which New Jersey elections now take place.

The Level of Political Knowledge

When statewide campaigns begin, a substantial portion of voters knows little or nothing about most candidates. Usually, less than half can actually name a candidate without prompting. Although more voters claimed to have at least "some" knowledge about Governor Tom Kean in 1985 than any other candidate in a statewide race between 1977 and 1989, more than two in five still knew little or nothing about him. Kean's fuzzy image persisted despite concerted efforts to keep his name before the public. In 1983, Kean argued successfully that $600,000 in party funds dedicated to that year's assembly races (most of which he had raised) should be spent on TV ads featuring a message from him.[3] Although unopposed in the 1985 Republican gubernatorial primary, Kean spent up to the legal limit during the spring primary season running commercials extolling his record. Early in the fall, the state tourism agency began a heavy advertising campaign featuring the governor. The ads ran through election day, concurrent with Kean's political ads. Roger Stone, one of the governor's political strategists, observed that all the TV messages were intended to "flesh out Kean. People knew him, but nothing about him."[4]

Kean's use of early advertising to "educate" voters was adopted by the 1989 Republican gubernatorial candidates. Atlantic County Senator William Gormley, relying on a southern base vote in the gubernatorial primary, spent $350,000 on Philadelphia television in 1987 to "defend" his safe senate seat. Courter, the eventual primary winner, spent more than twice that on 1988 ads painting him as a "new leader for New Jersey." The ads ostensibly supported his campaign for a U.S. House seat, which he regularly won with two–thirds of the vote.

Candidates who advertise heavily on TV do make an impression, albeit superficial, on voters. One need only compare the respective recognition rates of U.S. Senate candidates Frank Lautenberg in 1982 and Mary Mochary in 1984. Both were political neophytes whose opponents were the closest thing to political icons that New Jersey can muster. Mochary faced incumbent senator and former basketball great Bill Bradley. Lautenberg ran against Representative Millicent Fenwick, the model for Congresswoman Lacey Davenport in

Doonesbury and the subject of a story in *People* magazine.

Although only 2 percent of the public thought they knew a lot about Lautenberg in September 1982, 18 percent could name him as the Democratic Senate candidate, and another 48 percent recognized his name when it was presented. Lautenberg's "hard" recognition of 18 percent matched the 19 percent that could name U.S. Senator Clifford Case without prompting in October 1972, when Case was running for his third term. To achieve this level of awareness Lautenberg spent over $1 million of his own money on TV advertisements during the June primary. The ads sketched his rags–to–riches success story—the son of a Paterson silk mill worker who went to college on the GI Bill and founded a pioneer computer company. Each ad ended with the slogan, "Frank Lautenberg–New Jersey First." This chauvinistic campaign brought victory over nine other candidates.

Mochary had neither Lautenberg's money nor his inspiring biography. A successful lawyer and former suburban mayor, Mochary was recruited by the National Republican Senatorial Committee (NRSC), which was unable to find a more experienced candidate willing to take on Bradley. The NRSC delivered as much as it could legally spend, but neither it nor the candidate succeeded in persuading other donors to invest in her. As a result, Mochary began the general election campaign with fully three–quarters of the electorate ignorant of even her name.

As campaigns progress, the electorate learns more about candidates' personal qualities than their issue positions. Candidate advertising in New Jersey, as in other places, stresses valence rather than positional issues.[5] Positional stances "for" or "against" specific programs and policies can be electorally dangerous. The more complex or controversial the issue, the more difficult it is to lay out a reasoned position in a thirty–second ad, and the more voters the candidate may antagonize.

Valence issues, in contrast, are subjects about which everyone agrees. Economic opportunity, a safe and healthy environment, and less crime are all common valence issues. Campaigns emphasizing valence issues ask the voter to choose the candidate who seems most likely, based on personal qualities, to achieve desired ends. Political commentators decry "issueless" campaigns focused on valence issues, but the concept accords with life experience. People learn that taking a position is not enough to insure a desired outcome; success depends on the proponent's integrity, force of personality, negotiating abilities, and resolve.

Campaign messages, therefore, focus on valence issues and personal qualities, especially when candidates are running for an office in which they have no prior record. They do not use issues to present a policy agenda, but rather to make a statement about what kind of people they or their opponents are. Polls of the New Jersey electorate show that this is indeed the message that gets through.

In a mid–October survey during the 1989 gubernatorial contest, voters judged, by a margin of more than two to one, that "overall," Florio had "a better understanding of problems and important issues facing New Jersey." Yet when asked the candidates' positions on regulation of auto insurance companies—the crux of the issue they called most important—almost two–thirds admitted they didn't know or weren't sure. More than half offered the same response on the widely covered abortion issue, saying they did not know which candidate was personally more pro–choice.[6] When asked what personal quality most influenced their vote, the trait named most often was "honesty"—the attribute stressed, in both a positive and negative fashion, in the candidates' advertising.[7]

Thus, voters did not give Florio a policy mandate. Rather, they chose the candidate they felt had the personal qualities to address current problems most effectively. Thirty–second ads cannot transmit detailed issue analyses and, like all advertisers, political sponsors underscore their strengths and the competition's weaknesses. However, if voters cannot learn much about difficult issues from paid messages, why don't they get that information from print and television news?

The Role of the Mass Media

New Jersey's media patterns still hinder learning about state political affairs, even now when politicians try to be more visible and government in Trenton is doing more things of interest. In a 1984 study of eight states, only 51 percent of New Jerseyans described themselves as "very" or "somewhat" interested in state politics. This compared with an average of 72 percent in the seven other states, although the level of interest in national politics in New Jersey was similar to the others.[8]

New Jersey did not have a commercial VHF television channel licensed to the state until 1984.[9] It finally gained (from New York City) WWOR–Channel 9, an independent station. WWOR maintains offices as close to New York City as possible, and has no full–time Trenton correspondent. To distinguish itself in the crowded New York market and serving as a "passive superstation" for many cable–TV systems around the country, it runs syndicated entertainment–oriented programming like "The Arsenio Hall Show" and its sensational predecessor, "The Morton Downey Show." Other programming mainstays are New York Mets baseball games and network reruns. WWOR's evening news program covers the entire region and runs to "happy talk" news.[10]

Table 2: Sources of State Politics Information, 1971-1991

	News-papers	Tele-vision	Radio	Other, DK
Total 1991	84	55	13	24
Most valuable	60	20	3	17
Total 1971	90	35	20	21
Most valuable	70	13	5	11

Source: Eagleton Polls, specified years.

Note: Table entries are percentages citing a particular information source. Multiple responses are included.

New Jersey political news is practically nonexistent on the other New York stations (the justification used to move WWOR's license). Philadelphia stations do a somewhat better job but reach only a small proportion of the state's population. New Jersey Public Television airs an excellent nightly news program and other public affairs shows on four regional UHF stations. The state's political activists are attentive viewers, but these UHF stations in a VHF–dominated market draw small audiences.[11] The television situation produces an unusual dependence on newspapers for information about state politics, as seen in table 2.

Much of the print press, however, is not a good source of state news. Most New Jersey papers are heavily local in orientation. The state's culture encourages a local focus, as does the wide availability of New York and Philadelphia papers. A quarter of the population still reports that they read out–of–state news organs.[12]

A peculiar but telling characteristic of New Jersey newspapers is that most do not have locational mastheads. As the population moved out of the cities into the burgeoning suburbs, the *Newark Star–Ledger* became the *Star–Ledger*, the *New Brunswick Home News* became the *Central New Jersey Home News,* and so on. These papers now cover surrounding suburbs more heavily than their original places of publication. There are, for example, more than twice as many reporters in the *Star–Ledger*'s Morris County bureau than those covering Newark itself.[13]

New Jersey has never had a truly statewide newspaper and for some time has not had one of high quality. The *Newark Daily News*, which came the closest, went out of business in the early 1970s after a protracted strike. Since the *News*'s demise, the *Star–Ledger* (or simply the *Ledger*, as it is usually called) has aggressively sought to expand its presence in the northern and central areas of the state, and it is by far the largest state paper. Many New Jerseyans buy the *Ledger* because it is the best source for supermarket discount coupons and information about shopping mall promotions. It is so popular with advertisers that it literally turns some away.

The *Ledger*'s effective circulation area now covers almost two–thirds of the state and an even larger portion of the population. The eleven full–time reporters in its Trenton bureau constitute nearly a fifth of the entire statehouse press corps, which allows for considerable specialization. The *Ledger* publishes three times as much state news as any other paper. Some veteran reporters, particularly on the important education and environmental beats, are regarded as extremely influential. The *Ledger's* style has been described as "crusading," "populist," and heavy on state "boosterism."[14] Typically, beat reporters write multipart, front–page series on current issues. The drumbeat is then taken up on the editorial page, and action, or at least talk, follows in Trenton.

The *Ledger*, however, is prone to ignore issues that the editors believe do not interest readers (such as the many problems of Newark). Finding state news, spread almost randomly amidst the advertising on hundreds of unindexed pages even on weekdays, is daunting. Additionally, while tough on state government when in its "crusading" mode, the *Ledger* is also prone to cooperate uncritically with high officials as part of its "boosterism." Donald Linky, former chief counsel to Governor Byrne, has noted that governors "leak favorable stories to the *Ledger's* reporters, with the implicit understanding that the story will be considered by the paper's editors for the front page lead."[15]

As can be seen in table 2, the print media remain the leading source of state political news; this dependence has dropped significantly in recent years. During the 1989 gubernatorial race, as many voters—38 percent—cited TV news as their major source of information about the race for governor as cited print news.[16]

An interesting recent development is the emergence of a statewide radio station calling itself "New Jersey 101.5" (WKXW–FM). Based in Trenton, its signal reaches north to Bergen County. In 1990, WKXW changed its format to call–in segments dedicated exclusively to New Jersey affairs. The change catapulted it from seventh to first place in Arbitron's Trenton market ratings, and it became the nerve center of a statewide tax revolt. Talk–show emcees broadcast the telephone numbers of protest leaders; whipped up attendance at mass demonstrations in the capital; and played host to Governor Florio, who identified himself as "Jim from Drumthwacket"—New Jersey's governor's mansion.

More reliance on broadcast media makes New Jerseyans' knowledge about

Table 3: Rating of New Jersey as a Good or Excellent Place to Live

Year	Percentage
1977	62
1980	68
1984	80
1988	78
1990	59

Source: Eagleton Polls, specified years.

state affairs and its political leaders even more superficial and personality–based.[17] Two debates televised on New York and Philadelphia stations during the 1989 gubernatorial contest produced merely a parroting of the candidates' personalistic television ads. This was due as much to the reporters' questions as to the candidates' own proclivities. Heavily oriented toward personal rather than policy matters, they were aimed at producing "interesting" drama rather than "boring" technical discussions of auto insurance or budget shortfalls.

The Effects of State Issues and Images

Although New Jerseyans do not have much information about state policies or intense feelings about most politicians, during the 1980s they developed warmer sentiments about the state and more identification with it. Since 1977, Rutgers University's Eagleton Poll has conducted three major studies of how New Jersey residents view the state and its major institutions. In 1980, seven other university–based polling organizations sponsored similar studies in their states. The results depict changes in New Jerseyans' attitudes and permit interesting comparisons with other states.

As can be seen in table 3, perceptions of the quality of life in New Jersey improved notably through the 1980s, before crashing at least temporarily during the 1990 recession. At their high point, however, New Jerseyans were only approaching a level of satisfaction long present in other states. In surveys of residents of Connecticut, Delaware, Florida, Kentucky, Massachusetts, New Hampshire, and Texas in 1980, the average positive response to the same question was 83 percent, as compared to 68 percent in New Jersey. Among these eight states, New Jersey ranked next to last. Only 13 percent called life in New Jersey "excellent," while the average for the seven other states was 43 percent. Yet New Jerseyans did not perceive greener pastures elsewhere; few thought life was better in other states.

Table 4: Most Important Problems Facing New Jersey

	9/74	7/80	7/85	3/91	2/92
Economy	24	35	13	13	49
Taxes	34	18	13	39	46
Environment	48	34	60	8	9

Source: Eagleton Polls, relevant years.

Note: Table entries are percentages of all respondents citing a particular problem. Multiple responses are included.

Given the state's endemic localism, it is not surprising that until 1984, respondents consistently rated their own neighborhoods and towns more positively than they did the state.

However, the signal political events of the 1970s—the end of county–based politics, the onset of televised statewide campaigns, and the passage of the income tax—in essence made state politics and a state political culture possible for the first time. They also produced significant changes in the kinds of public issues New Jersey residents thought about.

Since the early 1970s, the Eagleton Poll has regularly asked what issues respondents regard as the most important problems facing the state.

For the past 20 years, three issues—the economy, taxes, and the environment—have almost always dominated the thoughts of New Jerseyans. The tax issue lost a long–standing position at the top of public concern during the 1980s until imposition of a huge state tax increase in the midst of recession in 1990. However, the public continued to think that taxes were too high and higher than in other states. Still, those who believed the services received were worth the tax dollars paid rose from 15 percent in 1977 to 32 percent in 1986 at the height of the state's economic boom and only fell back to 27 percent in 1990.

Despite strong distaste for state taxes, New Jerseyans grudgingly accept increases when a good case is made for them. In a 1977 Eagleton Poll, 57 percent agreed the state could not be run effectively without the recently passed income tax, and 56 percent approved of the 1982 increases in the sales and income taxes.[18] Unlike the wildly unpopular 1990 tax hike, both of the earlier increases were preceded by long periods of debate, during which the public was gradually persuaded they were necessary (see chapter 14).

Once the recession of the early 1980s ended, New Jerseyans focused increasingly on the environmental problems accompanying economic

Table 5: Party Identification in New Jersey

	1971	1978	1985	1992
Democrat	30	35	32	27
Republican	20	19	26	28
Independent	38	40	38	34
Other,Don't Know	12	6	4	10

Source: Eagleton Polls, specified years.

Note: Table entries are percentages of all respondents choosing a particular category.

growth. Only the combination of the national and state recessions and the largest state tax increase in history could temporarily drive environmental concerns to the back burner.

The picture that thus emerges is of an electorate capable of making judgments, but difficult to reach with detailed political information and arguments. New Jerseyans know the state's major problems and are willing to use their wealth to solve them in good economic times. They are eager to shed a historical inferiority complex, especially in relation to their larger neighbors and are prone to favor officeholders who make state pride a major theme.

Changing Patterns of Partisan Identification

Just as voters know little about candidates initially, candidates face great uncertainty about voters at the start.

The first thing apparent in table 5 is the state's large number of political independents. The percentage of New Jersey voters calling themselves independents has ranged from five to ten points higher than in the U.S. as a whole.[19] The second clear finding is the increasing tendency of New Jerseyans to call themselves Republicans. The shift toward the Republicans has not occurred evenly throughout the electorate. Between 1971 and 1990, the percentage of Republican adherents increased eight points and the parties reached virtual parity. However, among certain groups—whites, Catholics, those aged 18 to 29, and those in blue collar occupations, the number of self–identified Republicans at least doubled.

Candidates thus face a situation where the number of avowed partisans on each side is increasingly equal, and the battle is for the independent suburban vote. Swing voters in the suburbs, however, typically are not wealthy professionals who discuss political contests over weekend golf. Rather, as our analysis in chapter 4 suggests, they are "middle–middle class" residents of the older suburbs, more likely to talk politics over a beer at a bowling alley—the sort of voters political strategists refer to as "Joe Six–Pack."

Democratic voter–contact specialist Barry Brendel characterizes swing voters as belonging primarily to two groups. The first is former Democrats in skilled blue collar jobs, mostly Catholic, of Italian and East European extraction, and over 45. The second is their children—often more affluent, but not wealthy. They work at white–collar middle management jobs, play golf on public courses, and worry about being able to afford housing in the towns where they grew up.[20]

The swing vote (and for that matter, the partisan vote) is not notably ideological. Forty–four percent of New Jersey voters in the 1989 gubernatorial election called themselves "moderates," and another 10 percent were unable to characterize themselves philosophically. Only 27 percent called themselves "conservatives," and 19 percent styled themselves "liberals."[21] Candidates must devise campaign themes based on issues and images rather than on appeals to political philosophy or party loyalty. Certain types of issues and images—those that are "mainstream," pragmatic, and without strong ideological baggage—are the most persuasive.

THE EFFECT OF CONTEXT ON STATE ELECTIONS

Low levels of political information, the unique media environment, lingering sensitivities about New Jersey's image, a changing issue mix, high levels of political independence, and weak party ties have many effects on election contests. All other things being equal, they advantage incumbent and moderate candidates. They also make competitive races very expensive and often centered on personal and negative themes.

Advantaged Candidates

With partisanship and party organizations both in decline and a media climate that makes it difficult for newcomers to become known, voters usually choose the only candidates they have heard much about—the incumbents. The incumbency advantage feeds on itself. Strong challengers who might have run in the past because they enjoyed party organization support or sensed an advantage from the trends of the times are more loath to do so now.[22] They know how difficult it is to defeat an incumbent. Consequently, many incumbents do not face their strongest potential challengers.

In addition to challengers, two other kinds of candidates face difficulties:

those who think of themselves, or can be painted by their opponents, as ideologues and those who cannot make persuasive cases that they have the interests of voters at heart. The Republicans' 1989 gubernatorial hopeful, Jim Courter, who lost decisively, was seen as more conservative than the electorate he wished to represent. An identical 46 percent of voters described Courter's opponent, Jim Florio, and the outgoing governor, Tom Kean, as "moderate," a proportion similar to the voters' own opinions. Courter, however, was perceived as a "conservative" by 47 percent of the voters and as a "moderate" by only 29 percent.[23]

Senator Bill Bradley came close to a mortifying loss in 1990 when he refused to take a position on the issue overwhelmingly preoccupying his constituents—state tax increases—and ran an issueless campaign that "was out of touch with the New Jersey political reality."[24] Democratic legislators from suburban districts went down to defeat in droves in 1991. Even those legislators who did not support the tax increases or backed away from them lost, for this time low levels of information worked against incumbents. Voters wanted to blame someone, and since Florio was not on the ballot, his partisans took the hit indiscriminately.

Campaigns and Money in New Jersey

The recent hyperinflation in political campaign costs is well–documented.[25] Substitution of money–intensive campaign technology for labor–intensive party organizations is the major culprit. Until the late 1970s, party organizations were the dominant actors in New Jersey campaigns. Their abrupt collapse brought on expensive media campaigns very suddenly. The rise in costs is especially sensational in legislative races. Combined expenditures by the major party candidates in competitive U.S. Senate races rose from $3.1 million in 1978 to $16 million in 1988. A hotly contested House race in 1990 saw combined spending of over $2.5 million.[26]

Most states now see heavy spending in competitive federal races. Somewhat more unusual (although not unique) is the level of spending in New Jersey legislative races. Before the 1980s, legislative races were mostly cheap and largely invisible affairs, driven by party identification and organization and by coattails in gubernatorial election years.

The candidate–centered campaigns since then drove the median cost of a state senate race in 1987 to more than $236,000; the most expensive contest cost $378,000. In the assembly, the comparable 1987 figures were $28,000 and over $166,000. In 1991, three senate candidates spent over $400,000, and 10 assembly candidates topped $100,000. Total spending in legislative races increased by 34 percent over 1987.[27] The cost of competitive legislative races does not approach California's multimillion–dollar expenditures (state senate districts there are larger than U.S. congressional districts), but they are at the upper end of the 50 states.[28]

Public financing makes the picture in gubernatorial races somewhat different. New Jersey was, in 1977, the first state to adopt public financing of gubernatorial campaigns.[29] The goals were to remove special interests and their money from gubernatorial elections, allow candidates of modest means to run credible contests, and keep a realistic cap on spending.

Originally, the public finance law covered only the general election campaign and limited each candidate to a $2.2 million spending ceiling. Candidates became eligible for public funding after raising $40,000 privately. Contributions from individuals could not exceed $600. Once a candidate became eligible, the state matched every private dollar raised on a two–to–one basis until the limit was reached. For the 1981 election, the law was amended to include public financing of party primary contests—following the same scheme as for the general election, but with a spending limit of $1.1 million. The individual contribution limit was raised to $800, and candidates were required to raise $50,000 to qualify.

As with the federal law providing for public financing of presidential campaigns, gubernatorial candidates are not required to accept public financing and abide by spending limits, but there is a strong incentive to do so. All the major party general election candidates have participated, as have almost all primary election candidates.

As the 1989 gubernatorial election approached, the spending caps seemed inadequate in the face of $8 million campaigns on each side in the 1988 U.S. Senate race. Even in 1985, Governor Kean's staff had indicated he might opt out of the public finance system if a serious challenge developed. There was also a growing feeling that the $50,000 trigger "wasted" too much of the taxpayers' money on "fringe" primary election candidates.

Accordingly, in 1988, the legislature (which contained several gubernatorial aspirants) began protracted bargaining over a new law. The eventual compromise raised the 1989 spending limits to $2.2 million in the primary and $5.5 million in the general election. The limit on individual contributions rose to $1,500. Candidates had to raise $150,000 to qualify for public financing, and the first $50,000 raised was exempted from the two–to–one match. Those accepting public funds were required to participate in at least two televised debates in both the primary and general elections. The state Election Law Enforcement Commission was also empowered to raise future spending caps by the inflation rate.[30]

Although the new limits kept nominal costs somewhat below those for competitive U.S. Senate races, the numbers must be placed in broader perspective. In Michigan, the only other state with extensive public financing of governor's races, the 1990 candidates got by with general election budgets of roughly a third what New Jersey provides its candidates. Michigan's population is larger, but its media markets are much cheaper.

Further, a "soft money" loophole, similar to the one in presidential contests, permits New Jersey's state party committees to spend additional millions for "party–building activities" and "generic party advertising." Thus, the public finance law substantially understates real expenditures in gubernatorial campaigns. Informed estimates are that the actual spending by Democrat Jim Florio and Republican Jim Courter in the 1989 primaries and general election totaled $23 to $25 million, rather than the $14.4 million permitted by the public finance law.[31]

Finally, contribution limits in the public finance law have diverted large individual and "special interest" contributions to legislative candidates and state party entities. Although there are strict reporting requirements, through 1992, there were no limits on how much individuals, corporations, or political action committees could contribute to a legislative candidate or a political party. The wealthy donor who gave a gubernatorial candidate the maximum permissible $1,500 could (and often did) contribute $100,000 to a party group. The party contribution could then be recycled into a "generic" party mailing or TV ad reiterating the themes of the party's gubernatorial candidate.

Negative Campaigns

New Jersey's expensive campaigns, we have noted, are also often negative. These phenomena are not unrelated. Candidates must purchase broadcast time in two of the most expensive markets in the country. At this writing, a thirty–second spot in the New York market costs between $7,000 and $35,000 each time it is shown, depending on the size of a program's audience (Philadelphia is about 25 percent cheaper). Only about a third of the viewers in both media markets are New Jersey residents. The rest live in New York, Pennsylvania, Delaware, and Connecticut—a tremendous but unavoidable "waste" of a New Jersey candidate's resources.

The enormous costs cause television campaigns to start later than in most states. A New York ad buy that reaches the average viewer three to five times in one week costs nearly a million dollars. The cost of two ads on a top–rated program is roughly equivalent to the price of a whole week's buy in sparsely populated markets. Thus, a statewide candidate in Montana or North Dakota can be on the air for several months at less expense than a three–week buy in New York or Philadelphia.

These facts help explain New Jerseyans' low level of political knowledge and the especially negative tone of many campaigns. Voters usually "meet" statewide candidates barely two months before election day, while residents of most other states have been getting to know their aspiring officeholders and listening to their appeals much longer. Even the best–financed New Jersey candidates cannot afford a TV ad campaign that starts before mid–September, with perhaps a week or two of introductory advertising around the June primaries. Typically, at least 80 percent of the total budgets of statewide candidates are spent on this schedule of TV advertising.

Repetition is a key to effective advertising. People must hear a message several times before it "sinks in."[32] Because New Jersey campaigns start so late, candidates can transmit fewer different messages than in most other states. A well–financed campaign can only air seven or eight different messages with sufficient repetition to be assimilated, while candidates in states with cheaper media markets can run twenty or thirty different spots.[33]

Additionally, a credible negative message penetrates a viewer's consciousness more quickly than a positive one. For positive messages to be convincing, voters must know quite a bit about candidates and be favorably disposed to them to begin with.[34] This is rarely the case in New Jersey, particularly for nonincumbents. The limited number of messages candidates can air tempts them to spend more time and money criticizing opponents rather than promoting themselves. With little knowledge about most political aspirants, voters are prone to accept negative information that seems to have a kernel of truth. However, they also dismiss charges that are clearly preposterous, a point often lost on the many critics of negative ads.[35] Further, despite assertions that voter disgust with negative ads contributes to decreasing voter turnout, analysis of national turnout patterns gives this hypothesis little support.[36]

Negative advertising has even become a major factor in legislative races, where the messages get delivered in the mail rather than by television. Just as candidate advertising must "cut through" all the other advertising on TV, political direct mail must compete with the glossy catalog from L.L. Bean or Lands' End. As Richard M. Schlackman of the Campaign Performance Group of San Francisco, creator of Democratic legislative direct mail described his product, "We call it TV mail....Good graphics count quite a bit."[37]

Many legislative mail pieces feature pointed personal attacks on opponents. A few recent examples give the flavor. In Ocean County's Tenth District in 1989, Marlene Lynch Ford's Republican opponent sent a mail piece picturing a cereal box of "Ford Flakes," with a banner reading, "Free Inside–ACLU card." Inside was a picture of 1988 presidential candidate Michael Dukakis labeled, "Thanks, Marlene." The text noted that Ford had supported Dukakis "even when he defended letting criminals out of jail on weekend furloughs to run loose." The echoes of the 1988 presidential campaign were only too clear. Democratic attack pieces were no less pointed.   One piece critical of a Republican candidate's environmental record attributed to him the contrived quote, "Let them drink sludge."

Negativity also permeated the direct mail battle in 1991, but it was strongly shaped by continuing suburban outrage over Governor Florio's $2.8 billion tax hike.   GOP mail into every suburban district was virtually identical, varying only in the wording tying Democratic candidates to the tax hike and to Florio. Democratic mail attempted to distance candidates from the governor or attacked Republicans on local issues.   Strategists on both sides saw the campaign environment the same way.   Dave Murray, architect of the Republican mail assault, asserted, "The Republicans owe their success to Jim Florio, pure and simple.   New Jersey ignored the Bush recession because Florio glowed in the dark."   Democratic consultant Frank Robinson reported long discussions about a "generic" Democratic response, but concluded, "The problem was, what could we say?"[38]

THE ROLE OF POLITICAL PARTIES IN ELECTIONS

Our analysis so far could convey the idea that New Jersey's political parties are in an advanced state of decay, replaced by entrepreneurial candidates.[39] In some ways this is true; in others not.

Historically, New Jersey's strong party organizations were county–based rather than statewide. Earlier chapters detail the internecine battles between the Atlantic and Essex Republican organizations and the willingness of Hudson County Democrats to abandon or sabotage Democratic gubernatorial candidates insufficiently attentive to county patronage. Except for some county and local offices, however, county organizations play small roles in most New Jersey political contests nowadays.

They have been replaced by new kinds of state party organizations. To most political scientists and other political commentators, "state political parties" mean state party committees—independent social formations that are the constituent units of the national Democratic and Republican party organizations.[40] The really important party units in New Jersey, however, are not these organizations. Rather, they are other "party" bodies that are the creations of officeholders. Even the formal New Jersey state party committees are in essence

Table 6: State Party Expenditures on Legislative Candidates, 1977-1987

	Republicans	Democrats	Total
1977	.5	.1	.6
1981	2.1	1.5	3.7
1983	1.9	.8	2.7
1987	1.8	1.7	3.5

Source: New Jersey Election Law Enforcement Commission. Includes spending by legislative campaign committees.

Note: Table entries are millions of dollars expended.

holding companies for officeholders.

Each of the state's leading political figures—the governor, the senate president, and the assembly speaker—controls a separate political organization. Each has its own staff for political activities and for raising and allocating money. New Jersey is one of about 25 states where the leaders of the legislative party caucuses play a major role in the direction and financing of legislative campaigns and one of perhaps a dozen where leaders' power and continuation in office depend heavily on fund–raising abilities.[41]

The state Election Law Enforcement Commission reports the following increases in party expenditures on legislative candidates.

In 1983 and 1987, when both houses of the legislature stood for reelection, state party organizations contributed a larger proportion of candidates' campaign money (30 percent in 1983 and 24 percent in 1987) than any other category of givers—including individuals, political action committees, unions, or businesses.[42] However, very little of the money was raised independently by the formal state party committees, nor did they decide how to spend it.

On the Republican side, almost all of the $1.8 million spent by "party" entities in 1987 was raised by the Governor's Club and the legislative campaign committee controlled by Assembly Speaker Chuck Hardwick. The Governor's Club raised $1 million, and the Assembly Republican Majority Campaign Committee (ARM) raised $929,000.[43]

Kean funneled Governor's Club money through the Republican State Committee because reduced postage rates granted state party organizations made the money go further. However, the committee was staffed by Kean appointees who followed his directions about how to spend it. This was sometimes a matter of intraparty dispute, as in 1983, when $600,000 was spent on generic TV ads featuring Kean, although many candidates would have preferred

Table 7: Legislative Candidate Spending by Party, 1977-1991

	1977	1981	1983	1987	1991
Democrats	1.9	3.7	3.6	6.4	9.3
Republicans	1.9	4.2	4.6	5.1	5.7

Source: New Jersey Election Law Enforcement Commission.

Note: Table entries are in millions of dollars.

spending it on their own radio and direct–mail messages. Speaker Hardwick maintained control over the funds he raised as well and decided which assembly challengers and threatened incumbents would receive ARM money and services.

The Republicans followed a similar path in 1989. ARM spent more than $1.2 million on legislative races, a sizable portion of which came from its largest contributor, the Republican National Committee (RNC) in Washington. All of the RNC money, given as part of a program to gain control of state legislatures during the congressional redistricting period, had to be targeted to challenger seats. "Friends of Chuck Haytaian," the personal political action committee of the Republican assembly minority leader hoping to ascend to the speakership, contributed about $55,000 to ARM and $160,000 to individual GOP candidates.[44]

The 1980s were unusually flush times for New Jersey Republicans, but loss of the governorship and control of the assembly in 1989 brought difficulties. Courter's landslide defeat led to the removal of his designee as party chair in February 1990. Former Governor Kean assumed Drew University's presidency, which limited his partisan role. There was a vacuum at the party's top and many aspirants for its leadership. The potential for suspicion and competition was, however, considerably allayed through 1992 by the combative and partisan stance Democratic Governor Florio adopted toward Republican legislators, whom he often called "irrelevant."

The New Jersey Democratic party followed an opposite path through the 1980s. Before 1980, control of state government, a comfortable majority of party identifiers, and several powerful county party organizations made the state party organization an afterthought. It took the Democrats longer to see the virtues of cooperation. Governor Kean's second victory gave Republicans control of the assembly in 1985 and propelled the electorate in a noticeably more Republican direction. Individual Democrats began to look for anything that would help them.

Cooperative activities first began in the state legislature. Assembly Speaker Alan Karcher established a personal political action committee that raised

$125,000 for assembly candidates in 1983. The 1987 legislative elections saw a massive Democratic party spending increase. As shown in table 6, although Republican party spending on legislative candidates was down slightly from 1983, Democratic spending in 1987 more than doubled.

Almost all the 1987 party spending was generated by Senate President John Russo. Russo established the Senate Democratic Majority '87 political action committee, which raised $1.7 million and spent almost all of it in twelve targeted districts.[45] The Senate President's Ball, at which most of the money was raised, frankly imitated the Republicans' Governor's Ball and generated contributions from many of the same interests. Russo was intent on keeping his endangered senate presidency as the base for the 1989 gubernatorial campaign he then anticipated.

Russo persuaded candidates to add whatever they could raise on their own to the resources of Majority '87, and all the money went to campaign consultants for polling, broadcast media, and direct mail. The consultants worked with each campaign to devise a unique message. The twelve campaigns, although using the same consultants, averaged nine different individual direct mail pieces and set up individual phone bank operations.

All the campaigns benefited from Majority '87's statewide precinct voting analysis, opposition research, and production of get–out–the–vote lists and mailing labels. The central consultants also trained individual candidates' campaign staffs at a two–day seminar, and Majority '87 helped pay to update the state committee's voter files. These efforts resulted in a Democratic gain of one senate seat and eight assembly seats.

The 1987 strategy also resulted in Democratic legislative candidates outspending the Republicans for the first time since the Election Law Enforcement Commission began recording candidate spending totals.

The 1988 state Democratic campaigns also cooperated in an unprecedented way. Presidential candidate Michael Dukakis and Senate candidate Frank Lautenberg funneled $1.4 million through the state party. These funds supported 13 satellite party offices, each staffed with a Dukakis operative, a Lautenberg operative, and an area coordinator. Volunteers at each location made voter–identification and get–out–the–vote election–day calls for Dukakis, Lautenberg, and one county officeholder. Even when polls showed Dukakis would surely lose New Jersey, the Dukakis campaign kept its commitment to pour a final $60,000 into the state on election day.

These experiences led the Democrats to run the kind of coordinated gubernatorial–legislative campaigns in 1989 that the Republicans had perfected during the Kean years but were unable to repeat with Courter. An organization called Democratic Finance '89 consolidated fund–raising for both legislative candidates and Jim Florio. Florio met his fund raising target by Labor Day and was able to funnel almost $600,000 into eight targeted legislative districts before the end of October, passing it through the state committee.

All told, in 1989, Democrats raised $8.2 million above the public finance requirements, as compared with less than $5 million for the Republicans.[46] Democratic assembly candidates outspent Republicans in 27 of the 40 legislative districts. As a group, these Democrats spent more than twice as much as they had in 1987, while GOP spending was only up 18 percent.[47]

The Democrats' 1989 legislative strategy was a repeat of 1987, but with even more expensive consultants, slicker mail, and more elaborate get–out–the–vote programs.[48] To keep their state committee flush, Democrats charged an unprecedented $1,500 per person for the 1990 Governor's Gala—more than twice the tab at the last Kean Governor's Ball in 1989—aiming to raise all they could while still maintaining control of all branches of state government. Flat broke only two years earlier, the Democratic State Committee ended 1990 with $1.5 million in the bank.[49] Lack of money did not contribute to the Democrats' rout in the 1991 legislative elections. They were able to outspend the Republicans by three to two.

This survey of their recent activities explains why state party organizations in New Jersey (and many other places) can correctly be described as both weak and strong.[50] On the one hand, the state parties pay bills for numerous campaign services. On the other hand, these organizations no longer anoint candidates, set the direction of campaigns, or mobilize reliable partisans with the party symbol. Instead, they are the creatures of candidates and officeholders.[51] Weakened psychological ties to the parties make more offices competitive in previously one–party areas, but the competition now is between strong candidates rather than strong parties.

Casting about for support structures, candidates find organizational shells like the state parties especially useful. They can be staffed by loyalists; receive "soft money," which cannot legally flow to candidates; and be confined to functions that permit personal campaign organizations to control the candidates' presentation of self.

Debate about the vitality of party organizations is of the "is the glass half–full or half–empty?" variety. Are parties stronger because they are performing useful functions or are they weaker because they are not autonomous? Are they stronger because their staffs are increasing or weaker because they are no longer a strong link between voters and officeholders? Political scientists spend much time on these questions. Politicians intent on winning do not care much. For better or worse, politics in New Jersey is dominated by candidates and office-holders, and the parties can at best play a supporting role.

CHAPTER SIX

The Representation of Interests

If a group is wise, it goes to the party leaders and not to the committee members in charge of a bill.
— New Jersey state legislator, 1935[1]

In the old days...you needed a majority of the majority party....Now you have to worry about committees and even second committees. There are a lot more players in the process with life and death power over your bill.
— lobbyist, 1987[2]

Two recent descriptions of New Jersey's interest group system convey its essential features. From a veteran legislator's perspective, "Every issue around here has more than two sides. They are more a cube than a coin." From a leading lobbyist, "It's like eighteenth century Europe. There are no friends or enemies, just shifting alliances."[3] Interest group tactics are many and complex, and one cannot tell which players are on the same side at a particular time without a current scorecard. The myriad groups now bringing their problems to Trenton are all the more remarkable because half a century ago there were so few of them.

In the 1930s, Dayton McKean, a Princeton political scientist and Mercer County assemblyman, estimated there were about twenty lobbyists plying their trade at the state capitol. Most represented the business enterprises central to state politics, and their strategy was simple—purchasing officeholders. McKean noted of his fellow lawmakers, "It is perfectly well–known that some members represent certain interests"—including roughly a quarter of the entire legislature rumored to be on retainer by the Public Service Corporation, a holding company for most of the state's utilities and bus and trolley companies. Aside from a few other large corporations, interests then resident in Trenton included the labor, education, and local government groups present in most state capitols.[4]

What accounts for the recent changes? Largely, they resulted from the same factors affecting almost every aspect of politics and government in New Jersey after the 1960s—declining localism, growing state identity and government activism, and collapse of the county party organizations that brokered interests. Yet just as traces of the past remain in New Jersey's electoral politics, so too are they found in interest group politics. Home rule is wounded but not dead; the media environment still limits the ability of general public opinion to compete with narrow interests in setting policies. Every state has seen the explosion of interests that has occurred in New Jersey, but few experienced it so rapidly.[5]

THE INTEREST GROUP UNIVERSE[6]

More than 600 businesses, industries, and associations employ about 450 "legislative agents" or registered lobbyists in Trenton, as compared with the 20 McKean identified in the 1930s, the 70 who registered in 1971 when registration was first required, and the 254 who registered in 1976. About 10 percent of all the registered interests are associated with the health–care industry. Almost as many represent builders, developers, and other real estate interests, as well as banks and other financial institutions. They are followed closely by insurance concerns.

Smaller interest group sectors, each accounting for about 5 percent of the total number, include other regulated occupations (e.g., beauticians and morticians), pharmaceutical and chemical companies, education groups, energy companies, labor unions, the transportation industry, food and agricultural interests, beverage and tobacco distributors, local governments, the communications industry, and "good government" groups. Other business enterprises, including large corporations, constitute the small remainder.[7]

Lists of groups tell little about particular organizations or how their power has changed over time. Since the 1930s, four studies of varying precision have examined these questions. Although they are not directly comparable, significant shifts can be detected.

In 1938, McKean offered an informed if impressionistic judgment. He cited the New Jersey State Teachers Association (later renamed the New Jersey Education Association), the Chamber of Commerce, the New Jersey Manufacturers Association (later renamed the New Jersey Business and Industry Association), the Public Service Corporation, the New Jersey Taxpayers Association, and the American Federation of Labor (AFL) as the state's most influential groups.

These groups had different resources and sources of power. Teachers, the Manufacturers Association (representing smaller companies than the Chamber of Commerce), and unions were present in almost every legislative district. Unions engaged mostly in electoral reprisal or support, while teachers and businessmen also lobbied effectively in Trenton. The other three groups—large corporations or institutions representing them—contributed money to the parties and were thought to have lawyer–legislators on retainer. McKean also

Table 8: Interest Groups Most Frequently Cited by New Jersey Legislators, 1962

	Generalized Power	Group Merit
New Jersey Education Association	30	11
Chamber(s) of Commerce	20	25
AFL-CIO	23	10
N.J. Municipal League	7	17
N.J. Taxpayers Assoc.	5	21
N.J. Manufacturers Assoc.	7	2
League of Women Voters	3	12
N.J. Farm Bureau	4	2
PTA(s)	1	–

Source: John Wahlke, et al. *The Legislative System* (New York: Wiley, 1962), 318-19.

Note: Table entries are the percentage of legislators interviewed who mentioned the group. All groups mentioned by at least 1% of the respondents are included.

noted that business groups were more often fragmented and conflictful than mutually supportive. Finally, he praised the New Jersey Municipal Association and the Association of Freeholders for useful assistance with technical statutes affecting local government.[8]

A more systematic survey in 1962 confirmed McKean's impressionistic analysis. Scholars asked legislators in four states an open–ended question about "the most powerful groups" (termed "generalized power") in their states, and which groups' "advice ought to be considered whether they happen to be powerful or not" (termed "group merit").[9]

New Jersey legislators named 38 organizations, but only nine were mentioned by at least 1 percent of the respondents. Only the three groups with members in every legislative district—the state teachers' organization and the largest business and labor groups—were fairly widely regarded as "powerful." New Jersey legislators were also least likely to assign generalized power to business groups, most likely to say educational groups were powerful in their own constituencies, and named the lowest number of groups.[10] The results led to a widespread conclusion that New Jersey was a weak interest group state.

In 1979, Philip Burch conducted the next wide–ranging study, based on in–depth interviews with legislators, lobbyists, reporters, and former governors and cabinet officers. Respondents were asked "a series of questions ranging from an appraisal of the strength of interest groups and an assessment of the various major kinds...to a more detailed evaluation of all organizations...."[11]

Table 9: Effectiveness and Credibility of Selected Interest Groups:
Ratings by New Jersey Legislators, 1987

Group	Effectiveness Rating	Credibility Rating
NJEA (Teachers Assoc.)	4.3	3.5
NEWJOBS (NJ Business and Industry Assoc.)	4.2	4.0
Dental Assoc.	4.0	3.7
BPAC (Builder's Assoc.)	3.9	3.3
NJCAR (Auto Dealers Assoc.)	3.6	3.4
LEGAL (Trial Lawyers Assoc.)	3.6	2.8
School Boards Assoc.	3.6	3.8
AFL-CIO	3.5	3.1
Cable TV Assoc.	3.3	3.2
FAIR (Insurance)	3.2	2.9
Casino Assoc.	3.2	3.1

Source: Gallup Organization. *The 1987 Gallup Survey of the New Jersey State Legislature* (Princeton, N. J.: Gallup Organization, 1987), 2.

Burch singled out the New Jersey Education Association (NJEA) "as unusually effective" and the Chamber of Commerce and the New Jersey Business and Industry Association (NJBIA) as the most important business groups. He described the AFL–CIO membership as so large that it "cannot help but be a major force in New Jersey politics" but noted, "unlike the NJEA, it has never been able to translate most of its vast personnel and financial resources into any kind of equivalent political power." The League of Municipalities was cited for technical expertise within its special domain. Burch also noted the latent influence of the legal profession because of the many lawyer–legislators, rather than their organizational clout.

Burch also identified a number of other groups not mentioned in earlier studies, including senior citizens, builders and realtors, and the health professions. Although he did not rate them as particularly active or effective, their inclusion signaled the broadened scope and activity of New Jersey state government, which had already begun by 1979.

In 1987, the Gallup Organization, retained by several clients, conducted a survey of the New Jersey legislature and made some of the results available to the public. Although not the study's major topic, legislators were asked to rate "the effectiveness and credibility" of thirteen interest groups. Why these particular groups were chosen is not certain. However, they account for much of the PAC money contributed to legislative candidates over the last two decades and figure prominently in journalistic coverage of New Jersey's lobbyists and interest groups.[12] The relevant results of this survey appear in table 9.

The New Jersey Education Association continues to be strong. NJEA, whose impressive five–story headquarters is located across the street from the capitol, has over 130,000 members. It runs one of the state's best–financed political action committees, sends candidate endorsement letters to all of its members, and conducts effective election day get–out–the–vote operations. Legislators respect NJEA for its political clout and professionalism. As one legislator described it, "They represent a large constituency. They have a good research division. Good publicity; personal meetings; periodic information; luncheons; visible representatives in Trenton." Another added, "They are good in reaching out with their information—but also good in intimidation."[13]

The NJBIA, founded in 1905 by Paterson silk mill owners to oppose workman's compensation laws, matches NJEA in perceived effectiveness and has the highest credibility rating of any association listed. Like NJEA, the Business and Industry Association is respected for its knowledge, presence, and ability to help in campaigns. Another important similarity is the pervasive presence of both groups in legislators' districts. NJEA has 19 field offices and 37 field representatives. NJBIA has employer legislative committees (ELCs) in 20 of the state's 21 counties. County business leaders on these committees hold monthly meetings with association lobbyists to share information and concerns.

Compared to NJEA, NJBIA is more often cited as an "honest broker."[14] One legislator described NJBIA as having "a good research staff that provide detailed reasoning. They don't just say I'm for this or that." Another noted, "they give me both sides of the coin."[15]

The Gallup Survey also showed the continuing (but lesser) influence of the AFL–CIO, whose members are also present in many districts. Although their numbers are declining, New Jersey still has more than 600,000 unionized workers. Yet as Burch commented, organized labor has never played the political role their numbers might suggest—even in labor's boom times. New Jersey's unions have been unusually factious and often politically inept.

Discord in the labor movement stretches back to the bloody and prolonged strikes of Paterson silk mill workers and Passaic factory hands. The 137 strikes in Paterson between 1881 and 1900 amounted to "a virtual state of war."[16] The international anarchist movement made Paterson its U.S. headquarters. A five–month walkout by Paterson weavers in 1913 was taken over by the radical International Workers of the World (Wobblies). The IWW brought in leading leftists like Elizabeth Gurley Flynn, John Reed, and Upton Sinclair to inspire the strikers. A similar year–long work stoppage, involving 10,000 to 12,000 workers, occurred in Passaic in 1913. One reason leftists gained influence with these workers was that the conservative state AFL, dominated then and now by the building trades, supported the successful strikebreakers.

The relatively conservative bent of the largest labor federation and its uneasy relationship with other elements of organized labor continue to the present. The New Jersey AFL supported Jersey City Mayor Frank Hague's successful efforts to keep CIO organizers out of Jersey City (see chapter 3). When the AFL and CIO merged in 1955, only one state—New Jersey—refused to go along. Federation President George Meany forced the warring New Jersey unions to unite in 1961, but the old CIO unions withdrew again in 1964.

Today, there are two AFL–CIO organizations in New Jersey, which some-times cooperate and sometimes do not.[17] Charles Marciante, veteran president of the older and larger body, has served on the labor advisory council of the Republican National Committee, and his group endorses candidates of both parties. Marciante specializes in generating and supervising state construction projects and in lobbying on wage and benefits legislation.

Joel Jacobson, the long–time head of the smaller, more liberal body, the Industrial Union Council (IUC), was a fervent liberal Democrat active in the anti–Vietnam War and civil rights movements. While Marciante concentrated on pocketbook issues, Jacobson led labor's fights for right–to–know legislation and plant–closing notification. The IUC, although smaller, has been more politically sophisticated, with an active and well financed PAC and a more technologically advanced campaign operation for its endorsed candidates (almost always Democrats, who sometimes run against Republicans endorsed by the AFL). The IUC is aided by an informal alliance with the Communications Workers of America (CWA), which represents many state government employ-ees. With Jacobson's departure, the IUC moderated its stands somewhat.[18] It joined the AFL–CIO in a common effort on behalf of 1989 Democratic gubernatorial candidate Jim Florio, but the different strategies of the two major unions were apparent in their 1989 legislative endorsements. The AFL–CIO endorsed 52 Democrats and 19 Republicans in assembly races, while the IUC endorsed 52 Democrats and only two Republicans. In 1991, the AFL divided its endorsements evenly, supporting 18 Democrats, 18 Republicans, and an independent.[19]

Still, union members (who now constitute perhaps a fifth of all workers) are dwindling. Domination of the voting rolls and campaign contribution lists by businesses, nonunionized employees, and professionals explains why the

NJEA, for example, with many fewer members, has long been more politically effective than the AFL–CIO. It also explains why Democratic legislative leaders disparaged Marciante's threats to withhold 1989 legislative endorsements if the Democrat–controlled senate did not act on several labor bills.[20]

The most interesting aspect of table 9 is the appearance of many new groups, including several Burch described as politically feeble in the late 1970s—senior citizens, bankers, dentists, builders, and the organized trial lawyers. Others, such as the casino association and the cable television association, had barely come into existence at the time Burch wrote. Their rankings are further testimony to the expanding role of the state government.

Thus, a few New Jersey interest groups have been continuously influential for at least 50 years—the largest business groups, the major labor federation, and the teachers' organization. They have been joined by other groups whose economic interests are now more affected by state action. With the establishment of political action committees (whose dramatic growth we discuss below) and the waning of strong local party organizations, more interest groups have greater access to legislators, who are both free of party discipline and more in need of campaign contributions.

Large individual corporations, once the rulers of the legislature, now play a limited role because their principal concerns are dealt with by the federal government rather than state government. One recent exception is successful efforts by pharmaceutical companies—begun by Schering Plough and later taken up by Johnson and Johnson and Merck—to amend state law so as to make hostile takeovers of New Jersey corporations almost impossible.

More often, however, issues concerning large enterprises are handled by umbrella associations like the state Chamber of Commerce. Large corporations with New Jersey headquarters—Johnson and Johnson, AT&T, Beneficial Finance Corporation, and the Prudential Insurance Company—also make their presence felt more informally. As sources of campaign funds, employment, and managerial and fiscal expertise, they are important to New Jersey's political leaders.

No governor can ignore a company that employs thousands of the state's residents. Nor can a company like Prudential, a quarter of whose board of directors is appointed by New Jersey's chief justice, completely ignore Trenton.[21] Some corporations also take a benevolent interest in the state. Johnson and Johnson spearheaded redevelopment and revitalization in downtown New Brunswick, where its international headquarters is located. Prudential, Beneficial, Finance and New Jersey Bell are doing the same in Newark. Prudential's willingness to underwrite bonds for the New Jersey Sports and Exposition Authority was a key component in the development of the Meadowlands.

Some interests important in other states do not play a weighty role in New Jersey. The federal government is not a significant presence as landowner or source of employment, and the state sends more money to Washington than it gets back. New Jersey's religious organizations are denominationally diverse, predominantly mainstream, and liberally inclined. Although maintaining Trenton representatives to lobby on issues like state aid to parochial schools, they generally adhere to the principle of separation of church and state and seldom get actively involved in broader social policy.[22]

So-called "good government" groups, such as the League of Women Voters and Common Cause, often receive approving lip service for their activities but do not have the numbers or financial resources to lobby their issues effectively. Organized environmentalists, whose issues often dominate the public agenda, are not at the forefront of the environmental battle. Rather, in a state that has the country's greatest population density and largest number of federally designated Superfund cleanup sites, "Impetus for all of New Jersey's activism came from the apprehension and impatience of the general public."[23]

Political developments have enhanced the lobbying role of state agencies. State intervention in so many new policy fields forced agencies to develop their own agendas and appoint legislative liaisons. With more issues on state government's docket, governors concentrated their own lobbying efforts on a few priorities, leaving the agencies to deal with lesser ones. Divided government, a more assertive legislature, and Governor Kean's style often made the governor's office more reactive than proactive during the 1980s, with a need to turn to institutional memory and expertise.

Sometimes, governors foist unpopular decisions on executive agencies so as to avoid blame. For example, a solid-waste crisis forced some counties to accept trash from counties having no facilities. It was no accident that the Department of Environmental Protection rather than the governor took the lead and was identified with this highly unpopular policy.

Left without direction from the top on many issues during the Kean years, cabinet officials and agencies' legislative liaisons often joined with their clientele groups and opposed each other. Pesticide legislation, for example, found the Department of Agriculture allied with the industry against the Department of Environmental Protection and the Office of the Public Advocate. The latter two agencies joined with unions in support of another controversial bill regulating chemicals in the workplace. They were opposed by the chemical industry, the Chamber of Commerce, the NJBIA, and the Department of Commerce and Economic Development—whose commissioner was a major stockholder and former vice-president of American

Cyanamid, a leading chemical company. More interventionist chief executives could consolidate lobbying operations on more issues in their own offices or issue more directives to agencies. During the Florio administration, agencies' legislative liaisons were instructed to report to the governor's office on their activities.

Many laws must be implemented by administrative rules, and the agencies that promulgate them are another venue for lobbyists. Agency rules must be published in the New Jersey Register twenty days before they take effect. Joseph Gonzales, executive director of the NJBIA, explains the effect of regulations from an interest group's point of view: "A department is likely to take the bare bones of a bill and put meat, gristle and fat on it. As a result, you may be faced with something completely different than what the legislature intended, and that's a tough fight in itself. That's why it's important to develop a good relationship with people in the executive branch."[24]

One experienced lobbyist has estimated that there are 82 state government departments, divisions, commissions, boards, agencies, councils, and authorities empowered to issue regulations.[25] It is in this arcane and publicly invisible implementation phase that the experience of lobbyists who have served in the executive branch is most useful: "There are lobbyists who are extremely influential in this phase of the process. They tend to be highly skilled experts who are well-funded and knowledgeable about how to play an insider's game. They help to shape rules and regulations by providing research and background material to appropriate executive branch officials before a rule is promulgated."[26]

LOBBYISTS: A PORTRAIT

Most New Jersey lobbyists are employed full–time as government affairs specialists by individual businesses or associations or are contract lobbyists representing several clients. Large concerns often have sizable in–house lobby operations. Public Service Electric and Gas, the largest utility, has a twenty–person government affairs staff. NJBIA and NJEA both have about a half–dozen full–time lobbyists.

In recent years, the role of contract lobbyists has increased dramatically. Joseph Katz, the first such "hired gun," set up shop in 1966. In 1983, there were 22 registered individuals or firms with multiple, unrelated clients, collectively representing 181 concerns. By 1990 this had mushroomed to 45 different individuals or firms with 421 clients. Fifteen contract lobbyists had at least 10 clients, and three had more than 40.

Clients are not confined to enterprises without their own legislative agents; a number of firms hire contract lobbyists to augment in–house staff. Some firms without in–house personnel also retain more than one contract lobbyist. Among the businesses and trade groups represented by four or more individual and contract lobbyists are the Atlantic City Casino Hotel Association, the New Jersey Hospital Association, New Jersey Blue Cross, Ciba–Geigy, United Jersey Bank, the New Jersey Realtors Association, and Browning–Ferris Industries.[27]

Many contract lobbyists have held high positions in the executive branch of state government or on the legislative staff. Others are ex–legislators or former reporters for the state's leading newspapers. Principals in the largest contract lobbying firms have served as gubernatorial chiefs of staff or have themselves been gubernatorial candidates or legislative leaders. The major firms are bipartisan, including principals who have served governors of both parties. The only woman heading a major contract lobbying operation is the sole exception to this pattern; she began her Trenton career as executive director of New Jersey Common Cause. In 1990, contract lobbyists reported collecting fees of $7.7 million, more than a third of which was earned by only seven firms.[28]

A likely reason contract lobbyists doubled their client roster in the 1980s is that legislators regard them favorably. The Gallup legislative survey included a question about whether "in general," contract personnel, staff, or organizational volunteers were "most effective in communicating issues to you." Of the three–fifths of respondents indicating a preference, 47 percent chose contract lobbyists, 27 percent said staff lobbyists, and 26 percent picked the nonprofessionals.[29]

Another reason for the growth of contract lobbying is greater use of transient multigroup alliances to lobby major issues. Sometimes one of the participants' lobbyists assumes the lead role. In a major "right–to–know" controversy over what information chemical companies would be required to tell workers dealing with hazardous substances, the Chamber of Commerce, NJBIA, and the Chemical Industry Council (CIC) joined forces, led by the CIC's lobbyist. Opposing them was the New Jersey Right to Know Coalition, composed of environmental groups and their lead player, the IUC labor federation. More often, however, a contract lobbyist assembles the coalition or is hired to lead it, as in the case of FAIR, the Federation of Advocates for Insurance Reform. FAIR is a joint effort of insurance companies, professional groups, and corporations to change the state's liability insurance laws.

Generally speaking, therefore, the growth in the number and functions of contract lobbyists reflects the growth in the complexity of issues and the processes needed to resolve them.

Regulation of Lobbyists

New Jersey was one of the last states to regulate lobbyists. Not until 1971 were lobbyists required to register with the attorney general's office, disclose clients, report their interest in bills quarterly, and wear a badge while at work in the capitol. In 1973, when the Election Law Enforcement Commission (ELEC) was established to monitor party and campaign expenditures, the legislation also provided that lobbyists would have to file annual spending reports with ELEC. This portion of the law was immediately challenged in court by twenty lobbyists led by the Chamber of Commerce and was tied up in legal wrangles for six years. The legislature took up the financial reporting requirement again in 1981, when it became the most heavily lobbied bill of the year.[30]

The lobbyists objected to the bill's provision that expenditures be reported for any contacts with a legislator "without limitation." They argued that not only was it unreasonable to require reports of entertainment subsidies to legislators (such as free meals, drinks, tickets to sporting events, or convention trips) unconnected to specific measures, but that the law was so vague that it could include incalculable portions of office rent and utility bills. Some lobbyists also contended that the bill threatened freedom of speech. As Prudential Insurance's lobbyist put it, "We were being drawn into a situation that was not intended....If I am not talking to a legislator about an issue and I am just in his company, why report it? There are some First Amendment implications." Another lobbyist complained, "that is not lobbying as I understand it. It is building a relationship, not discussing legislation....No other people in the world are asked to quantify that."[31]

The session–long battle came to a mysterious end at literally the last moment. In the wee hours of the morning just before a new governor and legislature were to take office in January 1982, the outgoing legislature struck out the bill's "without limitation" wording and substituted language that only expenses connected "expressly" with discussions of specific legislation would have to be reported. The outgoing governor, who had previously vetoed several similar wordings, signed it at 8 A.M. on his way to the inaugural. All the participants later claimed surprise that the final bill was so favorable to the lobbyists. Most legislators said they did not realize what they were voting on in the year–end legislative blizzard, and the Chamber of Commerce lobbyist who had led the fight for seven years claimed it was a "Hail Mary" bill—one hoped for but never expected to happen.[32]

After a series of scandals during 1990, a blue ribbon Commission on Legislative Ethics and Campaign Finance, appointed by Senate President John

Lynch and headed by the director of the Eagleton Institute of Politics at Rutgers University, recommended lobbyists be required to report all good will spending. In 1991, the legislature finally passed a reform package removing the "expressly" wording, extending reporting requirements to lobbying directed at executive agencies and centralizing all reporting at ELEC.

The reforms could provide for more complete public disclosure. It has been difficult to access the information. The registration reports submitted quarterly to the attorney general's office were filed by assigned numbers rather than by name. Numbers—over 400 of them—were assigned by the date of an individual or firm's first registration rather than alphabetically or by clients. The data were compiled by hand and were not computer–retrievable. It was time–consuming to determine such simple facts as the names of all the lobbyists representing one organization or all those interested in a given issue.

Further, surmounting these hurdles yielded little useful information on the true scope of lobbying activity. Lobbyists were only required to report whether they supported, opposed, or sought to amend a particular bill—not the nature of the amendments. As a result of the "expressly" wording, the spending reports filed annually with ELEC since 1982 provided no information about "good will" expenditures like all–expenses–paid legislative trips to business conventions at luxury resorts. Nor were lobbyists required to report either legal fees paid to lawyer–lobbyists or expenditures on issue–related public relations campaigns.

The new law somewhat strengthens what many observers still regard as rather weak regulation of lobbyists. Certainly, as ELEC Executive Director Frederick Hermann said, the old law was "notoriously weak by comparison" with other states.[33] The head of New Jersey Common Cause called the new law "a real reform," but still "not as complete as it needs to be."[34]

INTEREST GROUP TACTICS

New Jersey's interest groups spend most of their time and resources cultivating access to legislators and executive branch officials. Two assured ways to gain access are providing campaign money and reliable technical information. Seasoned lobbyists hope to delay action in the legislature or executive agencies so as to maintain the status quo for as long as possible, insert amendments in bills or regulations that make unwanted legislation more palatable, or persuade the governor to exercise one of several different types of veto power.[35]

Technical information has long been the lobbyist's stock–in–trade. When the legislature met only once a week for a few months a year, had almost no staff, and was populated by amateurs with high turnover rates, lobbyists had a near–

monopoly on information and bill drafting.[36] More staff and a more professional legislature in the past two decades have not diminished the value of lobbyists' information because of the increase in the number of complex issues. As legislators' comments about NJEA and NJBIA indicate, they are quite willing to listen to lobbyists with reputations for knowledge and probity. As one assemblyman argues, the expertise of credible lobbyists is important in making it possible for legislators to understand many of the 10,000 bills that cross their desks in a typical session.[37]

The same is true at the governor's office, which often asks lobbyists for information on a bill's impact. The chief counsel to Governor Kean observed: "I believe my job is to give the governor every piece of information there is on a bill so he can make a judgment. No particular lobbyist has any particular influence, but certain ones have more credibility. We talk to both sides."[38]

As legislation has become more complex, technical expertise has become more important for lobbyists. However, as the backgrounds of the leading contract lobbyists make evident, political connections count for at least as much, and probably more, than technical knowledge. The leading players may depend on staff for data, but former officeholders and appointed officials do the important contact work.

Newer developments are lobbyists' increased reliance on political contributions to secure access to lawmakers and the growth in those contributions. In the past, interest groups contributed to campaigns, but the amounts were much smaller and directed to the county party organizations. Campaigns in New Jersey's pre–media age, which extended well into the 1970s, were relatively inexpensive. The collapse of the local party organizations and the era of high–tech candidate–centered campaigns dramatically escalated costs. Senate and assembly candidates spent $11 million on their 1987 campaigns—a 69–percent increase in constant dollars from 1983. In 1991, their spending reached a record $15.1 million.

PACs are a particularly attractive target for legislative candidates seeking funds because unlike more than two–thirds of the states, New Jersey has imposed no limits on either PAC or corporate contributions to legislative candidates.[39] Thus, $10,000 contributions to individual legislators are not unusual, and they have ranged much higher. The National Rifle Association probably set a state record when it contributed at least $61,000 in an unsuccessful attempt to defeat state senator William Gormley in his 1991 Republican primary election. Gormley, a 1989 gubernatorial contender, provided the single Republican vote needed to pass the toughest state ban on assault weapons.[40]

PACs have not been required to identify their interests, but only to report contributions. Some choose names not easily associated with a company or industry, making the identity of the givers something of a parlor game. In April

Table 10: Selected PAC Contributions to New Jersey Legislative Campaigns, 1983, 1987, 1991

Group	1983	1987	1991
NJEA (Teachers Assoc.)	100	270	268
NEWJOBS (NJ Business and Industry Assoc.)	86	128	199
Dental Assoc.	103	207	136
BPAC (Builder's Assoc.)	180	212	22
MJCAR (Auto Dealers Assoc.)	65	134	122
LEGAL (Trial Lawyers Assoc.)	84	188	243
Medical Action Committee	76	190	33

Source: New Jersey Election Law Enforcement Commission.

Note: Table entries are in thousands of dollars.

1991, ELEC's director admitted he was unaware that an eight–year–old PAC, which had already raised more than $30,000 in contributions for that November's elections, was organized by the New Jersey Restaurant Association.[41]

The 30 PACs that gave at least $1,000 and were thus required to report in 1979, contributed 14 percent of all campaign money that year. In 1987, 187 PACs met the new reporting threshold of $2,500 and accounted for 29 percent of all contributions. By 1991, there were 290 political action committees.[42]

As elsewhere, PACs in New Jersey usually contribute primarily to incumbents, although the level of competition in any given year has some effect. In 1987, when there were more hotly contested races than in 1983, incumbents received 71 percent of PAC contributions, as compared to 80 percent four years earlier. A small number of PACs contributes a large proportion of total PAC dollars. In 1991, the 20 largest PACs accounted for 63 percent of PAC contributions, up from 58 percent in 1987.

The PACs listed in table 10 are perennial heavy contributors to state campaigns. Other well–funded but more ephemeral PACs are controlled by particular candidates. The largest PAC in 1991, for example, was the Greater Camden County Committee (which contributed $983,000). The ninth largest, at $221,000, was the Greater Camden Committee, and the fifteenth, at $133,000, was New Visions for Cherry Hill—a wealthy Camden County suburb. All of these groups first appeared on the scene in 1989 and solicited funds from Governor Jim Florio's Camden County support base. Nineteenth on the list in 1991, at $82,000, was the Committee for an Affordable New Jersey, the personal PAC of Republican Christie Whitman.

Whitman, who came within a point of defeating U.S. senator Bill Bradley in 1990, was in 1991 an all–but–announced 1993 gubernatorial candidate.

Overall, these findings reflect the general conclusions about the current role of interest groups in the states. A more complex state economy does not lead, as was once thought, to weaker groups because of increasing pluralization. Rather, there are just more groups and continuing dominance, albeit even more fragmented, by business. The greater need for campaign money is met substantially by increased interest group contributions.

Of the traditional pressure groups, education and business remain strong, while agricultural and labor interests have lost ground. Some of the most important new actors are developers, the health care industry, and single–issue groups (e.g., tort reform advocates, or supporters and opponents of legalized sports betting), whose particular concerns land on the state's policy agenda from time to time. Less wealthy or well–organized groups must, as they always have, depend on the kindness of strangers.[43]

Although journalists and "good government" advocates regularly accuse the PACs of "buying" elections, the givers and recipients do not see it that way. Legislators freely admit that they indeed give "access" to "heavy hitters." John Russo, who as senate president from 1985 to 1989 raised well over a million dollars for Democratic senate candidates in 1987 and is now a contract lobbyist, said while in office, "If you call me up and if you've been a substantial contributor and supporter, I'll say that I'd like to see you. They listened to my plea, I'll listen to theirs."[44] The 1987 Gallup survey found that 45 percent of legislators thought PAC contributions had a positive effect on their relationship with interest groups, 7 percent thought they had a negative effect, and 48 percent expressed no opinion. Legislators cited good personal relations, more awareness of issues, and support for their own personal positions as the major positive effects.[45]

However, legislators strenuously deny being "bought." Raymond Lesniak, once chairman of a heavily lobbied senate committee and later chair of the Democratic State Committee, gives an example from his own experience: out–of–state bankers offered him a free trip to a Florida convention, which he accepted. Both before and after the trip, he led the opposition to the bankers' first priority: permission to open branch banks in New Jersey. After the bankers lost on the floor, Lesniak went back to them for a campaign contribution. Fearing loss of access, they gave it to him. He therefore argues, "It certainly doesn't get them what they want—their bills passed or not. What it does get them is time to build more support for their position if they ask for it or amendments to make the legislation more palatable. They get the frills, not the meat."[46]

Former Assemblyman Steve Adubato, Jr., now a journalistic crusader against

PACs, also believes legislators cannot be "bought" on issues about which they are knowledgeable and care deeply. But he enlarges on Lesniak's theme: "Did I vote against my conscience? Not really, but on legislation that I didn't have strong feelings on either way, I was inclined to support the position of a large contributor."[47]

One development militating against influence peddling is the increasing share of campaign funds raised by finance committees controlled by the governor and the legislative leadership, which are described in chapter 5. These committees spend their money on races targeted entirely on the basis of competitiveness, not candidates' issue positions. A lobbyist "hit up" for a contribution to, say, the senate president's committee, has no idea who will eventually wind up with the money.

These developments lead Alan Rosenthal, a prominent student of the legislature to conclude, "Lobbyists created a Frankenstein, and now they don't know how to control it. And I think the money they give doesn't buy them very much because people are expected to contribute and nobody gets anything special by contributing."[48]

Some of the crusaders against the PACs grudgingly agree that it is more image than actual malfeasance that is of real concern. After arguing that "The system lends the appearance of impropriety to the contributions process whether or not any lawmaker or candidate ever crosses that line," journalist Jeffrey Kanige, a frequent PAC critic, went on to concede, "There is ample evidence to suggest that campaign contributions matter less than the contributors might believe. There are any number of small organizations and lobbying groups that are well-respected and listened to in Trenton without handing out big checks."[49]

An indication that lobbyists may agree with this assessment is that NJBIA, seeing no end to the spiraling requests, has convened its own workshop on campaign reform. Even legislators seem weary of the endless fund-raising events. In the Gallup Survey, they favored "restricting PAC contributions" by a margin of 63 to 27 percent, with 10 percent expressing no opinion.[50]

In 1988, a Republican legislator introduced a comprehensive reform package, including public financing for legislative campaigns. Governor Kean's 1989 annual message also called for public financing. In 1990, after a lobbyist publicly accused four Democratic Assembly leaders of a "shakedown," the legislature convened a blue ribbon Commission on Legislative Ethics and Campaign Finance (mentioned earlier) to study the matter once again.

Public financing would not be without its own problems. In addition to the public's disinclination to bear the cost, a "level playing field" that gave all candidates the same resources would further advantage the better-known incumbents. States with limits on PAC contributions and the few that have recently established legislative public financing are already discovering PACs' ingenuity in getting around the rules.[51] The debate in New Jersey over the merits of various campaign schemes, as is the case nationally, is founded more on ideological preference than platonic virtue.

Although campaign contributions and legislative activity are lobbyists' chief stock–in–trade, other strategies are also employed to some effect. Grass–roots lobbying—in the form of organized mail and phone campaigns by members and sympathizers—is an increasingly common tactic. When Governor Florio proposed extending the state sales tax to monthly cable television bills, the New Jersey Cable Television Association orchestrated the mailing of "more than 125,000 anti–tax postcards, which were bundled in bags and delivered to the Statehouse in a wheelbarrow."[52] The cable tax was the only one of the governor's several unpopular sales tax extenders to be rejected by the legislature.

There are also frequent public relations campaigns on major issues like the long–running auto insurance morass. These campaigns involve newspaper, radio, and television advertising; commissioning of public opinion polls; and distribution of their results. Occasionally, interest groups also use litigation as a technique.[53]

New Jersey, like most other eastern states, has not had an important vehicle to advance group concerns—statewide initiatives placed on the ballot by public petition. The courts have also interpreted the state constitution as permitting the legislature to authorize ballot referenda dealing only with the state's bonded indebtedness or constitutional amendments.[54]

Most constitutional amendments address procedural issues such as the length of sheriffs' terms or the residency requirement for voting. However, because the constitution specifically prohibits all forms of gambling not approved by the voters, it must be amended to permit major changes like legalized casino gambling in Atlantic City (approved in 1976, after a referendum to allow casinos anywhere in the state failed in 1974), and also minor ones like changes in the rules for bingo, raffles, and boardwalk games of chance.

Voters have also passed judgment on numerous bond issues for public land acquisition, farmland preservation, wastewater treatment facilities, hazardous waste cleanup, and the like. Some bond issues, however public spirited, mean a great deal to particular interest groups. The construction industry, for example, is especially enthusiastic about frequent bond questions on state building projects.

Since 1985, when Governor Kean called for passage of a GOP–sponsored constitutional amendment permitting state initiatives, "I and R" (Initiative and Referendum) has been a frequent state issue. In 1989, public exasperation over high auto insurance rates produced a drive to put a nonbinding referendum on forcing down rates on the ballot in all 21 counties. The state supreme court, interpreting the constitution as it had before, refused to let it appear.

In 1990, Hands Across New Jersey, a citizens' group irate over tax increases, launched a million–signature petition drive to promote statewide initiative, referenda, and recall elections. Vocal support by a Trenton "talk radio" station and the *Trentonian* newspaper magnified their message. Over 30 county and municipal governments also authorized nonbinding referenda urging repeal of the taxes, but the state supreme court declared almost all of them unconstitutional.

Generally speaking, the Republicans in the legislature publicly supported I and R during the 1980s, while Democrats opposed it. Republicans hoped and Democrats feared that I and R's connection to the widespread tax protests would make for a potent issue in the 1991 legislative elections. Democratic Senate President John Lynch executed a politically astute strategy in the summer of 1991 to defuse the issue and take it off the political agenda until after the legislative elections.

Lynch believed some Republican senators publicly favoring I and R actually opposed it and were counting on the Democrats to kill the referendum. The senate president suspected GOP senators from small counties still feared their interests could be swamped by referenda votes from the populous north. Further, 99 influential lobbying groups, including the NJBIA and the NJEA, had banded together in a coalition called Citizens for a Representative Democracy to oppose I and R. Consequently "some of the [Republicans'] biggest financial backers were telephoning legislators...and telling them how unhappy they would be if they voted for I and R." [55]

Lynch thus offered 10 Democratic votes of the 21 needed to dislodge the proposal from committee, requiring the 17 GOP senators who had earlier voted en masse for I and R to provide 11 affirmative votes. Faced with this eyeball–to–eyeball challenge, the Republican senators blinked, providing only nine votes. However, the huge Republican majorities elected in 1991 contained many new members who had run on a promise to support I and R. New attempts ensued to put a constitutional amendment permitting I and R on the ballot.

CONCLUSION

Our analysis reveals several elements of continuity amidst vast changes in New Jersey's interest group politics. They are all related to the state's enduring localist orientations. The interest groups that have remained important over the past fifty years—education, labor, and small business—are those with large and relatively cohesive representation in legislators' districts. To explain oddities like New Jersey's status as the only state that until 1992 did not license physicians' assistants (although its state medical school trained them) or as one of only two states still without self–service gas stations, one need look no further than the many nurses, physicians, and independent gas station owners who are all legislators' vocal and well–organized constituents.[56]

Most of the issues state government deals with remain narrow and distributive in character or at least are defined that way. The newest groups with a Trenton presence are the targets of greatly increased state regulation—developers, the financial community, insurance interests (and their frequent nemeses, the lawyers), and the health care industry (and their largest clientele, senior citizens). Very rarely, aroused public opinion may intervene in debate on these "special–interest" issues. The most notable of these now are quality–of–life and environmental concerns and skyrocketing auto insurance rates. In a contracting economy, taxes also return to the forefront of the public's attention. However, the continuing absence of true mass media in the state—particularly its own mass audience television stations—makes it difficult for public, rather than special interest, opinion to form. As one journalist puts it, "The most powerful lobby in Trenton is ignorance."[57]

Today, unlike the heyday of the Camden and Amboy Railroad and the Public Service Corporation, no small number of interest groups dominates the state. Rather, in the continuing absence of strong aggregative institutions like political parties or statewide media, there is a myriad of small fiefdoms. Influence in Trenton, in the words of a local wag, has passed from the hacks to the PACs.

CHAPTER SEVEN

The Constitution

*The American constitutions were to liberty, what a grammar is to
language: They define its parts of speech, and practically construct them
into a syntax.*

—Thomas Paine[1]

*It shall be lawful...to conduct, under such restrictions and control as shall
_ from time to time be prescribed by the Legislature...the specific kind of
game of chance sometimes known as bingo or lotto, played with cards
bearing numbers or other designations, 5 or more in one line, the holder
covering numbers as objects, similarly numbered are drawn from a
receptacle and the game being won by the person who first covers a
previously designated arrangement of numbers on such a card....*

—Article IV, Section 7, New Jersey Constitution

New Jersey's three constitutions—of 1776, 1844, and 1947— successively
emphasize each of the three strains of American constitutionalism identified by
Daniel Elazar: communitarian, federalist, and managerial.[2] The 1776 charter
reflected early American faith in a weak executive and a strong legislature. The
1844 constitution responded haltingly to the emerging needs of an industrializ-
ing society and incorporated some aspects of Jacksonian populism. The 1947
charter stimulated development of an activist state government.

It has been said that "political decisions made by constitutional conventions
are really temporary truces in a never–ending conflict between social, economic,
political and sectional forces in the state."[3] This chapter describes how New
Jerseyans worked out those truces in each constitution.

THE CONSTITUTION OF 1776

On May 15, 1776, the Continental Congress requested the colonies to prepare
constitutions. New Jersey's Provincial Congress issued a call for delegates to
a constitutional convention on May 28. They convened in Burlington on June
10 and on July 2 approved a document drawn from colonial texts.[4]

Only 35 of the 65 delegates were present to vote on the charter, which was never formally engrossed, signed, or submitted for popular ratification. New Jersey's first governor, William Livingston, announced at his inauguration that "by tacit acquiescence and open approbation," the constitution "received the assent and concurrence of the good people of this State."[5]

Provisions of the 1776 Constitution

The brief charter, of about 2,000 words, was mostly devoted to the selection and duties of a legislature combining judicial, executive, and legislative functions. The vote was granted to "all Inhabitants of this Colony of full Age who are worth Fifty Pounds proclamation Money." Article 19 required officeholders to profess "a Belief in the Faith of any Protestant sect," but prohibited "Establishment of any one religious sect in this Province in Preference to another." Quaker influence made New Jersey one of the four original states that never had an established religion.

Citizens annually chose members of a bicameral legislative council and assembly, who had to meet stiffer property requirements than did voters (500 pounds for the assembly; 1,000 pounds for the council). Each county elected one member to the upper house and three members to the assembly, with the legislature authorized to adjust the composition of the assembly over time to reflect "more equal Representation."

The legislature, in joint session, appointed all other state officers (the governor, an attorney general, a secretary, and a treasurer), and members of the supreme court and inferior courts. Its upper house, the council, served as the highest appeals court. Although the governor, chosen annually, was granted "supreme executive power," he had no appointment or veto authority. The governor was commanding officer of the state militia, presiding officer in the council, and "Ordinary or Surrogate–Officer"—the highest officer of the courts.

The 1776 constitution was, therefore, a brief restatement of colonial governance documents, revised to account for independence and distaste for a strong executive. "The center of gravity was legally changed from governor to legislature, with as little change in form and familiar landmarks as possible."[6] This first fundamental law served the state for 68 years.

Deficiencies of the 1776 Constitution

Attorney William Griffith, writing as "Eumenes," set out most fully the rapidly apparent deficiencies of New Jersey's first constitution.[7] They included its ambiguous status as fundamental law, lack of an amending mechanism, absence of a formal bill of rights, questions about representation, and most critically, failure to provide for separation of powers.[8] Griffith's analysis served as the revisionists' bible for the next seven decades.

The document's status was ambiguous because public officials did not have to swear to defend or uphold it. They were limited only by the prescription of religious freedom, the provision for annual elections, and a guarantee of jury trials—which was violated many times during the charter's life.[9] Early acceptance of judicial review somewhat allayed concern about unbridled legislative authority. Judicial review was implied in *Holmes v. Walton* in 1780 and stated emphatically in *State v. Parkhurst* in 1802 when New Jersey Chief Justice Andrew Kirkpatrick wrote, "Now to say that the legislature can alter or change such a constitution, that they can do away with that very principle which at the same time gives and limits their power, is in my view a perfect absurdity. It is making the creature greater than the creator. It is establishing despotism without limitation and without control."[10]

However, this still left the question of how to alter a constitution without an amending procedure. Practical questions quickly arose, particularly about the franchise. Voters could simply state they met the property requirement "by proclamation." As Griffith put it, "Our polls swarm... with the worst sort of people from the neighboring States, fugitives from justice, absconding debtors." Griffith's ire, however, was directed primarily at the female vote. Women, he wrote, were not "fitted to perform this duty with credit to themselves, or advantage to the public."[11]

In 1807, female voters played a critical role in an electoral dispute over the location of the Essex County Courthouse. Unable to amend the constitution's grant of the franchise to "all inhabitants of full age," legislators decreed they could "interpret" or "explain" the document—and passed laws limiting the vote to adult white males on the tax rolls.[12] The immediate issue was resolved, but the fundamental problem remained.

Lack of a comprehensive bill of rights was another oft-cited deficiency. Colonial documents' promise of rights to life and property was absent. An 1816 writer asked, "What is there to prevent the majority from suspending the habeas corpus act, and practicing a system of tyranny against the minority?"[13] The framers likely believed such rights were subsumed in Article 22, which stated that "the common law of England heretofore practiced in this colony, shall still remain in force."[14] Still, concerns remained.

Representation was another issue. There was little discussion about allocating one seat in the upper house to each county regardless of population—

a proviso that survived for 200 years, with profound effects on state politics—but there was debate about the assembly's composition. Reapportionment based on population occurred periodically, but the charter included neither a schedule nor detailed rules for making such changes.[15]

The most glaring deficiency was the failure to provide for separation of powers, a widely approved doctrine by the late eighteenth century. In *Federalist No. 47*, James Madison wrote, "The accumulation of all powers, legislative, executive, and judiciary, in the same hands...may justly be pronounced the very definition of tyranny." Madison then observed, "The constitution of New Jersey has blended the different powers of government more than any of the preceding [states examined]."[16]

Griffith echoed Madison and described the legislature as: "a scene of intrigue, of canvassing and finesse, which baffles all description, and is too notorious to require proof, and too disgusting for exhibition. The members of a county in which an office is to be disposed of are beset by partisans and friends of the candidates....one grand scene of canvass and barter ensues."[17]

Local justices of the peace were too often, in the words of Governor Livingston in 1786, "partial," "groggy," and "courting popularity to be chosen Assemblymen."[18] Most power resided with these numerous local officials.

Attempts to Revise the 1776 Constitution

Despite sporadic discussion of its deficiencies, legislators concluded the constitution enjoyed public acceptance, that they had no authority to call a constitutional convention, and that tinkering might make it worse.

A state constitutional convention became an issue in 1800, by which time seven states had already revised their original charters. The newly formed Democratic–Republican party successfully opposed a convention because it suspected the motives of the Federalists supporting revision. Dissatisfaction continued to surface periodically. In 1827, citizens from nine counties composed a memorial requesting constitutional change. Lawmakers buried the appeal in committee. In his 1840 and 1841 messages to the legislature, Governor William Pennington argued that the increase in judicial business required separating the supreme executive and judicial offices. The legislature rejected Pennington's request because of "the hazards of a radical change."[19]

Thoroughgoing constitutional reform thus never generated widespread clamor. Rather, dissatisfaction with various provisions (or the lack thereof) bothered different politically active citizens at different times. The constitutional convention of 1844, which drew up New Jersey's second charter, likely came about because of the Whig party's political ineptitude.

During the 1842–43 legislative session, the Whigs defeated a compromise bill to submit the convention question to popular referendum. In all likelihood, the referendum would have lost. However, the Whigs' decision mobilized enough antagonists to elect a Democratic legislature in 1844, which passed a bill calling for a convention. Thus ended the 68–year life of New Jersey's first charter. Although imperfect, it served the society for which it was written. "Small, rural and conservative, the state drifted into and through the age of Jackson with her fundamental law intact."[20]

THE CONSTITUTION OF 1844

Although three times longer than its predecessor, New Jersey's second constitution, which endured for 103 years, did not depart dramatically from the 1776 document. It ameliorated some significant shortcomings, but the changes were modest compared to those in other states.[21]

The 1844 Convention and Its Delegates

Delegates to the 1844 constitutional convention, divided almost exactly between Whigs and Democrats, met in Trenton between May 14 and June 29. The 58 participants included three former governors, three state supreme court justices, two attorneys general and seven congressmen. Two other delegates later became governors, and 15 more would serve on the supreme court. Almost half were lawyers, and a slightly larger number were officers or owners of corporations or businesses.[22]

The framers spent seven weeks in session, 37 days in debate, and approved their handiwork by a vote of 55 to 1.[23] Newspapers in each county published the proposed text once a week for six weeks. In a special election on August 13, the document was ratified by a vote of 20,276 to 3,526.

Modest alterations and bipartisan amity contributed to the overwhelmingly favorable vote. New Jersey's Whigs and Democrats divided on national rather than state issues. "The one State and local issue constantly between the parties...was the distribution of jobs."[24] In 1844, the largest state enterprise was still the state prison, and the transit tax on through–state railroad passengers financed Trenton's modest needs. New Jersey's domination by New York and Philadelphia still "conditioned its economy, denatured its politics, and restricted the scope of its government."[25]

Constitutional Provisions

With little discussion, delegates wrote a bill of rights and extended the franchise to all white males save "pauper idiots," "insane persons," and unpardoned criminals.[26] The convention also adopted almost verbatim an amending article from the 1838 Pennsylvania constitution. It provided for submission of amendments to the people for ratification, but no more often than every five years and only after passage by two successive legislatures.

The convention's most important work dealt with separation of powers. An assembly committee on constitutional revision had noted in 1840 that "the governor of New Jersey has less power than is conferred by the constitution of any other state upon its executive."[27]

The convention made the governor a popularly elected official. He was given a three–year term and could not run for a second successive term. New appointment powers allowed him to nominate high court judges, the attorney general, and the secretary of state, subject to approval by the renamed upper house, the senate. The governor's judicial role was ended. A new court of errors and appeals replaced the senate as the court of last resort. Its unique membership consisted of a chancellor appointed by the governor as the presiding officer, the justices of the supreme court, and six lay judges appointed for six–year staggered terms. The lay judges preserved a role for nonlawyers, as had been the case when the senate was the highest tribunal. Otherwise, the judiciary remained a complex system grounded in English common law.

The new charter did not eliminate fused powers. The legislature continued to appoint, in joint meeting, the most important state officers–the treasurer, prison keeper, and the local common pleas judges. The same simple majorities in each house that passed a bill could override a gubernatorial veto. Members of the assembly continued to be elected annually. Senators, like the governor, were elected to three–year terms. The governor's new power to nominate judges stemmed partly from distaste for an elected judiciary, an idea gaining currency elsewhere.

Finally, the upper house continued to have one member from each county—one of the few provisions with obvious political implications. As one rural delegate said of proposed changes in the senate's composition, "I should be unworthy to represent the people of Cape May if I did not resist this in its incipient stage. They will never submit to it."[28]

The treatment of separation of powers therefore "represented no fundamental or drastic break with the past" and "indicated the conservative nature of the new structure of government."[29] The constitutional convention's delegates indicated they might "trust the legislature less," but they were "not disposed to trust the governor much more."[30]

Contemporary politics shaped the 1844 constitution. New Jersey's Democrats did not provide a populist, Jacksonian cast to the debate as they did in other states. Disputes over the franchise did not arise because of the provision for virtually universal male suffrage in 1807. The Democrats, allied with the dominant railroad, were hardly less friendly to business than were the Whigs. Strict limits on what the state could borrow reflected recent bank failures and skyrocketing public debt but had no effect on special business legislation. The increasingly common "long ballot," with election of judges and many state officials, was never seriously considered.

Unlike other state charters of the day, New Jersey's constitution did not become a policy compendium. It said little about the relationship between state government and county or local bodies. It remained a fundamental law, "containing only the bare outlines of a frame of government."[31]

Deficiencies of the 1844 Constitution

This new charter also soon proved inadequate for an increasingly urban and industrial state. The constitutional convention did not foresee social and political changes looming on the horizon. These included alterations in the state's political patterns, a growing role for state government, and massive pressures on the court system. New Jersey was, in Elazar's term, becoming a "commercial republic," but its fundamental law barely recognized it.[32]

At the center of new political debate was the senate composed of one member from each county. A motion in the 1844 convention to elect senators from five equally sized districts had failed by more than two to one. None of the counties was overwhelmingly dominant in 1844; the convention's delegates perceived themselves as "a family of little communities."[33] By the end of the century, the northern counties contained most of the population, most of the heavily Catholic recent immigrants, and most of the Democrats. Most southern and western counties were thinly populated, heavily Republican, Protestant, and "native." The population ratio between the largest and smallest counties was less than seven to one in 1840. It was 27 to 1 by 1910.[34]

Although New Jersey politics was competitive throughout the nineteenth century, only toward its end did that competition produce divided government. The Democrats of the populous north could elect the governor, but the numerous rural counties gave Republicans control of the senate. Republican senators regularly rejected Democratic governors' nominees for judicial and executive office. With few limits on their intervention in municipal affairs, legislators could emasculate Democratic city governments.

The state's weak chief executive and the urban Democratic majority were thus held hostage to the senate Republican caucus and the rural minority. In 1844, former Democratic governor and convention delegate Peter Vroom had expressed satisfaction that with newly elected local officials, the legislature would "come to make laws and not justices of the peace."[35] Now the legislature made judges, state commissioners, and prosecutors on a scale beyond what Vroom could have dreamed.

Amendments to the 1844 Constitution

During its 103 year life, the 1844 constitution was amended only four times. Five times between 1881 and 1913, the assembly called for a constitutional convention, as did three governors. The senate blocked all these appeals, fearing a convention would reapportion the upper house. Nineteen proposed amendments that did pass both houses were defeated in public referenda.[36] The four occasions on which voters did amend the constitution involved Catholics and Democrats lined up against Protestants and Republicans.

The first and most thoroughgoing revision—28 amendments affecting four of the constitution's ten articles—took place in 1875. In his 1873 inaugural address, Democratic Governor Joel Parker had called for an end to proliferating special and private laws. He noted that general public laws passed in the last legislative session occupied about 100 pages in the statute books, while 1,250 pages were devoted to special legislation—mainly business incorporations.

A bipartisan commission appointed to devise appropriate constitutional amendments quickly turned to other topics as well. These included absentee voting for members of the armed services, assessment of property at true value and under uniform rules, free public schools providing a "thorough and efficient education," increasing the governor's appointive powers to include common pleas judges and the keeper of the state prison, prohibition of legislative intrusion into internal municipal affairs, and an end to white–only suffrage.

The most controversial amendments—taxation at true value and municipal government autonomy—most affected heavily Catholic Hudson County and particularly Jersey City. The debate was sectarian and ugly. In revulsion, voters in a rare moralistic mood individually approved all 28 amendments in a special election on September 7, 1875.[37]

The victory was "incomplete and costly."[38] The legislature continued passing theoretically prohibited private laws, throwing them into the overburdened courts. Between 1875 and 1944, the courts overturned more than 300 statutes, two–thirds of which were special, private, and local laws.[39] "Thorough and efficient" public education and uniform taxation at true value remained items of hot dispute for decades.

Constitutional reform became dormant for almost seventy years. In the 1890s, a period of Republican (and hence rural) dominance began, with five successive Republican governors elected between 1895 and 1907. Voters endorsed an 1897 amendment prohibiting gambling by a margin of 801 in a total vote of 140,000 and at the same time approved a limit on the governor's recess appointments. The first amendment was a Protestant and Republican slap at Catholics and Democrats; the second a restraint on Democratic governors. Gambling also figured in a 1939 amendment legalizing pari–mutuel horse betting, which was supported by tourist interests in the Republican Shore counties. In between, the only other amendment approved (in 1927) gave municipalities the power to zone.

By the time Democratic governors started again winning frequently between 1920 and 1940, Hudson County boss Frank Hague had assumed control of the party. He had no interest in disturbing the status quo assuring his power. The 1927 and 1939 amendments met his qualifications. Hague's excesses and the eventual decline in his influence fueled a new movement for constitutional reform. It resulted in New Jersey's third and current constitution of 1947. The 1844 constitution was born of earnest nonpartisanship, but the government it created became the underpinning of partisan battles. In contrast, the 1947 constitution arose from fierce partisan battles but became a fundamental law admired for its nonpartisan integrity.

PRELUDE TO THE 1947 CONSTITUTION:
THE REFORM DRIVE OF THE 1940S

By the 1940s, the 1844 constitution was the despair of half New Jersey's political establishment and the source of power of the other half. Each of its deficiencies—a weak executive, an archaic court system, a malapportioned legislature, and a difficult amending procedure—had immense political implications. They were particularly resistant to change because important political cleavages crossed party lines.

A coalition of Hudson County Democrats and rural Republicans ruled New Jersey in the first half of the twentieth century. It derived its power from the system of weak state government and strong county government. As long as the governor was weak, the judiciary populated by county party appointees, and all legislation controlled by a senate safeguarding county interests, this ruling coalition could endure. It was in the interest of the Hague Democrats and the rural Republicans to form a winning alliance.

Opposed to this coalition were "reform" Republicans and anti–Hague Democrats. Reform Republicans controlled Essex, which rivaled Hudson as the most populous county. During most of the 1930s and 1940s, Arthur T. Vanderbilt led the Essex County Republican "Clean Government Association." A distinguished attorney, Vanderbilt eventually became dean of New York University Law School, president of the American Bar Association, and chief justice of the New Jersey Supreme Court.

Vanderbilt sought to make the Clean Government faction, which had some southern allies, a statewide counterweight to Hague and his confederates.[40] He favored constitutional reform because of its potential to modernize the court system. The Clean Government Association also wanted to rationalize the tangled state bureaucracy and make state government more efficient. This aim allied it with influential groups like the Chamber of Commerce and the New Jersey Taxpayers Association.

The Clean Government group had little success outside Essex County during the 1930s. It lost primary elections to the rural Republicans (who nominated and elected Governor Harold Hoffman in 1934) and general elections to the Hagueites (who elected T. Harry Moore governor in 1925, 1931, and 1937). However, its prospects improved with the election of Democratic Governor Charles Edison in 1940.

Edison, navy secretary under President Franklin Roosevelt, was imposed by Roosevelt on a reluctant Hague. Once inaugurated, Edison denounced Hague and called for constitutional revision.[41] A blue–ribbon citizens' group, the New Jersey Committee for a Constitutional Convention (NJCCC), formed within a month. It embraced the League of Women Voters, the New Jersey Educational Association, the Chamber of Commerce, the Taxpayers Association, the CIO, and the Vanderbilt Clean Government organization.

The 1941–42 Hendrickson Commission

The new drive for constitutional reform stalled when Edison suggested a constitutional convention should make legislative apportionment its first order of business. The Republican legislature took no action. In a token gesture, it appointed a seven member commission to study constitutional reform in late 1941. Most were Republicans, and all were opponents of Frank Hague. They were led by Arthur Vanderbilt and Robert Hendrickson—commission chairman and the Clean Government gubernatorial candidate Edison defeated in 1940.

The commission's closed sessions, beginning just after the bombing of Pearl Harbor, attracted little attention. Most members intended to compose "merely a few innocuous amendments," but Vanderbilt convinced them otherwise.[42] The commissioners emerged from seclusion with a full–blown draft constitution and suggested the legislature organize itself as a constitutional convention to ratify the draft and submit it to the public.

Their document provided for a simplified court system, a four–year term for a governor with increased appointment powers, abolition of most dedicated funds, and reorganization of all state agencies into nine departments. These measures reflected Vanderbilt's reform agenda. Other provisions continuing the legislature's appointment of the state treasurer and chief budget officer and the override of gubernatorial vetoes with a simple majority embodied the preferences of Hendrickson and the other legislators on the panel. Most notably, no changes were proposed for the senate.[43]

The commission explained its failure to act on frequent criticisms of the 1844 charter and its plan to move the document through the legislature rather than an elected convention as acquiescence to "political realities." Legislators would never release a document that tampered with the senate. An elected constitutional convention dominated by delegates from the large counties would try to alter the senate, endangering the prospects of the other proposals.[44] Concern for "political realities," however, did not extend to how the Hague Democrats and their Republican allies would receive the draft constitution.

Instead, the commission went out of its way to enrage the Hudson boss. Requiring all high court judges to have graduated from a law school at least ten years prior to appointment was a provision clearly aimed at Hague's son, a lay member of the court of errors and appeals. Frank, Jr. had finally passed the New Jersey bar exam but never won a degree from any of the several law schools he attended. Another provision authorized the legislature to investigate local officials. It would have overturned *In re Hague*, which quashed a legislative examination of Hague's affairs.[45] Even the gambling clause took a slap at Hague and his supporters. It permitted racetrack betting but banned the bingo games that were a favored Catholic fund–raising device.

These heavy–handed stipulations guaranteed Hague would move to thwart the commission's recommendations.[46] His chances were improved by failure to give rural Republicans any reason to support reform. A stronger governor with more appointive powers would diminish their legislative patronage and end legislative control of the Agriculture Department.

Once the proposal was transmitted to the legislature, the bipartisan coalition opposed to Vanderbilt and Edison took control. An eight–member committee appointed to study the draft constitution included two Hudson members and four rural Republicans. In the summer of 1942, it voted 6 to 2 to take no action until the end of the war.[47]

As 1943 opened, Edison was a lame duck, and politicians turned their attention to that year's gubernatorial election. Believing a new constitution important enough to "plant the seeds even if he was not around to reap the harvest," Edison made constitutional reform the centerpiece of his January legislative message.[48] In a calculated appeal to the heavily Republican legislature, he told it, "If we are honest with ourselves we cannot expect that the haphazard, inefficient and irresponsible State government that we have under the Constitution of 1844 will be half–way competent to deal with the new problems it will have to face. Washington will once more be compelled to act."[49] His words fell on deaf ears, but other political considerations eventually moved the Republican lawmakers.

First, annual rotation of the legislative leadership gave North Jersey Republicans command of the assembly and the senate. The new leaders were the two members of the 1942 joint legislative committee who had opposed its decision to abandon constitutional reform.

Second, after years of Democratic gubernatorial dominance, Republicans were hungry for victory in 1943. Walter Edge—governor during World War I and former U.S. senator and ambassador to France—agreed to be their standard bearer. Active in the NJCCC, Edge's price was Republican support for constitutional reform. Once Edge promised to retain county-based senate representation, a bill for a referendum on the legislature sitting as a constitutional convention sailed through both houses in May 1943.

Reformers were active between spring and election day. They were led by the umbrella citizens' group, now renamed the New Jersey Committee for Constitutional Revision (NJCCR). An offshoot, the New Jersey Constitution Foundation, distributed "educational" materials and had a weekly statewide radio program. It was said that "if three men stopped for a traffic light, someone would run up and make a speech for a new constitution."[50]

Opponents were less visible. Rural Republicans were silent in fear of Edge's wrath and possible damage to the simultaneous governor's contest. The Democratic gubernatorial candidate, Newark Mayor and AFL leader Vincent Murphy, was a trustee of the New Jersey Constitutional Foundation, but he was also aware of Hague's hostility to the measure and needed a huge Hudson vote. Murphy thus blamed the Republicans for past failures and otherwise avoided the subject. Hague himself decided to await the outcome of the referendum.

On election day, voters gave both Edge and the constitutional convention solid victories. The referendum won in 19 counties, losing only in Hudson and Ocean. However, a lack of real interest in reform was evident; only 55 percent of gubernatorial voters bothered to vote on the public question.

Having achieved victory, Edge moved quickly and decisively—in the opinion of many, too quickly and too decisively. The day after the election, he issued a "must list" for the new constitution—a reformed court system, a stronger governor, and an easier amending process. By mid–November, an unofficial legislative "Committee of Thirty" was constituted to go over the Hendrickson Commission draft.

Desiring speed and secrecy so that interest groups could not sabotage the document, Edge decreed enough public hearings had been held. To criticism that the members of the Committee of Thirty were all Republicans, he replied they were simply an advisory committee to the governor–elect. As a last–ditch effort, opponents contended in court that the constitution could only be amended by the cumbersome procedure in the 1844 charter. A supreme court justice agreed with Arthur Vanderbilt (deputized by Edge to argue for the state) that it was a "political question" between the people and the legislature and declined to hear the case.

Thus, a draft constitution, almost identical to that recommended by the Hendrickson Commission, was sent to both houses of the legislature on January 24, 1944, a few days after Governor Edge assumed office.[51] Edge refused to make patronage appointments or allow lawmakers to embark on their usual midwinter recess until they acted. On February 25, both houses agreed to put the document before the people at the November 1944 elections.

Opponents, led by Hague, now swung into action. Events over the past two years had made the Jersey City mayor even more determined to defeat his political enemies. With Edge's support, Governor Edison had pushed through a measure lowering the tax bill of New Jersey's railroads. It also retroactively relieved the railroads of $39 million in taxes–73 percent of which was due Hudson County, and 53 percent to Jersey City alone.[52]

Edge had also won several "ripper" laws—requiring use of voting machines in Hudson County (but not the solidly Republican rural counties), removing Hague appointments to the county election board and jury commissions, and reforming the county civil service system. The state's largest newspaper editorialized that Edge had delivered "more smashing blows" to Frank Hague "than all the other New Jersey governors combined during the last generation....The final blow will be delivered in November if the voters approve a new constitution."[53]

Supporters were confident of victory. Polls during the summer showed a comfortable lead. The Hudson voter rolls had declined by 71,000 since 1940. The presidential contest would bring out the "good–government" commuter vote that usually skipped other elections, and the 1943 referendum had passed easily. Republican presidential candidate Thomas Dewey taped radio spots endorsing the new constitution. However, the Republicans underestimated the Hudson County boss.

Mayor Hague proceeded to organize the opposition on a "magnet issue" basis. Hudson voters were whipped up on the railroad—tax issue and the "Edison–Edge–Railroad conspiracy." Labor unions were warned the constitution did not provide collective–bargaining rights, and women and minorities were told it had no specific anti–discrimination provisions. Abolition of the Chancery Court, conservative lawyers were advised, would turn New Jersey into a divorce mill. The Grange worried about loss of control of the Agriculture Department, and uniformed employees about the end of dedicated funds for their pension systems. Finally, in the last days, Hague characterized the whole document as anti–Catholic.

Most of the charges had little merit, but there were so many that they were impossible to answer fully. Also, the proponents' attention, and that of the critical independent voters, were centered elsewhere. Edge was distracted by wartime responsibilities and by national politics (he was thought to be a leading contender for the 1944 Republican vice–presidential nomination). D–Day and the Normandy invasion deflected the media's attention, particularly that of the New York and Philadelphia newspapers read by commuters.

On election day, the constitution was defeated by 54 to 46 percent. One in four presidential voters cast no vote on the charter. South Jersey Republicans rejected both Thomas Dewey and the constitution, and Hudson County buried both of them. The proposal was defeated in 12 of the 21 counties.[54] By presenting the constitution as a partisan issue, organizing the campaign for it in a partisan manner, and failing to lead that campaign, Edge suffered an embarrassing defeat. He was unable to mobilize the Republican–leaning commuter vote, reluctant rural Republicans, or enough Democrats.[55]

Edge declined to lead further reform efforts. The victorious Hague announced he would support a popularly elected constitutional convention. The legislature preferred a piecemeal amendment route. The NJCCR, still led by Vanderbilt, decided to concentrate on court reform by amendment. When the legislature devised an 18–amendment package, Vanderbilt, opposed to provisions for county courts that were a concession to Hague and the rural Republicans, instructed the Essex legislative delegation to block them. Edge's term ended with the constitution unchanged.

Governor Driscoll and Constitutional Politics

The choice of Alfred Driscoll as the 1946 Republican gubernatorial nominee revived reform efforts. Driscoll, from Camden County, had served in the Edge administration and had good relations with both the Clean Government and "Hague Republican" factions. He defeated a Hague Republican, former Governor Harold Hoffman, in the Republican primary and won Clean Government support by secretly promising Vanderbilt he would support constitutional reform.

Both gubernatorial candidates ignored the issue in their campaigns, but in his inaugural address Driscoll called the 1844 constitution "hopelessly out of step with the requirements of our modern industrial age."[56] He then sought support for a popularly–elected constitutional convention from all the important political factions.

Driscoll first mollified Mayor Hague by removing the Edge–appointed Hudson County election supervisor, ending a state investigation of Hudson bookmaking operations, appointing Hague nominees to Hudson county courts, and supporting bipartisan selection of convention delegates in each county— which would increase the number of Democratic delegates relative to their numbers in the legislature. He also promised to let Hague select the chair of the convention Committee on the Legislative Article. Rural Republicans won agreement that convention delegates would be apportioned among the counties on the basis of their numbers in the legislature–giving the small counties an "unrepresentative" delegate based on their Senate representation. The governor also assured small counties that the wording of the new constitutional referendum question would disallow tampering with the Senate during the convention.

Driscoll's bargains infuriated Clean Government Republicans. Edge deplored the concessions to Hague, which undid his own attacks on the Boss. Vanderbilt called Driscoll's actions a "grand double–cross."[57] In an April speech, the Clean Government leader said of the delegate composition,

"Every day the convention goes on, the people from the larger counties will be wondering what it is that they have done that should have led to their being treated as a politically inferior race....In one Republican county after another we have been treated to the spectacle of the Republican county committee accepting the recommendations of the Democratic county chairman, in each case the direct representative of the Hague machine....

The beaches are strewn with the bleached bones of Republican politicians who have listened to the siren voice of Mayor Hague."[58]

Knowing that Vanderbilt's main concern was that rural Republicans and Hagueites would undermine court reform, Driscoll won Vanderbilt's support by endorsing Vanderbilt's court reform plan, and giving him the choice of the chair and vice–chair of the convention committee on the judiciary. He also promised to make Vanderbilt chief justice of the new high court if the constitution was ratified.

With all factions on board, the second referendum for a constitutional convention in four years passed by a 5–1 vote on June 3, 1947. The major antagonists assured a smooth convention opening by departing the scene of battle. In a surprise move, Mayor Hague resigned on June 4, anointed his nephew, Frank Hague Eggers, as Jersey City mayor, and left for a summer in California. Vanderbilt departed for his Maine summer home to recuperate from a stroke. Edge withdrew to a hunting lodge in Canada.

THE 1947 CONSTITUTIONAL CONVENTION
AND THE NEW CONSTITUTION

With a somewhat anti–climactic air, 81 delegates convened in the Rutgers University gymnasium in New Brunswick on June 12, 1947. After a century of attempts, there was finally wide agreement on the need to produce a modern frame of government. The challenge was to do it while protecting all major political interests.

The Delegates and the Work of the Convention

The convention delegates numbered 54 Republicans, 23 Democrats and four independents. They included 25 with legislative experience (including 10 incumbent senators) 20 with judicial experience, 12 business executives, eight women, one black, two farmers and one labor leader.[59] Rutgers President Robert C. Clothier was elected convention president. For the first seven weeks, the delegates met in committee, convening periodically for progress reports. A small number of committees with complex charges kept members focused on their particular tasks. Lobbyists were banned from the floor, which helped delegates concentrate on major issues.[60]

Although the major committee chairs were strategic choices, representation for all factions prevented assignments from being a source of conflict. Many bipartisan county delegations and alphabetic rather than county roll call votes contributed to a purposeful atmosphere. Even the Hudson Democrats did not vote as a bloc on important issues. A firm September deadline for completion of their work also moved the process along. Each major committee reached quick agreement on once contentious issues, and spent most of their time on one or two points with weighty political implications.

For the Committee on the Executive, the question was "not whether the office should be strengthened, but to what degree."[61] Once it was agreed the Agriculture Secretary would remain a farm group nominee approved by the governor, there was almost no debate about reorganizing the state bureaucracy into no more than 20 cabinet departments otherwise headed by gubernatorial nominees.

The committee's toughest issue was gubernatorial succession. The one–term governors of the 1844 constitution were unable to become party leaders—to the satisfaction of the rural county organizations. However, even on this issue, the "conservative" position, which carried the day, was for a four year term with one immediate re–election try permitted, as opposed to no limit on successive terms.

The Committee on the Legislative Article began work with its major bone of contention—Senate reapportionment—declared off the table. They rapidly agreed on longer legislative terms (four years for senators instead of two; two years for the assembly instead of one); limiting legislative appointment power to the state auditor, and retaining annual sessions instead of moving to biennial ones. Their only difficult charge had nothing to do with legislative structure or process—they were handed the hot potato of legalized gambling.

Several factors contributed to the complexity of this issue, and its appearance in the constitution. First, gambling was a traditional way to entice New York and Pennsylvania money into an "economic" area where New Jersey could compete. Second, Jersey shore resorts desired horse racing and boardwalk games attractive to tourists. Most critically, gambling policy was a metaphor for Catholic–Protestant and Democratic–Republican conflict. The committee could not resolve the conflicts; in its report, it passed on a number of options to the convention as a whole.

The most technically complex work of the convention took place in the Committee on the Judiciary. The New Jersey court system was the most complicated in the nation, with overlapping jurisdictions at every level that confused even members of the bar. Everyone agreed on the need for reform, but lawyers were hopelessly divided on its shape.[62]

There were two principal stumbling blocks. The first was New Jersey's separate equity courts—present in only two other states. Younger attorneys wished to abolish them. Older ones pointed to the state bar's distinguished contributions to equity law. Judges on these courts feared for their jobs. The second issue was what to do about the county courts, beloved of patronage–minded (and prosecution–avoiding) county politicians. They were defended as "close to the people."

The judiciary committee began by hearing 40 expert witnesses, who conducted "law school seminars" on state court systems.[63] The teachers included eminent outsiders like Dean Roscoe Pound of Harvard and Judge Learned Hand, as well as New Jersey's governor, chancellor, chief justice, and leaders of the state bar. The choice of Vanderbilt allies as the committee's leaders tilted the committee toward massive reform. The celebrated visitors' impressive arguments for reform, and the less convincing ones by local jurists against it, persuaded the committee's lay members reform was necessary. Consequently, the committee recommended a unified and simplified court system. Hudson County delegates served notice they would oppose the plan on the floor.

The two other substantive committees also wrestled with predominantly political problems. The Committee on Taxation and Finance quickly agreed on a uniform fiscal year, a single appropriations bill, abolition of all constitutionally protected dedicated funds except the school fund, and the borrowing and spending language of the 1844 constitution.

The committee then had to face the interminable problem of railroad taxation, the only issue on which Hague seemed willing to wreck the convention. From his outpost in California, he warned that the people would "never permit Railroad influences to dominate the preparation of a new constitution."[64] On hearing of Driscoll's recommendation for uniform property taxation, a Hudson County delegate wrote in his diary, "This was about equivalent to His Excellency asking us to jump off the Empire State Building....What the irate taxpayers would do to us delegates if we were to agree to such a proposal is too horrible to contemplate."[65]

The tax issue was clearly headed for the convention floor. However, other potentially dangerous subjects—property tax exemptions for religious organizations and state aid for parochial school busing—passed easily, and another round of religious warfare was avoided. Patriotically inspired delegates also recommended a property tax break for recently returned veterans.

The last of the substantive committees—on Rights, Privileges and Amendments—had only a few charges, but serious disagreements about them. Most important were provisions for constitutional amendment. A Hudson County—rural county coalition quickly dispatched a provision, supported by the NJCCR, for automatic referenda on constitutional revision every 20 or 25 years. As a Hudson delegate observed, the "small counties thoroughly distrust Essex and Bergen Counties and believe that their fellow Republicans in those counties will liquidate them the first chance available....I too believe it is folly to believe that once turned loose the remainder of the State could be depended upon to decline to liquidate Hudson County....the fears of rural Jersey and our own are, in principle, similar."[66]

The small counties also wanted retention of the cumbersome 1844 amending procedures, but in a 6–5 committee vote, their opponents won amendment ratification by a three–fifths vote of the legislature, gubernatorial assent, and public approval. While hardly radical (amendment by public initiative, for example, was never considered), the amending process was greatly simplified.

The committee also had to consider contentious changes in the 1844 bill of rights. First was labor's demand for constitutional protection. The committee approved the right of private employees to bargain collectively, but did not extend it to public employees. It also drafted a general anti–discrimination statute, but rejected pleas of blacks and women for special protection.

The convention began general sessions on August 10. The changes in the legislative and executive articles were quickly accepted, and produced one of the strongest governorships in the nation. A poorly crafted Hudson amendment to save the equity courts was defeated easily, but the Hudson–rural Republican coalition was able to retain the county courts. Otherwise, the committee's design of a unified and simplified court system became the convention's major triumph.[67]

Still outstanding were the most "political" decisions—on gambling and taxes. Compromises were reached on both. Delegates voted to prohibit all gambling unless approved by public referendum or permitted in the 1844 constitution. However, they also endorsed a referendum on an amendment permitting games of chance conducted by charitable organizations. This satisfied Hudson County, and thus did bingo, lotto, and raffles achieve sanctification in New Jersey's fundamental law.

Delegates left negotiations on the tax article to those with the only hope of achieving an agreement—Governor Driscoll and Jersey City Mayor Eggers. The convention recessed for several days while Driscoll, Eggers and Convention President Clothier worked out a complicated deal to preserve uniform property assessments for all property, but ensure legislative action to provide more railroad tax money for Hudson County. Once this was done, "there was great rejoicing in Jersey City," and "for all intents and purposes, the constitution of 1947 was 'home.'"[68]

The draft constitution was then approved with only one negative vote, and the convention adjourned on September 10, ten days ahead of schedule. Two months later, voters approved it by a margin of 5–1. The southern rural counties were least supportive, but the heavily populated northern and central areas of the state—led by a 131,000 plurality in Hudson—confirmed it overwhelmingly.

Constitutional Developments Since 1947

Since 1947, the constitution has been significantly altered only with respect to the pivotal issue of legislative apportionment. A constitutional convention limited to that subject was held in 1966 because U.S. Supreme Court rulings in *Baker v. Carr* and *Reynolds v. Sims* required change. The legislature was enlarged from 81 to 120 members, and Senate districts, based on population, now cross county lines. In 1978, with the party machines enfeebled, voters also terminated the county courts. Adjustments have been made three times in how long a governor may consider bills and use the pocket veto. Otherwise, the frame of government created in 1947 has remained.

The framers succeeded in keeping New Jersey's charter a fundamental law. At about 17,000 words, including all amendments, it is one of the shorter state constitutions.[69] The constitution grants broad statutory powers to the legislature. It is silent on detailed regulation of county and local government—a legacy of a home rule tradition. Interest group provisions cluttering other state constitutions are confined to special property tax exemptions for veterans and senior citizens. Gambling's peculiar constitutional status has also produced several amendments. Well over half of all amendments since 1947 relate to legalized gambling and minor changes in taxation.[70]

The relative ease of the amending process is also noteworthy. From the 1950s through the 1980s, voters approved 38 constitutional amendments on 18 separate occasions, as compared with the four instances the 1844 constitution was amended over more than a century.

New Jersey's latest adventure in constitution–writing contains a number of lessons. Good timing contributes to success. The "times" were right in 1947. The end of World War II encouraged the state to look to its future. The waning power of the Hudson–rural county coalition made it possible to address previously intractable problems.

Political leadership is also crucial. Governor Driscoll conciliated the various political factions while never abandoning fundamental principles. Others who could have upset the process—Frank Hague, Arthur Vanderbilt, and former Governor Edge—ultimately showed restraint and statesmanship.

The 1947 constitution blends revolution and evolution. It has been described as a pathbreaking document that "became a model for other states," and also as "framed strongly by the past."[71] New Jersey's framers saw that the state was ready for far–reaching reform of the executive and the judiciary, and they seized the opportunity. Yet they also understood that assaults on legislative structure and home rule would doom the entire process. Their achievement was a fundamental law that would not shackle the state in the future, as did the earlier charters of 1766 and 1844.

CHAPTER EIGHT

The Governor

In the states the executive power is vested in the hands of a magistrate, who is apparently placed upon a level with the legislature, but who is in reality nothing more than the blind agent and the passive instrument of its decisions.

—Alexis De Tocqueville, 1830[1]

I have almost total control over the policy–making apparatus in the state. I am not unhappy about it. A good governor should absolutely dominate the political debate in the state and set its agenda.

—Governor Thomas Kean, 1988[2]

When John Adams described the U.S. vice–presidency as the most insignificant office ever conceived, he might have included the state governors of the time. In the postcolonial era, memories of the British sovereign and the colonial governor were a powerful argument for a dominant legislature.

New Jersey's 1776 charter devoted five articles to the qualifications, election, and duties of legislators. Only one article dealt solely with the governor. As to the chief executive's qualifications, the constitution specified only that the legislature should "elect some fit Person within the colony to be a Governor for one year."[3] As chapter 7 describes, the governor was given the "Supreme executive power," but that power was nowhere defined.

However, New Jersey's governor was apparently better placed than his contemporaries. "It is a notable circumstance," wrote one commentator, "that the powers of the governor of New Jersey under the constitution of 1776 exceeded those of any officer of the same rank in the United States."[4] The legislature often chose distinguished citizens to fill the post. William Livingston, the state's first governor, was reelected 14 times and sufficiently respected that he "even elevated to a position of influence the impotent office he held."[5]

The new constitution of 1844 provided for popular election of the governor to a three–year term, a weak veto, and some appointment powers. Still, some delegates at the constitutional convention feared that removing the governor from the judiciary would make the position so unattractive that distinguished citizens would shun it. One delegate worried, "I don't think the Governor ever will be a lawyer again. I mean a practicing Lawyer, for the office will not be worth the acceptance of a man with a good practice."[6]

The 1844 constitution did, however, contain the provision that Coleman Ransone suggests opened the way to gubernatorial participation in policy–making: "he shall communicate by message to the legislature at the opening of each session, and at such other times as he may deem necessary, the condition of the State, and recommend such measures as he may deem expedient."[7] Eventually, the governor's annual message became the vehicle for laying out a legislative program.

Under the 1844 constitution, governors were, for a century, subservient to the legislature. This first meant subservience to the railroads and later to county party organizations. Still, a few chief executives such as Woodrow Wilson (1910–1912) were able to affect the course of the state dramatically. What is true of presidents is also true of governors; force of personality, political skills, and the "power to persuade" often count as much as official powers.[8] However, the executive did gain major advantages under the state's third constitution of 1947. Governors could now succeed themselves, hold longer terms, and exercise strong veto and appointment powers.

With these new powers, New Jersey's governor is among the strongest in the nation.[9] He (all New Jersey governors to date have been male) has wide latitude to initiate by issuing executive orders—a prerogative of only nine of the nation's 50 governors. He has broad powers to reject. Along with more than 40 other governors, he can veto entire pieces of legislation or exercise a line–item veto. Like only 14 others, he may also issue a conditional veto, rejecting portions of a bill and suggesting new language.

The New Jersey governor is one of only three that are their states' only elected official. New Jersey does not have a lieutenant governor or an elected secretary of state, treasurer, or attorney general. In 27 states, elected officials hold all of these positions. The governor also appoints, and may remove, most members of his cabinet.[10] Only he can reliably command the power of publicity, with routine access to the state's media.

If these are his "sticks," New Jersey's chief executive also has many "carrots"—powers to provide. Each year, he dispenses about 500 appointments to boards and commissions and as chief party fund–raiser doles out generous campaign funds. If he also has the power derived from widespread popularity, New Jersey's governor seems almost, as columnist George Will described him, "an American Caesar."[11] It is thus not surprising that all of New Jersey's post–

World War II governors have achieved most of their stated objectives.

Yet these achievements have not come easily. Before the 1970s, the governor's imposing formal powers were still circumscribed by the informal realities of state politics. These were, in particular, the power of the county party organizations, the state's limited fiscal resources, and the governor's public invisibility. As late as 1973, Republican county leaders disenchanted with their sitting governor, William Cahill, could engineer his defeat in the party's nominating primary. Cahill's support for a state income tax was a prime cause of his downfall, and a similar proposal by Cahill's Democratic predecessor, Richard Hughes, was also thwarted by his own legislative partisans. Locally oriented newspapers paid little attention to Trenton and denied the governor a reliable communication channel to the public.

Many of these impediments disappeared in a remarkably short period during the 1970s. The U.S. Supreme Court's reapportionment decisions sapped the powers of the county organizations. Democratic county leaders were unable to unseat Governor Brendan Byrne in 1977, an incumbent they intensely disliked, as the Republicans had done only four years earlier. The New Jersey Supreme Court handed down decisions on school financing that virtually forced the legislature to enact an income tax in 1976.

These developments were crucial to making the governor the genuinely formidable chief executive envisioned by the framers of the 1947 constitution. However, some historic obstacles still remain, and new ones have arisen. Since the elected governorship began in 1844, chief executives have faced legislatures with at least one house under opposition control about 56 percent of the time, a figure that has varied little since inception of the constitution in 1947. Although divided government now occurs more frequently everywhere, it has always been more common in New Jersey, because there has never been a period when either major party was a helpless minority.[12] Legislators have increasingly independent power bases and less to fear from gubernatorial "punishment."

Further, New Jersey's chief executive continues to have the most difficult media climate in the country—with not a single commercial television station oriented primarily to New Jersey and no statewide newspaper. Until recently, the governor's staff was too small to be "commensurate with the additional authority granted the office."[13]

In this chapter, after profiling the people New Jerseyans have chosen to lead the state, we will look at how recent governors have attended to their fundamental tasks—achieving support for policy priorities and organizing their offices to seek those priorities effectively. Because the governor is now so central to almost every aspect of the state's politics, we also discuss the chief executive's role in many other places in this book. Chapters 4 and 5 deal with gubernatorial elections and the governor's role as party leader, chapter 7 concerns the constitutional development of the office and the governor's role in constitutional revision, chapter 10 deals with management of the executive branch, chapter 12 concerns the chief executive's growing participation in the federal system, and chapters 14 through 16 deal with gubernatorial policy formulation.

THE GOVERNORS—A PERSONAL PROFILE

The 37 men who have won New Jersey's highest office since popular election began in 1844 are similar in many ways to their counterparts across the country.[14] Most were married men in their late forties or early fifties when elected, and all have been white. The last of the few governors who was not a college graduate served in the 1930s; since the 1950s, all have had postgraduate education, and six of the seven were lawyers. Until the 1950s, every governor identified with a mainstream Protestant denomination, despite the state's large Catholic population. Since then, more Catholics—four of the seven most recent chief executives—have been elevated to the governorship than in most other states. Three of the four were Democrats, and all were at least partly of Irish ancestry.[15]

The most striking difference between New Jersey governors and those elsewhere is in the career paths they follow, and what they do afterward. New Jersey governors have always been more likely than average to come from the state legislature or the U.S. Congress. Even those who were not in the legislature when elected had served there earlier in their careers. Important recruitment channels in other states—elected statewide offices other than the governorship and elected judgeships—are absent.

Administrative officials were more likely to run for governor in the early part of the century, when they were chosen by the legislature and were often past members themselves. Since the 1947 constitution made all these positions gubernatorial appointments, administrative officials have less often had office-seeking backgrounds. Such recent gubernatorial hopefuls—most often attorneys general—have thus lacked the public recognition or political base to run successfully.

On leaving office, New Jersey's governors, like those in other states, have rejected downward political mobility. They are unlikely to seek lower state office or to enter the U.S. House of Representatives. Otherwise, however, the pattern in the state has been the reverse of the national one. Nationally, retired governors are now more likely than they were early in the century to go on to other high offices, particularly appointive ones, and about as likely to seek U.S.

Senate seats as they were in the past.

In New Jersey, however, no governor has sought a Senate seat since the 1920s, nor have any ascended to the federal bench or served as an elected federal official or cabinet secretary—all common aspirations in earlier years. A few have sought or been sought for such positions, but at this writing, none have yet ended up there. Going on the averages, a New Jersey governor is now likely to return to private life upon leaving Trenton.

THE GOVERNOR AND POLICY–MAKING—POWERS AND PROBLEMS

New Jersey's modern governors command many advantages in setting the state's agenda and determining major policies. Broad veto powers, domination of the budget process, use of executive orders, wide–ranging appointment powers, the likelihood of reelection, and the absence of a legislative veto constitute a formidable armaterium for the chief executive.[16] By the time most leave office, their dominant policy objectives have been enacted.

Additionally, recent governors have followed up rather systematically on many of their predecessors' chief concerns: "When few others thought the task was worth the trouble, the state's governors have had to struggle to build support for the recognition of statewide needs."[17] Through the 1960s and 1970s, three governors from both parties stubbornly persisted, at considerable political cost, in seeking approval of the statewide income tax finally enacted in 1976. The same three governors sequentially pursued the development of the Meadowlands. Their successors emphasized integrity in state government and politics, protection of the state's environment, and adequate funding of education.

Most have also honored their predecessors or gubernatorial opponents in remarkable ways. Republican William Cahill (1970–74) appointed his predecessor, Democrat Richard Hughes (1962–70), as chief justice of the state supreme court. Democrat Brendan Byrne (1974–82) appointed Republican Thomas Kean (1982–90) a commissioner of the State Highway Authority after Kean had left the Republican legislative leadership to run unsuccessfully for his party's gubernatorial nomination against Byrne in 1977. When Kean assumed the governorship four years later, he supported life tenure for Byrne's appointment as state chief justice (a former Democratic legislator and son of a leading Democratic county leader) against the opposition of many in his party. One of his last official acts was to name Byrne a commissioner of the state Sports and Exposition Authority. Despite palpable hostility between Kean and his successor, Democrat Jim Florio, Florio bestowed Kean's name on the new state aquarium in Camden.

Accomplishments, we have noted, have not always come easily for these "American Caesars." Victory on the income tax was achieved only when court decisions forced it, and the state underwent another major tax battle in the early 1990s. Initiatives in several administrations to help the state's decaying cities have made slow progress. Land–use regulation has moved glacially. Each governor has at least a short list of individual aspirations that went unrealized and a longer list of initiatives that underwent major modifications. The principal obstacles to gubernatorial success are the increasingly assertive state legislature and the peculiar difficulties in mobilizing public opinion in New Jersey.

The Governor and the Legislature

With mounting staff and personal resources, longer incumbency, and more continuous leadership (subjects addressed in chapters 4 and 9), state legislators have been able to oppose the governor more effectively in recent years. The most important elements affecting governors' abilities to deal with the legislature have been its partisan makeup, the personalities and styles of individual governors, and the nature of the times in which the governor serves.

All other things being equal, governors do best with the legislature when their own party controls both houses by comfortable but not enormous margins, and when they themselves have won a convincing electoral victory.[18] Between 1954 and 1993, only Republican William Cahill (1970–74) and Democrat Brendan Byrne (1974–82) had this advantage through most of their terms. Republican Thomas Kean (1982–90) was the only governor since the 1950s who did not enjoy a single year in which his party controlled both legislative houses. Kean also served in the period when the legislature's structural resources increased most markedly. Governor Jim Florio (1990–) had early legislative success with auto insurance, gun control, and tax proposals immediately after a landslide victory, and when his party controlled both houses by only a few votes.

The contrast between Kean's situation and that of his predecessor, Byrne, is captured well in the following anecdote. An official of the Kean administration was told that a Democratic assemblyman once inquired, "Which cliff does Brendan want us to jump off today?" The official retorted that in the Kean era, the question for Republican legislators as much as Democrats more often was, "Which cliff are we going to push the governor off today?"[19]

Whatever the partisan makeup of the legislature, the governor's relationship with lawmakers is affected by personal style and political experience. Some governors have been reserved, even taciturn or arrogant in their dealings with legislators and others; other executives have been gregarious, affable, and eager to be liked. There have been pragmatists willing to cut political deals or play political hardball to achieve major ends; others have rejected that strategy.[20]

Democrats Richard Hughes and Brendan Byrne represent recent polar extremes. Hughes loved people, and as a long–time county party politician, could cut a patronage deal with the best of them. As Hughes described himself, "My overall thrill at being governor was the relationship with the people....My wife says that if I got an invitation to see three Public Service Electric and Gas men open a manhole in Teaneck I would go...to cheer them up as part of our labor force." Hughes decided to run for a second term because there were "so many hundreds and thousands of people depending on you for jobs." Of his dealings with Republican senate leader (and three–time gubernatorial candidate) Charles Sandman, Hughes recalled, "We worked well together on patronage...and let's–get–this–bill–up–front stuff."[21]

Byrne's style was a sharp contrast to that of Hughes. Governor Byrne seemed unconcerned about his low popularity ratings, particularly after the passage of the landmark income tax. As he said of his second victory in 1977, "They probably didn't like me, but they recognized we were making decisions that had to be made....I wanted to get some things done, and I thought in the long run people would appreciate they had to be done. That was more satisfying to me than having people happy with me."[22]

Unlike Hughes, Byrne was not previously active in elective politics. As a veteran Democratic legislator observed of Byrne's prior experience, "He never had to deal in a compromise setting. He was always in a position to call the tune, as a county prosecutor, or on the Public Utilities Commission, and ultimately as a judge. The whole process was new to him."[23]

Uncomfortable bargaining with legislators, Byrne developed what his staff called a "Wizard of Oz" strategy—"sort of a mystical figure who's got some kind of power that as soon as you see it, it's gone." A top Byrne staffer described the preferred method of dealing with legislators: "I used to see them hiding under their desks. I'd go in and say 'Himself would like to speak to you,' and they would whine, and then you'd drag them into the hall."[24] Once the unhappy lawmakers arrived there, they would find not the governor, but his chief of staff or other major aides, ready to describe the governor's wishes and, perhaps, cut a deal.

Somewhere in between was the style of Byrne's successor, Republican Thomas Kean. Kean was a congenial and wily politician in the Hughes mold. He was not above making bargains with the Democratic senate president that he neglected to mention to the Republican assembly speaker—his ostensible fellow partisan but frequent nemesis. To the intermittent despair of his staff and the Republican legislative leadership, however, Kean steadfastly refused to deal in patronage or take political revenge.

In this sense, Kean resembled his predecessor Woodrow Wilson, who was blamed for allowing Frank Hague's rise to power because of Wilson's failure to use Democratic patronage to strengthen the reform element of the party.[25] When Kean suffered a major legislative defeat because almost half the Republican senators abandoned him, their floor leader reported he "pleaded passionately" with the renegades and "got nowhere" because, as one said, "We've gone against Kean before and he hasn't done anything about it." As the governor himself put it, "I know there were political favors that were promised and granted [in previous administrations], to a point where people had a reason to expect them. The first time I called some legislator and tried to get a bill through, the immediate reaction was—'this is the judgeship we want, this is the fellow we want for it.' I had a lot of problems for about a year and a half. People thought I was singling them out. It was over a year before people got the message business had changed."[26]

In addition to the legislature's partisan balance and the governor's personal style, the nature of the times—especially the state of the economy—affects the governor's success with the legislature. When the economy is good and there is more money to spend, governors have an easier time with their initiatives and can afford to let the legislature be more proactive. When times are tougher and the public is protesting inflation or tax burdens, the governor needs more creativity and resourcefulness. How the nature of the times interacts with the governor's own predilections is important as well.[27] Democrat Robert Meyner (1954–62) was a fiscal conservative who fit well into the Eisenhower era. His successor, Richard Hughes, had an expansive view of government's role in tune with the Kennedy–Johnson era in which he served. Kean's tenure coincided with the Reagan presidency; like the president, the governor had a gift for espousing a convincing rhetoric of fiscal conservatism while taking advantage of a boom economy during most of his term to engage in record spending.

In contrast to these happy matches of men and moment were the tenures of Republican William Cahill and Democrat Brendan Byrne, both of whom served during the economically difficult 1970s. Cahill's view of government's role was similar to that of Hughes, but the governor got caught in a mood change among his fellow Republicans. Additionally, as the Watergate scandal unfolded nationally, Cahill's own administration suffered scandal. All this contributed to his being the only postwar governor whose reelection bid failed. A combative person, Cahill called his greatest satisfaction in office "the battles I lost. I thought that what I was doing was necessary and right."[28]

Like President Jimmy Carter whose term overlapped his, Byrne was a moralistic "nonpolitician," elected at a time of popular revulsion toward "professional politicians." Like Carter, Byrne's meager political skills and austere personality did not inspire public affection. Byrne's innate caution and willingness to take unpopular stands helped the state through a difficult period, but like Carter, at the cost of personal unpopularity.

The 1990s opened with a national economic slowdown and debate about the wisdom of President Reagan's "trickle–down" economic policies. There were similar questions in New Jersey about Kean–era policies (although compared with Reagan, Kean had sought more of a downward flow than a trickle, if not quite a flood). For forty years, New Jersey's postwar governors had styles and policies that mirrored those of the president. Now, George Bush embodied a consolidation of the "Reagan Revolution" shorn of its rough edges, while Jim Florio came to symbolize those calling for more economic redistribution. The fate of the national and state economies as the 1990s progressed was likely to determine history's judgment of both Florio and Bush.

State Media and the Role of Public Opinion

As governors seek to guide their agendas through the legislature, they are both helped and hindered by the difficulty of mobilizing public opinion. Through the 1960s, few citizens identified with the state. Its economic leaders did not see New Jersey as a cohesive market, and county bosses dominated political life. "Public opinion" on state issues barely existed and was thus not a terribly important concern for the governor. If the bosses got their patronage, and large economic interests were inattentive, the chief executive had broad flexibility in setting state policy. He had only to deal with a small elite—in politics, the media, and the business community—who were all personally well–acquainted. The reverse side of that coin was that without widespread public support, the scope of his policy agenda could not be very ambitious.

Before the 1970s, therefore, a governor's most valuable attributes were extensive knowledge of the state's narrow power structure; a strategic sense of how its members would react to proposals; and perhaps most importantly, skills at persuasion and negotiation.[29] Consequently, it was not surprising that of these governors, "none were charismatic folk."[30]

State leaders have always known the power of public opinion aroused in support of the governor's priorities; the problem was how to arouse it. Republican Walter Edge, who served two terms separated by almost thirty years (1917–

1920, 1944–47) was a public–relations executive by profession. He used his business experience to advance his policy aims and wrote that "Much of the credit for any success my legislative programs may have had belongs to the press of New Jersey...the newspapers of New Jersey were extremely helpful in molding public opinion in support of administration policies."[31]

A few other earlier governors, notably the elegant orator and writer Woodrow Wilson, were also able to use the press to good effect. However, the locally oriented newspapers and lack of statewide radio or television stations led to the conclusion that "It naturally follows that no Governor except one with the most unusual qualities or remarkable good luck can make or keep himself the dominant factor in state government."[32]

In the 1970s, just as state government expanded, television became the dominant medium, and fewer people read newspapers. The county leaders were gone, and the need for an interested business community was greater. Governor Cahill stated the problem: "The state comes up short in affording a governor the opportunity to utilize the media properly. There is really no way that you can talk to all the people through any television medium. We do not...have the opportunity to get on television and speak to all the people at once. We also do not have a statewide newspaper....The regrettable part about it is that our citizens are not fully informed and therefore do not understand the problems and needs of the entire state."[33] Even if Cahill had had easy access to television, he was not the sort of warm or articulate person who could use it effectively. Neither was his successor Byrne, who described his own speaking style as "the oratorical equivalent of a blocked punt" and his monotonic voice as resembling a "dial tone."[34] Not until the arrival of Governor Kean in the 1980s did New Jersey's governors move into the media age.

Kean had considerable experience with television before taking office in 1982. After losing his first bid for the Republican gubernatorial nomination in 1977, he became a political commentator for the state public–television network. Kean also chaired President Gerald Ford's 1976 New Jersey campaign organization. He declined a similar post in the 1980 New Jersey Reagan campaign, preferring to cover it as a reporter. These experiences gave him exposure to the national media and leading Republican media consultants and further insight into how to use television effectively.[35] Once elected, Kean became New Jersey's first "media governor," displaying considerable ingenuity in getting around the state's special media problems.

Kean believed that "The most important power the governor has is the power of communicating. If that isn't done properly, you lose your power very fast." He saw the problem of mobilizing the public in much the same way Cahill had:

"It's more difficult in New Jersey. You haven't got TV—you can't go on TV like you can in 48 other states. In other states, if the governor wants something, he'll go on and do a message like the president. There are five TV stations in the state that will give him the time. You can do it [in New Jersey] but it's more difficult. It's more difficult to rev up the newspapers than to go on TV and get out a message."[36]

Kean used a variety of strategies to get his message out. He held hundreds of town meetings all over the state, giving people opportunities to make their concerns known and at the same time experience personally the governor's persuasiveness and charm. He regularly sought opportunities to participate in New York and Philadelphia radio and television programs. His frequent appearances on Sunday morning public-affairs shows got him the attention of the attentive public, while less politically aware citizens could often hear him on mass audience call–in programs and see him making public–service announcements on television. His widest audiences derived from heavy advertising campaigns featuring Kean—conducted by state agencies to encourage tourism and on behalf of the state lottery. These messages emphasized the governor's first priority of building pride in the state and identity with it and made him the symbol of that quest.

Kean did not ignore the more traditional avenues to the print press. Rather than holding periodic formal press conferences for an adversarial press corps with pent–up questions, he was available to reporters almost daily at the conclusion of some ceremony of the day. His days as a part–time reporter and as a legislative leader gave him a sure sense of media relations; as a reporter commented of the annual leading state story, "His years of experience in the political trenches of Trenton have taught him what sells in a budget. He knows exactly what ingredients the press looks for in those first budget stories, which are probably all that most people read."[37]

As Kean designed his many–pronged plan to reach New Jersey's relentlessly uninterested citizenry, he realized he was traveling uncharted waters: "You feel your way. I did a TV show on cable every week for a while....When you've done it for a year and nobody ever tells you they've seen you, you finally say— 'enough.' We changed it to radio. I just answered calls for an hour, and I heard about that all the time."[38]

Kean's successors will follow his path, for the state policy agenda and the attentive public have both expanded dramatically. Indeed, his immediate replacement, Jim Florio, attributed his 1981 loss to Kean to his own failure to use mass media well and to the public's perception of him as a cold personality. Within weeks of assuming office, Florio was on the air continuing Kean's

TV advertising campaign in support of state tourism. His outgoing wife, Lucinda, set up the first state Office of the First Lady. A former New Jersey school teacher, Lucinda Florio was the frequent subject of print and TV news features. Her visits to classrooms, scout troops, and the like helped take the "hard edge" off her husband.

In 1990, public reaction to the largest tax increases in New Jersey's history drove Florio's approval rating to historic lows. Florio requested free evening prime time from New Jersey's only television station to make his case and arranged for a Philadelphia station to receive and broadcast the transmission. Some 460,000 households tuned in—about 20 percent of all those in the state.[39] The broadcast had little effect on public opinion, but was an important addition to the array of gubernatorial media strategies. In 1991, for the first time, the governor's state–of–the–state message was delivered in evening prime time and carried on New York and Philadelphia network stations. Florio also used Treasury Department funds to pay for radio advertising reminding residents to file for property–tax rebates, had regular radio programs on two stations and a cable TV show, and held "office hours" in towns around the state.[40]

Thus, as governors pursue support for their policy agendas in the legislature and with the public, their methods depend on the climate of public opinion, the political climate in the legislature, and their own personal styles. Governor Hughes in the 1960s and Governor Kean in the 1980s were both veteran legislators with conciliatory styles who both faced long periods of opposition–dominated legislatures. But Hughes did not enjoy Kean's access to mass television audiences, and Kean did not enjoy Hughes's ability to succeed simply by persuading a few county bosses to get their legislative troops in line. In the 1970s, Governors Cahill and Byrne could both guide partisan legislative majorities with a heavy hand, as unknown legislators with few independent resources feared the governor's wrath or sought future executive–branch appointments. Governor Florio tried his own combination of these strategies—aggressively seeking quick legislative action and trying to explain it to the public later.

Florio soon found his early legislative majority to be a more assertive crew, less willing to "jump off cliffs" as they had for Brendan Byrne in the 1970s. He scored major victories early in his first year, when he persuaded frightened suburban Democrats to vote for massive tax increases and a new school–funding formula. Legistors hoped voters would forget their anger over the new taxes and reap the rewards of new state spending by the time the entire legislature faced them in November 1991.   .

Even in this "honeymoon" period, however, Democrats insisted on modifications critical to constituents in marginal districts.[41] Within a year, as massive opposition to Florio's tax and education policies continued, even Democratic legislative leaders abandoned Florio and sought major revision of his programs. Senate Majority Leader Daniel Dalton, a Florio protegé and sponsor of the revisions, said of the governor's office, "Their error was one of arrogance. They thought they knew all the answers."[42] When suburban Democrats in both houses suffered devastating defeats in the 1991 elections, they used a lame–duck session to attempt to repeal the entire Florio tax package. The plan failed due to lack of support from urban legislators.

ORGANIZING FOR SUCCESS: THE GOVERNOR'S OFFICE

Each recent governor's "front office" has grown in size and scope, so that the personal staff now numbers well over 150. The growing numbers of divisions and people reflect the increasing problems and functions New Jersey's governors must now address.[43]

Until the second Byrne administration of the late 1970s, the governor's office was run by a small and loosely organized collection of top aides. The chief counsel, assisted by a few lawyers, tracked legislation and prepared "passed–bill" memos advising the governor on appropriate action. A press secretary coordinated relations with reporters, overwhelmingly from the print press and usually the press secretary's former colleagues. An executive secretary dealt with the governor's daily schedule, hiring in the office and, perhaps most crucially, the allocation of gubernatorial patronage. Often the secretary of state, a cabinet official, served as the governor's chief arm–twister in the legislature. Occupants of this position seemed to have a propensity for getting indicted for various forms of corruption.

During the Byrne years, the enactment of the state income tax, the collapse of county party organizational power, and development of new institutional resources for the legislature occurred almost simultaneously. These developments made politics and policy–making infinitely more complex, and that was soon manifested in the organization of the governor's office. In his second term, Byrne was the first governor to appoint a chief of staff and a director of public information. His chief legislative counsel in the first term was named director of policy and planning, a new office intended to coordinate policy initiatives that crossed traditional departmental lines.

The new arrangements reflected widespread opinion in and out of the statehouse that the governor's nominal constitutional powers had "always been limited by the lack of staff to oversee what was going on."[44] Byrne's successor, Tom Kean, expanded the new components of the "front office" and added some others.

The staff in both the counsel's office and the office of policy and planning was greatly augmented. More help was needed in the counsel's office because of the increasing number of bills churned out by the legislature and also because Kean was the first governor not to enjoy an informal kind of pocket veto known as "gubernatorial courtesy." Although the state constitution called for the governor to act on a transmitted bill within ten days, the clock did not officially start running until the governor "called for" the bill. Many passed bills were dispensed with by never being "called for." A constitutional amendment at the end of 1981 ended that practice. More assistant counsels were needed to write more passed bill memos and veto messages in a short period of time, especially at the end of legislative sessions.

In the case of policy and planning, the growing complexity of state policy made many issues too convoluted for one cabinet officer to deal with and slowed down the whole policy process. The number of cabinet departments grew from 14 to 20 between 1950 and 1980, and their subdivisions mushroomed. Increasing fragmentation predictably produced duplication of effort, cross–purposes, and more things falling between the cracks.[45] As a Kean cabinet official described it, coordination was needed in the growing instances when, for example, "the policy of the environmental commissioner is radically different from the transportation commissioner's, or from Treasury, where revenue growth is affected. It's a hell of a lot worse than ten years ago."[46] Kean was disturbed by the ad–hoc nature of the process, recalling, "I had the impression that the most important function of the governor's office was to look ahead. I got the impression when I came there that any new governor was deluged with problems that should have been solved yesterday. We had to get ahead of the curve."[47]

The office of policy and planning also helps a governor decide which current issues should become thematic priorities, receiving close attention and the full weight of the governor's support. As one recent official put it, "There are only a certain number of hours in the day. The governor has five environmental issues, seven transportation issues, some banking issues–there's a limit to the number of issues you can manage from the governor's office."[48] The development of the policy and planning office mirrored events in other states, but the New Jersey office is one of the strongest and most wide–ranging.[49]

Kean's reorganization of the governor's office also included a massive increase in its outreach capacities. The director of public information was replaced with a director of communications and a larger staff to coordinate public relations. In the Byrne administration, one secretary was in charge of vetting the governor's mail from the public, and Kean's staff arrived to find a closet stuffed with unopened correspondence. Along with Kean's own expanded outreach activities, like town meetings and media appearances, an office of constituent communications was instituted to answer every piece of mail. Elaborate word–processing systems replaced the previous administration's typewriters. An office of intergovernmental affairs under the chief of staff continued to deal with county and municipal officeholders and party figures as in the past, but the new entities reflected the much greater attention to the general public.

The front office under Kean's successor, Jim Florio, further expanded on the Kean innovations, devoting even more resources to planning and coordination, legislative relations, and public outreach. The policy and planning office, renamed the Office of Management and Planning, served as a clearinghouse for the activities of all state agencies as well as being a policy–development body. The head of the office devoted herself to management and coordination, while a director of policy worked on programmatic initiatives.

The director of communications, while responsible for speech writing, public communication, and event planning, also supervised the press secretary. Florio's Office of Constituent Relations employed a staff of 23 to deal with as many as 1,500 pieces of mail and 8,000 phone calls daily. Staff writers addressed correspondence dealing with issues, while caseworkers followed up on individuals' problems.[50]

All governors now must grapple with a more complicated policy agenda, an assertive legislature, and a more interested public. In some ways, their staffs tend to be similar, composed primarily of policy generalists and old political acquaintances. Mobility and authority within the office are fluid, depending as much on political acumen and skills as formal titles. But each governor's office also reflects the individual.

Byrne's distaste for personal bargaining and the presence of some top aides whom legislators viewed as being as arrogant and unfamiliar with Trenton folkways as Byrne was, led to poor relations with the legislature in his first term. Things improved somewhat in Byrne's second term when the top staff changed, and the governor distanced himself more. Throughout his tenure, however, Byrne limited personal access and kept a tight rein on the agenda. No administration official went to a committee meeting or to the floor of the legislature without clearance from the counsel's office, and the administration bill list was always very large and very clear.

In contrast, Kean had an open door to a larger number of staff. Throughout his eight years as governor, the chief of staff, chief counsel, and director of policy and planning were a "troika," equally important in the office hierarchy. His press secretary also participated fully in policy debates. Kean welcomed written arguments and information from many sources. One old Kean hand observed, "The memos that go into him are just horrendous; I never understood how he could absorb all that information. But it's what he wants."[51] The governor himself explained, "I like information, I like to hear what's going on....People have different perspectives. It's not efficient and you do run into problems, but you don't get blindsided; somebody will bring everything to your attention. I like that, but most executives would not like it. Every governor has to design it for themselves.... Eventually you know your own style. It took me a year or two until I had exactly the office I wanted."[52]

Although Kean's top legislative priorities were clear, other issues were dealt with less tightly than in the Byrne administration. Cabinet officers had latitude to develop programs outside Kean's central agenda. It was not uncommon for commissioners to espouse different positions on crosscutting issues. The governor's office took no position on these kinds of bills as long as they were still in committee. It was only when they reached the floor that an assistant counsel would be dispatched to announce Kean's position to the Republican legislative caucuses and attempts ensue to keep unwanted bills from being posted or to get amendments.

Florio combined aspects of the Byrne and Kean styles. Even more than Byrne, the governor exercised tight control over cabinet departments. Even more than Kean, he was concerned with strategic planning for the future and domination of the media. Florio used his personal staff to monitor a wide variety of initiatives, ending what he regarded as the Kean cabinet's style of "free-lancing." Cabinet officers became "extensions of the Governor's staff, a distinct change from the traditional standing of them being an extension of the Governor."[53] Cabinet meetings were used to communicate Florio's agenda, rather than being the briefing sessions of the Kean era—leading Labor Commissioner Raymond Bramucci to tell Florio in exasperation at the end of one such meeting, "You treat us like mushrooms. You keep us in the dark and cover us with bull."[54]

In a move perhaps unprecedented in state or federal government, the new Florio administration did not permit cabinet officers to present their fiscal year 1991 departmental budgets to the legislature's joint appropriations committee. It argued that newly appointed officials did not know enough about the department budgets prepared by the governor and state treasurer (Florio's former campaign manager). When it was pointed out that Florio and Treasurer Douglas Berman were both new to Trenton, and at least three veteran commissioners had almost 30 years' combined experience as cabinet officials, a treasury department spokesperson said it would be "uneven" to have some commissioners testifying while others did not.[55]

Florio extended even further the use of the policy and planning office, which Kean had institutionalized. The Florio office of management and planning was not only a policy incubator, but a vehicle for coordinating cross–departmental programs in a manner Florio described as "horizontal" rather than "vertical." His managerial model was small groups of cabinet officers working with senior staffers in the governor's office to develop policies affecting several departments. For example, a Commission on Health Care Costs, chaired by the director of management and planning, involved the commissioners of human services, health, insurance, and labor, as well as the state treasurer and the public advocate. It reflected both Florio's preference for centralized management and the growing complexity of issues.[56]

GOVERNORS AND STATE POLICY: A SUMMARY ASSESSMENT

We end this chapter as we began it. The governor is a powerful official and can expect to leave office with many accomplishments. Yet victories are harder won and more extensively compromised than they would have been a few decades ago—even when the governor enjoys the most favorable combination of public opinion, partisan advantage, and external events. There are simply more people to satisfy, more complexities to overcome, and more players with more of their own resources than there have ever been before. This is particularly true of the legislature, which we examine in detail in the next chapter.

Because legislators know that their careers depend more and more on their own efforts and less and less on the governor or partisan considerations, neither gubernatorial threats nor rewards have much effect on their long–term propensity to cooperate. One former gubernatorial aide has said of the legislature, "Every governor has to understand they may say, 'This is fine for you governor, but how is it going to play in Woodbridge,' or another part of their constituency....If you've got a tough agenda...then you know you're going to be in for a long, very rocky road."[57]

In the end, achieving difficult policy priorities now depends most on the governor's own persistence and ability to mobilize public opinion and persuade the legislature that what is good for the governor is good for them as well. Or, as another executive branch official put it in explaining why the governor is likely to emerge bloody but usually unbowed, "If there's a crisis, they're in the boat with you and they've got to deal with it too. Eventually, something's going to happen."[58]

CHAPTER NINE

The Legislature

Speaker: Why do you rise?
Assemblyman: Mr. Speaker, I rise to aerate my shorts.
—colloquy in the New Jersey Assembly, 1976[1]

The truth is that without a strong governor, the New Jersey legislature is out to lunch.
—Duane Lockard, 1976[2]

The legislature today insists on sharing not only in the credit for state policy, but also its formulation. It no longer tolerates being excluded from the initiative and planning part of the process.
—Alan Rosenthal, 1986[3]

If New Jersey barely had a genuine state politics before the 1970s, one might also say that until then, it also barely had a state legislature. Until the adoption of the 1947 constitution, the legislature's powers far surpassed those of the governor, but before 1947 there was not much any element of state government was expected to do. State representatives, for annual salaries of $500, did the public's business at Monday night meetings five months of the year.

When the constitution granted the governor important new powers, and nothing about the legislature changed, its institutional role became even less significant. Today's stronger and more competent legislature arose as a result of external forces that compelled change—U.S. Supreme Court rulings ending malapportionment and the breakdown of the county party organizations that recruited and elected legislators—and rotated most of them out of office quickly.

John Wahlke's 1962 description of the New Jersey legislature makes the scope of change apparent. Its "essential features," Wahlke noted, were small size, extreme partisanship, dominance by the (Republican) majority caucus, an irrelevant committee system, the impersonalism of rotation, and a shut–out (Democratic) minority.[4] None of these "essential features" survive today. The New Jersey legislature of the past twenty years is an almost new institution— highly professionalized and with much greater capacity.

THE LEGISLATORS

Until 1968, the legislature had 81 members and was the sixth smallest in the nation. The size of the 60–member assembly was unchanged since the constitution of 1844. Members were elected at large until 1852, when multimember, county–based districts were created. At–large elections within the districts continued, enhancing the strength of a county's majority party. In 1953, for example, Republican candidates running for Essex County's twelve assembly seats received an average vote of 125,000, while their Democratic opponents averaged 117,000. Due to the at–large system, the Republicans won all of the Essex seats, although they received only about 52 percent of the vote.[5]

Assembly districts were apportioned by population, but each county was guaranteed at least one—a provision benefiting the Republicans who dominated most small, rural counties. Assembly members were elected annually, and most were rotated out after two single–year terms.

As it had been since 1776, the legislature's upper house comprised one member from each county, regardless of population. In 1954, New Jersey was one of only six states using counties as the basis for representation in the upper house; the other five were thinly populated and lacked urban concentrations.[6] The senate's size changed only as new counties were formed and stabilized at 21 after Union County's creation in 1857.

The senate was severely malapportioned. In the 1930s, members representing 15 percent of the state's population—fewer than the residents of the single county of Hudson—could put together a senate majority. Even by 1963, when migration to the suburbs had produced somewhat more even population distribution, an eleven–member majority could comprise senators representing about 41 percent of the public.[7] New Jersey senators served three year terms.

A county-based system of representation advantaged the Republicans, especially in the senate. So did elections in odd-numbered years, when there were no federal contests to draw casual voters to the polls. By the 1960s, the Republicans had controlled the upper house for all but three years of the entire century and the assembly for all but 13, despite frequent statewide election of Democratic governors.

"One–person–one–vote" court decisions of the late 1960s almost annihilated the counties as the basis of representation in both houses. Federal and state judicial mandates produced a new 120 member legislature of 40 senators and 80 assembly members, 2 in each senate district. Members of the assembly are now elected in odd–numbered years for two–year terms, while senate members are elected in odd–numbered years for nonstaggered terms, usually of four years [8] Many districts cross county lines.

Figure 2
New Jersey Legislative Districts

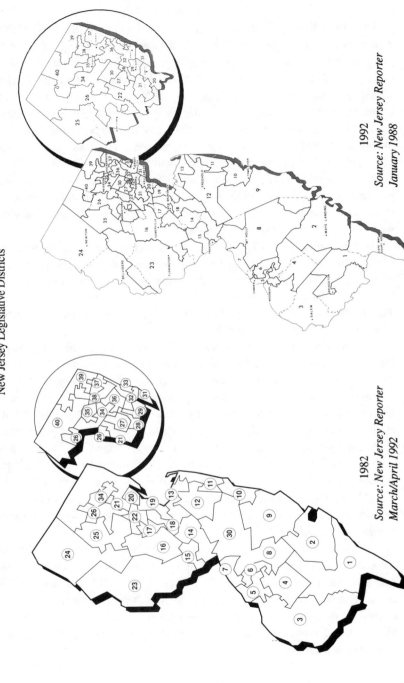

1992
Source: *New Jersey Reporter*
January 1988

1982
Source: *New Jersey Reporter*
March/April 1992

When the census requires legislative redistricting, a ten–member bipartisan commission named by the state party chairs is charged with drawing new district lines. If the commission cannot reach agreement within thirty days of receipt of official census figures, the state's chief justice appoints a neutral tiebreaker. In both 1980 and 1990, political scientist Donald Stokes, dean of the Woodrow Wilson School at Princeton University, was the tiebreaker who cast the deciding vote. Stokes's integrity is probably best demonstrated by complaints in both years that he was "unfair"—once from the Democrats and once from the Republicans.

As shown in figure 2, the lines drawn for the 1991 legislative elections created a new district in the southern half of the state, combined two in the north, and generally shifted districts south and west, reflecting population shifts.

In 1982, amendments to the federal Voting Rights Act mandated creation of "majority minority" districts where possible. They were an important factor in the 1990 redistricting process. Republicans and the NAACP called for two districts in Essex County with minority voting populations of over 60 percent. Tiebreaker Stokes agreed with the Democrats' proposal for three districts with minority populations of about 55 percent. The immediate effect was to protect white Democratic incumbents. The new map also contained a Hudson County district with a majority of Hispanics.[9]

Although about half the 40 senate districts now include municipalities in only one county, only in small rural Cape May are all county municipalities still represented by one senator. County lines do, however, continue to influence political thinking and organization, creating problems for the many politicians whose districts cross them. As a particularly unfortunate lawmaker whose district covered parts of five counties observed, "The result is five Lincoln Day fundraisers, five NJEA legislative dinners, and five of almost everything else, a needless waste of time and expense for a part–time legislator."[10]

The typical representative in both houses is about five years older than was the case from the 1940s through the 1970s. The average age of senators in 1992 was 53, and it was 50 in the assembly. In 1992, 95 of the 120 members of the 205th legislature had county or local government experience, and 21 held concurrent local or county office in addition to their duties in Trenton.[11]

Table 11 summarizes turnover and incumbent success rates since 1973, the first election with the complete, current electoral system in place.

Turnover in the assembly dropped steadily through the 1970s, and in the absence of redistricting, leveled off at one in four new members in each legislature, or even fewer. As the incumbent success rate shows, most of the new members were not successful challengers but rather won seats that opened

Table 11: Turnover and Incumbent Success, 1973-1991

	Assembly		Senate	
Year	Turnover	Incumbent Success	Turnover	Incumbent Success
1973	54	71	58	65
1975	29	84	NA	NA
1977	29	97	40	92
1979	21	86	NA	NA
1981	34	96	43	85
1983	18	97	25	88
1985	23	81	NA	NA
1987	26	97	13	97
1989	10	95	NA	NA
1991	43	75	45	79

Source: Calculated by authors from The New Jersey Legislative Manual.

Note: Table entries are percentages.

because of voluntary resignation (often to run for the senate) or death. Although turnover also dropped steadily in the upper house, it took a while longer for it to reach the level of continuity in the assembly. In both houses, incumbents running for reelection in most of the last several contests had about a nine–in–ten chance of being returned. The pattern of low turnover has only been disrupted in elections immediately following redistricting (in 1981 and 1991). In 1981, 47 incumbents did not return to the legislature, and in 1991, 52 incumbents did not return.

A few county or municipal party chairs still serve in the legislature, but most local party organizations no longer can single–handedly choose their delegations, nor rotate them out of office after a term or two. However, legislators still have deep local roots. In both houses, most are New Jersey natives, and many represent at least portions of the county where they were born. Most of the nonnatives arrived long ago from neighboring states and like the general population, are particularly likely to hail from New York City.

Although legislators are thus firmly embedded in their communities, not all of the state's communities are firmly embedded in the legislature. As with most other American legislatures, New Jersey's is heavily white and male and includes a narrow range of professions. Of the 120 members in 1992, 14 were women, 12 were African Americans, and 2 were Hispanic.[12]

Lawyers, at 30 percent, were the largest occupational group, followed by the 24 percent who reported running a business, and the 11 percent who were educators. Lawyers have long been prominent in Trenton, but the legislature is far less dominated by attorneys than it once was. More than half the state senators of the 1930s were lawyers by trade, and about three–quarters were in 1955. Almost half the assembly members that year were also from the legal profession, compared to 22 percent nationally.[13] Thus, the national decline of lawyer–legislators has occurred even more sharply in New Jersey, but the state had more of them to begin with.

A stiff conflict–of–interest law affects attorneys' ability to serve. Not only are legislators banned from doing legal business with the state themselves but also from membership in a firm in which other partners do such business. Although well–intended, the law bars many distinguished, politically active lawyers from legislative service. One example is former Assemblyman Robert Wilentz, scion of a prominent political family, and later chief justice of the state supreme court. Wilentz voted for the conflict–of–interest bill that ended his legislative career and left the assembly at the end of that term. The remaining attorneys are of the "Main Street lawyer" variety.

The legislature's unusual meeting schedule makes it rather easy to pursue another occupation while serving in Trenton. Some other geographically compact states have a "commuter legislature," but only New Jersey's is technically in session almost all year, yet meeting only weekly—on Mondays and some Thursdays. There are usually long breaks after the governor's February budget message, few sessions during the summer, and an election–time recess in the years legislators are running.

Members can travel to the capital in less than two hours from anywhere in the state and return home the same day. With recent scheduling improvements, many can make it home in time for dinner. Trenton thus largely lacks the "hangout" hotels, restaurants, and other components of legislative life common to most state capitals. After late sessions, legislators are as likely to stop for a hasty meal at one of New Jersey's ubiquitous highway diners on their way home as they are to go to a Trenton watering hole to talk shop with their colleagues.

Handsome salaries in many states lead an increasing number of lawmakers to make officeholding a full–time career. The National Conference of State Legislators found in 1986 that 11 percent of all state legislators reported political work was their full–time occupation, four times the number ten years earlier.[14] In states like California and New York, where base salary (often augmented by per–diem payments and extra pay for leadership positions) is well above average family income, almost all legislators are full–time.

Once New Jersey raised its long–standing annual stipend of $500 to $5,000 shortly after passage of the 1947 constitution, legislators began voting them-selves regular salary increases—to $10,000 by 1976, $18,000 in 1980, $25,000 in 1984, and $35,000 in 1990. The pay of the leaders of both houses is a third higher. Almost all members list themselves as holding another job, but informal estimates are that about a quarter are actually full–time politicians with, perhaps, a small insurance business or legal practice "on the side."

The Work Environment for Legislators

In the days of the amateur, part–time legislature, desks in the legislative chamber were most New Jersey lawmakers' "work environment." Only the senate president and assembly speaker had offices in the statehouse, and there were no rooms for committee meetings. A 1963 study observed, "Their present practice of considering important public business in the gallery during recesses is deplorable."[15] Former Governor Thomas Kean, who was elected to the assembly in 1967 and served ten years, recalls an early experience there: "My first year, there was some bill where I said, 'We've got to discuss this in committee before we even take it to caucus.' We had to go and negotiate for the ladies' room. They had a lady's cloakroom that was right across from the Assembly Chamber—so we sat in there, across from the chamber, because there was no other space."[16]

The legislative staff consisted of some part–time patronage employees performing the most basic administrative and secretarial functions at the behest of the leadership. This staff increased modestly in the 1950s and acquired the impressive–sounding appellation of "Legislative Services Agency."

The staff increases were partly the result of the recommendations of a legislative commission and partly due to the tendency to ignore legal limits. In 1957 for example, the rules called for 12 assembly clerks and 4 in the senate. The actual numbers of such employees were 44 and 19, respectively.[17] Little changed until the early 1970s, when a new breed of legislator less tied to party organizations began to arrive and assume leadership positions. Dramatic increases in all kinds of staff support followed quickly.[18] In the space of a few years, full–time, nonpartisan, professional staff; partisan staff; and personal staff were all created or grew markedly.

A 1971 Commission to Study the Legislature (spearheaded by, among others, then-Assembly Majority Leader Tom Kean) called for full–time staff to support the work of committees. The Legislative Services Agency, shortly renamed the Office of Legislative Services (OLS), assumed its current organizational structure in 1979—consisting of divisions of State Auditing, Legal Services, Legislative Information and Research, and Budget and Program Review. The first two offices perform the traditional tasks of postaudits of state agencies (constitutionally assigned to the legislature) and bill drafting. However, the divisions that have grown the most are those providing research and budget analysis.

These staff gave lawmakers independent information and support and ended their dependence on interest groups and the governor's office.[19] Governor Kean, in comparing the legislature in which he served in the 1960s and 1970s to the current body has observed, "The legislature had no fiscal capacity, and if we wanted anything, we had to go to [the state budget director]. If the governor didn't want us to do that, they'd just say no....[Now] they have the capability to do real research. They have the capability to know what they're talking about. They have the capability to look at the budget with a fine–tooth comb and ask really penetrating questions....That's what a legislative body should have, even if you have to question how they're using it." As governor, Kean personally experienced the contribution of the budget-reviewing Office of Fiscal Affairs to legislative autonomy, which as a legislative leader he had helped to create. He ruefully recalled, "I sometimes wonder if [Governor] Cahill wasn't right. I had to bargain with him to sign it—he said no governor should sign this bill."[20]

In 1968, the Legislative Information and Research Division consisted of nine professionals supporting a few committees. By 1971, the professional personnel had grown by half, so that five could be assigned to support key committees, and the rest worked for two committees each. By the late 1970s, every committee had its own nonpartisan full–time professional staffer. The OLS budget grew from $3.3 million in fiscal year 1975 to $11.3 million in fiscal year 1984 and $20.9 million in fiscal year 1991, when it had 337 employees.

At about the same time members strengthened the nonpartisan staff, they also began to turn the patronage employees into a more professional operation. Both parties appointed executive directors for the partisan staff in 1970. Most of the growth of this more overtly political operation, however, occurred in the 1980s, after the beefed–up OLS showed legislators how useful staff could be. As OLS head Albert Porroni put it, lawmakers developed "the sense that our function was too important not to be a political function."[21] Whereas OLS staff provides committee chairs with legal, research, and bill–drafting assistance, the partisan staff serves at the pleasure of the party leadership in each chamber. Its highest officials are a useful "institutional memory," especially on the Democratic side, with longer tenure than many legislators.

Although developing party policy and providing support to committees are part of its job, partisan staff spends much time running an elaborate press operation for leaders and members and serving as a more or less permanent campaign organization. Partisan workers compile voting and attendance data on the opposition for use in campaigns, write statements and speeches for members, and manage many campaigns.

The partisan staff's political activities became unusually public in 1990. The attorney general launched an investigation of a Republican assembly staffer who had "spied" on the Democrats by breaking into their data files on the legislature's computers. After admitting he knew of the staffer's activities and had done nothing about them, the Republican assembly staff director was forced to resign. Democrats could take little pleasure in their opponents' discomfort, however, because the files in question included records of Democratic campaign contributors—an obvious misuse of state property and possible official misconduct.[22]

After six months of study, a state grand jury found that while legislative employees of both parties improperly performed campaign work on state time, there were no "uniform guidelines" to provide grounds for criminal indictments. It proposed a draft law prohibiting the use of public funds "in furtherance of the nomination, election or defeat of any candidate for public office."[23]

As the partisan staff exploded in size in the early 1980s, the then–Republican minority subjected the Democrats to severe criticism. When the Republicans took over the assembly in 1985, however, they cut the Democratic staff from 45 (30 full–time, 15 for session days) to 17—but gave themselves 55 full–time staffers and another 27 for session days. Democrats, who reassumed control in 1990, first swore similar vengeance. However, upon reflecting on the possible consequences of this staff "arms race" in a competitive state, they granted themselves 39 full–time staff and the new Republican minority 28. In the senate, where interparty hostilities are not as great, the majority traditionally allocates itself about 25 partisan staffers and awards 17 to the minority. Republicans were similarly generous to the minority when they took control of both houses in 1992.

Along with all the aides legislators share, each lawmaker has a budget for personal staff and a district office. By the mid–1970s, to enhance communication with constituents, each member already received funds to rent and furnish a district office, a telephone credit card, stationery, and 5,000 stamps (increased to 10,000 in 1989). The allowance of $15,000 for personal staff aides in 1976 has grown steadily, increasing fastest in recent years. The $25,000 members awarded themselves for this purpose in 1985 became $45,000 by 1987 and $70,000 in 1991. Rules for allocating this money are often honored in the breach. Although supposedly limited to a total of six "legislative aides" in 1984, more than half the members reported employing more than six people; the top three made payments to a total of 52 people.

The nature and use of personal aides vary widely. Generally speaking, legislators from competitive suburban districts turn district–office staff into a well–honed constituency service and personal political organization. District representatives often pool their funds to pay a relatively small number of full–time employees, who run professional and smoothly functioning offices.

On the other hand, some legislators from safe districts with remnants of a county party organization hire large numbers of "very part–time" or no–show employees whose offices are hard to find and seldom open. Many "aides" receive annual "salaries" of $500 to $1,000, whose real value is to the employee's eventual state pension. Pension payments are highly dependent on the number of years of state, county, and municipal employment, and these small stipends count toward those years. Thus, one Essex County representative reports small wages to such aides as his father, a former president of the Newark City Council, Essex County voting registrars, rent collection and zoning officers, and a Newark Democratic ward leader.[24] Whatever kind of district office members choose to have, they are all connected by computer to the partisan staff in Trenton.

Overall, New Jersey ranks high in its provision of legislative staff of all varieties. In 1979, it was one of only three states providing full–time personal staff to members of the lower house and one of ten allotting such staff to senators. New Jersey then ranked thirteenth nationally in the size of its state legislative staff, and by 1988, it was ninth.[25]

THE ORGANIZATION OF THE LEGISLATURE: COMMITTEES AND LEADERSHIP

In the era when New Jersey legislative committees had no staff, the absence of staff was unremarked. Although formally numerous, committees were merely paper organizations. Rules called for weekly committee meetings, but they were seldom held. Many committees had no bills referred to them, and no records were kept of attendance or actions. Although the 45 senate committees and 54 assembly committees of 1953 were soon severely reduced, the smaller number was not much more effective. The 21 senators were still nominally assigned to nine to twelve committees each, leading the authors of one survey of legislative work to comment, "One can only wonder what would happen if in fact the Senate committees did attempt to meet regularly."[26]

The legislature's work, such as it was, got done not in its committees but in the majority party caucuses, particularly in the senate—which is to say, by the Republican senators. As it was described in the early 1960s, "When Senators arrive on Monday morning, the Republicans go into caucus and the Democrats wait around wondering what is going to come out of caucus."[27] The senate Republican caucus of this epoch, as we noted in chapter 3, was similar to the despotic U.S. House Rules Committee of the same era, and was called the "most powerful majority party caucus in any state legislative chamber."[28]

When the senate doubled in size (and the Democrats assumed control in 1974) the Republican caucus lost its power to delay or defeat. With no alternative institutions to play the caucus's role, control of the legislative agenda passed for a brief time to the governor's office. New Jersey's legislative committees, as compared to those in other states, were described as "very passive"—with light work loads, few bills referred, and even fewer amended. The committees had "little to do with policy and program formulation."[29] However, the 1971 Commission to Study the Legislature, which had launched the development of a professional staff, also began the process of constructing a genuine committee system for the staff to serve. Over the next few years, the commission's recommendations to establish committee rooms, record committee actions and attendance, open meetings to the public, refer bills routinely to reference committees, and hold legislative sessions two days a week were all adopted.

In the 205th legislature (1992–94), there were 13 standing reference committees in the senate and 19 in the assembly, numbers that have varied somewhat since committees were reduced to 12 in both houses in 1954. There were, for example, 10 senate committees in 1974 and 14 in 1990; 13 in the assembly in 1974 and 24 in 1990. The trend, however, as these numbers show, is an increase, especially in the assembly, since the severe pruning of the 1950s. Traditionally, the membership and leadership of the various committees resembled the game of musical chairs, with new players constantly entering the game. High turnover ensured a lot of new members and open slots, and continuing legislators migrated to "better" committee slots and then to the leadership ladder. At least half the members of the "desirable" and important committees dealing with taxation, finance, and judicial appointments changed from one session to the next between 1948 and 1967.[30]

Turnover is usually lower now, especially on the committees dealing with financial affairs, and changes occur less often because of members' departure from the legislature. Rather, they are occasioned more by alterations in party balance (and thus their proportions of committee members) and the creation of new committees on which to serve. All bills of any import now go through committee screening and public hearings, and a growing number of committee meetings and public hearings are held on nonsession days so there is time for more careful consideration.

All these logistical alterations and the proliferating staff would still not have given the legislature more control over its own affairs if it had not, at roughly the

Table 12: Average Number of Meeting Days Per Legislature, 1948-1989

	Assembly	Senate
1948-57	50	52
1958-67	43	46
1968-73	63	61
1974-81	74	74
1982-89	67	65

Source: New Jersey Legislative Manual

same time, begun to develop more continuous leadership. Before the 1970s, there was a long tradition of leadership rotation in both houses and both parties. The few lawmakers who stayed around more than two or three years followed a preordained leadership ladder—one year as chair of the appropriations committee, then one year each as assistant majority leader, majority leader, and finally, assembly speaker or senate president. Occupants of these positions often achieved them less because of political or legislative skills than because of their county of residence. The most powerful county organizations in each party saw to it that they shared in the leadership spoils. A look at the Democratic leadership as late as the end of the 1970s and into the early 1980s makes the point. The senate presidents were from the politically potent counties of Mercer and Essex successively; the assembly speakers from Hudson and Middlesex.

Republican leaders in the early 1970s began ending the tradition of annual leadership change, when Senate President Raymond Bateman (Republican gubernatorial candidate in 1977) held office for an unprecedented three years between 1970–72, and Assembly Speaker Thomas Kean (governor, 1982–90) served for two years in 1972–73. It briefly appeared that a tradition of one leader per legislature (i.e., a two–year term), was developing. However, beginning in 1978, successive senate presidents and assembly speakers from both parties established a "new tradition" of two–term leadership, or four years.

It is uncertain how long the new four–year tradition will endure, or if future legislative chieftains will try for the semipermanent positions of the leadership in some states and in the U.S. Congress. A force working against this is the absence of many other places for ambitious careerist politicians to go, since New Jersey has no statewide elected officials other than the governor and only five county executives. Thus, at present, leaders get to serve two terms. If they remain in the legislature thereafter—and many do, at least for a while—they are awarded titles like president pro tempore or assistant majority leader.

It seems clear, though, that the time–honored means of ascent to the top posts

Table 13: Average Number of Laws Passed Per Legislature, 1948-1989

Years	Laws
1948-57	650
1958-67	448
1968-73	686
1974-81	662
1982-89	703

Source: New Jersey Legislative Manual

have changed in important ways. Democratic Senate President John Russo and Republican Assembly Speaker Chuck Hardwick, who led the 202nd and 203rd legislatures from 1986 through 1990, broke the mold. Neither Russo (from Monmouth) nor Hardwick (from Union) represented traditional, partisan, powerhouse counties. Rather, their skills at public relations, political strategy, and especially campaign fund–raising played a critical role.

Certainly Hunterdon Republicans or Middlesex Democrats are not shut out of the leadership in this new era, but they need virtues other than place of residence. Indeed, the Democratic leaders of the 1990–91 legislature all came from traditional Democratic bastions. Senate President John Lynch was a Middlesex County native. Assembly Speaker Joseph Doria hailed from Hudson County and Assembly Majority Leader Wayne Bryant from Camden County. All, however, had respected political skills. Doria's election denied the speakership to the former minority leader from the flagship Democratic county of Essex, because of that person's perceived lack of effectiveness.

When Republicans assumed control of both houses in 1992, Lynch and Doria continued as leaders of the minority. Assembly Speaker Garabed ("Chuck") Haytaian had previously been minority leader in the lower house. However, the former senate minority leader from strongly Republican Morris County lost a contest for senate president to the more moderate Donald DiFrancesco and had to settle for the majority leader position. Haytaian and DiFrancesco, from Warren and Union counties, respectively, further demonstrated that residence in a partisan "flagship county" is no longer a requirement for leadership positions.

LEGISLATIVE WORK: THE NATURE OF THE PRODUCT

The first thing one notices in considering the work of the legislature is that it is doing a lot more of it than it used to. One measure of effort is how much time legislators spend in session.

During the governorship of Republican Tom Kean (1982–90), the legislature did not maintain the record meeting pace it set during the tenure of his Democratic predecessor, Brendan Byrne (1974–82). Still, the contrast between the last two decades and earlier years is apparent in table 12. Generally speaking, the legislature is meeting half again as often as it did in midcentury. More meeting days mean more opportunities to pass laws, and members have done just that in recent years.

Until 1982, the numbers of laws rose and fell quite regularly with the shared or divided partisanship of the governor and the legislature. The years of lowest average volume, 1958–67, were a time of Democratic governors and mostly Republican legislatures. In the other time periods, one party monopolized state government almost all the time. The divided government of the entire 1980s, however, did not bring renewed stalemate, at least as reflected in the amount of legislation produced. This was not due only to Governor Kean's consensual style, since Democrats Robert Meyner and Richard Hughes, facing mostly opposition legislatures, had similar styles.

Rather, the increase in the legislature's staple product is due to its new resources, growing autonomy, and need for credit–taking in campaigns. The effect of more control over the "means of production" is apparent in a huge upsurge in the number of bills introduced. Between 1931 and 1935, the average number of bills introduced per session was 1,000, and the average number passed was 350, or slightly over a third of the total. By the 1978–79 session, 5,142 bills were introduced, and only 13 percent made it into the lawbooks. Ten years later, in the 1988–89 session, the number of bills had doubled, but only 4 percent became statutes.[31]

To be sure, most of the laws produced in recent years—those about issues not part of the governor's legislative agenda—are unlikely to change the life of New Jersey citizens. Other chapters (particularly 14–17) describe the legislature's growing role in shaping the state's more important public policies; we concentrate here on the rest of their output. Among the less–than–earthshaking measures the legislature has solemnly passed are extension of the raccoon–hunting day from midnight on Saturday to sunrise on Sunday, creation of a commission to investigate the surplus population of cats and dogs, reimbursement for $662.65 worth of damage caused by an escaping state prison inmate who stole a motorist's car, and free admission for guide dogs of the blind to public facilities.

As these examples suggest, special–interest concerns take up much of the legislature's time. If there are vocal proponents, no opposition, and little cost, the legislature will acquiesce to their desires. But if there are determined groups on both sides, such issues can haunt lawmakers year after year. Some recent perennials include battles to allow self–service gas stations, which are permitted in 48 other states (independent station owners vs. the oil companies); regulation of leghold traps (hunters vs. animal–rights activists); prohibition of disposable soft–drink containers (soft drink manufacturers and South Jersey glass manufacturers vs. environmentalists); and permission to dispense contact lenses (physicians and optometrists vs. opticians). When faced with these kinds of disputes, the legislature often assumes the role of referee. Requests for new or expanded functions for licensed professionals are a frequent example. When occupational therapists, for instance, sought licensure, they were bidden to strike a deal with hospitals and physical therapists, the other interested parties.

The governor rarely intervenes in such matters, unless they will cost the state money—the reason Governor Kean gave when he vetoed the surplus pet commission. A rare exception was Governor Cahill's 1972 rejection of a bill designating a melody called "I'm From New Jersey" as the official state song. Cahill dismissed this composition, approved after its author sang it from the assembly gallery accompanied by a six–piece musical group, with a succinct veto message: "It stinks."

A veteran analyst of the legislature ascribes its style of dealing with special–interest legislation to the crush of bills, the limited time to deal with them on sporadic Mondays and Thursdays, and the fragmented sessions: "For the legislator, life in Trenton is discontinuous, and the legislative process moves by fits and starts. It is almost impossible to give anything much attention for any significant length of time."[32] The nature of the legislative day illustrates the problem. Members leave home early in the morning to get to the committee sessions scheduled for 10 A.M. Around noon, party conferences on the day's agenda begin. About two in the afternoon, floor action is supposed to start. All the while, there are constituents and visiting schoolchildren to greet, lobbyists to consult, and calls to make from one's floor desk phone (since there are still no offices for the rank and file).

Because all these activities constantly run behind schedule, the body operates on what is known as "legislative standard time"—about an hour behind scheduled clock time. Members may not know until the last minute what bills the leadership will post that day, or in what order they will come up. Assembly members who wish to gain the floor are at the mercy of the speaker, who controls not only recognition, but also the chamber's microphones. As sessions draw to a close, there is always a last–minute blizzard of "must–pass" legislation, and the thirty–bills–per–day official limit is often waived.

Nor is it simple for legislators (or anyone else) to reflect back on what they have done. Unlike 31 other states, and despite the presence of the necessary equipment, legislative sessions are not recorded. When the state supreme court and later the U.S. Supreme Court ruled on a New Jersey school–prayer case requiring "a moment of silence," judges had to rely on newspaper clippings to assess legislative intent.[33]

THE LEGISLATURE: AN ASSESSMENT

We began this chapter with a description of the legislature of thirty years ago— a small body composed of a few distinguished public servants and a large number of party hacks who left quickly; an institution almost without structure; a formally co–equal branch of government that did little when it had constitutional power, and willingly ceded that power to an executive branch eager to seize it when the constitution changed—just as state government began to develop into a vital instrument. Like most reforms, the legislative reforms of the past three decades have had unintended consequences. And many were thrust upon the legislature by external forces rather than by members' conscious designs.

The New Jersey legislature today is not the best in the nation, but it likely ranks higher than it did in the past. In a national study in the late 1960s, it placed 32nd overall among the fifty states. Even then, however, it was already graded 14th in its capacity for legislative and administrative oversight and 18th in terms of information resources. Much lower ratings on independence from the governor and interest groups (31st), representativeness (35th), and public accessibility to its documents and proceedings (42nd) pulled down the overall rank.[34] New Jersey legislators themselves, in a seven–state survey, confirmed this general picture.[35] Although there are no recent systematic comparative studies, the legislature has improved greatly in all these respects and others.

There is first the change in its membership. Legislators today come to Trenton with more officeholding experience, usually stay longer, and get to know their jobs better. Buffoons and hacks are fewer; substantive experts and persons of thoughtful mien may be more numerous. If they are more personally ambitious, they are also more likely than they were to build careers based on policy accomplishments or constituency service, rather than service to corporations or political machines.

The thread of personal ambition and political entrepreneurship runs through all the other changes in the legislature. More staff positions were created so that legislators could help formulate policy rather than rubber–stamp it. Nonpartisan staff was supplemented—some say elbowed aside–by partisan and personal staff that could better serve ambitious members' political ends. The director of the Office of Legislative Services complains that his personnel are overwhelmed by a system that allows every member to request research, legal opinions, or bills. He suggests that, as in many other states, some clearance—perhaps from the leadership—should be required.[36] "Good–government" types look askance at the no–show "district aides" and political operatives on the state payroll. Yet thanks to the staff, as a lobbyist and former Republican staff director points out, "Today, even unspectacular legislators can be incredibly well–informed on issues in bills coming up." A Democratic counterpart agrees, saying that legislation goes "to a more argumentative fate, but better argued than ever before."[37]

Similarly, committee chairs and senior members stay in place longer because of genuine policy interests and expertise, and also because their path to house leadership is slowed by colleagues serving longer there. Effective legislative leadership is a sure ticket to a serious gubernatorial candidacy, if desired, and all the leaders of the 1980s did so desire.

Leaders have an independent power base derived from the gratitude of their partisan colleagues for fund–raising prowess and other campaign assistance. They are thus less likely to work in harness even with a governor of their own party. Further, almost every member of the majority party in each chamber has some claim to be a "leader," for all of them in the last few legislatures have been chairs or vice–chairs of some committee—the impetus for the growth in the number of committees.

Does nothing remain of the New Jersey legislature of old? What have been the effects of the careerist, professional legislature on the institution and its performance? The answer to the first question is simpler than the second. Commuting lawmakers, discontinuous meetings, and "off–off–year" elections keep the old localist political culture going to a considerable extent. They hobble a drive to genuine excellence. The answer to the second, broader, question is more obscure.

Although the number of legislators living off county organization patronage has declined sharply, there are new ways of making a living from a long–term political career that may be no less problematical. Reelection now often depends on being able to raise large amounts of campaign money, and much of it, particularly for incumbents, comes from "special–interest" sources with concerns before the legislature. Former Governor Kean has described the possible dangers graphically: "They parlay the [money for staff and from salary] into another $200,000 they get from representing a couple of towns, and you have a small town lawyer making a quarter of a million dollars or more—from the seat in the legislature. The same applies to an insurance agent or a real estate person who gets local business. It's all based on the assembly seat and therefore they'll do anything to keep it. If they lose the assembly seat, they're liable to lose all the rest too. It makes people cast votes I don't think they ever would have otherwise."[38]

The price of stronger committees and more staff—especially partisan staff—is considerable legislative behavior that is more political or self-serving than it is useful, as when assembly Democrats were recently perceived as designing their legislative agenda primarily to "showcase" threatened incumbents, while the Republican leader allegedly told his assembly troops to oppose any bill sponsored by a targeted Democrat.[39] As both leadership and staff take on political as well as governing roles, the line between "politics" and "government" becomes increasingly blurred and sometimes erased.

The autonomy most legislators enjoy and the profusion of "leadership" positions mean that the governor must deal with an almost unmanageable number of actors. Governor Kean exaggerated little in saying of the assembly, "When I ask for a meeting of the leadership, there are forty people in this room. When I was in the assembly [for ten years beginning in the mid–1960s], we had three leaders—the speaker, the majority leader and the minority leader. Maybe that was too few. But 40 is too many."[40]

Another prominent Republican who served in the legislature in the same period as Kean recalls how Democratic Governor Richard Hughes (1961–69) dealt with a body often led by the opposition: "He met not with the gang that is now the legislative leadership, but with the Speaker, the President of the Senate, and the majority and minority leader of each house before every session; on agendas that were related to the Governor's program....People from both sides of the aisle could let their hair down with respect to what they could do, what they couldn't do, and what they didn't want to do."[41] Contrast this with the description by a Kean administration official of the leadership meetings Kean endured: "Many of those sessions were just posturing sessions. People had an agenda and they were using the governor as a mechanism to further their own agenda. And Governor Kean did not want to be used to provide a forum for someone else's agenda, so those meetings were terminated fairly rapidly."[42]

Nor did this Republican governor endure slings and arrows only from the opposition. In his last year in office, two Republican senators and the assembly speaker were avowed gubernatorial contestants, interested first in furthering their own candidacies. The governor's last proposed major tax package was supported by Democrats in the Democratic–controlled senate, but the Republican assembly speaker refused to release it from committee.

Such tales are far from unique in state legislatures these days and led one prominent analyst to entitle a recent study, "The Legislative Institution—

Transformed and at Risk."[43] It argues that while the legislature's focus used to be on governing, it is increasingly on politics and campaigns, as extraparliamentary party organizations decay, and leaders are distracted from their governing jobs by the requirements of their new political jobs.

Yet surprisingly enough, this analysis concludes, "if performance is the standard, then state legislatures are in better shape than they were twenty years ago....thus far, they have even been able to shape policies needed by the state."[44] Leaders that stay in their jobs because of their political skills thwart governors not only for political reasons, but often for good policy reasons. As a former legislator–turned–lobbyist says, "Continuing leadership gives the leadership greater power and clout, and you need that to balance the power of the governor's office."[45]

Legislative actions that are too obviously partisan and obstructive redound to the discredit of all incumbents as they face their frequent "job reviews" by the electorate. Association with good public policy helps them. If the process is not as pure and legislators less high–minded than "good government" requires, still the improvements over the past half–century are striking. Legislatures "reflect fundamental tensions of political life and fundamental contradictions in political institutions, not just human failing."[46]

CHAPTER TEN

The State Bureaucracy

The governor's ability to exert control over the state government has remained his most difficult challenge.
— Donald Linky, former director, state Office of Policy and Planning[1]

I think one of the things all of us would secretly like to do is to come back in another life and find out what the bureaucrats permitted us to do during our tenure that we might have thought we were enormously successful at doing. The bureaucrats will say, "Remember the time we didn't tell you about X?...The next commissioner, maybe we'll tell them, because it will be important at that time from our point of view to let them know."
— reflection by former cabinet official[2]

Creating a strong and efficient executive branch was a major goal of New Jersey's 1947 constitutional convention. Since then, executive agencies have grown at a pace the framers could hardly have envisioned. Bureaucracies by nature are concerned less "about the overall architecture of government" than they are with "the narrow sliver they believe they represent."[3] This chapter looks at the factors that shape New Jersey's executive branch—constitutional, cultural, historical, and political.

To reinforce a newly powerful chief executive, the 1947 constitution limited cabinet departments to no more than twenty. They were to contain "all executive and administrative offices, departments and instrumentalities of the State government" and be "under the supervision of the governor."[4] The charter's framers took aim at the myriad departments, boards, and commissions that began to multiply after 1900. No one oversaw their work. Governor Franklin Murphy (1902–1905) thought about reestablishing a governor's mansion in Trenton because, if he were in town regularly, "the department chiefs might be shamed out of their apparent notions that the State was paying them big salaries only to have them serve as State House ornaments....the chiefs of the State House had gone to their offices in Trenton only—well, they were always there on paydays, at any rate. The work of their departments—even the supervision of them—was left entirely in the hands of their deputies and clerks and assistants."[5]

In 1929, a National Institute of Public Administration (NIPA) study found that New Jersey state government consisted of "a grand total of ninety–four agencies....many are practically independent of the governor, either because of the nature of their appointment or the length of their terms of office. The seventy–two boards and commissions consist in the aggregate of approximately 500 members."[6] The writers of the report recommended abolishing many of these bodies and putting the rest into twelve cabinet departments responsible to the governor. They recognized that strong executive leadership was at least as important for successful state government as the "neutral competence" exemplified by independent commissions.[7]

In his 1932 inaugural address, Governor A. Harry Moore endorsed the recommendations. As it usually did, the legislature ignored the governor. Unusually forceful chief executives like Woodrow Wilson (1911–1912) and Walter Edge (1917–1919, 1944–1947) achieved some administrative consolidation, but the chaotic and antiquated bureaucracy remained largely in place until 1948.

Although the new constitution permitted 20 cabinet departments, only 14 were established. However, within thirty years, the 20–department limit was reached de jure and breached de facto. To maintain the nominal limit, authorities and operating commissions "in but not of" cabinet departments proliferated— formally assigned to departments but operating virtually autonomously. Thus, for example, the Hackensack Meadowlands Development Commission, which regulates development in 14 municipalities in two counties, is "in but not of" the Department of Community Affairs. The 500 appointments to boards and commissions that NIPA decried in 1929 are about the same number as today.

The complex bureaucracy of the 1990s differs sharply from that of the 1930s however. The governor now appoints and removes almost all top officers at will, and almost all leave office when the governor does. It is now the governor who controls the 500 patronage appointments to boards and commissions, rather than legislators or county party officials. Although the senate must confirm many gubernatorial appointments, rejection is virtually unheard–of.[8] Obstacles to executive leadership are now logistical and political, rather than statutory.

Still, the career employees just below the top layer of gubernatorial appointments, who actually run agencies, have considerable resources. These "be– heres" ("when this governor and his appointees are gone, we'll still be here") command civil–service protection, technical expertise, and the agency's institutional memory.[9] State government is so vast that a thin layer of political appointees can never entirely master the larger departments.

Moreover, career managers' knowledge, close relationships with clientele groups, and their own short tenure tempt political appointees to "marry the

natives"—to join subordinates in opposing gubernatorial programs with negative effects on the agency. The tension between control and cooperation, as the
governor and cabinet officers strive to lead the state's permanent government,
is a major theme of this chapter.[10]

STATE BUREAUCRACY: SIZE AND STRUCTURE

To begin with the basics, it is difficult to provide a deceptively simple figure—
how many workers the state employs. In 1992, the authorized work force
in cabinet agencies was about 67,500. Adding employees of the judicial branch,
the legislature, commissions, authorities, and the state college system—most
of whom also take home state paychecks—increases the number to around
110,000. To complicate matters, thousands of these employees are paid
with pass–through funds from the federal government, counties, and other
non–Trenton sources. All that is certain is that New Jersey has about five
times as many state workers as it did in 1950, and about 85 percent of them
are career employees.[11]

Despite this growth, the home–rule culture is still apparent. In comparative
terms, New Jersey government is not large. The work force is the seventh
smallest among American states. State employees make up only a quarter of
combined state and local employment, third lowest in the nation. There is some
trend toward centralization. In 1967, New Jersey had only 65 state employees
per 10,000 population, which was the lowest ratio in the country.[12]

Compared to other states, New Jersey assigns proportionally more employees to regulation, control, and oversight (ranking sixth highest) than it does to
providing services.[13] It ranks eleventh in the number of corrections employees,
twenty–fourth in those employed in higher education, and thirty–second in those
engaged in managing natural resources. Some of the disparity stems from public
clamor for regulation—of the insurance industry, the environment, and legalized gambling, for example. Still, the bureaucracy has historically been "mired
in its own red tape, devoting enormous time and energy to internal paper
shuffling rather than to actual delivery of services."[14]

Departments of State Government

New Jersey currently has nineteen cabinet departments. Table 14 shows their
dates of creation or most recent major functional reorganization and their
number of employees when Governor Jim Florio took office in 1990.

Only five of the nineteen departments—Agriculture, Treasury, Law and

Table 14: Cabinet Departments of New Jersey State Government

Department	Date of Creation or Reorganization	Employees November, 1990
Agriculture	1948	218
Banking	1970	142
Commerce and Economic Development	1987	353
Community Affairs	1966	1,057
Corrections	1976	10,010
Education	1967	1,278
Environmental Protection	1970	3,631
Health	1948	1,693
Higher Education	1967	313
Human Services	1976	22,086
Insurance	1970	445
Labor	1981	3,850
Law and Public Safety	1948	9,199
Military and Veterans Affairs	1987	1,422
Personnel	1986	474
Public Advocate	1974	1,036
State	1948	474
Transportation	1966	5,339
Treasury	1948	5,946

Source: New Jersey Office of Management and Budget, November, 1990.

Public Safety, Health, and State—remain as they were created in 1948. These departments perform essential state government functions.

Eleven of the remaining fourteen departments have been collapsed, spun off, or reorganized—sometimes repeatedly—since 1948. Four (Banking, Commerce and Economic Development, Insurance, and Labor) cover areas once part of a single Department of Labor and Industry. Commerce and Economic Development, created in 1981, absorbed the now defunct Department of Energy in 1987, which itself existed for only a decade. All four regulate or promote economic enterprise—a growing concern in all states.[15]

The Departments of Education and Higher Education were separated in the 1960s when increased state–tax revenue gave Trenton a greater role in education finance and policy–making. Corrections and Human Services are two of the largest departments. They were created by a breakup of the original Department of Institutions and Agencies.

The remaining three departments in this group—Military and Veterans'

Affairs, Personnel, and Transportation—have been renamed and reorganized to reflect new emphases or missions. The old Defense Department was renamed Military and Veterans' Affairs in 1987 when veterans' offices in other agencies were transferred there. The old Civil Service Department was restyled as Personnel in 1986, when some hiring and management functions were transferred to individual departments. Transportation grew out of the old Highway Department; the new name reflected growing state responsibilities for mass transit.

Only three departments represent genuinely new cabinet–level areas of state activity. The oldest, the Department of Community Affairs, was established to manage programs for local communities and clientele groups spawned by the War on Poverty in the 1960s. As these initiatives lost favor in Washington, New Jersey continued many as state programs.[16]

The Department of the Public Advocate, created in 1974 in the midst of the Watergate reform climate, is unique to New Jersey. Its largest component is the Office of the Public Defender, a conventional state function, but more innovative offices include the Divisions of Public Interest Advocacy, Citizen Complaints and Dispute Settlement, Rate Counsel, Mental Health Advocacy, and Advocacy for the Developmentally Disabled. They represent the public at regulatory hearings and regularly sue other cabinet departments on behalf of the poor, the disabled, and prisoners.[17]

Finally, the Department of Environmental Protection, created in 1970, expresses the state's resolve to deal aggressively with harmful aspects of its industrial past.

Reorganization Schemes: Panacea or Placebo?

Every New Jersey governor since the 1960s has rearranged some of the cabinet departments, seeking stronger executive direction of policy.[18] Democrat Richard Hughes (1962–70) saw an expansive role for government. He created the Departments of Higher Education and Community Affairs and reorganized the old Highway Department into the broader Department of Transportation. A decade later, another Democrat, Brendan Byrne, focused on better management of health and welfare services. He broke up the huge Department of Institutions and Agencies, separating it into Human Services and Corrections. Byrne created the Department of the Public Advocate because of concerns he developed about public representation when he served on the Board of Public Utilities in the 1960s.

Republican governors have tended to reorganize agencies dealing with economic development and tried to introduce private–sector management techniques. This latter effort goes back to 1913, when Governor Walter Edge ran on the slogan of "A Business Man With a Business Plan." In 1970, in the Edge spirit, Governor William Cahill appointed a blue–ribbon Government Management Commission led by a vice–president of the Prudential Insurance Company. It suggested ways to save $80 million through administrative orders and consolidation of the 17 existing cabinet departments into six superagencies. The legislature declined to pass this plan, and Cahill instead increased the number of cabinet offices. He separated the Banking and Insurance departments, and inaugurated the Department of Environmental Protection.

When Tom Kean became governor in January 1982, he launched the most ambitious of the Republican management studies—the Governor's Management Improvement Program, known familiarly as GMIP. GMIP was headed by executives from AT&T, Johnson and Johnson, and First National State Bancorporation. They raised $2.6 million from New Jersey's business community to fund the project and recruited 250 executive volunteers to help run it.

Most GMIP funds went to a business consulting firm, which compiled detailed information about departments and agencies. Computerized "house plots" were produced for each unit, charting organizational structure, cost per worker and manager, and ratio of managers to workers. At the same time, volunteer executives, paired with department career personnel selected by the governor's commissioners, did extensive interviewing and brainstorming in the departments. The GMIP team submitted its findings and recommendations in late 1983.

Opinions vary about GMIP's success in cutting government spending and introducing increased efficiency.[19] Official reports document modest reductions in management–worker ratios, some intradepartment reorganization, and user–fee increases. The governor's office claimed the program saved $102 million in the ensuing 1984 fiscal year. Independent analyses ascribe some of the "savings" to reduced inflation and debatable budget–projection techniques.[20] GMIP, however, is given more credit for other outcomes. It produced a strategy for increased gubernatorial control of programs—through a new budget process and better data management and information systems.

Before GMIP, division and bureau managers made budget recommendations to department heads, who transmitted them to the governor. Traditionally, requests would range 10 to 15 percent above the pool of available money. Working with the Treasury Department's Bureau of the Budget, the governor would balance the budget, as required by the state constitution.

Under the new process, an Office of Management and Budget in the Treasury Department and the director of Management and Planning in the governor's office work together to set mandatory budget targets for all agencies. The

OMB's Office of Telecommunication and Information Services (OTIS) consolidates all data collection and analyses in the budget agency. Previous budget powers had looked impressive on paper, but the governor had "never had the staff, the administrative apparatus, to exercise that power within the bureaucracy. The creation of the OMB gives him the potential to probe the operation of the departments."[21]

Kean's successor, Democrat Jim Florio, proposed substantial reorganization to create "a smaller and smarter" state government. He called for consolidation of the Banking, Insurance, and Commerce departments into a new Department of Regulated Commerce. The Personnel Department was to be absorbed into the Treasury Department, and the Board of Public Utilities was to become part of a broadened Department of Environmental Protection and Energy (DEPE).

Massive budget deficits resulting from economic recession were another factor in Florio's thinking. The plan to reduce the cabinet departments to 16 also envisioned an 8,000–person reduction in the state work force. The legislature reacted coolly. Florio achieved only the absorption of the Board of Public Utilities into the DEPE, which could be accomplished by executive order rather than statute.

Despite frequent reorganization, the size and complexity of cabinet departments still work against executive control. Judith Yaskin, Florio's first Environmental Protection commissioner, learned that monitoring only one large industrial plant's dealings with her department required going through three assistant commissioners, eight program offices, and dozens of computers. It was well known in Trenton that hostile subordinates, resentful of Yaskin's close supervision, "retaliated" by sending her encyclopedic amounts of information she could not possibly absorb.[22]

Administrative chaos and poor morale in her department drove Yaskin out of office within a year. The Kean administration also suffered a major embarrassment demonstrating the limits of gubernatorial monitoring. It took place in the sprawling Department of Human Services (DHS) during his second term.

One of DHS's most difficult tasks is placing the developmentally disabled in community care facilities, overseen by its Division of Developmental Disabilities. After being sued by the public advocate, the division acknowledged clients' constitutional right to such placement and pledged that waiting lists would be erased by July 1987. When the deadline arrived, there was still an official waiting list of 1,800 and 1,500 more who were ready to leave state institutions.

The following year, it was discovered that Eddie Moore, the career head of the division, had "resolved" the waiting list problem by overspending his budget for community care by at least $21.5 million. Moore knew the paper forms used to submit data on over 1,000 contract accounts were not compatible with either department or OMB computer systems. He also knew that the commissioner routinely covered division deficits at the end of the year with accounting transfers or fiscal year rollovers.

When Moore's overspending was discovered, the OMB budget operations manager explained, "The volume of information on that form made it hard to decipher, and it's not automated." The state auditor noted that no one seemed aware of postaudits of the division from 1983 to 1986 that showed problems in its accounts.[23] A frequent legislative critic of the department (who got himself hired as an attendant at a state mental institution using the name and address of a convicted sex offender and the social security number of another felon convicted of armed robbery and drug violations), observed, "DHS may very well be unmanageable. It is just too big and too vast to really have a handle on it. It's a cabinet position, but you never hear of political leaders who are going to kill to get that job."[24]

Although an extreme example, the DHS fiasco demonstrates that despite reorganization schemes and elaborate monitoring systems, management problems can still become crises requiring political solutions.

THE POLITICS OF THE BUREAUCRACY

Bureaucratic functioning depends ultimately on political processes. They include the governor's relationship with political appointees, the appointees' relationships with career officials, and the role of clientele groups.

Selection of Cabinet Officers

An appointed official heads each of New Jersey's cabinet departments. Almost all are nominated by the governor and confirmed by the state senate.[25] Some departments are traditionally led by policy experts, others by politicians, and some by persons from a variety of backgrounds.

Policy professionals always head the Departments of Education, Higher Education, Corrections, Health, Military and Veterans' Affairs, Banking, and the Public Advocate. New governors sometimes continue expert incumbents in office. The current corrections commissioner has led the prison system since 1973, after serving as superintendent of the largest penal institution. First nominated by Governor Cahill, he has been reappointed by three succeeding governors. Between its founding in 1967 and 1990, two higher education chancellors served four different governors of both parties.

Other departments in this group change leadership when a new governor arrives, but their commissioners are seldom political activists. Since the public advocate's post was established, for example, all its occupants have been members of prominent minority groups (two African Americans and three Hispanics) with prior careers in public–service law or legal education.

At the other end of the spectrum are the heads of the Departments of Law and Public Safety, Community Affairs, Labor, and State. Their leaders are the governor's political associates, representatives of department clientele groups, or both. Until the 1970s, the attorney general and the secretary of state were the executive's chief political agents, coordinating relations with the legislature and dispensing patronage.

With the development of the counsel and chief of staff roles in the governor's office, the Department of State's political role became diminished. However in 1992, Governor Florio appointed a longtime political ally to the post, whose job was defined once again as "chief political operative."[26] The attorney general has lately devoted more attention to administering the vast Department of Law and Public Safety. An expensive professionalization of its Division of Motor Vehicles, which was until the mid–1980s "the state's last great monument to the political patronage days of old," symbolizes the attorney general's changing role.[27]

Career politicians are most regularly found at the Department of Community Affairs, which dispenses money and advice to localities. When Governor Hughes created the DCA in the days of the Great Society, he nominated noted social scientist Paul Ylvisaker as its first commissioner, but this did not begin a tradition. Governor Cahill appointed the Republican mayors of Maplewood and Paterson to head the agency. Governor Byrne elevated the Democratic mayor of New Brunswick. Governor Kean chose first the Essex County Republican chair and last a seven–term Republican assemblyman. Between them was the only echo of Commissioner Ylvisaker, a black Republican with a graduate degree from Harvard's Kennedy School. Governor Florio's first appointment was the Democratic mayor of Camden; his second, a black assemblywoman from Essex County.

Departments where commissioners shift back and forth between politicians and professionals—notably Labor, Insurance, Transportation, Treasury, and Environmental Protection—handle issues that are technically complex but politically potent. Governors place at their head technical experts with strong political skills or skilled politicians who can control the department's career technical experts.

Environmental Protection Commissioner Christopher Daggett, for example, had earlier been federal EPA commissioner for New York and New Jersey but also Governor Kean's cabinet secretary and deputy chief of staff. While Kean's first treasurer was a professional economist and nominal Democrat, Governors Byrne and Florio appointed their campaign managers (a former professor of public policy and an attorney, respectively) to head this department. Labor commissioners come from the state's union leadership in Democratic administrations, while Republicans appoint political supporters or business executives with personnel backgrounds.

The governor's party and own political style influence the balance of career professionals and politicians in each administration. Commissioners with political backgrounds are more numerous in Democratic administrations. This difference is partly due to Republicans' stronger links to the business community but also to the Democrats' recent dominance of the governor's office and the large county governments. Democrats held the governorship 70 percent of the time between 1953 and 1993. Thus, when a new Democratic governor arrives, many Trenton veterans are available.

When Republican Tom Kean became chief executive in 1982, there had been only one other GOP governor in the prior three decades. Thus there was no large pool of experienced statehouse hands at the ready. An election recount did not confirm his victory until the end of November—barely six weeks before he would assume office. Kean had also promised to base major appointments on merit alone.

Kean's solution was to employ an executive search firm to seek out talented cabinet officers. It screened candidates and recommended finalists to his transition team, which forwarded names to the governor. The first commissioners of Health, Insurance, Education, Environmental Protection, Commerce and Economic Development, and the state treasurer all emerged from this process. They were professionals the governor had not known personally.

The procedure had mixed results, producing some of the administration's finest commissioners and others who departed rapidly. A key variable was the commissioners' political skills or lack thereof. Some business leaders in the Kean administration, as in others, had trouble learning "that the frustrating circumstances with which they must contend—lack of formal authority, meddling by legislators, pressure from interest groups—are features of the duly constituted political order."[28]

The Democratic governors who preceded and followed Kean used different strategies. His predecessor, Brendan Byrne, drew heavily on a talent pool from the Hughes and Meyner administrations, in which he had served himself. Among these veterans were his first appointments as treasurer, attorney general, labor commissioner, chancellor of higher education and public advocate. With polls showing Byrne on the way to a landslide victory, the administration could make a quick start. As his treasurer (and campaign manager) Richard Leone commented, "We had the advantage of a few people who knew exactly what they were going to do 24 hours after the election."[29]

Florio enjoyed somewhat similar conditions in 1990. His first commissioners of Environmental Protection and Human Services had also served in the Byrne administration, and Richard Leone resurfaced as commission chair of the Port Authority of New York and New Jersey. Although Florio asked an executive search firm for pro bono aid in finding some commissioners (in contrast to Kean, who used much of his transition budget for this purpose), he relied more on his own team's contacts with professional networks to find cabinet members with appropriate expertise.

The Democrats' larger pool of experienced people does not necessarily produce better cabinet officers or a more smoothly functioning executive team. When Kean appointees from the nonpolitical world did not work out, the "businesslike" atmosphere permitted quiet departures. Some of Byrne's "political" appointees, with independent power bases and finely honed skills at bureaucratic infighting, were more difficult to remove. Byrne's own lack of political acumen contributed to the difficulties.

It was widely reported, for example, that former New Brunswick Mayor Patricia Sheehan refused to resign from the Department of Community Affairs and successfully mobilized mayors and other Democratic activists on her behalf.[30] In another instance, Governor Byrne dispatched someone from the governor's office to act as deputy commissioner in another agency in which the leader was uncooperative. The governor's operative reported the results: "The governor said, 'go over and be deputy commissioner for six months.' Well, I arrived, and the night before, [the commissioner] took the [deputy commissioner's] office and cut it in half, put up a wall literally, so the size of the office I was going into was half of what [his predecessor] had....the message was clear. I had only spent three days there when I fully realized that I was going to be less valuable to the governor enmeshed in the bureaucracy than I could be with some independence back in the governor's office, and I called and begged to get back."[31] Thus, whatever the process used to select cabinet officers, their political skills and style and that of the governor are critical in determining their effectiveness.

The Role of Politics and Clientele Groups

Politics influences many other important decisions about the bureaucracy, as evidenced by a variety of events in the Kean governorship of the 1980s. Kean did elevate merit over patronage in some important appointments. He surprised many by naming Democratic economist Kenneth Biederman as his first state treasurer. (One of the most surprised was the Republican senator representing the treasurer's home county, who learned of it in the newspapers). Biederman, identified by Kean's executive recruiters, chose his own subordinates: "The governor made it very clear up front that's what he wanted....resumes would find their way to the circular file real quick. I never once got a call from the governor."[32]

On the other hand, Kean ignored advice to dismantle or reorganize the patronage-heavy Departments of State and Community Affairs. As a member of his transition team said, "Democrats have enjoyed that patronage a quarter of a century. Let's use it before thinking about doing away with it later."[33] "Later" never came, because, as Kean's first chief of staff, Lewis Thurston, observed, all administrations must "find a place to bury your most loyal but least talented supporters....They don't have much talent but they have a lot of persistence."[34]

If dislodging a single official is difficult, dismantling an entire department would seem impossible. Kean did, however, manage to eliminate the Department of Energy in 1987. His success, when contrasted with Brendan Byrne's failure a decade earlier to abolish the Department of Community Affairs, yields instructive lessons about the role of clientele groups in bureaucratic politics.

Byrne established the Department of Energy—an agency similar to the federal cabinet department created in response to the rise of the OPEC oil cartel—late in his first term. Its mission was "perceived as unnecessary by many people and as boring by most."[35] The department's chief promoter, however, was an important state senator from Byrne's home county of Essex, who was critical to the governor's difficult campaign for a second-term nomination. That, along with federal subsidies for most of the department's costs, persuaded Byrne to endorse its creation.

A decade later, weak leaders had still not defined a mission for the department. Rationing was gone, and the prime energy concern was its effect on the business climate. New Jersey's energy prices were the eighth highest in the nation, trailing only the New England states. The department was perceived as "doing little or nothing at all. At the same time, it has incurred the wrath of the utilities and the segments of the business community it has attempted to regulate."[36] At Kean's suggestion, its functions were absorbed by the Board of Public Utilities and the Department of Commerce and Economic Development, whose mission and clientele guaranteed that regulations would be scrutinized for their economic impact. Few mourned its passing. As the Democratic assembly speaker said of Energy, "The department doesn't have a constituency."[37]

Quite the opposite was true when Governor Byrne, citing an end to federal funding for many of its programs, sought abolition of the Department of Community Affairs in January 1976.[38] Local officials and legislators protested vociferously. Despite large majorities in both houses, Byrne could not find a legislator to sponsor his initiative. He withdrew the proposal and transferred the key Division of Local Government Services to the Treasury Department by executive order. Overturning an executive order requires a two–thirds vote in each house of the legislature. Despite the Democrats' dominance, the assembly easily mustered the votes, and Byrne was forced to concede failure.

Byrne's inability to eliminate or weaken DCA and Kean's success in abolishing Energy are especially surprising because Byrne's Democratic colleagues controlled the legislature, which had to pass the reorganization plan, while Republican Kean had Democrats in charge in the senate and the narrowest of Republican majorities in the assembly. The explanation lies in the difference in the departments' clienteles.

Business interests most affected by the Energy Department were hostile to its basic mission. In contrast, Community Affairs "comes closer to being all things to all people than any other department of state government."[39] It dispenses technical assistance to municipalities preparing their budgets or writing grant proposals, disburses funds to pay for police and firefighters, and underwrites public–works projects benefiting bankers and developers. DCA's supportive clientele has all the hallmarks of a strong constituency base—it is large, geographically dispersed, prestigious, committed, knowledgeable, and well–organized.[40]

The "Other Governments": Authorities and Commissions

Although the number of cabinet departments has remained at or below the constitutionally mandated limit, there are still numerous boards, commissions, and authorities—many buried "in but not of" cabinet departments. In 1990, there were at least 21 operating commissions, 35 temporary commissions established by the governor or the legislature, and 29 "authorities, compacts and other special purpose agencies."[41]

The commissions and authorities may be divided into permanent multistate agencies (such as the Port Authority of New York and New Jersey), temporary bodies that satisfy clientele groups (such as the Holocaust Victims Memorial Commission, the New Sweden Commemorative Commission, or the Martin

Luther King, Jr. Commemorative Commission), and those that manage large state enterprises (such as the New Jersey Sports and Exposition Authority, the New Jersey Transit Authority, or the New Jersey Highway Authority). We will concentrate here on the last group. (Multistate authorities are addressed in chapter 12). Of the clientele–based groups, it only bears mention that governors and legislatures have seen fit to increase their number greatly since 1980.

The important authorities and commissions present an interesting paradox. On one hand, their functions and funding are insulated from the vagaries of politics because most issue their own bonds and do not have to depend on tax revenue and legislative appropriations.[42] On the other hand, they are accused of being unaccountable empires and patronage dens. To monitor authorities better, Governor Kean established an Authorities Unit in his office. More gubernatorial intervention in "independent" authorities' operations, however, can create its own problems. A good example involves the New Jersey Highway Authority, which manages the Garden State Parkway.

The problems arose when the Highway Authority began considering large parkway toll hikes. Unlike travelers on the state's other major toll road—the New Jersey Turnpike—Parkway patrons are mainly in–state commuters rather than through–state travelers. These toll hikes had special political significance because they would occur in 1987—an election year when the Republicans' tenuous control of the assembly was at stake. Some of the state's most competitive legislative districts—in Monmouth and Ocean Counties—contained large numbers of parkway commuters.

Although the authority began its discussions in mid–1986, the decision to double tolls was not announced until two weeks after the November 1987 legislative elections. A predictable public outcry followed. Governor Kean expressed outrage at the size of the increase. He noted the state treasurer's criticism of the authority's financial management and using his power to veto authority minutes, rescinded the toll increase. He also replaced the authority's chairman and made the state transportation commissioner an ex–officio member of the Parkway and Turnpike authorities for the first time.

There matters might have remained if a highway authority commissioner was not upset about other happenings at the authority. Commissioner Julian Robinson, a black Hudson County Democrat, was first appointed to the authority in the 1970s by Governor Byrne. Kean reappointed Robinson, who headed "Hudson County Democrats for Kean" in 1985.

Robinson was unhappy with the authority's record on affirmative–action hiring. None of the well–paid political appointees, consultants, or bond–house employees were members of minority groups. Robinson also knew the authority pressured a consultant to provide dubious traffic projections to buttress the request for the toll hike. He observed that media consultant Roger Ailes's firm, which produced the ads for Kean's 1985 campaign, was paid $49,000 for advice on how to announce the toll increases.

In November 1987, Robinson, whose commission term expired immediately after the 1989 gubernatorial elections, hosted a fund–raiser for Democratic gubernatorial candidate Jim Florio. In March 1988, after Kean indignantly vetoed the toll hike, Robinson went public. His most damaging accusation was that Kean had been present when the Authorities Unit director (whose prior jobs had been in Republican campaigns) decreed that the hike not be announced until "after November"—that is, after the legislative elections. "All of us in that room, being political people," Robinson recalled, "knew he was not talking about Thanksgiving."[43]

Investigations by the public advocate and a legislative commission followed. The public advocate found the authority had violated the Open Public Meetings Act and had "decidedly unconventional accounting procedures."[44] The legislative commission's report, unanimously endorsed by its bipartisan membership, confirmed Robinson's account. The Democratic chair of the legislative commission reported, "The Governor's fingerprints are on everything. This authority is clearly not an independent authority. This is an authority being run out of the Governor's office. Many decisions remained totally within his control, and at times, political motives were the primary agenda."[45]

The governor not unreasonably saw some "political motives" in the release of the report a month before the 1989 legislative elections, calling it "a political document" that was "not worthy of comment." He pinpointed the crux of the problem: "Some people said I had too much oversight, some people said I had not enough." Kean's transportation commissioner commented cryptically that Julian Robinson had "focused everybody's attention on how independent the independent authorities are."[46]

When Governor Florio assumed office in 1990, he moved decisively to gain control over the authorities. He quickly forced the resignations of the chairmen, executive directors, and several commissioners of the Turnpike and Parkway authorities. The transportation commissioner was given more power to coordinate the activities of the various transportation–related authorities. Florio also reappointed Julian Robinson to the Highway Authority. In a clear reference to the parkway toll imbroglio, Florio acknowledged giving up the "option of deniability," but said, "if something is going to come home to roost back here in my office....I will be happy to take the praises and the black eye....But I am not going to do that unless I have the ability to monitor."[47]

A year later, the issue of autonomy arose again. To balance the fiscal year 1992 budget, Florio proposed selling to the Turnpike Authority, for $400 million, state access roads to the turnpike. Bondholders questioned whether the funds, raised for turnpike expansion projects, could be so used, and the Standard and Poors' bond–rating survey lowered the state's prized AAA bonds a notch when the one–time revenue source was included in the budget. Debate about the place of authorities thus continues, but it is clear that New Jersey governors are now inclined, more or less forcefully, to bring them under greater control from Trenton.

A leading student of public authorities notes that they often reflect the politics of the areas in which they are located.[48] Although classic examples of old–style corruption occur more often now in some of New Jersey's county and local authorities, it is not surprising that the state transportation authorities are plagued with political problems. From its earliest days, transportation has been a major element of the state's economy, providing an enticing source of capital and too often, opportunities for questionable political activities.[49]

THE CAREER PERSONNEL SYSTEM

Toilers in the bowels of the bureaucracy rarely affect major state policies. Yet, it is possible for "the fourth level bureaucrat whose life depends on being able to shut down the War Memorial or whatever to come in and destroy everything that everybody else is trying to do."[50] Additionally, civil servants' pay and benefits are a significant portion of the state budget, swallowing up over a fifth of the general fund. For that reason alone, the career civil service deserves scrutiny.

New Jersey's civil service was long "among the most archaic systems in the country."[51] By 1987, there were more than 12,000 job classifications, some covering only a single person—more than triple the number 15 years earlier.[52] Until 1986, a Department of Civil Service administered the career employee system. Unreformed since the beginning of the century, it managed "to withstand virtually every onslaught."[53] The strongest veterans'-preference provision of any state moved veterans with a passing score on "merit" job exams to the top of appointment lists, ahead of nonveterans with higher scores. Some job descriptions were notoriously designed so that only political appointees first hired as noncareer "provisionals" could meet them. In 1987, about a sixth of the entire work force had been appointed or promoted provisionally.[54]

Over time, public employees negotiated increasingly favorable pension and benefit arrangements. State pensions became vested in 10 years, and a method of calculating pensions based on the five highest earning years was lowered to three. Annual pension COLAs were raised to 60 percent of the consumer price index. Retirees retained full health benefits, and the cost of their fully paid health insurance quintupled in two decades.[55]

The Kean administration's GMIP exercise, described earlier in this chapter, brought about the first major civil service reform act in 80 years, replacing the old Civil Service Commission with a Department of Personnel. The act was intended to: (1) make merit the sole basis for hiring, firing, and promotion; (2) give managers more authority to carry out program responsibilities; (3) enhance equal opportunity in state employment; and (4) guard against political coercion and protect employee bargaining rights.[56] A powerful clientele kept the absolute veterans' preference in place and unchanged. Despite expressions of concern in the GMIP study and Governor Kean's warnings about spiraling pension and benefit costs, they were not addressed.

The Senior Executive Service

One feature of the Civil Service Reform Act was creation of a Senior Executive Service. The SES was established to "enhance State government by fostering and developing a cadre of high–level potential managers and executives" and to provide "an appropriate avenue of mobility and influence for those who have demonstrated their dedication and ability in the Career Service."[57] It resembled similar programs in about a dozen other states and the federal government.

By the end of the Kean administration, the Senior Executive Service had 564 members averaging 17 years of government service and working in 12 of the 19 cabinet departments and the Board of Public Utilities. At least 85 percent had to be career personnel, and all were to have "substantial managerial, policy–influencing or policy–executing responsibilities."[58]

In return for higher base salaries, more vacation days, continuing education opportunities, and that greatest of perks—a reserved parking space—SES members had to agree to possible transfers and salary adjustments entirely dependent on annual merit evaluations.[59] Most members of the SES (85 percent) occupied "key positions" identified by department leaders and were "encouraged" to join the SES. Other positions were posted and their current occupants moved to regular civil–service jobs. A bipartisan Merit Systems Board had to approve each SES position, and the commissioner of personnel had to approve each nominee.

A review of the SES's first years by the Institute of Public Administration praised its quality, high level of enthusiastic acceptance, and freedom from political interference. The review warned, however, that future success would depend on keeping SES appointments unpoliticized, not breaking faith on employee rights, and using mobility to reward rather than punish.[60]

When Jim Florio took office in 1990, the SES was one of the first programs examined by the new Governor's Management Review Commission. State employee unions, hostile to "merit" schemes and facing layoffs due to budget shortfalls, charged the Senior Executive Service contained too many political appointees receiving inflated salaries and "unnecessary layers of management."[61]

The Management Review Commission found the number of SES unclassified employees to be well below the statutory limit and little evidence of salary inflation. However, it criticized a "departmental focus" that permitted each cabinet unit to determine its own participation level, implementation strategy, and positions to include in the SES. The commission concluded that while of value, the Senior Executive Service was "fragmented, decentralized, diffused and unstructured." Shortly thereafter, the administration removed 385 members from the SES. Reflecting Florio's greater preference for centralized control, the management commission recommended that SES serve as a mobile "SWAT team," guiding policy "in a manner consistent with the goals and objectives of the Administration, and with full loyalty to the Chief Executive and his key unclassified appointees."[62]

The SES addressed two civil service reform goals: enhancing the role of merit in career advancement and strengthening managerial personnel and processes. Significant progress was also made on a third goal—equal opportunity. Between 1982 and 1989, the number of minority employees increased from 26 percent to almost 32 percent of the state work force.[63]

From the viewpoint of public employees, the record on the fourth reform goal—removing apparent political preferences and protecting collective bargaining rights—is more mixed. The number of "provisionals," often patronage appointments, has dropped dramatically. The myriad job classifications—also alleged to have political implications—were reduced from over 12,000 to about 8,000 by mid–1989. A new Labor Advisory Board, meeting bimonthly, routinized communication between the personnel commissioner and union leaders.[64]

Yet there are still concerns. Rank and file and administrators alike find the mechanism for shrinking classifications and titles difficult and time–consuming. Employees fear downgrading and salary reductions. The moratorium on new titles is frustrating, as new programs requiring new skills come on line. Unions worry the Department of Personnel will become even more of a management tool than it was in the past. They also see conflicts between merit provisions and collective bargaining. The outcome of these issues remains to be seen.

As his second term drew to a close, Governor Kean reflected on his experience managing the vast executive branch. Kean had achieved the first meaningful civil service reform in a century. He had brought some oversight of independent authorities into the governor's office. The reformed budget process gave the governor unprecedented control of state policies and programs. But in pondering his jousts with the bureaucracy, Kean thought first of an anecdote about another chief executive: "There's a quote by Truman where he said, talking about the transition [from the Truman to Eisenhower presidencies] and the administration, 'Poor Ike—he's used to being in the Army where he said something and it got done. He's going to get into this office, and he's going to say something—and nobody's going to pay any attention to him!'"[65]

CHAPTER ELEVEN

The Courts

*If you want to see the old common law in all its picturesque formality,
with its fictions and its fads, its delays and uncertainties, the place to
look for them is not London, not in the Modern Gothic of the Law
Courts in the Strand, but in New Jersey. Dickens, or any other law–
reformer of a century ago, would feel more at home in Trenton than
in London.*

—D. W. Brogan, 1943[1]

*New Jersey's [judicial] system embodies a combination of the features
proposed as models....[They] have placed New Jersey in the vanguard of
the states.*

—Sheldon D. Elliott, 1959[2]

The 1947 constitution brought change to all of New Jersey's political
institutions, but especially to the courts. The popular phrase "Jersey Justice"
was a pithy description of the pre–1947 judicial system. It was a contemptuous
allusion to "the most complicated scheme of courts existing in any
English–speaking nation."[3] Based on a model Britain abandoned in
the nineteenth century, an archaic structure of separate law and equity courts
and a welter of inferior courts reflected the state's innate parochialism
and hostility to change.

Yet "Jersey Justice" also had a positive meaning. Politics infused
the judiciary as it did everything else, but a certain propriety obtained
when choosing high court judges. When making nominations, governors
followed a tradition of bipartisan balance. Even reformer Arthur Vanderbilt—
first chief justice under the new constitution and long–time opponent
of the Hudson County machine—admitted that county party organizations
lifted up talented jurists. Vanderbilt thought it wrong to foresee "a governor
and a senate appointing bad judges to the court of last resort" because "with
a very few exceptions over the last hundred years" this had not happened.[4]
Organizational deficiencies, not the caliber of the justice dispensed, were
the major impetus for the 1947 judicial reforms.

CHIEF JUSTICE VANDERBILT AND COURT REFORM

The new constitution's judicial clause called upon the new chief justice to implement massive reforms. The job fell to Arthur T. Vanderbilt—dean of the New York University Law School, long–time Essex County political leader, and nationally known court–reform scholar. Vanderbilt's ten years as chief justice left an indelible mark on the organization and administration of the courts.

The State Court System

Before 1947, New Jersey had separate law and equity courts; several county and state courts with overlapping roles; a misleadingly named "supreme court"; and a court of errors and appeals, to which cases from the supreme court and some other courts could be appealed. The court of errors and appeals had 16 members, including ten lay judges. A 1947 constitutional convention delegate described it as a "little larger than a jury, little less than a mob."[5]

The new constitution abolished the separate law and equity courts that required resort to the law courts and their adversarial process for assessing damages and to the equity courts for fact–finding, injunctions, and other court orders. Instead, it created a single three–tier court system, with equity and law divisions. The system was also reorganized functionally and geographically.

The superior court has jurisdiction over all matters originating in the state courts. Its law division handles all civil and criminal actions, including small claims cases assigned to the special civil part. The equity division deals with requests for injunctions, orders compelling performance of contracts, probate of contested estates, and family concerns (e.g., juvenile delinquency, domestic violence, adoptions, and divorces).

Superior court judges sit in 15 vicinages, headquartered in county court-houses. Eleven counties have separate vicinages. There are two multicounty vicinages in the south (Atlantic and Cape May; Gloucester, Cumberland, and Salem) and two in the west (Morris and Sussex; Somerset, Hunterdon, and Warren). In each vicinage, an assignment judge devises the calendar for all its judges. Judges generally hear cases of a single type (civil, criminal, or equity). Superior court cases are heard by a single judge, and only murder cases must have jury trials.

The appellate division of superior court sits in Hackensack, Newark, and Trenton. Two or three judge panels hear appeals of lower–court and adminis-trative-law decisions and publish written opinions. The appellate division may not overturn such decisions but may reduce sentences or damages. Appellate judges review procedures, jury instructions, and statutory interpretations.

Atop the system is the seven–member supreme court, sitting in Trenton. It is the only New Jersey court in which all of the member judges hear all of the cases. The high court only accepts cases with substantial constitutional questions, a dissent in an appellate court decision, or the imposition of a death sentence. At least three justices must agree to hear a case. Because of the court's strict interpretation of its jurisdiction, it hears fewer cases than most state supreme courts.[6]

The supreme court's procedures put a heavy burden on the appellate division of superior court, since each loser in the lower courts is permitted one appeal. In 1988–89, the appellate division disposed of 6,500 appeals and had 5,100 pending—21 percent of them for more than a year. Mandatory sentences for certain crimes, particularly drug–related offenses, which account for 40 percent of all sentences, are largely responsible for the backlog, which is even worse in the district courts. In 1988–89, superior court judges disposed of a record 46,000 cases, but there were 53,000 new cases—more than half of them drug–related. It was the third consecutive year that new cases exceeded the number resolved.[7]

Despite heavy use of pretrial intervention, plea bargaining, and experimental probation programs for nonviolent offenders, an ever–worsening backlog prompts repeated calls for more judges to cope with the burden. In 1987, the Essex County vicinage took an average of 307 days to dispose of a criminal case, while Wayne County, Michigan (Detroit), with similar crime problems and of similar size, took 71 days. A 1990 report by the National Center for State Courts called the Essex Court one of the slowest and least efficient in the nation.

In response to such criticism, Hudson and Essex Counties established special remand courts to hear criminal cases. They were among eight counties that saw the permanent transfer of 17 superior court judges from the civil to the criminal divisions. This further aggravated the civil case backlog, which in 1991 included over 70,000 cases on file for over a year—leading the Essex County assignment judge to threaten cancellation of all civil trials. The legislature then passed a bipartisan measure to fund 36 new superior court judgeships through increased court filing fees.

Compounding the crisis is a shortage of public defenders. New Jersey was the first state to guarantee a free legal defense to any indigent charged with a crime. Primarily because of the upsurge in drug–related arrests, the cases pending in the public defender's office increased by 50 percent between 1982 and 1990, without any additional resources to deal with them.

The state's 42 administrative law judges, who hear about 12,000 cases a year, sit in Newark and Trenton. They are housed in the Office of Administrative Law of the Department of State, but are "independent of any supervision or control by the department or any personnel thereof."[8] The Office of Administrative Law was established in 1978 to systematize the work of hearing examiners assigned to investigate complaints against state agencies. Administrative law judges make recommendations to agency heads, who can accept or reject them. A complainant dissatisfied with the final agency decision can appeal to the courts.

The only post–1947 blot on this simple organization was the general–purpose county court, a concession by the constitutional convention to powerful county political organizations. A 1978 constitutional amendment abolished the general–purpose county courts, and county juvenile and domestic relations courts were similarly terminated in 1983. These county courts were absorbed into superior court (hence its name, although there are no state courts below it).

Bearing most costs of the state court system has been the one vestige of the counties' judicial role and a constant source of friction between state court administrators and county governments. Disparate population size and crime rates produce an inequitable distribution among the counties of the $200 million annual cost of running the state courts. When Essex County filed suit in 1991 to force Trenton to assume all costs of the state court system, Essex taxpayers were subsidizing it at a rate more than twice that of Bergen County residents. In 1992, voters approved a constitutional amendment that will phase in the state's assumption of all court costs by July 1997.

Despite the pressures on it, simple and rational organization makes the court system a prototype for court reformers in other states. Aside from a tax court established in 1979 to hear appeals of property tax assessments, there are no special courts outside the basic system.[9] Most states have many more special courts.

Judicial Rulemaking and Administration

When Arthur Vanderbilt became the new system's first chief justice, he thought his administrative role was just as important as deciding cases. Vanderbilt established the first state Administrative Office of the Courts.[10] Its rules required that cases be decided within four weeks of submission. Vanderbilt personally kept track of the rate at which judges were clearing cases and rode herd on dilatory jurists. He personally admonished a judge who took a day off to drive his son to college and wrote another, "I am considerably concerned to note that you have five undecided cases, the oldest of which dates back to August 25th. There is no other county judge in the state who has a single undecided case back of September tenth."[11] His concern for speedy trials led him to advocate removing or even disbarring justices who falsified their weekly reports.

This efficiency campaign prompted Felix Frankfurter to describe the New Jersey chief justice as "a pompous martinet who treats his court as a factory where men punch clocks."[12] However, Vanderbilt's stringent rules addressed the defects of a system in which twenty years could pass before a case was settled. In the first year of the new system, the superior court law and chancery (equity) divisions doubled the average number of cases heard by each judge. The appellate court heard 70 percent more cases and the supreme court 50 percent more.[13]

Vanderbilt's spirit lives on; New Jersey remains the only state requiring judges to make weekly reports. Vanderbilt's three successors have given court administration varying degrees of attention, but Robert Wilentz, chief justice since 1979, is in the Vanderbilt mold. Like Vanderbilt, Wilentz is seen as a strong jurist and administrator but weaker at the "public relations" aspect of his job.

As in the Vanderbilt era, judges still complain about "menial tasks" such as filling out weekly reports, and timely disposition of cases is still a problem. In reviewing his first decade in office, Wilentz admitted, "on occasion, the things I asked [judges] to do were put to them in a command style that was inappropriate."[14] On becoming chief justice, he made speedy trials his first priority. The average resolution time for criminal cases of 12 months in 1981 was reduced to seven months by 1985, but the legislature's imposition of mandatory sentences for drug–related offenses threw the system back into disarray. Remand courts and more judgeships are Wilentz's latest efforts to achieve swift justice.

Thanks to Vanderbilt, in addition to their administrative powers, New Jersey's chief justices also have unusual control over the rules of judicial procedure.[15] The 1947 constitution appeared to divide this power between the chief jurist and the legislature when it stated, "The supreme court shall make rules governing the administration of all Courts in the State and, *subject to law, the practice and procedure in all such Courts*."[16] At the start of his tenure, Vanderbilt precipitated a constitutional crisis by testing the limits of statutory law on the courts' rules of conduct. The contest went on for almost a decade. It involved both constitutional law and politics, particularly the historic clash between the "moralist" forces Vanderbilt represented and their perennial antagonists in Hudson County and the rural counties.

Two weeks before the new constitution's judicial article was to take effect, the legislature passed a bill that limited the supreme court's right to make rules for other courts and permitted judges to continue private legal practice. Governor Driscoll vetoed the bill, as well as another measure recreating the equity courts. Soon thereafter, in a contentious opinion in *Winberry v. Salisbury*, the court asserted its right to determine time limits for filing appeals. The case became a symbol of the conflict between the judiciary and the legislature.

Winberry generated critical articles in seven law reviews, including those of Harvard, Rutgers, and Vanderbilt's own New York University. A bipartisan legislative coalition, led by Democratic state senator Robert Meyner of Warren County, threatened a constitutional amendment to reverse it. Politicians and legal scholars alike agreed that *Winberry* did violence to even the most expansive reading of the constitution.

The public, however, supported Vanderbilt, even if he did not have a legal leg to stand on. For them, it was not a question of legal niceties, but suspicion of the political forces—Hudson County and the rural Republicans—arrayed against him. Senator Meyner's proposed constitutional amendment died in committee, and he was defeated for reelection in 1951 when his opposition to Vanderbilt became a major issue.

The legislature abandoned attempts to control the court's procedural rules, but the underlying dispute soon flared anew. Meyner won the 1953 Democratic gubernatorial primary by 1,500 votes and went on to defeat Vanderbilt ally Paul Troast in the general election. Troast sued to overturn the results, based on irregularities in the Hudson County primary vote. A superior court judge threw out the case. On appeal, the supreme court decided six to one for Meyner, with Vanderbilt the lone dissenter. This "left the implication that [Vanderbilt's] motives were blatantly political."[17]

Governor Meyner renewed his conflict with the chief justice in 1955, when he insisted that the legislature had the constitutional power to determine rules of evidence. Vanderbilt appeared before the legislature to argue the contrary, saying his visit did not violate separation of powers because the legislature had invited him.[18] Although Vanderbilt contended that rules of evidence were procedural, the U.S. Supreme Court had treated them as matters of substance. The issue remained unsettled until Vanderbilt's sudden death in 1957. Meyner's appointment of his former counsel, Joseph Weintraub, as the new chief justice improved the court's relationship with the legislature. In a three–branch compromise, New Jersey became in 1960 the first state to adopt nationally proposed uniform rules of evidence.[19]

Death did not end the long debate about whether Vanderbilt was a "leader" or a "boss." Vanderbilt was devoted to the law and the advancement of the courts, but his behavior also reflected years of battle with Hudson County's Boss Hague when Vanderbilt was leader of the Essex County Republicans. Looking back, Governor Meyner observed, "I am sure he felt that the end justifies the means. Vanderbilt in the Winberry case was so fearful of legislative action that he was willing to distort the language of the constitution." A Vanderbilt biographer concluded he was "a moralist who used less than moralistic means to attain his goals."[20]

In any case, there is wide agreement that only Vanderbilt could have institutionalized the 1947 reforms, because other candidates were less than forceful personalities or outright opponents of reform. Twenty–five years after his death, a leading judicial scholar ranked New Jersey first among the states in judicial power over rulemaking and third in centralized management of the courts.[21] This is Arthur Vanderbilt's legacy.

NEW JERSEY JUDGES AND HOW THEY VIEW THEIR WORK

New Jersey's judges have long been noted for their high caliber and profession-alism. The new judicial system made these characteristics even more prominent. Under Vanderbilt's leadership and thereafter, the state supreme court also developed a reputation for activism and innovative decisions.

In part, this distinctive ethos results from the "moralistic" aspect of the state's political culture early finding its strongest expression in the courts. Under New Jersey's first constitution of 1776, the governor was chief magistrate, and the legislature gave this role to the state's most distinguished citizens. Even during the heyday of the party machines under the second constitution of 1844–1947, there was respect for the role of judges. The court has continued to "insulate itself from the prevailing political culture in the state and created a distinctive state legal culture."[22]

If history institutionalized the tradition of a high–quality judiciary, recent developments have advanced the newer tradition of activism. Since 1947, each of New Jersey's chief justices has previously served as an elected or appointed official, and none has disdained "the political thicket." As party organizations weakened and the legislature's power centers fragmented, the courts were increasingly called on to resolve difficult political issues. Further, as the legislature gained independence from the governor, both branches looked to the courts to resolve disputes between them.

Judges: Selection, Credentials, and Professionalism

All New Jersey judges must be members of the bar for at least ten years when named to the bench. All are nominated by the governor and confirmed by the senate. After a seven–year probationary period, judges reconfirmed by the senate receive tenure and may serve until mandatory retirement at age 70. The system is unusual in several respects. Only seven other states have no judges elected by the public or the legislature. In most states, judges undergo periodic review. Only Rhode Island grants life tenure initially; only Massachusetts and New Hampshire, in addition to New Jersey, grant tenure after a probationary period until age 70.[23]

Despite their diminished role, county party organizations are still active in naming judges. Vacancies in the lower courts are first identified as "belonging" to the Democrats or Republicans, in accord with bipartisan tradition. Informal negotiations among county party organizations, bar organizations, and local state senators produce names to submit to the governor, who may also have other candidates in mind. In this competition for judgeships, "rarely does the individual without 'connections' and without a record of partisan political activity do well."[24] Notwithstanding the politics involved in their selection (or perhaps because of it), judges are proud of a strong code of ethics, which they follow de facto as well as de jure. No sitting judge may teach in a law school, much less have a private practice. A survey of supreme court justices in four states found New Jersey's most likely to emphasize the importance of "proper judicial behavior."[25] In publicly reprimanding two superior court judges for accompanying politically active spouses to Governor Jim Florio's 1990 inaugural ball, Chief Justice Wilentz acknowledged many jurists' past political activity, but asserted, "that stops completely and without exception on becoming a judge....The prohibition is absolute."[26]

The court also takes seriously its policing of the state bar. In many states, disbarred lawyers are actually only suspended. Only in New Jersey and Ohio are they permanently prohibited from practice in the state. More than 200 New Jersey attorneys were disbarred during the 1980s. Only 3 of those expelled from the state bar in this century have won reinstatement—the last in the 1950s.[27]

Traditionally, "senatorial courtesy" allowed state senators to delay or kill judicial nominations, but using this custom for blatantly political reasons is now strongly condemned. Senator Gerald Cardinale's 1983 attempt to deny tenure to Judge Sylvia Pressler, before whom he had personally appeared (and lost) twice, was a watershed event. Chief Justice Wilentz held his first press conference to denounce Cardinale's action, calling it "the most important thing that has happened during my tenure."[28] The *New Jersey Law Journal* published an extraordinary front page editorial criticizing senatorial courtesy. The senate voted thirty–five to two to reconfirm Pressler, and Cardinale's previous victory margin of 11,000 votes fell to about 1,200 when he ran for reelection that year.[29]

Senators tried to preserve the concept of senatorial courtesy by saying it was inappropriate in the Pressler case because of Cardinale's conflict of interest. The issue arose again, however, when Chief Justice Wilentz came up for tenure in 1986. Republican Senator Peter Garibaldi, from Wilentz's home county of Middlesex, opposed reconfirmation—nominally because Wilentz did not actually live at his legal residence in Perth Amboy, but rather in an apartment in New York City. The chief justice explained that he was in New York to be with his wife, who was receiving advanced medical treatment there.

Some senators were clearly using the residence issue as an excuse to deny confirmation to a judge whose "liberal" and "activist" opinions they abhorred. Furthermore, to live in New York for any reason was political dynamite. Republican Governor Tom Kean, who gained respect for Democrat Wilentz when they served together in the legislature, and who renominated him, wrote of the furor, "beneath the patina of new [state] pride lay a two hundred–year–old case of insecurity. To have the chief justice live out of state was bad enough. But in Manhattan! To listen to some senators, one got the impression that it was grounds for impeachment."[30]

After Kean's last–minute intervention in the protracted battle, the senate reconfirmed Wilentz by the narrowest of margins, 21 to 19. Garibaldi was the only incumbent to suffer defeat in the 1987 elections. Observers concluded that using senatorial courtesy to block judicial confirmation might be "approaching extinction."[31]

Initial supreme court nominations are the choice of the governor, and recent governors have usually chosen trusted allies. Five of the seven current justices, appointed by three different chief executives, previously served in the governor's office, cabinet, or both. The two exceptions are notable. As an assemblyman in the late 1960s, Chief Justice Wilentz promoted strict conflict–of–interest regulation that forced his own departure from the legislature. The other exception is Marie Garibaldi, a former president of the state bar association who became New Jersey's first female justice when Governor Kean appointed her in 1982.

Each time governors have selected a new chief justice, they have passed over the sitting justices. Governor Driscoll chose Arthur Vanderbilt to head the reformed supreme court rather than the sitting chief justice or the chancellor of the court of errors and appeals. After Vanderbilt's death in 1957, Governor Meyner chose his counsel, Joseph Weintraub, to replace him. When Weintraub retired, Governor Cahill also named his counsel, Pierre Garvin, to head the court. Garvin died soon thereafter, and Republican Cahill amazed many by then nominating his gubernatorial predecessor, Democrat Richard Hughes. Hughes's retirement in 1979 led to Governor Byrne's nomination of Wilentz.

New Jersey's supreme court justices have less judicial experience than in many other states and are also less likely to have attended in–state law schools. Nationally, almost half of the state supreme court justices have had prior service on the bench, and about two–thirds are graduates of in–state law schools.[32] Of New Jersey's current justices, only one previously served on a state court, and all attended out–of–state "national" law schools.

THE TRADITION OF SUPREME COURT ACTIVISM

Outside observers and the justices themselves repeatedly describe the New Jersey Supreme Court as a leader among "activist" state courts. "Activism" has many guises. One is a reliance on state grounds to find new or expanded constitutional rights. Another is limited attention to precedent. Most fundamentally, an "activist" court involves itself heavily in public policy.

New Jersey's high court meets all these criteria. Its justices are much less likely than those of other states to say that precedent is important and are more likely to say that policy–making is a proper judicial function. The New Jersey court also more often has before it issues depending on state statutes. Arthur Vanderbilt was a devotee of "sociological jurisprudence" in the tradition of Oliver Wendell Holmes, Louis Brandeis, and Roscoe Pound. The court has always welcomed "Brandeis briefs," replete with social, economic, and political information. It makes strong efforts to reach unanimous decisions that will have particular force.[33]

In a 1965 decision, the justices observed, "The law should be based upon current concepts of what is right and just and the judiciary should be alert to the neverending need for keeping its common law principles abreast of the times."[34] In a 1975 case, they invited a defendant to argue that the state constitution provided more stringent limits on search and seizure than does the U.S Constitution, despite identical wording. The court asserted its "right to construe [the] state constitution in accordance with what we conceive to be its plain meaning."[35]

New Jersey's high court is often "unwilling to defer to the expertise or stature of the United States Supreme Court."[36] In a 1990 search–and–seizure decision contravening federal high court rulings on the right of police to search household trash, the five–to–two majority argued that the state constitution made privacy the "right most valued by civilized man." Therefore, "the equities so strongly favor protection of a person's privacy interest that we should apply our own standard rather than defer to the federal provision."[37] The same year, the justices offered similar language in a decision that smokers or their survivors could sue cigarette manufacturers for damages, despite numerous federal court rulings that cigarette label warnings bar such claims.

The New Jersey Supreme Court as Policymaker

Mary Cornelia Porter and G. Alan Tarr provide a useful list of the major categories of state supreme court policymaking. First, courts may be innovative by overturning or filling in gaps in state policy and imposing a specific policy. Second, they can set a policy agenda by upsetting traditional policies without specifying a new alternative. Third, their decisions may be complementary by aiding legislative policy goals or "taking the heat" for the legislature. Fourth, they may be elaborative by extending federal precedent. Alternatively, they can be restrictive by limiting or evading U.S. Supreme Court decisions. Finally, they can seek to advance the judicial institution by preserving the autonomy and integrity of the courts and seeking sufficient financial support for the court system.[38] The New Jersey Supreme Court has involved itself in all these activities.

Innovation. The high court has pioneered in setting state policy through judicial decisions, particularly when defining individual rights. Abortion rights in New Jersey are among the broadest in the nation, based on the right to privacy the justices find in the state constitution. They also find a right for poor women to public funding of therapeutic abortions. In *In re Quinlan* in 1976, the Court was the first to find passive euthanasia legally permissible for "*brain dead*" patients in a "persistent vegetative state" with no hope of recovery.[39] Quinlan was described as "undoubtedly one of the most activist [decisions] handed down by any court in the nation."[40] In the highly publicized *Baby M* case, the court issued the first major decision on the rights of surrogate mothers.

The New Jersey Supreme Court is not alone in its recent tendency to use state grounds in cases involving individual civil rights.[41] Since the advent of the Burger and Rehnquist U.S. Supreme Courts, more individual–rights cases turn up in state courts, in the hope of finding a more hospitable home in "the new judicial federalism."[42]

Agenda Setting. Two controversial policy arenas in which the court has heavily involved itself are school funding and land–use regulation. These interventions, which affect every municipality and many individuals and which challenge New Jersey's home–rule tradition, have brought the court to public attention. (We treat court involvement in these areas later in this chapter and again in chapters 15 and 16). In both arenas, the court's early decisions overturned traditional policies but left it to the legislature to devise new ones. Justices often try to "combine active participation in the determination of state policy with appropriate deference to the prerogatives of elected officials" and "mandate attention to pressing problems without foreclosing the exercise of discretion and political judgment."[43]

Complementary Decisions. When state courts make complementary decisions, they support other branches of government, particularly the legislature, in advancing policy goals or assist them by deflecting public criticism or buttressing controversial decisions. Many such cases involve liability law and consumer protection. In a study of the speed with which post–World War II state supreme courts adopted 14 tort law innovations through 1975, the New Jersey high court ranked first.[44] A 1960 landmark case dealing with implied warranties is often viewed as the "effective beginning of strict liability."[45]

The long struggle to reform New Jersey's troubled car–insurance system demonstrates how the court buttresses other public officials. When public furor over insurance rates reached a peak in late 1989, a coalition of activists managed to place a referendum on rate rollbacks on the ballot in all 21 counties. The court called the strategy unconstitutional and left auto–insurance reform to the governor and legislature about to be elected.

Upon taking office in early 1990, one of Governor Florio's first acts was to speed through the legislature yet another attempt to reform auto insurance. The insurance companies rebelled, and several announced they were leaving the state. Within weeks, the supreme court had upheld a superior court restraining order against one of the companies. It ordered the company to continue doing business in New Jersey until it came up with a plan, approved by the state insurance commissioner, for replacement coverage for its customers.

Elaborative and Restrictive Decisions. Elaborative and restrictive decisions involve deviations from U.S. Supreme Court decisions, most often in the field of criminal law—either to expand the rights of the accused or to limit or evade such rights. In contrast to its expansionary views in other areas, the New Jersey high court has a mixed record in this area. Despite enthusiasm for other expansionary decisions, Chief Justice Vanderbilt was a conservative on criminal law, and his successor, Joseph Weintraub, was sharply critical of the Warren Court's expansion of defendants' rights. The Weintraub court's consistent denial of motions to suppress evidence based on a claim of unreasonable search and seizure led lawyers to joke that in New Jersey, the Bill of Rights had one less amendment than in other jurisdictions.[46]

Weintraub's successors as chief justice did not make defendants' rights a priority, although the court has moved in a more liberal direction in recent years.

It relies more on common law than constitutional rights when it weighs the rights of criminals and has given full force to legislative decisions when it cannot find vital constitutional issues.[47] Of recent criminal law issues, the court's position on the death sentence has received the most public attention.

After outlawing the death penalty from 1963 to 1982, the court accepted a revised capital–punishment statute. However, through 1992, no state prisoner had yet lost or exhausted final appeals and actually been executed. After reversing or remanding for retrial 25 capital–murder convictions, in 1991 the court let stand the conviction of Robert Marshall, whose case was the subject of Joe McGinniss's best–seller, *Blind Faith*.[48]

Institutional Advancement. Beginning with Vanderbilt's long campaign to ensure the chief justice's control over judicial administration and procedures, the state supreme court has been active in protecting and advancing its own prerogatives.

Chief Justices Weintraub and Hughes maintained the system Vanderbilt established but were less interested in judicial administration. Wilentz, however, gives Vanderbilt–like attention to his administrative role. In 1990, Wilentz refused to permit motion picture filming at the Essex County Courthouse that depicted blacks rioting in a courtroom. The chief justice, backed by the state NAACP, said the scenes were offensive to African Americans and could undermine confidence in the justice system.

The Essex County executive and the American Civil Liberties Union sued Wilentz in federal court, accusing him of censorship. Underlying the dispute, however, was the right of the chief justice to control the use of county court buildings. When a U.S. district judge ruled that Wilentz's action was "offensive to the principles of the First Amendment" and "unconstitutional" and ordered the chief justice to pay the county's legal fees, the chief justice appealed the decision to the U.S. Circuit Court of Appeals. It ruled for Wilentz on the grounds that only the film company had standing to sue. Although it declined to address them directly, the court noted that the case had serious First Amendment implications.[49]

One of only 15 state chief justices who appoint the head of the Administrative Office of the Courts, Wilentz has overseen its expansion to a 300–person professional bureaucracy—about six times larger than the similar office in neighboring and more populous Pennsylvania.[50] Wilentz and the AOC also created the first task forces to consider how the courts deal with gender bias, minority concerns, and linguistic minorities. Many states followed New Jersey's lead.

Each year, the AOC also sponsors a state judicial conference on a major legal issue. Recent topics have included mandatory sentencing, speedy trials, dispute resolution, and municipal–court reform. Although chaired by the associate justices in rotation, the AOC staff organizes the meetings and prepares the background materials for the conference reports. In general, the chief justice depends heavily on the AOC and its executive director to administer the courts.

The chief justice has also been a crusader for higher judicial salaries and the creation of new judgeships. His persistent efforts bore fruit when the legislature raised Wilentz's own salary from $95,000 to $120,000 in 1991, granted equivalent raises to all other state judges, and finally provided funds to support a substantial number of new jurists.

In manifold ways, therefore, the New Jersey high court has not hesitated to involve itself in state policy–making. Its role, however, is even greater than this inventory suggests. When called upon, as it frequently is, to referee disputes between the branches of government, it also affects policy significantly. Further, despite disinclination to impose remedies in agenda–setting decisions, the court has not hesitated to do so when it perceives legislative irresolution or irresponsibility.

The New Jersey Supreme Court as Umpire and Referee

State supreme courts serve as umpires and referees when they resolve conflicts about separation of powers; disputes about day–to–day government operations; and issues of public policy, large and small.[51]

When disputes about the power of the governor as against the legislature reach the supreme court, its rulings are almost always in the governor's favor. In 1982, the justices unanimously upheld the governor's use of the line–item veto to delete or reduce legislative appropriations and to delete legislative language limiting executive latitude in spending appropriated funds.

Another unanimous decision in 1984 struck down the legislature's power to delay or nullify executive branch rules and regulations. The court asserted that a legislative veto interferes "with executive attempts to enforce the law. The chief function of executive agencies is to implement statutes through the adoption of coherent regulatory schemes. The legislative veto undermines performance of that duty."[52] (However in 1992, voters passed a constitutional amendment authorizing a legislative veto).

Even activist high courts are wary of offering specific remedies for policy problems. The extent to which the New Jersey court has become directive has depended on two factors: the ability of other branches of government to find solutions to difficult problems the court lays before them and the disposition of the court's members at a particular time. These influences are apparent in the most conspicuous problems the high court has faced repeatedly over the last two decades: school finance, land use, and zoning.

School Finance: The Robinson v. Cahill Decisions

New Jersey has always put unusual reliance on local property taxes to fund its public schools. Beginning with California's 1971 *Serrano* decision, many state courts have directed government officials to devise school funding plans providing greater fiscal equality across school districts with unequal property-tax resources. The issue first came to the New Jersey Supreme Court in 1973, in *Robinson v. Cahill*. At the time, several justices had reached or were nearing the end of their careers. Only three members of the Weintraub court, which served through the 1960s, were still sitting. By the fall of 1974, they would all be gone.

Weintraub's dealings with other officials were less stormy than those of his predecessor, Vanderbilt. Rather than direct confrontation, he preferred a three-pronged strategy. First, he thought it important to leave lawmakers wondering—and worrying—what the court would do next if they did not act. Second, he believed interim remedies should be distasteful enough to all parties to provide a strong incentive to act. Third, to encourage quick action, any remedy should also withhold government benefits from everyone affected.

Weintraub successfully employed this strategy to achieve a constitutionally acceptable legislative reapportionment plan in the late 1960s and early 1970s. By 1960, due to legislative deadlock, the assembly had not been reapportioned since 1941, and in the mid-1960s, U.S. Supreme Court decisions required even more politically painful redrawing of the senate as well. The court never specified detailed reapportionment plans, but rather used Weintraub's devices to compel politicians to come up with them.[53]

The strategy was clearly at work in the early *Robinson v. Cahill* rulings. The first two decisions, over which Weintraub presided, struck down the school-finance formula but offered no specific remedy. The court left every municipal government, taxpayer, and parent anxious for a solution. Shortly thereafter, however, both Governor Cahill and the chief justice departed the political scene, and the legislature was hopelessly divided. A huge Democratic majority was split between urban legislators seeking property tax relief and more state aid and suburban lawmakers whose constituents did not want to divert local funds to urban schools.

The new chief justice, former governor Richard Hughes, had the politician's bent for compromise and was willing to give the legislature more time to solve the problem. The new governor was, oddly, much less "political" than Hughes. Brendan Byrne was himself a former superior court jurist of activist bent (he had, for example, participated in declaring the death penalty unconstitutional). Byrne "viewed the legislature with contempt and the supreme court with esteem" and made an unprecedented appearance before the court to argue for "aggressive judicial action to resolve the legislative deadlock." The legislature was not happy with Hughes's tactics either. As one member observed, "This never would have happened under Vanderbilt or Weintraub...Weintraub would have told us what to do and we would have done it."[54]

For two years, legislative disarray kept the case before the court. With Hughes replacing the more imperious Weintraub, its vaunted unanimity began to fray. A five–to–two decision in May 1975 directed that $300 million in state aid to wealthy towns be redistributed to less wealthy ones; the two dissenters saw this as improperly aggressive action that still left root problems unresolved. In the next decision in January 1976, unity completely disintegrated. Two justices joined in a Hughes opinion, two wrote concurring opinions, one dissented, another joined except for one part of the decision, and the last joined only in that part.

In March 1976, after three years of school budgetary chaos, the assembly finally passed New Jersey's first income tax, but the senate refused to go along. In May, *Robinson v. Cahill* returned to the court for the seventh and last time. The court finally applied a Weintraub–like stratagem, ordering that no public funds be spent for education after July 1, 1976, without a constitutional funding scheme in place.

Although less draconian than shutting the schools down in September, the ruling immediately affected 100,000 students planning to attend summer school and many handicapped students in year–round programs. On July 9, the legislature passed an income–tax package and funding plan acceptable to the Court, and *Robinson v. Cahill* came to an end. But it was only an apparent end, for the plan still contained constitutional defects justices had previously criticized. Only a few years later, in 1981, what might be termed "the son of *Robinson v. Cahill*" began making its way through the judicial system.

The new case, *Abbott v. Burke*, brought against Education Commissioner Fred Burke on behalf of 20 students in Camden, East Orange, Irvington, and Jersey City, charged that the new formula still left those in poorer communities without equal protection of the law. The progress of *Abbott*, described in chapter 15, reveals the strategies of yet another set of justices and elected officials in dealing with the dilemmas posed by educational funding schemes.

Local Zoning: The Mount Laurel Decisions

Despite a few rhetorical threats to impeach all the justices or to amend the constitution to delete its "thorough and efficient" clause as a result of *Robinson v. Cahill*, "no one mounted an assiduous effort to take on the Court or reverse its direction." However, "If *Robinson*'s stand had stood explicitly to benefit...adults trapped in poverty, a legislative counterattack would have been more likely."[55] Public reaction to the court's next entry into the policy arena, in the cases collectively known as *Mount Laurel*, proved this prediction correct.

Mount Laurel I was decided by the Hughes Court in 1975, after three years in the lower courts. The local branch of the NAACP had sued the township of Mount Laurel, saying that its large–lot zoning ordinances restricted residential choice. Historically, New Jersey courts had stayed out of local zoning matters. In 1952, they sustained the right of wealthy Bedminster Township to zone 85 percent of its developable land in minimum five–acre lots.[56] When *Mount Laurel* came before the Hughes court, it was in the midst of the controversial school–funding cases, and the more activist firebrands of the Weintraub court had departed.

In a unanimous decision, the court supported the NAACP's contention that exclusionary zoning was unconstitutional. The decision became a topic of debate for legal scholars and was frequently cited by other courts.[57] Liberals praised it as a courageous step toward equal opportunity, while conservatives saw it as the worst kind of judicial social engineering. Its practical effect, however, was negligible. As in the early school–finance cases, the court offered no particular remedy or method of enforcing its decision. The legislature avoided the issue, and by the 1980s, *Mount Laurel I* had become a dead letter.

The plaintiffs pursued the matter, however, and in 1982, *Mount Laurel II* returned to the supreme court. The court majority now consisted of more aggressive judges appointed by Governor Byrne and led by Chief Justice Wilentz. This time, the court unanimously imposed a sweeping remedy. It ordered municipalities to change their zoning ordinances to permit construction of a specified number of low and moderate–income housing units.[58]

If municipalities refused to comply, a "builder's remedy" came into play. Developers would be allowed to exceed the density local zoning ordinances permitted if they included a specified proportion of low and middle–income units. It was widely believed that the court inserted this proviso to get the state's politically influential housing industry behind the push to open the suburbs. New Jersey builders were the largest single group of contributors to legislative campaigns.

As then–Governor Thomas Kean described it, "*Mount Laurel II* exploded in the state like a giant hand grenade."[59] An avalanche of lawsuits followed the decision. Deluged with complaints from constituents, the legislature threatened a constitutional amendment to remove the court's power to intervene in local zoning matters. Kean also entered the fray, saying the decision smacked of "judicial dictatorship" and "stomped on the toes of the executive and legislative branches of government."[60]

Lawmakers took more than two years to respond, but finally, in 1985, passed the Fair Housing Act. The act created a Council on Affordable Housing (COAH) to replace judicial oversight and also provided alternatives to the builder's remedy. Wealthier suburbs could "buy out" of half their affordable–housing obligation by subsidizing such units in any other municipality that would accept them.[61] The result was a rush by wealthier suburbs to finance construction in poorer areas.

In 1986, the supreme court decided *Hills Development Co. v. Township of Bernards* (often called *Mount Laurel III*), a case challenging the Fair Housing Act. The court unanimously declared the Fair Housing Act constitutional, and gave control of all pending cases to COAH.[62] In a later decision, "fully developed communities" were exempted from the obligation to provide or subsidize new low and middle–income units. *Mount Laurel III* seemed to reverse the court's earlier determination to "open up the suburbs." Those favoring *Mount Laurel II*'s sweeping mandate argued that transferring cases to COAH vitiated the effects of twelve years of pro bono legal work on behalf of the poor.

Although eventually backtracking from its position, the court's intrusion into actual "policy–making" was thus greater for a time in the zoning arena than it was in school funding. The personalities on the court at the time of each key decision and the actions of other branches of government seem to explain the action of the court. Significantly, however, in both instances, one of the nation's most activist state supreme courts acknowledged its policy–making limits and accepted legislative solutions difficult to reconcile fully with their reading of the constitution. *Robinson v. Cahill* thus inevitably spawned *Abbott v. Burke*; as we discuss in chapter 16, *Mount Laurel* cases also continue.

The supreme court's ventures into the political thicket bring it criticism from both ends of the political spectrum. When it shut down the schools in 1976, it drew the ire not only of local conservatives, but of syndicated columnist George Will. Will called the decision a classic example of how "progressives" and their "allies in the judiciary circumvent democratic processes."[63]

Others said that an unwilling court was forced to act because the governor and legislature had "ignored" the constitution's thorough and efficient mandate since 1875 and simply "passed the buck" to local governments. In the view of these critics, the court did not go far enough, and missed a golden opportunity to order a uniform, statewide school tax.

Similar arguments greeted the succession of zoning cases. One set of *Mount Laurel* III critics saw the decision as a sellout and a "blueprint for delay." At the other extreme, there were arguments that COAH incorporated too much court dicta about planning and land–use regulation, areas some believed should be left entirely to local and state governments.[64]

THE NEW JERSEY COURTS AND THE POLITICAL THICKET

The New Jersey judiciary is not partisan, but it is political, in the finest sense of that word. Justices with earlier political careers are unlikely to develop political amnesia, nor is the cast of characters there likely to change much for some time.

Only the justices hear their own deliberations or know their thoughts about politically potent cases. Was it mere chance that the court first chose to remand *Abbott v. Burke*—and give elected officials a lost opportunity to deal with the school–funding issue—at a time when the court was facing political attacks because of its involvement in local zoning decisions? Was it coincidental that *Mount Laurel III*, which seemed to contravene the same judges' *Mount Laurel II* decision, was decided just as Chief Justice Wilentz's tenure fate hung in the balance in the legislature? Was the timing of the *Abbott v. Burke* decision, expected for months, unrelated to the timing of the open–seat governor's race of 1989?

As the examples mount, it is difficult to ascribe them all to coincidence, rather than to essential qualities of today's "Jersey Justice." New Jersey's judges are respected for their integrity and professionalism. The state high court "has eagerly embraced opportunities to promulgate policy for the state and doctrine for the nation, confident of its own abilities and of the legitimacy of the activist posture it has adopted."[65] Today, however, as they did fifty years ago, New Jersey's courts still show many signs that they follow the election returns.

CHAPTER TWELVE

Government and Politics in Localities

New Jerseyans must love local governments; they created so many of them.
—Thomas M. O'Neill[1]

New Jersey is "a state governed by 567 municipalities," runs a famous aphorism. It has more local governments per square mile than any other state—more than Arizona, Delaware, Hawaii, Maryland, Nevada, New Mexico, Rhode Island, and Wyoming combined. Forty–sixth in size among the states, New Jersey ranks eleventh in total number of municipalities. Their average size is the smallest of any state. Governor Brendan Byrne once observed that "home rule is a religion in New Jersey," and a journalist has called it "as indigenous to New Jersey as the tomato, the Eastern Goldfinch and the Pine Barrens tree frog."[2]

Curiously, given New Jersey's homage to home rule, experts rank municipalities' control of their functions and personnel at about the national average and their control of local government structure and financial authority well below the national average. The executive director of the New Jersey League of Municipalities acknowledges "a strong legal and constitutional argument that there is no home rule" in New Jersey. In *Trenton v. New Jersey* in 1923, the U.S. Supreme Court ruled that "in the absence of state constitutional provisions safeguarding it to them, municipalities have no inherent right of self–government beyond legislative control." In 1971, the state supreme court, in *Ringlieb v. Parsippany–Troy Hills*, similarly found that "Municipalities have no powers other than those delegated to them by the Legislature and by the State Constitution."[3]

New Jersey's distinctive history accounts for the difference between de jure and de facto home rule. In the past, communities had few cultural or economic links. Reliance on the local property tax to finance public services reinforced localism. Weak state government offered no counterweight. However, three current trends move home rule toward rhetorical principle rather than actual practice: a new state pride and identity, a growing number of urgent problems that cross municipal boundaries, and recent broad–based state taxes producing increased state aid to localities and thus more state control.[4]

The role of the counties is also changing. Traditionally, county political organizations were extremely important, while county government was extremely unimportant. Simply to transpose those adjectives now would be too strong a statement. Yet, as county party organizations have subsided into relative impotence, county government has become more meaningful. Trenton has assigned the counties growing responsibility for regional policies, from transportation planning to solid–waste disposal to public higher education. This chapter looks at political change and continuity in New Jersey's localities.

MUNICIPALITIES

Municipal Development in New Jersey

By 1800, every inch of New Jersey was already in an incorporated place. The first township law, in 1798, authorized but did not require support of the poor, building and maintenance of roads and animal pounds, and determination of township boundaries. The early form of local government, as in New England, was the town meeting.[5]

North Jersey municipalities became satellites of New York City as soon as there was reliable transportation across the Hudson River. Before the introduction of the steamboat in 1813, the mile–long trip by sailing ferry between Manhattan and Paulus Hook (later Jersey City) could take as long as three hours. By the mid–19th century, New York's population growth brought separation of business and residential areas and the start of commuting. Every New Jersey population center was linked to New York (and Philadelphia) by railroad, canal, boat, or turnpike. By 1860, a million rail passengers traveled annually between Newark and Jersey City, where ferries conveyed them across the Hudson.

The industrial revolution created a demand for unskilled workers, and foreign immigrants flocked to the cities. In 1850, only 38 percent of Jersey City males were native–born; an equal number were Irish immigrants. By 1860, over a third of Newark's population was also foreign–born. It was the nation's eleventh largest city and its most industrialized, with 74 percent of the work force engaged in manufacturing. Industrialization also brought primitive sanitation, high accident rates, drunkenness, and crime. These problems were of little concern to urban and suburban elites and the rural leaders of the state legislature.

Newark's city fathers first hired municipal firefighters and police officers and funded some sidewalks and lighting in the 1850s. Descendants of

Newark's founding Puritans, they saw individual effort as God's work. This attitude, combined with the growing number of immigrants, paved the way for ethnic–based urban political machines and their bosses. Jersey City elected its first Irish–Catholic mayor in 1869. By the 1890s, many cities had Irish or German officials.

It was crucial to New Jersey's development, however, that the bulk of the population never lived in cities or developed empathy for them. Thirty percent of the state's residents dwelt in Newark, Jersey City, and Paterson in 1890, a high water mark never reached before or since. The wealth cities produce created bedroom suburbs like South Orange, Montclair, and Morristown and seaside resort towns such as Long Branch and Atlantic City.[6] By 1920, the suburban population was as large as the rural population and about half that of the major cities.

The outlying shore communities could ignore urban problems, but alarmed suburbs on city borders fought "to contain the trolley, the saloon and the tenement radiating out from Newark" during the "Greater Newark" movement of the 1890s.[7] Montclair required saloons to have expensive licenses and bonds. Well–to–do Republicans controlling Essex County won state legislation that mandated consent from 50 percent of all property owners along proposed trolley routes. They described such strategies with reformist catchphrases like "regional and county–wide planning."[8]

European immigrants and migrating southern blacks remained largely confined to older cities. Jersey City's black population had grown from 39,000 in 1880 to 69,000 in 1900, when a state report expressed shock at their living conditions— "one of the most vexing urban problems of the 1960s had become manifest by the turn of the century."[9]

Constitutional language and legislative politics bred large numbers of small municipalities. The 1844 constitution allowed for unrestricted, ad–hoc legislative charters of both businesses and municipalities. If legislative representation had been based on towns rather than counties—as in Connecticut, for example—proliferation might not have occurred. But since it was not, "the balkanization of local government had the political merit of increasing the number of offices and jobs" without disturbing the partisan balance in Trenton.[10]

In 1800, New Jersey had about 100 municipalities. Township fragments broke away to escape rising taxes or social problems, and Trenton granted incorporation to avoid having to provide public services itself. Municipal incorporations followed the business cycle, spiraling upward in the 1840s, 1890s, and 1920s, and essentially ending by the 1940s. So many small localities developed that while the state's population in 1967 was 26 times larger than it was in 1810, the average municipal population was only 2.5 times larger.[11]

The Rise of the Suburbs

New Jersey's cities never had a high noon, but they entered their twilight years in the mid–20th century. Each succeeding decade brought another blow to the cities. By the end of the 1920s, zoning and master plans protected suburbs from "infiltration" by low–income urban workers. By the late 1930s, three major highways whisked commuters out of New York City across the George Washington Bridge and into the Bergen County suburbs; three others led from the Lincoln Tunnel to the far reaches of Essex County. In the 1940s, construction began on the Garden State Parkway and the New Jersey Turnpike. In the 1950s, the federal highway program authorized three interstate highways. The state toll roads enabled rapid travel from north to south; the interstates from east to west. Until World War II, cars were mainly feeders to the commuter railroads. When the new highways came, industry and population dispersed in new patterns: "the off–ramp replaced the trolley stop and commuter station as the active node of suburbia."[12] Newark provided a fifth of all jobs in 1909 and paid a quarter of all wages but was reduced to less than 10 percent of both by 1939. As the economy grew, businesses moved to suburbs, which, unlike those in many other states, did not fall victim to urban annexation.

Suburbs became more than bedrooms for city workers. They grew around industrial plants (e.g., Ford Motor facilities in Edison and Mahwah; Squibb Pharmaceuticals in North Brunswick), research parks (CIBA–Geigy in Summit; Colgate in Piscataway), or shopping malls (first in Bergen County; later almost everywhere). Many workers now commute from homes in one fringe suburb to jobs in another and never need enter a city. They give New Jersey its distinctive character as the nation's most suburban state.

More than half of New Jersey's 567 municipalities are genuine "small towns" with less than 10,000 residents. Only about a quarter of the population lives in communities of more than 50,000. Bergen County, home to more than 1 in 10 New Jerseyans, epitomizes the state. Its northern half is semirural, rich, and Republican; its southern portion bordering Hudson County is industrial, blue collar, and Democratic. With over 800,000 people—more than Boston or San Francisco—Bergen could qualify as one of the nation's larger cities. Instead, its residents live in 70 municipalities with an average population under 12,000. In the 1990 census, Bergen supplanted Essex (home of Newark) as the state's most populous county.

New Jersey's suburbs are thus remarkably diverse. Bergen, Monmouth, Morris, and Somerset County towns with luxurious homes and weekend retreats are among the nation's wealthiest. Others, like Dover Township in Ocean County, Parsippany in Morris County, or East Brunswick in Middlesex County, consist mostly of comfortable housing developments for transient corporate middle managers attracted by their proximity to highways. Still others are company towns for blue–collar workers or offer housing for the so–called "cops and firefighters" market.

Although much of New Jersey's minority population remains locked in the cities, there are also suburbs with sizable or majority black populations. Some, like East Orange, border on Newark. Others, like Lawnside in Camden County, were stops on the Underground Railroad during the Civil War. Still others, like Montclair, Plainfield, and Morristown, house descendants of nineteenth–century domestic servants and professional families drawn by existing minority populations and exceptionally attractive housing. There are also historically black rural communities, like the hamlets of Little Rocky Hill in Somerset County and Bivalve in Atlantic County.

Types and Forms of Municipal Government

A confusing feature of New Jersey municipal government is the frequent lack of correspondence between types of municipal incorporation and forms of government with the same names. The word "city," for example, refers to both a type and a form, but a municipality can be a chartered "city" with a different form of government. Such disjunctions between form and type produce locutions like "the township of the village of South Orange"—township referring to governmental form; village referring to the type of incorporation.

Types of municipal incorporation include cities, towns, boroughs, townships, and villages. New Jersey is unique in that these types do not differ in their rights, powers, or duties.[13] Forms of government refer to organizational structure—the principal government officials, their powers and duties, and how they are selected. There are five types of municipalities and twelve forms of government in current use.

Municipal types are determined at the time of incorporation, but types did not have clear legal definitions until the end of the 19th century, when most municipalities were already established.[14] Even then, types and forms with the same name were only loosely related. Types remained the same, while forms changed. By type (but not form), Newark is a city, and so is Corbin City (population 412). Most boroughs—the most common type of municipality—

arose in the late 1800s when parts of townships split off to avoid taxes. Ease of incorporation produced "boroughs" like Tavistock, with 12 current residents. Tavistock consists of a golf club, which split off from Haddonfield in 1921 when the latter banned Sunday play. Shrewsbury Township (one–tenth of a mile in size; population 1,098) is composed entirely of two federal housing projects.[15]

The earliest forms of government were the nineteenth–century categories with the same names as the types—city, town, township, borough, and village. All provide for partisan officials elected from wards or at–large for two to four–year terms and weak executives. In some, the mayor and council are elected separately; in others, the council chooses the mayor. All have been criticized for combining legislative and administrative powers.

In 1911, the Walsh Act added the commission form, in which individually elected and nominally nonpartisan commissioners head government departments. After 1923, municipalities could also choose a municipal manager form. In this form, nonpartisan elected council members appoint a manager who makes all other municipal appointments. The council may remove the manager for cause after three years. Unlike the commission form, this option, emphasizing nonpartisanship and neutral competence, never caught on and has had few adoptions.[16]

Seeking to enhance municipalities' managerial capacity, Governor Alfred Driscoll established a Commission on Municipal Government in 1948. Two years later, the commission recommended an Optional Municipal Charter Law, which the legislature passed overwhelmingly. Known as the Faulkner Act (after Montclair Mayor Bayard Faulkner, chair of the commission), its intent was to professionalize municipal government by separating executive and legislative functions and giving the executive stronger powers.

The Faulkner Act offered municipalities a "veritable delicatessen" of governmental alternatives.[17] There were two basic designs: a mayor–council plan, and a council–manager plan. Each included many options—for the timing of elections (general elections or regular municipal elections), the size of the council (five, seven, or nine), partisan or nonpartisan elections, concurrent or staggered terms for officeholders, and wards or at–large seats (although no plan provided for wards only).

The various permutations were designated as options A through F under both basic plans. There was also a simplified version of the mayor–council system for small municipalities. Finally, municipalities could still petition the legislature for special charters. All the Faulkner plans also provided for the local initiative, referendum, and recall of elected officials.[18] In 1981, the legislature revised the Optional Municipal Charter Law, allowing municipalities to combine the various alternatives for election timing and districts, council size, and partisanship in whatever way they prefer.

Under the mayor–council plan, the mayor is chief executive, directing preparation of the municipal budget and appointing all department heads (which are limited to ten). One appointee must be a business administrator who oversees a centralized purchasing system and the personnel system and helps with budget preparation. The mayor may attend council meetings and veto ordinances, which require a two–thirds vote of the council to override. The council functions purely as a legislative body. It can reduce items in the mayoral budget by a simple majority and add items by a two–thirds vote.

The council–manager plan is based on popular election of council members who choose a mayor from among themselves. The mayor's duties are limited to presiding at council meetings. A professional manager chosen by the council is the chief executive officer, making all municipal appointments and preparing the budget. The council may remove the manager at any time.

Municipalities can adopt a Faulkner Act form by one of two routes: voter approval of a charter study commission, placed on the ballot by ordinance or direct voter petition; or by direct voter petition to place a particular form on the ballot for immediate approval or rejection. If a study commission is established, it must make a recommendation within nine months. A public referendum must confirm the recommendation.

More than half the state's municipalities have considered a charter change under the Faulkner Act, and about half of those have adopted a new government form. These include most larger municipalities, so 47 percent of the state's population lives in places with Faulkner Act charters. In 1992, there were 120 municipalities with Faulkner Act charters and 17 others with special charters. The most frequent change has been from the commission form to the mayor–council form. More than 80 percent of municipalities still hold partisan elections, and more than half of those using nominally nonpartisan forms report that partisanship still figures in local elections.[19]

Functions of Municipal Government

Titles 40 and 40A of New Jersey's public laws delimit the functions of local governments. One large category is regulation of personal conduct—from loitering to begging to "the ringing of bells" and "the crying of goods." Municipalities may also regulate the use of private property in various ways, of which the most important is zoning. "Control over land use is the principal tool by which local governments maintain their individual character and pursue their particular goals."[20]

A 1927 constitutional amendment gave municipalities zoning powers, and for many years they had almost total discretion to decide land use. Recent court rulings on exclusionary zoning, the state Fair Housing Act, and Trenton initiatives fostering regional planning and environmental protection have eroded municipal autonomy (see chapters 11 and 16). Despite new constraints, decisions by local zoning boards remain of great community interest. The surest—perhaps only—way to generate a crowd willing to attend public meetings through the wee hours is to bring a controversial variance request to a local zoning board.

Historically, New Jersey had few state–mandated municipal services. Robert Wood wrote in 1958, "The pattern of state–local relationships is traditionally one of the state giving limited financial aid, but abstaining from control, providing resources in a policy framework so broad as to fit any conceivable local attitude."[21] That has changed somewhat in recent years (see chapter 14). Each locality must have a disaster–control director, a local defense council, a local assistance board, and a department of health. Many communities have a recreation commission, a shade–tree commission, and so on, but they are not required.

Almost all municipalities have a paid police force. Many have paid firefighters, although volunteer squads, along with volunteer ambulance squads, remain a source of social life and organization in many communities. Water and sewer service, garbage removal, and street maintenance are provided by some municipalities. These services are often regionalized or individually purchased. Even in densely populated New Jersey, the well and septic system have not yet vanished.

Most municipal employees are civil servants, but the professionals retained by many communities are not. All municipalities must have a full–time clerk, and most retain a municipal attorney, engineer, and accountant. Commonly, those on retainer are political appointments—especially the attorney, who usually has political ties to council members and a policy–making role.

Municipal attorneys are often past or present members of the state legislature or have other connections to Trenton. Many communities also retain other lawyers to work with their zoning and planning boards. With civil service and competitive bidding requirements limiting the classic forms of political patronage, lawyers are the most ubiquitous patronage beneficiaries.

To provide services, municipalities must levy taxes and prepare a budget. New Jersey's local governments depend almost entirely on the local property tax, which provides 98 percent of locally raised revenues as compared to about 74 percent nationally.[22]

Property taxes are collected by municipalities, but their governing bodies receive and spend a rather small portion. Municipal governments are the collection agents for counties, whose budgets also depend heavily on property taxes. A large share of local taxes goes to finance local public schools, and this money is allocated by separate boards of education. New Jersey has even more school districts (610) than it does municipalities (567) and more mostly elected school–board members (4,780) than elected local officials (3,376).[23] Most municipalities have fiercely resisted proposals for regionalized schools.

Although municipalities have some discretion in choosing the services they provide, the state monitors their fiscal affairs closely. A 1917 municipal budget law (the first in the nation) began state audits of municipal accounts but did not require cash–basis budgets. There were no limits on how municipalities estimated revenues or requirements for a surplus fund. This was not a problem during the boom years after World War I, but the Great Depression brought massive difficulties.

By 1931, tax delinquencies in Camden, Newark, and Paterson approached 30 percent. Vast public works construction during the 1920s increased municipal and county debt from $400 million in 1922 to over $1 billion in 1933. The stock–market crash prevented municipalities from converting bond anticipation notes into long–term bonds. In 1934, New York City banks refused to bid on New Jersey municipal bonds not backed by cash–basis budgets, and the state government received aid petitions from 128 municipalities unable to meet local relief bills.

Faced with this crisis, Trenton finally acted. The 1936 Local Budget Law set up a Division of Local Finance (later renamed the Division of Local Government Services) located first in the Treasury Department and after 1962, in the newly created Department of Community Affairs. Each year the division sets the important deadlines for municipal budget–making and produces a manual of required budget titles, sequence of items, and the like. It also certifies the revenue estimates of all municipal budgets and their compliance with statutory expenditures.

Municipal budgets must be certified annually by the Division of Local Government Services and enacted by ordinance no later than March 31. If municipal officials do not meet this schedule, the division will write the budget, adjusting the past year's document. If municipalities experience financial trouble as defined in the law, the division takes control of the local budget and taxes until the problems are rectified. Between 1931 and 1948, this occurred in 24 municipalities. During the 1980s, the division engaged in full or partial takeover in 6.

Many more municipalities flirt with missed deadlines—not because they are inept, but because Trenton budget battles leave them unsure of how much state aid they will receive. Municipal budgets operate on a calendar year, while the state fiscal year begins in July. In 1989, over 200 municipalities gave this reason for missing the state deadline for introducing their budgets, and 54 were in the same position in 1990.[24] In 1991, the legislature required 69 municipalities either with populations over 35,000 or receiving extraordinary state aid to move the start of their fiscal year from January to July so as to match the state fiscal year and mitigate these problems.[25]

Most municipalities now enjoy good credit ratings; the 1936 state budget law provided a prototype for the National Municipal League's model cash–basis budget of 1948, and the Department of Community Affairs' professionalism and service to local governments, after a period of decline in the mid–1970s, is once again highly regarded.[26]

Another factor affecting municipal budgeting is the state's municipal cap law. The cap law was passed in 1976 in conjunction with the state income tax and was supposed to ensure that the new tax proceeds went for property tax relief rather than municipal "spending sprees." For a few years, the allowable annual increase of 5 percent seemed adequate. Then hyperinflation, withdrawal of federal CETA and general revenue–sharing funds, and sharp increases in insurance costs made the cap unrealistic.

Like Washington's Gramm–Rudman law "mandating" reduced federal budget deficits, New Jersey's municipal cap law became a charade. Thanks to creative evasion (e.g., creating local authorities to take services "off–budget") and 46 amendments specifying exemptions (e.g., for state–mandated garbage and recycling costs and compliance with the state Fair Housing Act), at least half the typical municipal budget became exempt from the cap. By 1986, the real annual increase in municipal expenditures was estimated at 11 percent.

The New Jersey League of Municipalities argues that the cap law should be repealed if there is no state aid to pay for an ever–growing list of state mandates. In 1988, Governor Kean conditionally vetoed a three–year extension of the cap law. The legislature agreed to his proposed one–year continuation through 1990, handing the issue to incoming Governor Florio. Cap–law history then seemed to repeat itself. A $2.8 million state tax increase in 1990 unleashed the same public outrage as had the 1976 income tax, and Trenton looked to local spending caps as a device to placate voters.

Florio tried to dampen anger about increased state taxes by promising they would stabilize rapidly rising local property taxes. He requested and won an even tougher cap law, which limited annual municipal budget increases to 4.5 percent, and removed costly items like insurance, garbage collection, and recycling costs from the exemption list. However, the law also permitted municipalities to apply for an increase to 5 percent and the Local Finance Board of the Department of Community Affairs to grant exceptions to the law. Bickering over the cap and "smoke and mirrors" seems likely to continue.

Municipal Politics

New Jersey's reputation for local political corruption may be a case of "guilty with an explanation." One exculpatory factor is the sheer number of elected local officials—with 3,376 of them, a small percentage of bad apples can be highly visible. Amateur and poorly paid officeholders in small towns and the patronage tradition in larger ones also make some officials susceptible to bribery. Finally, the moralistic strain in the political culture—never dominant but always present—sends the state into periodic fits of "reformism."

While Governor Kean preached the "politics of inclusion," and Governor Florio often spoke of creating "one New Jersey for all of its citizens," in many municipalities politics is still best described as tribal, with race and ethnicity playing prominent roles. Big–city mayors used to figure prominently among New Jersey's more celebrated crooks. From the 1950s through the early 1970s, various Atlantic City, Camden, Jersey City, and Newark executives all spent time in federal correctional facilities. With the exception of Atlantic City, where four of the last seven mayors have been indicted and convicted (leading an old political hand to comment that "Atlantic City makes Jersey City look like something out of Plato's Republic"), most recent big–city leaders have been models of rectitude.[27]

A spate of white urban reformers in the 1960s (e.g., Mayors Arthur Holland in Trenton, Paul Jordan in Jersey City, and Lawrence "Pat" Kramer in Paterson) were succeeded by similar black leaders (Melvin "Randy" Primas in Camden, Kenneth Gibson and Sharpe James in Newark, and Douglas Palmer in Trenton). As elsewhere, most successful city politicians, both black and white, are Democrats. The state's Republicans suffered a tragic disappointment when their highest–ranking symbol of "the politics of inclusion"—James Usery, mayor of Atlantic City and president of the National Conference of Black Mayors—was arrested in 1989 on bribery and extortion charges.

However, Usery—and Jersey City Mayor Gerald McCann, who was convicted in 1992—are now the exception rather than the rule. Less prominent officeholders generate the notoriety New Jerseyans would like to put behind them. One such national headline grew out of the 1990 scandal at the U.S. Department of Housing and Urban Development (HUD). First, the

Passaic Housing Authority was found to have $1.6 million in questionable expenditures, including the $245,000 salary paid to its executive director (with more to his wife). This was followed by guilty pleas to bribery and tax evasion by former housing directors in the Middlesex County communities of Carteret, Perth Amboy, and Woodbridge. A HUD task force took up residence in the Newark regional office to look for further instances of malfeasance by New Jersey's 80 housing authorities.

At roughly the same time, the 44,000 residents of Manchester Township in Ocean County (80 percent of them senior citizens living in self–contained complexes) learned that a ring led by the township administrator had defrauded the municipality of $10 million over 13 years. In taking over the township's finances, the hardened director of the Division of Local Government Services said that in 20 years, he had "never seen fiscal mismanagement and very probable criminal activity of the scope that exists in Manchester Township....They simply wrote checks to themselves whenever they wanted."[28]

In addition to continuing sagas of local corruption, "tribal" politics, with its ethnic and racial overtones, continues unabated where it has flourished. Jersey City was famous for internecine warfare between Protestants and Irish Catholics—followed by conflicts between the Irish and later—arriving Italians and Poles. Now that Jersey City's white Catholics have achieved an uneasy truce, there are new feuds. Blacks and Hispanics have been unable to elect a mayor as yet, and the state took over the city's welfare and police departments for a period in 1988 following complaints of incompetence and discrimination.

There is also tension between blacks, Hispanics, and Jersey City's newest large immigrant group—Indians. In 1987, the Jersey Journal published on its front page a letter from a group calling itself "Dotbusters," which proclaimed, "We will go to any extreme to get Indians to move out of Jersey City." Neighboring Hoboken experienced a yearlong series of assaults against Indians at the same time, culminating in the murder of a bank manager beaten to death by four Hispanic teenagers.[29] In a conciliatory move Frank Hague would doubtless find incredible, an Indian woman was named vice–chair of the Hudson County Democratic party in 1988.

Tribalism also plays itself out in voting patterns. Atlantic City Mayor Usery used overtly racial appeals in his unsuccessful 1990 reelection campaign, suggesting the criminal charges against him were a racist plot. Jesse Jackson came to town to back up this interpretation. Douglas Palmer's Italian opponent in Trenton swept the city's Italian wards while Palmer did the same in black wards. New Brunswick's politics often involves coalitions of Irish and Hungarians pitted against the city's blacks and Hispanics.

Tribal politics does not dominate everywhere. University towns like Princeton and Highland Park (near Rutgers) have declared themselves nuclear–free zones, adopted sister cities in Nicaragua, and taken positions on the Gulf War. Many municipal contests revolve around which candidates will do better at keeping unwanted incinerators, corrections facilities, or highways out of town; or conflicts between tenants and homeowners. But in the yeasty politics of blue–collar and ethnic New Jersey, the tribal tradition continues.

COUNTIES

The Development of Counties in New Jersey

Thirteen of New Jersey's 21 counties were created in the colonial period, with the earliest—Bergen, Essex, Middlesex, and Monmouth—dating from 1682. Counties were formed and divided for the next 175 years, ending with the establishment of Union in 1857. Created from a portion of Essex, "Union" was an odd name for a county whose founding stemmed from the 200–year–old competition between Newark and Elizabeth.

Development of counties was haphazard. The legislature usually acted for political reasons, such as majority–party schemes to gain another state senate seat or as in the case of Union, wrangles over the location of the county courthouse and its patronage jobs. Governmentally weak but politically strong county units encouraged balkanization.[30]

New Jersey's counties began as popularly elected governments with some responsibilities; they were never merely state judicial or administrative units.[31] Weaker than counties in the southern and western states, they were still of more import than in New England, where towns were dominant.

Forms of County Government

Until the 1970s, elected boards of chosen freeholders governed all counties. A colonial term for property owner, freeholder is a job title unique to New Jersey. State law on the composition of county freeholder boards was largely unchanged from 1798 to 1912. Until 1851, all counties elected two freeholders per township. As townships splintered into cities, towns, boroughs, and villages, the electoral system became less uniform, although the most common arrangement was one board member per municipality. By the turn of the century, boards in the larger counties had become unwieldy, with as many as 40 freeholders in Essex and 38 in Camden. Consequently, in 1902 and 1912, the legislature passed optional "small board" statutes, providing for three to nine members.

By 1912, 12 of the 21 counties with four–fifths of the state's population had "small boards." Most of the holdouts were in the south. In the 1950s, there were still more than 20 freeholders in Cumberland and Gloucester and 34 in Atlantic County. A 1965 superior court decision flowing from the U.S. Supreme Court's "one person–one vote" mandates finally produced a uniform system of 3 to 9 freeholders (based on population) and at–large elections for staggered three–year terms.

The freeholder board resembles a commission form of government, combining administrative and legislative functions. It operates through committees, with members chairing one committee and holding membership on several others. Freeholders choose one of their number as director; he or she is a presiding officer with voice and vote but no veto. They also appoint a board clerk and a number of county officers, such as a counsel and treasurer. Freeholder salaries in 1991 varied from $26,000 in Essex to $15,000 in Cumberland.

In addition to the freeholders, voters elect three other county officials. The sheriff, who is primarily an officer of the court, oversees the service of legal papers, transport of county prisoners, and conduct of foreclosure sales. The surrogate probates wills and appoints legal guardians. The clerk keeps county records, registers deeds, and processes passport applications.

Dramatic change in county government became possible in 1972 with the passage of an Optional Charter Law that was a kind of Faulkner Act for counties. As with the Faulkner Act, the new county charter options encourage more executive responsibility.[32] They offer four alternatives to the traditional free-holder board: a county executive plan, a county manager plan, a county supervisor plan, and a board president plan. The first provides for a separately elected county executive; the second for a manager selected by the freeholders, with broad appointive and administrative powers. Both retain the freeholder board as a legislative body and the other elected county officials. The third plan divides executive power between an elected supervisor and an appointed manager, and the fourth gives one freeholder some executive powers.[33]

As with the Faulkner Act, counties may adopt a new form by voter approval of a county charter study commission and its subsequent recommendation or approval of a specific plan placed on the ballot by voter petition. Like the Faulkner plans, each of the basic county charters offers a "cafeteria" of options for the size of the freeholder board (5, 7, or 9 members), concurrent or staggered elections, and district or at–large seats. All of the plans provide for partisan elections and the initiative, referendum, and recall.

Within three years of the law's enactment, nine counties—with two–thirds of the state's population—had held charter referenda. Only half initially passed.

Atlantic, Hudson, Mercer, and Union approved charter changes, while Bergen, Camden, Essex, Middlesex, and Passaic rejected them. Essex reversed itself two years later, as did Bergen in 1985. Thus, six of the 21 counties, including most of the largest, now have reformed charters. All but Union, which adopted the county manager plan, chose the county executive option. No county has yet approved either of the other two plans.[34]

Functions of County Government

In recent years, county government's functions have expanded somewhat. The current list of responsibilities includes operating county jails; financing the state justice system, except for judges' salaries; administering elections, county library systems, mosquito control commissions, and welfare services; maintaining county roads; providing parks and recreation services; overseeing weights and measures; and establishing planning boards.[35]

This basic list is little different from that of the 1930s.[36] However, as state government began providing more services and state aid, it delegated more tasks to the counties. Education is a prominent example. The legislature authorized establishment of county colleges in 1962. Nineteen of the 21 counties now have such institutions, serving 125,000 students. By statutory formula, the state is to provide for 43 percent of their cost but actually contributes less than 20 percent—a level that is 45th among the 48 states with county colleges.

Since 1975, the counties have also had perhaps the most unpopular job in New Jersey government: devising solid–waste disposal plans. These plans, which must be approved by the state Department of Environmental Protection, require highly charged decisions about the siting and use of landfills, incinerators, and trash–transfer stations. In 1988, the counties also became transportation planning districts. These developments are discussed further in chapter 16.

Over 60 percent of county revenues come from property tax receipts. State aid contributes most of the rest, with a small portion from fees and fines. Municipal collection of the county share of property taxes has the political virtue of making county taxes relatively invisible but the vice of providing a weak public check on how counties spend money. County budgets undergo fiscal scrutiny by the state Department of Community Affairs, similar to the process for municipal budgets.

County Politics

For most of New Jersey's history, county politics was in effect state politics.

County party bosses like Democrats Frank Hague of Hudson and David Wilentz of Middlesex and Republicans Arthur Vanderbilt of Essex and Enoch "Nucky" Johnson of Atlantic "made" governors, legislators, and state policy (such as it was). Court intervention, a changing population, and candidate–centered campaigning ended the dominant role of the counties in state politics, but a diminished and less visible system of organizational politics and patronage still operates in the counties. County party organizations can no longer name the governor, but they can still anoint the sheriff.

Some counties of strong partisan bent seem little changed from 50 years ago. Hudson may elect a Republican freeholder when there is a statewide GOP tidal wave at the top of the ticket or Somerset a similar Democrat, but they will likely be gone in the next election. Other counties are competitive across long periods of time (like Union) or have competitive eras (like Camden).

County charter reform since 1972 has had mixed political effects. "Good–government" activists hoped for more efficient and less patronage–ridden county management. The more cynical thought charter reform was just another change that could be deflected by party bosses. Some saw the county executive position as an added step on a state political ambition ladder with few rungs, while others believed the executive would be a glorified freeholder director. There is evidence for all these theories, as a few county vignettes will show.

"Good government" got its severest test in Union County, where the Elizabeth newspaper led a crusade to endorse the county manager plan and end widespread patronage. "Reform" forces won in a close race, and George Albanese was named the first county manager in 1976. Albanese was a rare combination of talented administrator and gifted county pol: formerly the county's well—regarded director of criminal–justice planning, he also had years of experience in Union County politics.

Within a year, Albanese had achieved a Triple A bond rating for Union, the lowest per capita county budget in the state, and respect from a fractious freeholder board of six Democrats and three Republicans. The latter resulted partly from the manager's close cooperation with a longstanding bipartisan patronage ring headed by the septuagenarian director of the Department of Buildings and Grounds.

Writing about the Union experiment in 1977, a journalist reported local concern that finding the next manager would "be far more difficult." She speculated that it was "unrealistic to expect county politicians to kick the patronage habit overnight, or ever," and that the "structural strengths" of the manager plan were its "political weaknesses."[37] After Albanese became state commissioner of human services in 1982, Union County government indeed became a continuing sea of political intrigue and litigation. This record may explain why no other county has adopted a governing plan only public administrators could love—or at least, one not likely to appeal to county politicians.

Essex County seemed at first a better example of how to make reform work in New Jersey counties. The leading local newspaper, the *Newark Star–Ledger*, led the two battles to adopt a new charter. The dominant Democratic organization was in decline due to the crumbling power of longtime boss Harry Lerner and the aspirations of Newark blacks for a larger organizational role. It nonetheless managed to raise $103,000 to fight charter reform for the second time (against the proponents' $35,000), and Lerner thundered that the change was "a scheme to break up the greatest Democratic organization in the United States since that of [Chicago] Mayor Daley."[38]

When reformers eked out a victory, Lerner retired to Florida. The Democratic organization fragmented, and nine candidates, eventually winnowed to four, entered the 1978 executive race. Reform candidate Peter Shapiro, an assemblyman in his mid–twenties, won the Democratic nomination (tantamount to election) with 36 percent of the vote against two Italian organization candidates and a Newark black.

After running a model county government for seven years, Shapiro unsuccessfully challenged incumbent governor Tom Kean, another Essex resident, in 1985. Ensuing events seemed a parody of the old politics. When Shapiro forced incumbent sheriff Nicholas Amato off the Democratic ticket in 1986 to make room for a black candidate, Amato switched parties and ran for county executive as a Republican. He defeated Shapiro, who had postponed a big increase in county taxes until after the gubernatorial campaign.

As 1990 approached, Amato's polls showed he could not win reelection as a Republican. He thus announced he was returning to the Democratic fold and gave an early endorsement to gubernatorial candidate Jim Florio. The Democratic organization rejected his renomination and supported the sitting Democratic sheriff—the eventual winner—instead.

In Bergen County's first executive race in 1986, there were hopes the contest would produce an energetic young reformer. Instead, the Democrats nominated a veteran state senator, and Republicans chose the current sheriff. Both had been active in county politics for thirty years. Despite his nickname, "Wild Bill" McDowell, the Republican victor, ran a low–key administration that continued traditional patronage practices.[39] McDowell declined renomination, and a poll for the successful 1990 Republican candidate, Assemblyman "Pat" Schuber, revealed that only 20 percent of Bergen County voters could identify the county executive as the highest county office. Even when asked directly, only 50 percent claimed to have ever heard of it.

Although county executive races have so far attracted more traditional political veterans than ambitious, younger officeholders, the political community believes the office could become a regular track for credible gubernatorial candidates. Bergen's Schuber is one example. Another is Democratic Hudson County Executive Robert Janiszewski, also a former legislator. Janiszewski came up through the Hudson Democratic organization but has smoothness and public–relations sense his predecessor, a more traditional machine politician, lacked.

County politics and government are thus in flux. Most people know what county they live in but have little reason to identify with it. Counties are hampered by low public visibility, weak statutory powers, and resistance to regional policies and planning. The county executive has only partially replaced the strong party boss, who used to personify the county and give it political clout. Expanded duties granted to counties must be weighed against the heavy controls imposed by state government.

HOME RULE: RHETORIC OR REALITY?

Academic disccussions of home rule begin with the opposing arguments in two famous nineteenth–century court cases. *Dillon's Rule*, promulgated by an Iowa justice, holds that municipal corporations derive all powers and rights from the legislature and are creatures of the state: "As it creates, so may it destroy. If it may destroy, it may abridge and control."[40] The *Cooley Doctrine* of a Michigan jurist holds that American local governments, which existed before state governments, have inherent rights deriving from common law and historical tradition that cannot be abridged.[41]

In many states, and certainly in New Jersey, *Dillon's Rule* describes the legal case, while *Cooley's Doctrine* is the more accurate picture of reality.[42] In the years between 1870 and 1920, when New Jersey municipalities proliferated, the legislature let them shape themselves as they pleased. An 1875 constitutional amendment prohibited the legislature from passing "private, local or special laws" that regulated "the internal affairs" of towns and counties.[43] The 1947 constitution describes legislative power over local government as follows: "The provisions of this Constitution and of any law concerning municipal corporations formed for local government, or concerning counties, shall be liberally construed in their favor. The powers of counties and such municipal corporations shall include not only those granted in express terms but also those of necessary or fair implication...not inconsistent with or prohibited by this Constitution or by law."

Thus, the constitution makes clear that local governments are ultimately bound by constitutional and statutory law but just as clearly indicates that liberal grants of home rule are in order. In general, the legislature and the courts have issued detailed procedural guidelines (as for local finance), but otherwise allowed municipalities and counties wide latitude (as in the "cafeteria" choices of the optional municipal and county charter laws).

This choice comports with New Jersey's history and localist culture and with a legislature so full of former (and sometimes current) municipal and county officials. Legislative politics is an important prop to home rule. Legislative candidates base their electoral strategies on towns, because unlike county lines, town lines have generally been honored in redistricting plans (Newark and Jersey City are the only municipalities split between legislative districts).

Yet, as public problems increasingly cross municipal boundaries, as state government increasingly finances municipal activities, and as citizens identify as residents of the state and not just their hometowns, New Jerseyans are forced to rethink a 300–year–old "theology" of home rule. Poised against distrust of state government and fears of losing community identity is recognition that municipal services are uneven, inefficient, and significant contributors to New Jersey's high local property taxes. Governing a city–state of 567 municipalities that cling to a strong home rule tradition is now New Jersey's central political challenge.

CHAPTER THIRTEEN

New Jersey in the Federal System

*It seems proper, in treating of the vast population occupying the cities of
New York, Brooklyn, Jersey City, Newark, and Hoboken to consider them
as...one great metropolitan community....The villages and towns strung
along the railways for 50 miles from New York...are very largely made up
of persons doing business in the city or occupied in manufactures which
find there their market.*

—U.S. Census Report, 1880[1]

*New York and New Jersey will grow together or we will perish together.
The sooner both states realize that, the better off the whole region will be.*

—Governor Thomas Kean, 1988[2]

Historically, the interests of New Jersey's citizens rarely extended beyond their
own communities. During the American Revolution, they saw Britain as their
protector from New York. In the Civil War era, there was sympathy for the
Confederacy's position on "states' rights." When the rest of the country was
engaged in trust–busting, New Jersey was called "the traitor state" for inviting
corporations in on favorable terms.

Many states have sent citizens to Washington who became significant actors
in American history, but few New Jerseyans are among them. Garret Hobart
of Paterson, elected vice–president in 1896, might have become an accidental
president had he outlived William McKinley, but he did not. Grover Cleveland
was born and died in New Jersey but spent most of the time in between in
New York. The state's most famous contribution to the nation, Woodrow
Wilson, lived there less than 20 years—all of it in Princeton, which was
regarded, and was pleased to regard itself, as a place apart from the rest of
New Jersey.

The New Jersey congressional delegation labored in obscurity, breaking into
national consciousness only on the frequent occasions when members were
accused of corruption.[3] Strong local party machines kept most talented politicians at home where the real action was.[4] Always quite wealthy, New Jersey
received modest federal largess.

Relations with other states were limited mostly to neighboring New York and Pennsylvania and were often hostile. New Jersey financed its state government by taxing those traveling between New York City and Philadelphia. When Charles Dickens made the trip in 1842, he had this to say about New Jersey: "The journey from New York to Philadelphia is made by railroad, and two ferries; and usually occupies between five and six hours."[5] New Jerseyans both profited and suffered from the quasi-colonial relations with their neighbors, particularly New York.

Although New Jersey still receives less federal aid than many other states, today it aggressively seeks help in areas such as environment and transportation. Its congressional delegation has recently been well-placed to get it, and during the 1980s, its governor enjoyed ready access to the White House. New Jersey also takes a more assertive posture toward New York and Pennsylvania and fares better in competition with them. It has strengthened its federal lobbying operation and become more active in interstate organizations. In the past, New Jersey reluctantly adopted innovations pioneered in other states; now it is often the pioneer. No longer insular, it seeks national and international markets for its goods and services.

NEW JERSEY IN THE FEDERAL SYSTEM

American federalism has passed through a number of phases. The idea of "dual federalism," with different functions for national and state governments, held sway for over a century. "Layer cake" was the favored metaphorical description of this system. The actual separation between the "layers" was, however, less complete than the theory implied.

From about 1913 to 1964, "cooperative federalism," a "marble cake" of grants-in-aid and bargaining between governments, was the dominant relationship. Lyndon Johnson's Great Society policies (1963–1968) made Washington, D.C., the dominant actor in the federal system between the mid–1960s and 1980. The states became perceived as instruments of national purposes, and direct federal aid to local governments increased, often bypassing state capitals. Richard Nixon encouraged a "new federalism" with fewer strings and a larger role for state governments but provided even more federal money.

Ronald Reagan and George Bush championed federal extrication from many programs. Fiscal transfers from Washington to the state capitals declined or grew at a slower pace; categorical grants with strict requirements were replaced with block grants that provided less money but more discretion about how to spend it. In a controversial five-to-four decision in *Garcia v. San Antonio Metropolitan Transit Authority* in 1985, the U.S. Supreme Court seemed to withdraw from its historic role as arbiter of federal relations, ceding it to the U.S. Congress.[6]

All these phases were clearly evident in New Jersey. Dual federalism was warmly embraced. When Andrew Jackson's administration deposited excess federal funds in state banks for discretionary use, Mahlon Dickerson, U.S. senator from New Jersey, approvingly noted that the "states may be safely trusted to make the best use...as their interests or exigencies may require."[7]

In the era of cooperative federalism, New Jersey welcomed New Deal programs that saved many communities and political machines' patronage jobs. Richard Hughes, governor during the Kennedy–Johnson administrations, was a confidant of both presidents and a strong supporter of Great Society initiatives; President Johnson chose to hold the 1964 Democratic National Convention in Atlantic City.

Thomas Kean, whose governorship spanned the Reagan years, endorsed a "kinder, gentler" version of supply–side economics and applauded the discretion given to state governments. An intimate of figures in the Bush and Reagan administrations, such as HUD Secretary Jack Kemp and Treasury Secretary Nicholas Brady, Kean delivered the keynote address at the 1988 National Republican Convention. His successor, Jim Florio, emphasized, even more than Kean had, the importance of aid from Trenton to poorer communities bearing the brunt of federal budget cuts.

New Jersey continued strong support for many programs abandoned or reduced by the federal government during the Reagan and Bush years. The state employed a dual strategy of forceful competition for the remaining federal dollars and replacement of federal dollars with state funds. A study of 14 states' responses to the sharp cuts during President Reagan's first term put New Jersey in the group with the "most pronounced" actions to replace lost federal assistance, both fiscally and institutionally.[8]

Like other states, New Jersey first employed "coping" strategies, such as fund carryovers and shifts between accounts. To ameliorate federal cuts in programs for children, New Jersey transferred some new aid for low–income energy assistance. It used federal highway trust fund money, which increased after the 1982 hike in the federal gasoline tax, to soften the impact of reduced grants for mass transit operations. Money was also shifted from the state unemployment trust fund to cover medical bills for the poor.

In most states, programs targeted specifically at the poor, such as AFDC and food stamps, suffered most in the Reagan years. Programs with broader constituencies fared better in local "coping" and replacement efforts. New Jersey showed a mixed picture. Stricter federal eligibility requirements did result in a sharp drop in food stamp recipients, whose numbers declined from 577,000 to 503,000 between fiscal years 1981 and 1984. Some of the decline, however, was attributable to the state's improving economy. Unlike many other states, New Jersey increased AFDC benefits in both 1985 and 1986.

New Jersey was among 31 states imposing tax hikes in 1983, increasing both its income and sales taxes. New revenue flooded in as the economy recovered. A state budget surplus of $450 million in 1984–85, and even larger ones in the next few years, permitted the state to expand many programs. As a result, Newark's effective tax rate declined during the early 1980s, a pattern not seen in hard–pressed cities elsewhere.[9] In 1985, the governor and legislature enacted a pioneering "medically needy" program assuring hospitalization coverage for non–Medicaid qualifiers. A new transportation trust fund financed with federal highway money, contributions from the state's three toll road authorities, and new state appropriations gave transportation funding some stability and held down mass transit fare hikes. Another new trust fund, partially financed by a state bond issue, replaced lost federal funds for wastewater treatment.

The governor's significant control over both the state budget and the allocation of federal funds made Kean chiefly responsible for designing New Jersey's response to Washington's actions. Kean agreed with the Reagan administration that the "best social program" was vibrant private enterprise but differed from many other Republicans in favoring a larger role for government in expanding economic opportunity. As he described his approach, "if there was a problem with the War on Poverty, it was that it was designed to give people things. That can sustain life, but it doesn't give them anything else. We had a philosophy that you had to turn these programs into opportunity programs."[10]

Programs directed at poor and urban areas during the Kean years bore the stamp of this philosophy. Before 1982, New Jersey used Community Development Block Grants for housing and neighborhood revitalization. Kean redeployed them to development projects aimed at leveraging private investment. He admired President Carter's Urban Development Action Grant (UDAG) program, which was directed to similar ends but eliminated during the Reagan administration. The Kean administration sponsored a 1982 state bond issue to finance a state UDAG–type program.

While federal urban enterprise zone legislation languished in Washington, New Jersey established state enterprise zones in 1983. Businesses in most of the zones, of which there were 11 by 1990, may charge only half the state sales tax, which is retained by the host municipality for development in the zone. The program appears to be cost–effective and to produce economic improvements in the host communities.[11]

As much as possible, Kean sought to finance such programs outside of the state's general fund through vehicles such as bond issues. As he explained this general strategy, "We tried to keep them out of the general budget for fear that the same thing would happen to them in the state budget that happened to them in the federal budget—when the cuts came, those would be the first things cut because they didn't have a lot of voters attached to them. Where we could, we tried to fund them in ways that wouldn't make them dependent on the vagaries of economic cycles."[12]

An economic slowdown hit New Jersey as Kean's second term was ending. His successor, Democrat Jim Florio, responded even more definitively than Kean had to the 1982 recession. In 1990, Florio proposed the largest tax increases in the state's history, including an increase in the sales tax and a much more progressive income tax. Accompanying cuts in state spending were, like many of the proposed tax hikes, targeted at middle and upper–income residents. His predecessor's concern for those most affected by Washington's budget cuts was one of the few Kean policies Florio did not condemn but rather continued and expanded.

While Trenton acted to replace declining or disappearing federal aid, New Jersey's congressional delegation made the best of the situation in Washington. They faced major difficulties in attracting federal funds during the Reagan era. Two principal forces shaping federal spending in the states during the 1980s were massive defense expenditures and redirection of domestic aid to the very neediest. Never a leading recipient of defense contracts and with the second highest per–capita income in the nation by the start of the 1990s, New Jersey did not begin in a favorable position.

Indeed, from 1981 to 1988, New Jersey ranked dead last among the fifty states in terms of return on federal taxes, getting back 73 cents on the dollar in 1981, and 62 cents by 1988. At the same time, the state's share of the federal tax burden rose from 3.9 percent to 4.6 percent even though its proportion of the national population decreased slightly, from 3.2 percent to 3.1 percent. Federal officials attributed this pattern to New Jersey's high per–capita income, low unemployment, and healthy economy.[13]

Another contributing factor was New Jersey's relative paucity of defense contracts during a period when the Pentagon absorbed about one–third of all federal expenditures and engaged in almost three–quarters of all federal procurement. Still, military spending contributed more to New Jersey's economy than many realized.[14] In 1987, the state ranked seventeenth among the 50 states in the number of military personnel, sixteenth in military compensation, and thirteenth in value of military contracts. In 1986, 32 New Jersey firms, led by companies like RCA and ITT, had prime source defense contracts amounting to more than

$3.2 billion. The Lakehurst Naval Air Engineering Center and the Picatinny Arsenal do important military research and development work, and McGuire Air Force Base is the largest military air transport facility on the East Coast.

However, the $3.2 billion in defense contracts amounted to barely more than 2 percent of all such Pentagon spending and lagged far behind California's $28 billion, Texas's $11 billion, or Massachusetts's $8 billion. Further, a 1989 bipartisan congressional base–closing commission recommended big cutbacks at Fort Dix, the state's largest military installation. In 1991, a second base–closing commission, headed by former New Jersey Representative Jim Courter, saved Fort Dix from the complete shutdown recommended by the secretary of defense, but left in place elimination of its basic training mission and 90 percent of its personnel. Although Courter had been a senior Republican on the House Armed Services Committee and a strong proponent of increased defense spending, he also could not support the kind of "pork" he had opposed as a leader of the congressional Military Reform Caucus. Along with every other member of the delegation save Jim Florio, Courter had supported establishment of the original 1989 base–closing commission.

Other members of the delegation did not share Courter's philosophical distaste for federal assistance. James Howard, chairman of the House Public Works and Transportation Committee from 1975 to 1987 and known as the "Colossus of Roads," was a legendary Santa Claus. Twice in the Reagan years, Howard guided major highway and mass transit bills through the Congress. The 1987 legislation contained 100 "demonstration projects" immune from state formulas. Typically, they included projects in Howard's Monmouth County district and also that of Paterson–area Representative Robert Roe, another senior member of Public Works. Among the larger projects Roe generated as chairman of a subcommittee on water resources was a long–term effort by the Army Corps of Engineers to remove rotting piers and derelict vessels. It benefited Jersey City, Elizabeth, and Hoboken, as well as Newark Bay, Raritan Bay, and the Hackensack and Passaic rivers. Over 15 years, the project garnered $43 million in state and federal funds.

While Howard and Roe attended to the classic forms of federal pork, Jim Florio led in gaining newer federal funds for environmental programs. Florio was a prime mover in creating the federal Superfund in 1980, which provides money to clean up toxic waste sites. New Jersey led the nation in designated Superfund sites. Superfund was reauthorized in 1985, and by 1989, federal funds were providing 44 percent of the $307.8 million New Jersey spent on environmental programs, as compared with 21 percent of the $55.1 million expended in 1985.[15]

In the space of 11 days in 1987, Jim Howard died suddenly, and Judiciary Committee chairman Peter Rodino announced his retirement. The delegation seemed transformed "from a political powerhouse to a political basket case."[16] Florio's departure for the governorship in 1990 was a further blow. However, New Jersey's senators stepped into the breach. Bill Bradley used his seat on the powerful Senate Finance Committee to amend the tax code in ways favorable to New Jersey businesses. When the Democrats regained control of the Senate in 1986, Frank Lautenberg acquired two critical chairmanships—of a new Environmental and Public Works subcommittee overseeing Superfund operations and other environmental programs and an Appropriations Committee subcommittee on Transportation and Related Agencies, with jurisdiction over funding for Amtrak, airports, roads, and buses.

Lautenberg began producing Howard–like projects, such as $7 million from the Urban Mass Transit Agency for feasibility studies of a Newark Airport rail link. He had an especially banner year for the state in 1988, when his electoral vulnerability made the Senate Democratic caucus particularly willing to help him. In 1991, Roe moved to the chairmanship of the Public Works and Transportation Committee when the House Democratic caucus ousted the California representative who had replaced Howard. That year, he was the chief architect of a transportation bill that granted New Jersey $5 billion over six years for road, bridge, and transit projects.

Other members of the delegation were also well–placed. Bernard Dwyer and Dean Gallo sat on the Appropriations Committee and Frank Guarini on the tax–writing Ways and Means Committee. Robert Torricelli did not hurt his district's interests when he gained President Bush's gratitude for being one of the few prominent House Democrats to vote in favor of the 1991 Gulf War.

Events in 1992, however, made the effects of Rodino's and Howard's departures in 1987 pale in significance. A combination of unfavorable redistricting decisions, the miasma surrounding the House of Representatives, and the Republicans' resurgence in state politics led Representatives Dwyer, Roe, and Guarini to announce their retirements. Beginning in 1993, New Jersey's House delegation, for the first time in many years, would neither hold nor be in line for significant committee chairmanships, and even more responsibility would fall on the state's Senators.

Like most states, New Jersey has a Washington office. The Washington office coordinates communication between the state and federal capitals, tracks the progress of relevant bills, lobbies legislators and agency officials, prepares detailed analyses of the effects of federal legislation, and serves as the chief contact point with organizations such as the National Governors Association.

The prominence and activity of the Washington office depends on the governor. Republican Tom Kean used the Washington office to coordinate his close association with the Reagan and Bush administrations. As Kean described it, "There were a lot of things that weren't public—there's a lot of discretionary money down there....It is not unhelpful to have a president and an administration of your own party. In most cases, there was a visit or a phone call from the governor to the [cabinet department] secretary, and sometimes when the secretary was not particularly responsive, I'd write to the [presidential] chief of staff."[17] The state's Washington office would brief Kean on opportunities and follow up on his calls and letters. The director of the state office was a Washington professional who had previously headed another state's office.

The Washington office loomed less large in the Florio administration. Florio—and members of his congressional staff who followed him to Trenton—had established contacts in the Congress but little access to the Republican White House. Florio appointed a junior member of his congressional staff to direct the Washington office. His administration used the office primarily for its bill–tracking capabilities during the Bush administration.[18]

INTERSTATE COMPACTS

Just as New Jersey has stepped up its relations with the federal government in recent years, so too has it entered into more formal compacts with other states. Most are with its immediate neighbors—Delaware, Pennsylvania, and especially its historical nemesis, New York.

The most crucial of the compacts is the Port Authority of New York and New Jersey. Its creation in the 1920s has been called "the most important single event in the rise of the modern compact." For its members, the Port Authority is the "most visible manifestation of both the gulf that separates the two states and the complex weave of economic and physical ties that bind them together."[19] The authority's annual revenue of $1.7 billion is more than the entire GNP of China.[20] It is of vital importance to New Jersey.

This behemoth began inauspiciously. In 1916, New Jersey interests began lobbying the U.S. Interstate Commerce Commission for lower railroad rates in the port district, and in 1920 an interstate study commission recommended establishment of a port authority. The authority district extended for a 25–mile radius around the Statue of Liberty. Its purposes were to end counterproductive railroad competition and coordinate rail terminals, promote the economic well–being of the port cities, and create a comprehensive transportation plan for the region. Governor Walter Edge, who joined New York Governor Alfred E. Smith in endorsing the compact, called it "a large step toward interstate amity."[21]

The first authority enterprises were not money–making ventures. Three bridges linking Hudson and Middlesex counties with the New York City borough of Richmond (Staten Island), for which the authority received approval in 1925, were financial failures. Meanwhile, the Holland Tunnel between Hudson County and Manhattan—a potentially more successful venture— opened in 1927 operated by dual commissions from New York and New Jersey that did not involve the authority.

The authority's position improved dramatically after 1930, when it proposed issuing revenue bonds for new projects—whose toll receipts would repay the bonds and produce no burden on the states' credit. Both states accepted this idea and transferred the Holland Tunnel to the authority. The George Washington Bridge between Bergen County and northern Manhattan opened under budget and ahead of schedule in 1931. The new bridge and the Holland Tunnel generated funding for the Lincoln Tunnel, a third Hudson River crossing completed in 1937.

The Port Authority of New York, as it was named until 1972, was now launched for continuing success. Under the leadership of Executive Director Austin Tobin (1942–72), it took over both states' major airports—Newark, LaGuardia, and Idlewild (later John F. Kennedy)—just as air travel began spectacular growth. The New Jersey marine freight terminals at Port Newark and Port Elizabeth were also profitable investments.

During the three decades of Tobin's rule, authority commissioners were prominent business executives, often from the banking industry. Tobin believed that business people would be "apolitical"; that diverse opinions would be disruptive and deflect the organization from its goals; and that elected officials, including the governors, should stay out of the authority's decision making. Governors followed Tobin's lead, appointing their partisans who met his criteria. By 1965, the average length of service on the commission was 11 years. The real action took place in closed committee meetings; formal ratification, usually unanimous, occurred in brief "open" commission meetings.

Although at least three commissioners from each state had to approve any action, and either governor could stop an action by vetoing the commission's minutes, in practice Tobin made all important decisions. Consolidated bond offerings and pooled accounting practices made it impossible to track the performance of individual facilities or projects. By the end of Tobin's tenure, these included four airports; eight marine terminals; four bridges; two tunnels; two truck terminals; two bus terminals; two heliports; the PATH rapid transit system between Manhattan and New Jersey; and nine trade development offices, including outposts in London, Tokyo, and Zurich.

Covenants in the authority's bonds, ostensibly to protect investors, permitted the commissioners to sidestep gubernatorial requests, particularly from New Jersey, that "excess money" be devoted to mass transit. PATH, which the authority grudgingly took over in 1962 to get New Jersey's approval to build the World Trade Center in lower Manhattan, was the sole exception. Another small but symbolic victory was that the two World Trade Center buildings, briefly the tallest in the world, were built on Manhattan's Lower West Side facing New Jersey, rather than on the Lower East Side facing Brooklyn as originally planned. The price for PATH, however, was a promise that no other mass transit projects would be proposed or approved.[22]

By the early 1970s, New Jersey officials were increasingly frustrated by Tobin's arrogance, the authority's lack of cooperation, and its deleterious effects on coordinated transportation planning. Resentment grew over the favoritism New Jersey believed was shown New York, starting with the authority's name. Consequently, the next several governors became much more aggressive toward the authority.

Republican William Cahill (1970–74), who came to the governorship from the U.S. House, enlisted the Nixon White House to help kill an authority plan for a major jetport in Morris County's Great Swamp—an ecological treasure located amidst some of New Jersey's wealthiest suburbs. He was the first governor to study authority minutes carefully and regularly threaten use of his veto power. Cahill also forced the agency to change its legal name to the Port Authority of New York *and New Jersey*.

Cahill also appointed more "political" commissioners, including a former state party chair, a former state senator, a Hudson County politician, and the vice–chair of the New Jersey Turnpike Authority. Unfortunately, this message was somewhat vitiated when two had to resign after being indicted. However, Tobin's irritation at commissioners' "meddling" finally led to his resignation in 1972.

For the next few years, the authority was in flux as Cahill resisted appointment of an executive director close to New York Governor Nelson Rockefeller. A deal struck in 1977 between New York Governor Hugh Carey and New Jersey Governor Brendan Byrne broke the stalemate. That agreement, followed ever since, awards the commission chair to New Jersey and the executive director to New York. Governor Byrne was the first to add some transportation expertise to the commission—appointing his own state transportation commissioner, who eventually became authority chair. Other Byrne appointees included members whose businesses as well as homes were in the state.

Governors Kean and Florio followed suit in their appointments and actions. After their low bid to clean the bus terminals was rejected for not conforming to prevailing Manhattan wage rates, Kean forced the hiring of a New Jersey minority business firm by vetoing authority minutes. His 1989 threat to veto toll and fare hikes on PATH, the bridges, and the tunnels—mainly destined to finance improvements at New York's Kennedy Airport—resulted in the authority withdrawing the plan.

In 1990, Florio chose Governor Byrne's former state treasurer, Richard Leone, as commission chair. Leone cautioned that policies had to "evolve out of the priorities set by the governors so that the governors will be willing to do the politically difficult task of allowing the tolls to go up."[23] Florio's transportation commissioner further warned: "We have to look at linkages. This is one system for our state and citizens, and they don't care about modes or authorities....This spending for [capital improvements] can't be driven just by what meets the needs of the Port Authority or what gives it the maximum rate of return....It also has to meet the needs of the states."[24]

Seventy years after its founding, the Port Authority has indeed become a titan but more reliant on support from more forceful governors. The influence of New Jersey, once the clear junior partner, has grown along with the state's role in the regional economy. Newark Airport has passed LaGuardia in traffic volume; Port Newark and Port Elizabeth strongly dominate the authority's marine terminal business.[25] The executive director and commission chair must now "maintain a delicate balance between the states, with each reaping equal dividends from the agency's activities."[26]

In 1983, in return for gubernatorial approval of fare hikes, the authority set up a $250 million Fund for Regional Development, of which New Jersey got 55 percent, based on its proportion of users paying tolls. Further toll hikes in 1987 resulted in another $150 million set aside for regional economic development, evenly divided between the states. Kean and New York Governor Mario Cuomo negotiated these agreements without the participation of authority personnel.[27] In 1990, $200 million more came to each state from the authority's buyout of 50 floors of World Trade Center office space, after New Jersey protested its rental at below–market rates to New York State offices.

In the 1980s' boom years, the authority invested in new areas, such as an Essex County trash incinerator; industrial parks in Elizabeth, Yonkers, and the Bronx; and a legal office center in Newark (dubbed "Tort Port"). The leaner 1990s brought renewed attention to the authority's core activities, as Los Angeles eclipsed New York/New Jersey as the nation's largest maritime port, and Kennedy Airport's share of international passenger traffic dropped. The authority's current priorities are renovations at all the airports and new light–rail linkages between them and existing mass transit facilities. A departure tax on airport passengers, which Congress passed in 1990, will finance the mass transit projects.

NEW JERSEY AND ITS NEIGHBORS

Although New Jersey has increased relations with other states and even other nations, New York and Pennsylvania—particularly the former—have always been of special concern.

Along with Washington Irving, who left New York's "disease and dust" to "breathe the fresh air of heaven and enjoy the clean face of nature" in Newark in 1807, New Jerseyans long viewed their largest city, along with the rest of the northern part of the state, as a dependent of New York City.[28] During the nineteenth century, as Newark became less bucolic and more industrial, many of its goods were stamped "Made in New York." A city newspaper editorialized, "We are only a workshop, a community of manufacturers rather than merchants."[29] Newark's Branch Brook Park, designed by Frederick Law Olmstead, never achieved the fame of Olmstead's Central Park in Manhattan, and the University of Newark (later absorbed into Rutgers–The State University) was once a branch of New York University.

New Jersey's resentment of its second–class status and the state's traditional method of dealing with it are seen most clearly in its economic rivalry with New York. New Jersey had thrust upon it or sometimes sought the least desirable money–making ventures. These included shadowy enterprises like illegal gambling (an early harbinger of Atlantic City's casinos) and legal ones like huge garbage landfills loaded with trash from New York and Pennsylvania.

Generation of state revenues was predicated on location. Well into the twentieth century, the state budget was largely financed by levies on railroads and their interstate passengers. In 1961, fifteen years before imposing a general income tax, Trenton began taxing New Jerseyans who worked in New York. The justification was that commuters forced the state to provide otherwise unneeded transportation facilities, and the money was earmarked for transportation projects.

After New Jersey passed a general income tax, it continued to tax commuters at a higher rate. By 1983, when the state supreme court declared the commuter tax unconstitutional in a case brought by New York, it was bringing in $55 million annually. New Jersey's own tax experts estimated that over twenty years, the state collected $380 million from the commuter tax but spent only $183 million on commuter services.[30]

Each time New Jersey alters its tax system, debate ensues about how the changes will affect its economic competitiveness with New York and Pennsylvania. Governor Kean called this consideration "determinative" for his fiscal policy, asserting, "I'm a very strong supply sider when it comes to state government. People move because of incentives. If you can keep taxes on individuals and firms lower than your neighbors, you don't have to do anything else."[31]

When Governor Florio imposed several new and increased taxes in 1990, there was much unfavorable comparison of New Jersey's new tax rates with those in Pennsylvania and the possible effects on the state's economy. The New Jersey Business and Industry Association's 1991 annual poll found that 71 percent of the 3,100 responding companies thought business conditions were worse in New Jersey than the rest of the nation, up from only 27 percent the previous year. Another survey by the state Chamber of Commerce and Price Waterhouse found that 87 percent of the 500 respondents thought state government actions would hurt their businesses over the next five years.[32]

Generally, however, as suburbs have become more attractive places to live, work, and spend leisure time, New Jersey has fared better in regional competition. Lost commuter–tax revenues during the 1980s were more than replaced by the net outflow of jobs from New York City to New Jersey. On average, about 70 firms a year moved across the Hudson; in 1985 alone, that resulted in New York's loss of 14,250 jobs to its neighbor.[33] These firms found that New Jersey's rental and utility costs were half those of New York City. Even in the souring economic climate of 1990, 51 New York companies moved or expanded across the Hudson.[34]

Although some relocations were glamorous and high–profile (like AT&T's sprawling world headquarters in the wealthy Morris County suburb of Basking Ridge), more important and numerous were the financial "back offices" that left Wall Street for Jersey City and Hoboken. This was a competition between historically blue–collar New Jersey towns and New York City's similar outer boroughs like Brooklyn, rather than places like Basking Ridge and Manhattan.

During the late 1970s and early 1980s, the federal government's Urban Development Action Grant program—which provided funds to leverage private investment in depressed urban areas—was a potent weapon in the regional battle.[35] Through 1984, New Jersey won $225 million in UDAG grants, and New York only about two–thirds that amount. In 1983 an alarmed New York City persuaded U.S Secretary of Housing and Urban Development Samuel Pierce (a former Wall Street corporate attorney) to cancel a $9 million UDAG grant to

Jersey City that was key to moving 1,300 Bankers Trust Company back–office jobs. New York City called the proposal job piracy rather than new economic development. New Jersey's claim that "piracy" was not an issue, because all the locations were in the same metropolitan statistical area, was not successful.

Sports and entertainment facilities are another source of rivalry. In the past, New Jersey sports fans rooted for professional teams in New York City and Philadelphia and had to travel there to see them, just as they did to attend most cultural events. During the late 1980s, Governor Kean greatly increased public support of the arts, and New Jersey orchestras, theaters, and ballet companies burgeoned.[36] For the mass public, however, the Meadowlands sports and entertainment complex developed in the late 1970s was pivotal.

The Meadowlands provided a site for rock concerts and popular entertainment such as the Ice Capades and Barnum and Bailey's Circus, which used to give area performances only in New York City. Its racetrack cut into revenues of older New York tracks. Most significantly, the complex attracted both of New York City's professional football franchises (the Jets and the Giants) as well as the Nets basketball team. New York made aggressive attempts to prevent the Meadowlands development, including environmental suits and pressure on New York City banks not to buy Meadowlands development bonds.

Typically, citizens resent the football teams' continuing refusal to identify themselves as New Jersey teams, but the fans and their money are now in the state. Trenton has also sought, so far unsuccessfully, to attract a major–league baseball franchise.[37] When Governor Florio, a South Jersey native, took office, he renewed efforts to attract Philadelphia sports franchises. However, negotiations aimed at moving the 76ers basketball franchise and the Flyers hockey team to Camden did not succeed.

Once the butt of humorists' allusions to the "landfill capital of the world," New Jersey is now a garbage exporter rather than importer, and out–state trash no longer receives a warm welcome (see chapter 16). State law in the 1970s banned the importation of out–of–state hazardous waste. Unfortunately, from New Jersey's perspective, the U.S. Supreme Court supported Philadelphia's claim that the legislation violated the interstate commerce clause.[38]

During the 1980s, New Jersey forced the closing of a New York City ocean dumping site off Sandy Hook. Its congressional delegation led the way in achieving a national ban on ocean dumping in 1992 and fought to end oil drilling off the entire Atlantic coast. A campaign to get New York City to close down the Fresh Kills landfill on Staten Island—reputedly the largest in the world— seems a lost cause at least through the 1990s, but New Jersey did manage to get New York State to impose strict requirements to prevent further debris from escaping and turning up on Middlesex County shores.

Other air and water pollution issues, which usually involve New York's "export" of noxious substances to New Jersey, frequently make news in both states. In recent years, New Jersey has threatened to bring suit against New York City's Javits Convention Center's sewage systems emptying into the Hudson, if New York continued to sabotage development projects in Jersey City. It has also castigated New York State for violations of the federal Clean Water Act.

The U.S. Environmental Protection Agency gives its lowest rating to New York waterways entering New Jersey's northern border. Part of northern New Jersey's water supply, they are particularly galling because New York waterways on its Connecticut border are rated "pristine." New York resists a New Jersey area upgrade because it might prevent future development of office and research facilities in Sterling Forest, a recreational preserve that crosses the states' borders but is primarily in New York.[39]

New Jersey's relations with New York are not uniformly hostile. In addition to frequent contacts between the governors, the Port Authority, New Jersey Transit, and New York's Metropolitan Transit Authority work together to develop joint "problem statements" for long–range improvements in the regional transportation system. One recent proposal envisions extending the New York City subway system into the Meadowlands.

The tri–state Regional Plan Association, founded in 1929 and financed by Connecticut, New Jersey, and New York businesses, is another example of regional cooperation. At its founding, the RPA recommended an ambitious plan for building bridges, highways, and tunnels over the next thirty years—a plan largely realized by Austin Tobin at the Port Authority and Robert Moses at New York's Triborough Bridge and Tunnel Authority. In the 1960s, a second major plan called for action on commuter railroads and the development of regional business centers like Stamford, Connecticut; New Brunswick, New Jersey; and White Plains, New York. That regional development did occur, and New Jersey and New York both took over bankrupt commuter lines.

The third major RPA plan, for the 1990s, calls for keeping the region "competitive in the global economy and livable." While earlier plans focused on capital infrastructure, the current plan addresses social infrastructure—preserving open space and fighting high housing costs, congestion, pollution, and homelessness.[40]

NEW JERSEY, THE NATION, AND THE WORLD

A more confident New Jersey has expanded its influence beyond its immediate borders and also beyond the nation. A 1969 study of the diffusion of policy innovations among the American states ranked New Jersey fourth behind New York, Massachusetts, and California. The study suggested, however, that this high ranking might be due merely to proximity to New York.41

Later research casts doubt on this thought. One analysis accords New Jersey the same overall ranking but shows the effects of the state's culture. Although New Jersey ranked second in its speed of adopting civil rights innovations, it was only tenth in the area of welfare policies and twenty–second in educational policies. Another study breaks out time periods and controls for missing data, small numbers of adoptions, and universal adoption due to federal mandates. It finds that New Jersey adopted more innovations from New York before World War I, but that afterward, New York was actually more likely to adopt New Jersey innovations, as were its other neighbors, Delaware and Pennsylvania.42

During the 1980s, Governor Kean found organizations like the National Governors Association and the Education Commission of the States important sources of new ideas flowing in both directions. As he commented of his discussions with other chief executives at NGA meetings, "the private exchanges are often extraordinarily productive. Governors are not rivals; we don't run against each other, and very few of us are especially partisan."43

From Governor Jim Hunt, Kean learned of North Carolina's summer governor's schools, where talented high school students study with college professors on their campuses. Kean launched four governor's schools at New Jersey colleges—for the study of the arts, science, public policy, and the environment. His proposal for parental choice of schools was originally a Minnesota idea.

Kean also shared New Jersey's innovations with other governors. One was the "alternate route" program, which permits otherwise qualified teachers to take education-methods courses after they begin teaching. About 20 states adopted some version of New Jersey's transportation trust fund. The federal welfare reform law is modeled on New Jersey's program, and its sponsor, New York Senator Daniel Patrick Moynihan, credited the National Governors Association with enabling its passage.

Kean also won a term as chairman of the Education Commission of the States, a compact that New Jersey had earlier been among the first to join. Kean's "talks with teachers" program, to learn instructors' views on how they could best do their jobs, was copied by more than twenty governors.44

During the 1980s, Kean, like most governors, saw an increasingly important connection between the health of the state's economy and the international economy.45 He increased the budget of the Division of International Trade from $400,000 in 1982 to $2 million in 1988. The number of foreign companies doing business in the state doubled in this period, and $9.5 billion in foreign investment put New Jersey fourth among the states. More than 200,000 state residents and foreign nationals now work for foreign firms, which contribute $200 million annually in corporate and property taxes.

New Jersey's foreign trade strategy emphasizes both imports and exports; about a third of its 11,000 manufacturers (of machinery, chemicals, and electronics particularly) engage in one or both of these activities. During the Kean years, over 200 companies participated in trade shows in 15 countries, and the state also opened trade offices in Montreal and Tokyo. Reluctant to lead overseas trade delegations during his first term because of press criticism of his predecessor's so–called "junkets," Kean made his first such trips to China and Korea in 1986 and others several times thereafter.[46]

Although Governor Florio closed the Tokyo outpost as an economy move, his appointment of an international banker as his first commerce commissioner, who came to Trenton directly from his bank's London office, signaled continuing interest in foreign trade. The Florio administration focused on the new markets in Eastern Europe.

More than 1,400 resident foreign subsidiaries take advantage of reduced or eliminated tariffs in international free trade zones at Port Newark/Port Elizabeth and the Mount Olive International Trade Center. The International Trade Center boasts 2.5 million square feet of space in 15 buildings on 667 acres. Aside from Rockefeller Center itself, it is the largest real estate enterprise of the Rockefeller Center Development Corporation, a part owner of the trade center. Tenants include Germany's BMW; Japan's Hattori watch company; and the Netherlands' Naarden International USA, the world's second largest producer of flavors and fragrances.

Businesses from 40 different countries—the most in any state—have facilities in New Jersey. Their numbers are dominated by Japan, Germany, the United Kingdom, and France, which together and in rank order account for almost two–thirds of all foreign subsidiaries. Although the 31 Japanese manufacturing plants of the late 1980s paled in comparison to California's 153, New Jersey has attracted about a third more than either New York or Pennsylvania. Sony, Panasonic, and Sharp are among the Japanese firms with corporate headquarters in the state. Honda, Nissan, Mitsubishi, Sanyo, Toshiba, and Toyota also have a New Jersey presence. They join Britain's Rolls Royce, Jaguar, and Viking Penguin; Germany's American Hoechst; France's L'Oreal, Michelin, Peugeot, and Renault; and Italy's Olivetti.

Aggressive courtship contributes to this success. In addition to the work of the International Trade Division, foreign companies such as Britain's Laura

Ashley and Japan's Kenwood Corporation profit from low–interest loans from the New Jersey Economic Development Authority. However, New Jersey also offers deep–water ports, good transportation networks, and overnight motor access to 40 percent of the nation's population. It is a leader in R–and–D spending, average number of patents granted, and number of high–technology firms. A historically polyglot population makes newcomers feel at home.

Finally, there is the ever–present proximity of New York City. In a new version of an old story, many foreign firms maintain corporate headquarters in Manhattan and locate manufacturing and distribution centers in northern New Jersey. The six northern counties of Bergen, Essex, Hudson, Middlesex, Passaic, and Union are home to 70 percent of all New Jersey–based companies engaged in foreign export, with Bergen alone accounting for 40 percent. In 1989, the value of exported goods was $8.6 billion, ranking New Jersey twelfth among the states.[47]

New Jersey banks concentrate on facilitating international finance transactions, such as letters of credit, on which they undercut New York prices by half. Seventeen New Jersey banks have international divisions. The largest, First Fidelity, has 125 employees and offices in London, Hong Kong, Mexico City, and Bogota.

New Jersey has also had sporadic ventures into what might be called "foreign policy." Governor Kean made international news in 1983 when he and New York Governor Mario Cuomo refused to let Soviet Foreign Minister Andrei Gromyko, headed for the United Nations, land at the Port Authority's Kennedy Airport shortly after the Russians shot down a Korean Airlines plane. Although popular with the public, a State Department official called the action "preposterous," and the New York Times editorialized about "a hallucinatory disorder that causes local politicians to imagine themselves President or Secretary of State."[48]

In 1985, Kean was urged to withdraw $2 billion in state pension funds invested in businesses with interests in South Africa. As Kean contemplated divestment, the Reagan administration made known its unhappiness with state "meddling" in foreign policy and the political implications of a big–state Republican governor opposing them on a visible and contentious issue. In the end, both moral considerations and the South African government's then recalcitrant stance on apartheid led Kean to order total divestment.[49]

New Jersey's new role in the federal system and in the world reflects new economic strength and new confidence. In 1964, two analysts wrote, "New Jersey is strategically located to become a major seat of economic and social power for the nation. The extent to which this happens may depend upon whether or not it can also become a major seat of political power."[50] Stronger state government has contributed powerfully to New Jersey's new presence in the nation and the world.

CHAPTER FOURTEEN

The Politics of Taxing and Spending

*The passage of a law equalizing taxation seems to be imperatively
demanded by the people, and I respectfully but earnestly commend it to
your early consideration and prompt and efficient action.*
— Governor Daniel Haines's message to the legislature, 1851

*Our whole system of taxation, which is no system at all, needs overhauling
from top to bottom.*
— Governor Woodrow Wilson's inaugural address, 1911

*We're going to talk about taxes today, which Yogi Berra would say is deja
vu all over again.*
— Former Governor Brendan Byrne at a conference on state tax policy, 1987.

In 1900, New Jersey state government collected and spent less than $3 million.
The general public paid none of the state taxes of the time—on bank stock,
insurance companies, railroads, corporate franchises, or large inheritances. Nor
did most benefit directly from Trenton's paltry services. More than half the state
budget supported "charities"—aid to the blind, deaf, and mentally troubled—
and "corrections"—judges and the state prison. Local governments spent four
times as much, raising virtually all of it from property taxes.

In 1992, however, state government collected and spent more than $15
billion. Broad-based taxes, levied at rates among the highest in the nation,
produced the majority of revenues. Direct state aid to local governments
accounted for the majority of spending. The "big three" state taxes—on income,
sales, and corporate profits—together produced as much revenue as all local
property taxes. Invisible and insignificant state taxing and spending at the
century's beginning had become highly visible and significant at its end. What
state government spends its money on, and from whom it raises it, are now
important questions to everyone in New Jersey.

THE BUDGET AND BUDGET POLITICS

Before the 1947 state constitution banned them, a morass of dedicated funds made it "impossible for the state to mass its fiscal resources and direct them to the points at which they are most needed."[1] As a group of Princeton scholars further observed, "no living person knows what expenditures have been authorized....Only by the merest accident can the needful expenditures of a department coincide with its receipts from particular fees or taxes."[2]

Formal budget procedures today are deceptively simple. The state's fiscal year begins on July 1. By that time, the legislature must pass a balanced budget. The state constitution requires a single general appropriations bill. It also proscribes the creation of state debt exceeding 1 percent of the fiscal year's appropriations without approval in a public referendum.

The Role of the Governor in Budget Making

Generally, the legislature plays a greater role in determining how revenues will be raised than in how they will be spent. Legislators usually can do little but tinker with the governor's expenditure recommendations. A line–item veto allows the governor to remove appropriations he or she does not favor. The governor can also prohibit or limit expenditure of any appropriation "when he determines that it is not in the best interests of the state or if revenue collections fall below the certified amount."[3] It is the governor who must "certify" the revenue predictions. Presidents must envy a New Jersey governor's ability to impound, sequester, and rescind.

To an ever greater extent, the governor's office rather than the extended executive branch develops spending recommendations. Until the 1980s, cabinet officials proposed whatever they thought they could get away with, guided by the informal mandates of an incremental budget process. The budget director, the treasurer, and the governor would then review the cabinet's recommendations. Everyone understood department requests would be cut 10 to 15 percent and acted accordingly. With the civil servants in the budget bureau playing a larger role than the understaffed governor's office, policy aims got rather short shrift.

Governor Kean instituted a tighter and more focused process beginning in 1983. Departments file budget requests with the Office of Management and Budget in October of the previous fiscal year. They must be predicated on specified target amounts, and arrayed in "priority decision packages." The OMB director (a civil servant directed by the governor's office) "examines each request and determines the necessity or advisability of the appropriation requested."[4] The cabinet's actual role in this process was rather starkly illustrated in 1990, when state Treasurer Douglas Berman presented all fiscal year 1991 department budgets to the legislature, and cabinet officials were not permitted to testify.

To some extent therefore, the annual budget is now a statement of the governor's priorities. It can also be an instrument to reward or punish departments and constituencies. However, governors have far from a free hand. Mandated expenditures constitute well over half the budget and have been rising rapidly. Between 1984 and 1990, expenditures for employee pensions and benefits rose by 78 percent and now account for about fifteen cents of every budget dollar. Health-and age-related entitlements almost doubled in cost in the same period. Medicaid alone consumes 10 percent of the budget.[5]

Additionally, much of the revenue flowing into the state treasury is for mandated purposes. Although the constitution bans dedicated revenues, amendments have overridden that provision for most of the new revenue sources of the last three decades. Income tax moneys are dedicated to property tax relief, casino revenues are dedicated to programs for the elderly and handicapped, lottery revenues are dedicated to education and state institutions, and a portion of the gasoline tax is dedicated to transportation.

Combined with legislative entitlements for pensions, benefits, Medicaid, and aid to local governments, "the amount of state revenue not encumbered by prior 'commitments' is relatively small."[6] Discretionary spending constituted only 27 percent of the fiscal year 1992 budget.[7] However, dedicated revenues are assigned to broader categories than they were before 1947 and are far more "comingled."

Patterns of Spending Growth

During the 1980s, New Jersey's governments increased spending faster than most other American jurisdictions. Between 1982 and 1988, federal spending rose by 49 percent, in comparison with Trenton's 64 percent growth. Only Connecticut posted sharper increases. The average rise in spending by American state and local governments in the same period was 58 percent. In New Jersey, it was 70 percent, eighth highest in the nation.[8]

These increases continued a trend begun in the 1970s, which moved New Jersey toward the top of the state spending pack from its traditional place near the bottom. Table 15 tells the tale.

Although New Jersey's overall state and local expenditures are now well above average, Table 16 depicts the considerable variation across areas of expenditure.

New Jersey has long spent handsomely on its public schools, already ranking fourth among the states in 1939. High population density, many poor and urban areas, and large numbers of municipalities account for high levels of spending

Table 15: Average Per Capita Expenditures, State and Local Governments, 1962-87

Year	N.J.	U.S.	N.J. as % of U.S.
1962	$302	$321	94
1968	$452	$512	88
1972	$801	$802	100
1978	$1,402	$1,355	103
1982	$1,950	$1,868	104
1987	$2,009	$1,665	121

Source: Significant Features of Fiscal Federalism, relevant years.

on public welfare, police officers, and firefighters. Higher education and health facilities have historically been starved, as their clienteles were directed to or took advantage of institutions in New York and Pennsylvania. To a declining but continuing extent, they still do.

These data raise two intriguing questions. First, what accounts for New Jersey's sudden shift during the 1970s from a miserly state to a rather free–spending one? Second, what explains handsome spending in some areas and relative stinginess in others? The answers to these questions are not unrelated.

State government cannot spend money it does not have. As we discuss in detail later, New Jersey imposed broad–based state taxes later than most other states. A strong home rule tradition assigned Trenton a minor role in both taxing and spending. Before 1947, the governorship, which might have represented larger state interests, was a weak office. The legislature, dominated by an upper house in which each county had one senator, favored fiscally conservative rural interests.

New Jersey's urban Democrats were concentrated in a few counties. They focused their attention on the local governments that provided most fiscal and patronage resources. To have any influence in Trenton, urban Democrats had to make common cause with rural Republicans. This county–based political system was not a recipe for activist state government.

The 1947 constitution greatly strengthened the governor's office, but a quarter century passed before governors could really exercise their new powers. The structure of the legislature was left undisturbed, and county–based politics continued. Lacking both political will and broad–based state taxes, the pattern of modest state budgets and activities persisted into the 1960s.

When federal court decisions in the late 1960s ended county–based legislative representation and weakened county party organizations, governors could

Table 16: New Jersey Average Per Capita State and Local Expenditures, Selected Functions, as Percentage of U.S. Average, 1977 and 1987

Function	1977	1987	1987 Rank
Elementary/Secondary Education	107	115	(5)
Higher Education	67	79	(39)
Highways	72	91	(27)
Public Welfare	106	114	(14)
Health and Hospitals	72	79	(34)
Police and Fire	119	131	(6)

Source: Significant Features of Fiscal Federalism, 1987

actually exercise their constitutional powers, and the legislature could professionalize. Democrats could gain more seats, and with migration and population growth, they were no longer as concentrated in only a few counties. These changes made it possible to pass broad–based taxes during the late 1960s and 1970s. Once the state commanded more resources, it began spending them.

Increases in overall spending have followed the twists and turns of the state and national economies. Broad–based taxes are elastic—their revenues rise and fall along with the economy. In periods of recession, state governments, most of which are constitutionally required to balance their budgets, often raise taxes to compensate for declines in revenue. When the economy improves, greater amounts of tax money flow in, and the temptation is to spend on new or expanded programs rather than to lower taxes.

As shown in table 15 when New Jersey raised its sales tax in 1970 to cope with economic difficulties, an improving economy brought in new revenue, which the state promptly spent and continued spending. Imposition of an income tax in 1976 did not have a big immediate effect, because the tax was at first quite low and completely offset by decreases in local property taxes. In 1983, faced with the worst recession since the 1930s, New Jersey raised both of its broad–based taxes. The deep economic trough was followed by a strong and sustained recovery. Along with much of the Northeast, New Jersey prospered even more than the nation as a whole. With the strongest economy in its history and less federal aid, New Jersey, like its neighbors, went on an unprecedented spending spree. As recession loomed again in the early 1990s—this time hitting the Northeast the hardest—the cycle repeated, and state taxes were raised once again.

The pattern of expenditures in table 16 reflects historical legacies. Even before the 1970s, policies that benefited localities and for which revenue was raised locally enjoyed high levels of support. Wealthy suburbs had long been amenable to taxing themselves to support their public schools. Municipal employees that were the foot soldiers of local party organizations were well–paid. However, none of these parochial entities was much interested in subsidizing higher education or health facilities benefiting the whole state.

When Trenton acquired additional resources, the home rule tradition insured that money would flow to the places it always had. If local tax dollars had always gone first and foremost to local schools, new state dollars would too. Transportation systems, colleges, and health or cultural facilities would have to wait their turn. Further, the tax system did not shift away from localities toward the state overnight; indeed, the shift is still more incomplete than in most other states. Broad–based state taxes began at modest rates and increased rather slowly. Understanding expenditure patterns requires an understanding of the evolution of the tax system.

TAXES AND TAX POLITICS

The most prominent characteristic of New Jersey's tax system is its strong reliance on the local property tax. Taxes on property began in 1670. Three centuries later, the local property tax was still the linchpin of government finance. As late as 1962, it generated 65 percent of all own–source (state and local) tax revenues in New Jersey, compared to a 38 percent average for all the states.

Even in 1989, long after New Jersey imposed broad–based sales and income taxes, property taxes still accounted for 43 percent of state and local tax dollars, as compared with a national average of 30 percent.[9] Only three states—Montana, New Hampshire, and Oregon—collected a larger proportion of income from this source. New Jersey still relies more heavily on the property tax than any other state with both sales and income taxes.

Midcentury State Tax Policy

By the mid–1950s, 31 states had a state income tax, 33 states had a general state sales tax, and only three—including New Jersey—had neither. About two–thirds of New Jersey's state revenues came from excise taxes and fees (e.g., on public utilities, motor fuels, vehicle registrations, cigarettes and alcohol, and racing); most of the rest from corporate taxes. In 1956, New Jersey state taxes, as a percentage of all own–source revenues, were at half the national average.

High local property taxes accounted for the divergence. On average, state and local taxes contributed about equally to a state's own–source revenue in the 1950s. In New Jersey, local revenues—virtually all from the property tax—still contributed four times as much. Its county and local leaders saw broad–based taxes as the "greatest threat to the endurance of the home rule tradition."[10]

Although some states began earlier, the majority imposed broad–based taxes in reaction to the Great Depression. In 1935, as one municipality after another went bankrupt, Republican Governor Harold Hoffman proposed a 2 percent sales tax and an income tax at half the federal rate. The legislature summarily rejected an income tax. The sales tax squeaked through in June with help from Democratic boss Frank Hague rather than Hoffman's Republican colleagues but was repealed in October after loud public protest. Despite a stone wall against new forms of taxation, existing taxes rose apace. An economist observed in 1960, "Taxes are not low in this state. Heavy property taxes and taxes adverse to business impede growth."[11]

Stung by the violent reaction to Hoffman's tax proposals, the entire New Jersey political establishment assumed "that endorsement of new taxes constitutes political suicide."[12] A state tax commission issued repeated criticisms but had an express policy of not advocating a reform program "until it is politically possible to pass it." Each year the legislature attempted "to get by without any reform of what is one of the worst tax systems of any wealthy state."[13]

One strategy to avoid new taxes, especially after World War II, was unusual reliance on public authorities. Legislative appropriations provided only $300 million of the $512 million state agencies spent in 1956. The remainder came mostly from highway authority tolls, and from license fees and tuition. New Jersey's penchant for authorities helped shape—one might say distort—priorities. Controlled for inflation and population growth, state spending between 1946 and 1956 grew at exactly the national average—174 percent. However, the rate of increased spending on highways was more than 50 percent above average, while the rate of increase for education and public welfare was well below average.[14]

The authorities responsible for the Garden State Parkway and the New Jersey Turnpike could issue bonds and spend huge sums without troubling the taxpayers; moreover, they could continue the tradition begun with railroad taxes—of extracting much of their income from out–of–state residents. That income retired the authorities' bonds and widened the highways, but there were no such handy funds available for mass transit, education, or social programs. The authorities' effect on public policy, however, paled in comparison to that of massive reliance on local property taxes.

Midcentury Tax Structure and the State–Local Finance System

Extraordinary dependence on the local property tax produced vast inequalities among counties and municipalities. Residents with low or fixed incomes suffered especially from a tax that had a limited relationship to ability to pay and no protection against housing inflation. Further, the tax system discriminated against urban areas with shrinking tax bases and increasing demands for public services. In 1951, assessment ratios (that is, the assessed valuation of a property as a proportion of its market value) were at least 50 percent above the state average in eight of the 13 largest municipalities.[15]

As cities imposed high tax rates to pay for constantly growing needs, businesses and middle–class residents fled, intensifying a vicious cycle.[16] Developers seeking cheap land and home buyers and businesses seeking low taxes produced "a premature spreading out of urban development, the creation of an automobile–dependent society, and the deterioration of established cities."[17]

Thus, in midcentury, the tax system relied on local property taxes that were insensitive to economic fluctuations, had little relation to ability to pay, and covered only a small proportion of income–producing assets. It accelerated cities' decline by depressing urban property values and was based on unstandardized and inequitable assessments.[18]

State Tax Policy and Politics: 1960 to 1989

By the mid–1960s, the climate finally seemed right for cautious tax reform.[19] The economy was booming. Recent migrants (especially from New York) were accustomed to higher levels of state services (and taxation). Democratic Governor Richard Hughes, who favored tax reform and more state services, began an eight–year tenure in 1962, part of the time with a Democratic legislature.

Hughes managed to get assembly approval of an income tax in 1966 after a big reelection victory but could not persuade the senate. Much of the opposition was framed as a preference for a sales tax, however, and Hughes was able to enact a 3 percent sales tax—New Jersey's first permanent broad–based tax—in April 1966.[20] It was less regressive than many state excise taxes in that it exempted both food and clothing.

When Republican William Cahill succeeded Hughes in 1970, the Republican–dominated legislature grudgingly—but quickly and by a large margin—approved Cahill's request to meet pressing revenue needs by raising the sales tax from 3 to 5 percent. Although in dollar terms the increase was as large as the tax's original imposition, there was much less controversy. It reaffirmed the common wisdom that it was easier to raise an existing tax than to impose a new one. A state–run lottery—another "painless" source of revenue—was also established that year.[21]

Along with the sales tax proposal, Cahill established a Tax Policy Committee to study the entire tax system. It recommended generating state and local revenue in approximately equal proportions from income, sales, and property taxes. The proposals called for shifting much of the tax burden from localities to the state, from property to income, and for an overall increase in revenues. The plan cut local property taxes by about half the amount of an increased state tax burden of $1.5 billion, and the committee also recommended a ceiling on property tax rates.

Cahill sought passage of this proposal at a special legislative session in 1972, but only nine of the 39 assembly Republicans would vote for it, and prospects in the senate were even worse. Republican displeasure with the plan played a major role in Cahill's primary–election defeat when he sought a second term in 1973.

In April 1973, a state supreme court decision in *Robinson v. Cahill* declared New Jersey's school funding mechanism—heavily reliant on the local property tax—unconstitutional. Substantial revenues from another source were needed to meet the court's requirements. Democratic Governor Brendan Byrne, who took office in January 1974 after campaigning on a platform of no new taxes in "the foreseeable future," fared no better than Cahill in his attempts to push further tax increases and tax reform through a now heavily Democratic legislature.

After the 1975 legislative elections, there were more months of protracted bargaining and more crises—most significantly, a July 1976 court order closing all public schools until a satisfactory funding mechanism was in place. Faced with this directive, and after more than three years of chaos, the legislature finally passed a state income tax a few weeks later.[22] A constitutional amendment specified that all revenues from the income tax were to be applied only to property tax relief. Most of the "relief" was supplied by the state assuming a larger proportion (about 40 percent) of the costs of the public schools.

To ensure that residents saw the connection between the income tax and property tax relief, all homeowners began receiving an annual property tax rebate check (averaging about $180) from Trenton. Even renters got a smaller amount. Senior citizens got larger rebates, helping many on fixed incomes. The rebate program did little to remedy the basic problems with the property tax because it was not linked to ability to pay. In the first year, however, total property taxes, including the rebates, did indeed drop by 17 percent.[23]

Compared to most other states' levies, the new income tax of 2 percent on the first $20,000 of income, and 2 1/2 percent above that, was quite modest. During Byrne's eight years in office, corporate income taxes were also raised twice (in 1975 and 1980), and some less progressive business taxes were repealed or

Table 17: Revenue Sources, New Jersey and U.S. Average, 1962-1987

Year	United States			New Jersey		
	Federal	State	Local	Federal	State	Local
1962	14	41	46	9	28	63
1968	17	43	40	12	35	53
1972	19	42	39	16	36	48
1978	23	43	34	20	41	39
1982	20	46	34	17	49	34
1987	17	46	37	14	52	34

Source: Significant Features of Fiscal Federalism.

Note: Table entries are percentages of revenue from each source.

phased out. Finally, Byrne also oversaw the passage of a public referendum legalizing casino gambling in Atlantic City in 1977. The principal motive behind the casino policy was to revitalize the ailing resort and tourism at the shore, but it was also yet another "painless" revenue–generating measure.[24]

Although Republican Tom Kean, Byrne's successor, ran on a tax–cutting platform and rejected any new taxes during his two terms, he did significantly extend the broad–based taxes. Greeted with major cuts in federal aid and the worst economic climate since the Great Depression when he took office in January 1982, Kean went along with increases in the sales tax (from 5 to 6 percent) and the income tax (raising the rates to 3 1/2 percent on income over $50,000) in 1983. In his first term, Kean also phased out the inheritance tax and some minor taxes businesses found particularly annoying.

A sharp rebound in the economy soon produced huge budget surpluses and partisan wrangling about how to return some of the bounty to taxpayers. Kean and the Republicans suggested returning some money directly through lower taxes. In September 1985, the Democratic majority in the legislature instead passed its own proposal for a credit against income tax bills of $65 for homeowners and $35 for tenants.[25]

With the improved economy and his own enormous popularity, Kean came under increasing pressure to perform major surgery on a tax system still overly reliant on the inequitable and inelastic property tax. His response was acquiescence to a bipartisan legislative proposal for yet another State and Local Expenditure and Revenue Policy Commission, known familiarly as the SLERP Commission.[26]

The SLERP Commission, created in December 1984, was asked to study the effects of mandated spending, the impact of the tax system on the economic

Table 18: Index of Tax Capacity

Year	1967	1975	1979	1981	1986	1988
N.J.	97	103	118	112	121	124
National Rank	(25)	(13)	(8)	(10)	(8)	(7)

Source: Significant Features of Fiscal Federalism, various years; Measuring State Fiscal Capacity (1986).

Note: Table entries are index numbers where 100 is the U.S. average.

viability of the state, its long–term adequacy for funding major state services, and the equity and efficiency of the state and local tax system. Plagued by delays in selecting an executive director and the governor's appointees, SLERP did not begin work until September 1985. The commission was directed to report in January 1986, a date conveniently after the 1985 gubernatorial and legislative elections. This assured that taxes in general, and property tax reform in particular, would not become a "front–burner" issue in the election. Because of its slow start, SLERP did not finish its work until 1988.

The effects of recent changes in the tax structure that SLERP was studying can be seen clearly in table 17.

Since the 1960s, New Jersey has lagged behind the national average in the proportion of revenue derived from the federal government. There has been a striking transformation in the proportion of revenues raised by local governments (which, relatively, dropped by close to half) and the proportion raised by state government (which rose concomitantly). The first big change is seen in 1968, two years after the imposition of the sales tax. Sales tax revenues, combined with increased intergovernmental transfers from federal Great Society programs, accounted for the 10 percent drop in the local share. The next big change, in 1978, reflects the establishment of the state income tax and still– increasing federal revenues, with a continuing decline of the local share.

By 1987, the effects of the Reagan–era federal cuts are obvious. The state share of revenue continued to rise as a result of increased sales and income tax rates. Tax elasticity in a boom period permitted Trenton to replace some of the revenues no longer available from Washington and to do so to a greater degree than most other states. The need for local governments to take up some of the slack is reflected in the failure of the local share to decline further after 1982, although local governments escaped the increases that occurred nationally.

Two other comparative measures provide further illumination. They are

Table 19: Index of Tax Effort

Year	1965	1975	1980	1982	1986	1988
N.J.	87	94	101	100	103	101
National Rank	(40)	(29)	(18)	(21)	(16)	(17)

Source: Significant Features of Fiscal Federalism, various years; Measuring State Fiscal Capacity (1986).

Note: Table entries are index numbers where 100 is the U.S. Average.

New Jersey's ratings in terms of tax effort and tax capacity. The tax capacity index measures the amount the state would raise, relative to all other states, if it applied a national average set of tax rates to 26 commonly used tax bases. Tax effort is the ratio of actual collections to tax capacity. These ratings are shown in tables 18 and 19.

In table 18, we see New Jersey's growing ability (relative to other states) to extract revenue from its citizens. From a middling position in the 1960s, New Jersey has risen much closer to the top. In table 19, we see the extent to which, particularly during the 1980s, political leaders were willing to do so, and the public was willing to pay.

Unlike the earlier Cahill commission, which reported before the imposition of the state income tax, SLERP concluded that new taxes were not required, and that tax reform should be revenue neutral. But as the Cahill commission had, it advocated a massive shift of the tax burden (about $1.2 billion in current dollars) from local property taxes to broad-based state taxes. The idea was that state rather than local revenues should be used to pay for what should be state rather than local government functions.[27]

SLERP recommended that Trenton assume the costs of the state court system, the local share of welfare costs, and county expenditures for psychiatric hospitals and centers for the developmentally disabled. Additionally, the state was to contribute a greater proportion of the costs of the public schools and county colleges.

All this could be accomplished, the commissioners suggested, by raising marginal income tax rates to 4 percent on income between $50,000 and $100,000 and 4.5 percent on income over $100,000 and by sales tax extensions. They also proposed means-tested "circuit breakers" on property taxes, thus making the existing property tax rebates passed as part of the 1976 income tax package more progressive.

The State–Local Tax System, 1960–1989

The SLERP proposals would have done much to create an equitable and efficient tax system. The broad–based taxes had moved the state somewhat in that direction, but the distortions caused by the property tax had become even worse than they were in the 1960s. The problems were the continuing disparity in assessment ratios and tax rates across the state; growing controversies about state–local responsibilities; and toward the end of the 1980s, skyrocketing local property tax increases everywhere, despite the presence of broad–based state taxes.

The issues related to assessment ratios and tax rates were many. First, although the state constitution mandated annual assessments of property at true value, in 1986, 133 of the state's 567 municipalities had not conducted revaluations for at least ten years. Cities like Newark and Trenton had not revalued for more than 20 years, causing enormous tax shocks when the revaluations were finally accomplished.[28] The director of the State Division of Taxation called "our utter failure, over a period of 200 years, to meet the standard of annual assessments of property for tax purposes" the "central issue of property tax administration."[29]

Growing disparities in effective tax rates between cities and suburbs were even more troublesome. In 1986, the effective tax rate in Princeton was $1.94 per $1,000 of assessed valuation, while Trenton, in the same county, had an effective rate of $4.85—as against a state average of $2.38. A former state treasurer calculated that if all municipalities were taxed at the statewide average rate, Newark's rate would drop by half and the rates in Camden and East Orange by two–thirds.[30]

Other factors also helped suburban property owners and hurt their urban counterparts. For one, businesses (cherished by local governments as "ratables") paid 30 percent of all local property taxes. Increasingly, they sought to locate in places like the Princeton area—with its low rates, open space, and prestigious address—and to leave places like Trenton. For another, tax exemptions and special rates also favored rural areas and discriminated against urban areas. Cities contained most tax exempt property devoted to public use (10 percent of the total property in the state; almost two–thirds of Newark's 24 square miles) such as government buildings, public universities, parks, airports, and seaports.[31]

Conversely, rural areas contained the open land subject to the much lower rates of the Farmland Assessment Act, which covered 25 percent of all state property in 1988. Intended to maintain open space, in effect it permitted the state to "rent" such space at very high costs. For example, one 106–acre parcel in Plainsboro—a rapidly developing area between Princeton and Trenton—was taxed at $1,300 per year under the Farmland Assessment Act when the annual levy would have been $419,000 at a market value rate.[32] It was thus no wonder that SLERP recommended a graduated property tax with lower rates for urban areas and higher rates for less developed sections. The state director of taxation called this proposal "the single most important proposal in the SLERP report."[33]

Gross differences in county tax effort and tax capacity indices resulted from this overall property tax system. Tax capacity was especially high and effort low in wealthy Bergen, Cape May, and Ocean Counties; capacity was low and effort high in the poorer counties of the south (Burlington, Camden, Cumberland, Gloucester, and Salem) and the urban north (Essex, Hudson, Passaic, and Union). Setting the state average at 100, the county tax capacity index ranged from 27 in Cumberland to 317 in Bergen, while the tax effort index ranged from 78 in Ocean to 139 in Essex and Hudson.[34]

Local officials also became increasingly irate about state mandates and state aid formulas. Mandates with price tags flooded out of Trenton without accompanying funds to pay for them. Municipalities were directed to engage in mandatory recycling, close local landfills, transport their solid waste as far away as Texas, increase public–employee salaries and pensions, and carry expensive insurance policies.

Not only were there no state funds to meet these costs, but existing aid was cut. A particular case in point was the franchise and gross receipts taxes paid by utilities and distributed pro rata to municipalities. In 1980, payments to individual municipalities were capped and the excess used for a new "distressed cities" aid program. Pleasure that Trenton began collecting these revenues for them in 1980 faded quickly when, beginning in 1982, the state began keeping a large portion for its own purposes.

Similarly, the state established a revenue–sharing program in 1977 pegged at 7 percent of income tax receipts which, in the tax's first year, yielded $50 million. In subsequent years, Trenton kept the fund at $50 million, although if it had distributed the 7 percent of receipts specified in the law, the amount would have reached $195 million by 1988.

Because local governments almost never received what the statutes said they should get—according to the school aid, county college, revenue–sharing, and other statutory formulas, property taxes escalated sharply. Between 1982 and 1988, they rose as a percentage of true property value from 3.25 percent to 5.9 percent. Property taxes more than doubled during the 1980s, capped by a 13 percent average increase in 1989. Increases had lagged behind inflation and income growth in the late 1970s and early 1980s, but that ended as the 1980s progressed.[35]

The Florio Tax Plan

When Governor Jim Florio assumed office in 1990, he faced a large budget deficit and growing anger over property tax increases. Further, the state supreme court was about to render another school–funding decision in the case of *Abbott v. Burke*. The court was expected to declare again that a school–funding mechanism based heavily on local property taxes was unconstitutional. Florio chose to take on these two major challenges—the major shortfall in the state budget and the impending school finance decision—together and immediately.

In his first months in office, Florio proposed massive tax changes embodying almost every recommendation students of the tax system had suggested over the past thirty years, and then some. The income tax was to become sharply progressive, with the highest marginal rate rising from 3 1/2 to 7 percent. The new rates were projected to produce about $1.4 billion in additional revenue.

Another point was added to the sales tax, whose 7–percent rate would be the second highest in the nation. It was to be extended to nonfood grocery items such as paper goods (ridiculed as the "toilet paper tax"), and also heavy trucks, janitorial services, cable television, telephone calls, and telecommunications services. There was a new tax on the gross receipts of oil companies and increases in "sin taxes" on smoking materials and alcohol. These excise taxes were to produce about the same amount of revenue as the income tax and close the budget gap.

The new income tax revenues were dedicated to property tax reform. Florio's plan scrapped universal property tax rebates and credits and substituted larger rebates for the least wealthy and no rebates for the most wealthy. Only taxpayers with under $65,000 in family income, paying more than 5 percent of gross income in property taxes, would be eligible for a rebate of up to $500 on a sliding scale.

The rest of the new income tax revenue was dedicated to a similarly redistributive program of school aid, intended to address the anticipated decision in *Abbott v. Burke*. Florio proposed pouring $1.4 billion more into school aid, almost half of it for the state's 30 poorest districts—mostly urban and with large numbers of minority students. "Middle–class" districts would receive the rest. About a third of all school districts, with a quarter of the students, were deemed wealthy enough to receive no general school aid. Finally, the governor proposed taking over the counties' costs for welfare and social services. He emphasized that 83 percent of taxpayers would pay no more in income taxes; the wealthiest 17 percent of the population would bear the entire new income tax burden.

The many elements and complicated scheduling of the Florio plan confused the public. It had two major phases. The excise taxes would take effect in July 1990, to close the $550 million gap in the fiscal year 1991 budget left by Kean. Balancing the fiscal year 1991 budget also required unpopular cuts, such as funding the existing school–aid formula at only 83 percent of the statutory requirement (10 percent below fiscal year 1990) and shortening hours at Division of Motor Vehicles facilities. There were also to be no property tax rebates at all in fiscal year 1991.

Although already announced, neither the income tax increase nor the new property tax rebate program were to go into effect until July 1991. A nervous Democratic legislature, though not up for more than a year, knew voters would experience short–term pain but no short–term gain. During 1990 and much of 1991, they would pay more every time they went to the supermarket or the drugstore, bought a six–pack, made a phone call, or stopped at a gas station. Most would also be hit with higher property taxes to cover the shortfall in state school aid. Their annual rebate checks would be nowhere in sight, and it would be another year before any benefited from the promised property tax reform.

Consequently, the legislature tinkered with the plan— advancing the start of the stiffer income taxes to January 1991 to pay for a reduced old–style rebate that fiscal year, exempting cable television and over–the–counter drugs from the sales tax, upping some more "sin taxes," and raising the significant cutting point in the income tax rates to $70,000 for families. After three attempts, the income tax increase finally received the requisite 41 votes (one more than an absolute majority) in the assembly, as did the sales tax increase and the budget as a whole. The senate also passed all three pieces of legislation with the minimum necessary 21 votes. Not a single Republican voted for any of the measures in either house.

When July 1990 came, and the price of cigarettes, beer, paper towels, and gasoline all went up at once, the public erupted in anger not seen since the Hoffman tax increase of 1935. A poll found that 80 percent gave the governor negative ratings on his tax policy and 65 percent similar marks on the budget. Three–quarters could not cite anything positive Florio had done since he took office and believed the governor's economic plan would hurt "people like yourself." Despite his assertions that the plan was the greatest property tax relief measure in history, only 2 percent thought their property levies would go down, and 70 percent thought they would go up.[36]

The 1990 elections showed the depth of public anger. U.S. Senator Bill Bradley, who had refused to comment on the tax plan, came close to defeat. Republicans easily won a special state senate election widely seen as a referendum on taxes and deposed local Democrats all over the state. Middlesex County elected Republican freeholders for the first time in 20 years, and the GOP took control in Florio's home county of Camden.

The next morning, the governor described the results as "a strong message directed at me and the policies of my administration." He acknowledged that "leadership" required not only "hard decisions," but also "bringing people to build a consensus, to build a mandate....The other part of leadership in a democratic society entails doing more of what I did not do."[37]

Property taxes did decline in more than half of New Jersey municipalities in 1991 (partly as a result of the legislature later moving a substantial portion of the new school–aid money into additional property tax relief). However, in April, 70 percent of residents still rated Florio's tax policy as "poor." Fewer than a third gave him positive marks for anything. His approval rating sank to 17 percent, tied for historic worst with Governor Byrne's showing when the income tax was first passed in 1976. However, the hostility to Florio was even deeper. At his lowest point, 34 percent had termed Byrne's performance "poor." A full 48 percent gave Florio this rating in the spring of 1991.[38]

That November, the Republicans, running on a promise to roll back the sales tax increase, gained veto–proof majorities in both houses of the legislature, and more local offices fell to the GOP. Huge legislative majorities permitted the Republicans to rewrite much of the governor's fiscal year 1993 budget on a line–item basis and to override Florio's veto of their handiwork. The 1 percent sales tax rollback had left a $600–million revenue hole. Half of it was made up by lowering property tax rebates to a flat $90 for homeowners and $30 for tenants and restricting them to households making less than $40,000. Only the politically potent senior citizens and the disabled were still able to collect as much as $500.

Amidst all the hostility and political drama, there were indications that a smaller tax package or one introduced over a longer period of time would have fared better with the voters. It was less what Florio did than the way that he did it that enraged his constituents.

First, instantly forsaking his "no new taxes" campaign pledge and promise to conduct a thorough state audit gave the governor severe credibility problems. More than two–thirds of the state's residents believed Florio "didn't tell all he knew" about state fiscal problems during the campaign. An equal number admitted taxes had to be raised, but most felt the increases could have been much smaller.[39]

Second, the heavily graduated income tax rates, along with the plan to spend much of the new revenue in a small number of urban school systems, rekindled the historic animosity between cities and suburbs. Many suburbanites—the large majority of the population—had serious doubts that long mismanaged and corrupt urban school systems—now with heavy minority populations—could absorb so much new money so rapidly and use it wisely. This "class warfare," which historically had ugly religious undertones, took on more explosive racial ones when Education Commissioner John Ellis suggested that racism accounted for some of the opposition.

On learning that "wealthy" school districts would have to replace lost state aid with higher property taxes, and much of the ballyhooed new aid to "middle–class districts" would be swallowed up by a shift in teacher pension costs from the state to municipalities, even many sympathetic to helping poor children abandoned the governor. Some "wealthy" districts scheduled to lose all aid were actually heterogeneous communities. Unlike Alpine in Bergen County, where average family income is over $400,000, other ostensibly "wealthy" towns like Hackensack or Edison had thousands of lower and middle–income residents.

Many citizens also disagreed with Florio about how his plan would affect various segments of the population. A majority of those with family earnings of $70,000—the cutoff for the highest income tax rate—believed that to be a "middle–class" income. Despite the administration's messages and constant journalistic references to the governor as Robin Hood, two–thirds of New Jerseyans thought the plan would hurt the poor, and 71 percent thought it would "make no difference" to the rich.[40]

Shortly before the 1989 gubernatorial election, former Governor Byrne had listed four keys to the passage of the state income tax in 1976. First, a tax plan must be simple—too many things at once led to confusion and provided targets for criticism.[41] Second, in politically competitive New Jersey, tax measures had to have bipartisan support. Third, a tax plan had to emphasize "salable" issues. Finally, the public had to believe a real crisis would occur without new tax revenues. By following these guides, the governor derisively dubbed "One–Term Byrne" in 1976 had won landslide reelection in 1977, when his opponent could not convincingly explain how the state could function without an income tax.

The Byrne and Florio tax plans stood in sharp contrast when measured by Byrne's criteria. The Byrne plan involved one simple tax—a modest and virtually flat income tax–rather than the many levies and graduated rates of the Florio scheme. It gained significant Republican support and was largely crafted in the legislature after three years of negotiation. Florio instead pushed his plan through within five months of taking office, without a single Republican vote.

The 1976 plan promised property tax relief to all, which appeared almost immediately in the form of rebate checks. The 1990 plan gave increased property tax relief to about half of New Jersey's taxpayers, while the other half

Table 20: Percentage of Family Income Paid in State and Local Taxes, New Jersey and U.S., 1985 and 1991

	N.J. 1985	N.J. 1991	U.S. 1991
			(Average)
Top 1% earners	6.8	9.7	7.6
Middle quintile	9.3	10.8	10.0
Lowest quintile	13.3	15.2	13.8

Source: Citizen's for Tax Justice 1991 Study.

received either smaller rebates or none at all. There was also a long period of higher taxes before the new rebate checks arrived.

Finally, the Byrne tax reform eventually passed in the midst of a genuine crisis—the state supreme court's shutdown of the public schools in July 1976—but a crisis Byrne expected and indeed encouraged. As he recalled, "Everybody says New Jersey adopted a state income tax because there was a crisis. Actually, I created that crisis. I asked [the state supreme court] to close the schools in 1976. If I hadn't, I don't think New Jersey would have a state income tax today. So maybe to get tax reform we're going to have to find a candidate who can create a crisis."[42] With a decision looming in *Abbott v. Burke*, Florio, like Byrne, could have used the ruling to force legislative action and made some Republicans his reluctant partners. Instead, when the decision was handed down, it was obvious that the Florio taxes greatly exceeded the court's requirements.

To make the governor's life even more difficult, deep economic recession left the administration lamely explaining why, despite all the new taxes, the fiscal year 1991 and 1992 budgets had projected deficits larger than the fiscal year 1990 deficit "inherited" from Tom Kean. More new levies to deal with true crises—for example, a payroll tax proposed to fund a hemorrhaging trust fund for the million New Jerseyans without health insurance—became impossible in the short run.

Lost in the furor—and subject to partisan or ideological interpretation—was the real shape of the New Jersey tax system after the Florio reforms. The data in table 20, from the annual study by the national tax study group Citizens for Tax Justice, cast some light on this matter.[43]

At every income level, New Jerseyans are taxed more heavily than the national average–overall, more heavily than the residents of 41 other states. High sales and property taxes make low–income residents fare poorly in absolute terms. However, doubling the income tax rate for the state's wealthiest residents has increased their tax burden by much the largest proportion. The "middle middle," which led the tax revolt, fares little worse than such earners do nationally. State taxes are high, but for partisans of a progressive tax system, fairer than they were.

The complete story of the tax battles of the 1990s remains to be written. It is already clear, however, how the latest New Jersey tax saga reflects both continuity and change.

Taxing and spending continue to centralize in Trenton, and tax effort draws closer to tax capacity as New Jersey's fiscal system comes more to resemble that of other wealthy states. Still lurking beneath the surface, however, are the strong home rule tradition, the public's "guilty until proven innocent" attitude toward tax–raising politicians, suburban indifference to the plight of New Jersey's struggling cities and their residents, and the vestiges of class warfare. As the early years of the Florio administration demonstrated, politicians ignore this historic legacy at their peril.

CHAPTER FIFTEEN

The Politics of Education

*The Legislature shall provide for the maintenance and support of a
thorough and efficient system of free public schools for the instruction of
all children in the state between the ages of five and eighteen years.*
— 1875 amendment to the New Jersey Constitution

*Whether the state acts directly or imposes the role upon local government,
the end product must be what the constitution commands....If local
government fails, the state must compel it to act, and if local government
cannot carry the burden, the state must itself meet the continuing
obligation.*

—New Jersey Supreme Court in the *Robinson v. Cahill*
landmark school funding case, 1973

Home rule versus state direction, cities versus suburbs, local property taxes vs. broad–based state taxes, how to achieve economic development and social justice—nowhere are these debates more prominent than in the politics of public education.

The 1970s mark a major dividing line for New Jersey education policy. Before then, coalitions of local leaders made state policy. After the 1970s, the clarion call of "one New Jersey" referred to nothing so much as public education and its direction from Trenton.

EDUCATION POLICY IN HISTORIC PERSPECTIVE

Public education in New Jersey assumed its distinctive characteristics by World War II. It was handsomely supported; New Jersey spent at a rate a third above the national average by the 1920s. Teachers enjoyed above–average salaries and state–financed pensions. As the rest of the country saw a massive wave of consolidations, New Jersey, with its home rule tradition, increased the number of school districts.[1]

Trenton's contribution to local education budgets through the 1940s was 3 to 6 percent. Next door, Albany already provided a third of the funds for New

York's schools.[2] Over nine in ten New Jersey education dollars came from local property taxes. Most districts approved their budgets in annual elections and at the same time, elected school–board members. In urban areas, appointments to the school board and jobs in the school system were important patronage resources for local politicians.

State education commissioners came from the local educational establishment. Although controlling little money, they approved curricula, certified teachers, appointed county education superintendents, and chose the administrators and faculties of the state teachers' colleges. This role in higher education was uncommon in other states. Commissioner Frederick Raubinger, appointed by Republican Governor Alfred Driscoll in 1952 and reappointed by Democrats Robert Meyner and Richard Hughes in 1957 and 1962, was often cited as an example of how state education commissioners, in symbiotic relationships with interest groups, could dominate educational policy–making.[3] Raubinger "established himself as a separate entity in state government."[4]

Every few months, Raubinger met at a Princeton inn with leaders of the New Jersey Education Association, the School Boards Association, the PTA, and the superintendents' association. They discussed "tactics, general strategy .and intelligence on the political climate."[5] Among the participants, NJEA, with its large membership and research capacity, ranked second in influence to the commissioner.

Raubinger presided over a system in which local preferences and resources produced wide regional disparities. By the late 1950s, New Jersey was second to New York in per–capita expenditures for elementary and secondary education. However, in terms of state aid, it ranked 37th among the 48 states. Hudson and Essex counties in the north spent almost twice as much per student as did Camden and Cumberland counties in the south.

A Transition Period—The Hughes and Cahill Years

When Democrat Richard Hughes won easy reelection and control of both legislative houses in 1965, he obtained passage of the first broad–based state tax to support education and could seek dominance over state policy. A showdown with Raubinger arose over Hughes's resolve to strengthen higher education.[6] New Jersey's public institutions for the most part had neither quality nor quantity to recommend them. County college legislation was not passed until 1962, the six teachers' colleges each enrolled only about 2,000 students, and Rutgers—the nominal state university—had only 11,000 students on three campuses.[7]

Other public higher education systems in the Northeast developed late because of a sizable private sector, but New Jersey's private institutions were relatively few and mostly small. Almost half of high school graduates seeking higher education attended colleges elsewhere. New Jersey was known in education circles as the "Cowbird State"—after a creature that places its young in others' nests.

Hughes won creation of a cabinet–level Department of Higher Education, which struck at the heart of Raubinger's empire. The commissioner resigned in protest and orchestrated a comeback attempt. He failed, and Hughes' appointment of new commissioners of education and higher education in 1967, along with resources from the new sales tax, produced a new state role in education.

The new education commissioner, Carl Marburger, served in a time of turbulence. During his five–year term, the legislature began to develop the capacity to influence policy. The federal government demanded an end to de facto segregated schools in central and southern New Jersey. A property tax rebellion led to rejection of 170 district school budgets in 1969.[8] And just as Marburger arrived with a mandate to wrest power from the education establishment, NJEA was being transformed from a professional organization into a union. As with many other milestones in New Jersey affairs, this change had its roots in New York City.

In December 1961, the American Federation of Teachers (AFT) won recognition as bargaining agent for New York City's teachers. A New Jersey offshoot organized some urban districts but had only 1,600 members in 17 locals, as compared with NJEA's 46,000 members. AFT criticism, however, led NJEA to try to counter charges that it was not aggressive enough and to seek a "professional" bargaining law. The legislature passed the measure in 1965, but Governor Hughes vetoed it.

Concurrent efforts by all state employees to unionize and gain bargaining rights complicated matters for NJEA. To fight AFT expansion in urban districts, NJEA supported teacher strikes in Newark and Perth Amboy in 1965–66 while still seeking a separate bargaining law for teachers. In 1968, in a loss for Hughes as well as NJEA, the legislature overrode a gubernatorial veto and passed the Public Employee Relations Act (PERA).

PERA specified that grievance procedures, wages, and hours for all public employees, including teachers, be negotiated between employee bargaining agents and a new state Public Employee Relations Commission (PERC). None of the "professional" rights NJEA had sought—such as its traditional voice in curricular, class size, and teacher–transfer decisions—were included. An even less malleable Republican governor (William Cahill) and legislature took office in 1970. In response, NJEA transformed itself from a professional association to a trade union practically overnight.[9]

Before PERA, NJEA sponsored professional publications, an annual conference on professional issues, selective benefits for members, and lobbying. With teachers' interest now centered on favorable contracts, NJEA radically reoriented itself to vanquish the AFT. By the mid–1970s, the field service division, which helped with contract negotiations, comprised more than half of NJEA personnel and almost as much of its budget.

Although unable to gain a "closed shop," NJEA did win a dues checkoff and increased its membership to about 80 percent of all teachers. Declining attendance at the annual conference—from 55 percent to 28 percent of members—reflected changing interests. Although all New Jersey public schools still close for two days when NJEA holds its annual November convention in Atlantic City, most members now regard this time as just another paid holiday.[10]

Finally, NJEA reorganized its political operations. Its political action committee, created in 1972, became a major source of funds and campaign workers for legislative candidates. NJEA lobbyists who had operated as the "public relations" division became the mainstays of a renamed "governmental relations" office, signaling a new formalism in their relationship with the Department of Education and a shift in focus from the department to the legislature.[11]

Before coming to New Jersey, Commissioner Marburger had served President Lyndon Johnson, specializing in educational programs for the disadvantaged. Marburger shared Governor Hughes's special interest in minority education and Governor Cahill's determination to weaken NJEA influence and encourage broader participation in educational policy–making.

Thus began a rare period when urban reformers and fiscally conservative Republicans found common cause. The urban reformers embraced state assessment tests and merit pay for teachers as ways of holding educators responsible for students' performance. They also championed community participation in decision–making. Republicans also liked the ideas of educational accountability and local control. The unusual coalition inaugurated three enduring policy changes.

First, Marburger's "Our Schools" program introduced broad public participation, as thousands of citizens attended meetings to set goals for local schools. Second, despite NJEA opposition, the state began testing students' reading and mathematics skills. Third, the State School Incentive Equalization Law of 1970 (known as the Bateman bill, for its chief sponsor) provided special state aid to districts with many disadvantaged students and inadequate tax bases. It guaranteed each district the average tax capacity in the state and awarded extra funds for each student on the welfare rolls.[12]

The changes generated heated debate. NJEA, allied with legislators irate about imposed integration plans, supported the senate's refusal to reconfirm Commissioner Marburger when his term expired in 1972—the first such rebuff of a gubernatorial nominee in New Jersey's history.[13] NJEA's court challenge of the state assessment tests, although eventually unsuccessful, delayed release of the results.[14]

Most crucially, the new school funding law—the first state effort to aid poor and mostly urban school districts—was immediately challenged as inadequate by those it professed to assist. On February 13, 1970, a suit was filed in Hudson County Superior Court on behalf of Kenneth Robinson, a sixth grade student in Jersey City's public schools. The issues in *Robinson v. Cahill* remain at the center of New Jersey's major political battles.

A New Role for the State in Education Policy

Robinson v. Cahill and its aftermath produced massive change in the state's role in education policy, and spilled over to other areas. Education funding is central to the long–standing controversy, described in chapter 14, about the entire state–local finance system. The tax system is inextricably connected to home rule—another perennial issue. Home rule in the context of education deals with citizens' rights, by voting on school budgets, to determine resource commitments to their local schools. Those resources determine much about districts' curricula and other programs. New Jersey is one of only four states that allow voters a say on school spending.[15]

Home rule also accounts for the presence of over 600 separate school districts, a third of which serve fewer than 500 students. Texas, with twice the population and 34 times the landmass, has 188 districts. New Jersey has more school districts than Delaware, Pennsylvania, Maryland, and West Virginia combined.[16]

Home rule is also linked to the dark side of New Jersey's "tribal politics." Once a hostile rivalry between Protestant suburbs and Catholic cities, by the 1970s, the rivalry was between largely white suburbs, mostly middle–class or wealthy, and largely minority urban areas, mostly poorer. The *Robinson* plaintiffs argued that educational quality strongly affected social and economic mobility. The state thus had an obligation to equalize quality across communities irrespective of their resources. New Jersey's recent governors have offered different but increasingly aggressive responses to that contention.

State Education Policy in the Byrne Years

When Democrat Brendan Byrne took office in January 1974, there were already three court rulings in the matter of *Robinson v. Cahill*. The legislature's rejection of Commissioner Marburger and Republican primary voters' rejection of Governor Cahill (not unconnected events), had also left the education department leaderless for over a year.

In January 1972, Superior Court Judge Theodore Botter found the Bateman bill violated the equal protection clauses in the federal and state constitutions. A funding formula so dependent on local property taxes discriminated against pupils in districts with low property wealth and imposed unequal burdens for "a common state purpose" on taxpayers in different localities. While acknowledging it was not the only factor, Botter wrote, "More money should make a significant difference in many poor districts....much can be done and doing more will cost more. Education is no exception to this fact of life."[17]

Botter also accepted an amicus argument that the state constitution's guarantee of a "thorough and efficient" program of instruction for all pupils required the state to ensure a still indeterminate level of educational quality. State policy thus had to address both funding strategies and the quality of education provided.

Botter's decision was immediately appealed to the state supreme court, which first ruled on *Robinson v. Cahill* in April 1973. By then, the U.S. Supreme Court had found in *Rodriguez v. San Antonio School District* that a Texas law similar to New Jersey's did not violate the federal constitution's equal protection clause. The New Jersey Supreme Court also rejected an equal protection argument grounded in the state constitution. However, it upheld Botter based on the "thorough and efficient" clause. The decision was unanimous.

The state supreme court accepted "the proposition that the quality of educational opportunity does depend in substantial measure upon the number of dollars invested" and further observed, "we have been shown no other viable criterion for measuring compliance with the constitutional mandate." The justices added, "the State must define in some discernible way the educational obligations and must compel the local school districts to raise the money necessary to provide that opportunity. The State has never spelled out the contents of the constitutionally mandated educational opportunity. Nor has the State required the school districts to raise money needed to achieve that unstated standard....our present scheme is a patchy product reflecting provincial contests rather than a plan sensible only to the constitutional mandate."[18] In another ruling in June 1973, the court required legislative action by December 31, 1974.

To address these decisions, Governor Byrne and the legislature had to devise an acceptable distribution scheme for state school aid and fund it. They also had to define a "thorough and efficient" education and how to measure and monitor it. All proved to be agonizing exercises.

The December 1974 court "deadline" was only a beginning. New court deadlines, failed tax plans, and unacceptable funding schemes came and went for two more years. With no satisfactory legislative action, the supreme court, in its seventh ruling in *Robinson*, closed all public schools on July 1, 1976. Eight days later and three years after the court's first "deadline," an acceptable school funding plan was enacted. It was embodied in the Public School Education Act of 1975 (known as Chapter 212) and the income tax law of 1976.

The new funding scheme used state aid to further equalize school districts' tax capacity. Whereas the old plan favored districts with poor children, the new scheme favored districts with low property values per pupil—which, along with cities, included middle–class residential suburbs with few commercial ratables.[19] As Jersey City, Kenneth Robinson's home district, illustrates, poorer urban districts gained little additional revenue when Chapter 212 replaced the Bateman bill, but the state picked up a larger proportion of their costs.

By 1975–76, when the Bateman bill was fully phased in, Jersey City got 43 percent of its total school funds from Trenton and spent at a rate 94 percent of the statewide average. A year later, under Chapter 212, the state financed 58 percent of its budget, and Jersey City was spending at a rate equal to 97 percent of the average district.[20]

With tax capacity equalization accomplished, it was left to individual districts to decide how much capacity to tap. Districts could choose their own local taxing and spending levels and thus maintain or even exacerbate expenditure disparities. Some Chapter 212 provisions made disparities likely to develop.

Equalization aid based on prior–year expenditures favored wealthier suburbs losing students in a period of "birth dearth" at a rate faster than cities. Further, only about half of state aid fell under the equalization formula. The other half— for compensatory education, transportation subsidies, and especially teachers' pensions and social security costs—also tended to favor suburbs with intradistrict busing, smaller classes, and better–paid teachers. Even the compensatory aid formula advantaged wealthier districts, because it provided a fixed amount per student, regardless of whether the student had one special need or several.

Finally, "minimum state aid"—an equalization aid floor for every district regardless of wealth—was included to get suburban support for the entire package. For similar reasons, state aid was held to an average of 40 percent of education costs, as opposed to the 50 percent national average.

The new plan bespoke political pragmatism. To achieve property tax relief for urban taxpayers, it distributed considerable aid to middle class suburbs. It respected home rule by leaving to municipalities decisions about the level of resources to commit to education. It gained support for the income tax from NJEA (which had earlier opposed it in fear of antagonizing some legislative allies) after veiled threats to end full state payment of teacher pensions. While not a perfect plan from a "good government" point of view, it had the political virtue of leaving everyone feeling they had won something.

Similar prudence characterized the approach to defining and monitoring "thorough and efficient" education. Cahill's conflicts with the legislature made Byrne leery of state standards. NJEA, which gave Byrne its first formal gubernatorial endorsement, was leading the charge against state testing.

Still, Byrne needed some Republican votes for the income tax that was the linchpin of the funding scheme—both to pass it and to give it legitimacy. Ever suspicious of "throwing money" at social problems, the Republicans demanded "accountability" in return for new state school funds—through measurable education standards and testing.

In 1975, while still dickering over funding schemes, the legislature had passed a "T&E law" defining "a thorough and efficient education." Key phrases in the law—"reasonable levels of proficiency in the basic communication and computational skills," "program breadth to develop individual talents and abilities," "evaluation and monitoring of programs at both state and local levels," and "annual testing for achievement in basic skills areas"—were left to bureaucrats to clarify—in this case, in regulations to be developed by the Department of Education.[21]

Educational "progress" can be gauged by means of "input," "output," or "process" measures. "Inputs" are quantitative measures of facilities, staff, curricular richness, and other tangibles—all easily translatable into money. "Outputs" are also quantitative measures, such as dropout rates and test scores. "Process" measures focus on qualitative relationships between teachers, children, schools, and the community. They emphasize consensual goal setting and curricular planning. All these approaches had their partisans in New Jersey.

In *Robinson*, the supreme court justices had said that inputs—defined as more money, more equally distributed—were the only "viable criterion" they had been shown for assuring a "thorough and efficient" education. NJEA also favored input measures implying more and better-paid staff, more materials, and improved physical plants. Teachers asserted quantitative testing did not measure different kinds of abilities or creativity and encouraged mediocrity and "teaching to the test." NJEA also argued that failing state tests would contribute, particularly in the case of minority students, to a sense of inadequacy. Unspoken was the fear that student test scores might also be used to evaluate teachers.

Output measures were favored by the unusual alliance that had coalesced around Commissioner Marburger—Republicans, urban reformers, the school boards association, and business groups. Republicans and school board members saw test scores as a way to enforce accountability. Business groups thought them the best way to assure a trained work force. The reformers—led by Newark's Urban Coalition and the Education Law Center (which had prepared the "thorough and efficient" amicus brief) believed testing could identify children needing help and make the state responsible for setting skill floors and providing the resources needed to reach them.

Developing the administration's position on T&E fell to Fred Burke, who became education commissioner in 1975. Burke was acutely sensitive to the politics of the issue. In devising the administrative code for T&E, Burke strongly inclined toward "process" measures. He argued that "education" was too subtle to measure by either inputs or outputs and emphasized local goal setting and curricular decisions as the key elements of T&E. Process measures were less easily quantifiable and avoided the political minefields of the other choices.

Those favoring "outputs" won the first battles. In March 1976, Republican Assemblyman Tom Kean introduced a bill drafted by the Education Law Center, mandating "minimum basic skills" tests and state standards. The bill had 18 Republican cosponsors. Although Burke opposed it, Governor Byrne knew it was the price for Republican support of the still–unpassed income tax and endorsed it. Within two weeks, it passed the assembly overwhelmingly.

However, when the bill reached the senate two months later, NJEA allies managed to amend it to allow local districts to establish local "interim goals" and remediation programs. This amendment accorded with Commissioner Burke's plan for "state guidelines and local standards" and was widely seen as an NJEA victory.

The seventh draft of the administrative code, finally adopted by the State Board of Education in February 1978, defined T&E primarily in process terms. The state was to monitor all schools annually on over 300 items, including financial management, curriculum planning, goal setting, and facilities planning, as well as basic skills achievement. Passing scores for the basic skills tests were set low enough that urban pass rates would not be fatally embarrassing, but high enough to require more tangible support for schools. A study of participants in local goal–setting meetings found many to be

NJEA members or their relatives.[22]

Thus, all the criteria for assessing a "thorough and efficient" education and their supporting clienteles got some attention, but "process" measures—those least subject to easy quantification—dominated. By the time Byrne left office in January 1982, advocates of outcome measures had again made some headway. High school graduation requirements were increased, and plans were in the works for stiffer assessment tests.

Despite its Trenton lobbyists and campaign contributions, NJEA suffered repeated setbacks. Its campaign contributions modestly affected assembly votes on union—favored issues but had little effect on senate voting.[23] After losing a key bargaining rights case in the state supreme court in 1978, NJEA lost again on the same issue when the senate rejected an assembly–endorsed measure.[24] These defeats pushed NJEA even further into a "union mentality." Membership swelled to over 130,000 with a 1979 decision to admit school clerical workers, bus drivers, cafeteria workers, and aides.

State Education Policy in the Kean Years

When Republican Tom Kean succeeded Brendan Byrne in January 1982, the governorship passed to a leading advocate of "outcome" measures. A former teacher, doctoral candidate in education, and chair of the assembly education committee, the new governor had unusual expertise in education policy.

American schooling was becoming a national concern as Kean took office. *A Nation at Risk*, a federal study likening the effects of American educational failures to destruction by an invading enemy, was published about a year later, and the National Governors Association made education a special focus. As "the education governor," Kean sponsored more than 40 initiatives that drew national attention.[25] The Kean years had all the requirements for policy breakthroughs— a widely recognized problem, a receptive national mood, specialists with proposals at the ready, and an entrepreneur to push them.[26]

Rather than the "state guidelines and local standards" of the Byrne era, Kean preferred "state standards and local guidelines." When he and Education Commissioner Saul Cooperman issued a "Blueprint for Educational Reform" in 1983, NJEA called its exclusion from the plan's formulation "insulting."[27] This recalled Commissioner Marburger's desire "to establish that there was a Commissioner, that I was the Commissioner, that the NJEA was not determining policy for education for the state."[28]

The Kean administration inaugurated a more difficult high school proficiency test all students had to pass in order to graduate. An annual School

Report Card, sent to each student's home, gave comparative information on schools' test scores, dropout rates, percentage of graduates pursuing higher education, and the like.

The 300 items on the "process" advocates' monitoring list were reduced to 52. Districts passing monitoring gained certification for five years rather than one. In return for this reduced intrusiveness, failing systems had to remedy deficiencies in a reasonable time or face state takeover of their schools for at least five years. The controversial plan spawned a long legislative battle but finally passed when grievance procedures and job security for teachers and administrators were included.

In May 1988, Commissioner Cooperman moved to take over the Jersey City school system on the grounds that it was "not providing a thorough and efficient education for its children." Cooperman accused the district of fiscal mismanagement, political interference, and inadequate response to monitoring.[29] In October 1989, after more than a year of administrative law hearings, state takeover of the district occurred—the first in American history—with Governor Kean condemning Jersey City for committing "educational child abuse."[30] (In 1991, Paterson became the second district taken over by the state).

Many of Kean's initiatives focused on attracting and keeping good teachers, whom he saw as the key to quality education. An "alternate route" plan permitted college graduates to teach in the public schools before completing the education courses required for teacher certification. New Jersey's "alternate route" teachers had better college records, had higher pass rates on the National Teachers Examination, were more likely to be members of minority groups, and were more willing to teach in urban schools than were "conventional route" teachers.[31]

Kean also sponsored higher minimum teacher salaries and state academies where instructors could study educational innovations. Parents annually nominated an exemplary teacher in each school who received a $1,000 discretionary grant for instructional materials. With the accountability provided by state testing and takeover, the governor's constituents were willing to fund these initiatives. State aid to education almost doubled during the eight Kean years, constituting a quarter of the state budget in fiscal year 1986, and a third four years later.

Kean's basic philosophy was that disadvantaged students should have the same opportunities and be held to the same standards as those in wealthy suburbs. By the year 2000, minority students would constitute almost a third of New Jersey's children. All children had to learn the higher–order academic skills and cultural values needed to compete in the new "high–tech" economy and provide a work force whose skills matched the available jobs. To think they could not, Kean asserted, bordered on racism.[32]

Kean pointed pridefully to improved educational "outcomes" during his tenure. The proportion of students passing all sections of the High School Proficiency Test (HSPT) on their first attempt rose from 38 percent in 1986 to 68 percent in 1989. Average scores on the Scholastic Aptitude Test rose 30 points from 1981's historic low—the seventh highest increase among the 22 states where the SAT was the dominant test for college–bound students.[33]

Noted for civility and reluctance to criticize, Kean became sufficiently confident of his political support and policy accomplishments to issue a savage public attack on NJEA and step up condemnation of local school boards and administrators he believed were "ripping off the taxpayers."[34] However, the governor's opponents had not disappeared, just as Kean had bided his time while advocates of "local standards" and "process" measures held the upper hand.

When appraisals of Kean's record began to appear in 1989, so did the arguments of the 1970s. Former allies of Fred Burke called his accomplishments "modest." Their contention that better test scores, particularly in urban areas, were partly a product of "teaching to the test" or statistical artifice had some confirmation.[35]

More broadly, however, the critics reproached Kean for forcing the same standards on all students "regardless of their interests or aptitudes" and for failing to recognize that test failures "may be discouraging." Urban schools, they argued, were pouring scarce resources into "teaching to the test" and ignoring curricular depth and breadth. Seventy percent of Jersey City's school buildings predated World War I, and Newark's Burnett School, where Abraham Lincoln gave an informal address on his way to his 1861 inauguration, was one of nine Newark schools still in service after at least 120 years. New Jersey was one of only two states where de facto segregation was increasing. Its schools were the fourth most segregated in the nation, making "the term urban schools...a euphemism for minority schools."[36]

Although spending in some urban school districts had reached—and even exceeded—state averages, the gulfs between them and the "lighthouse" districts in the wealthiest suburbs had grown. For example, spending per pupil in the city of Camden, which was 79 percent of that in neighboring Cherry Hill in 1975–76, had dropped to 68 percent of the Cherry Hill level by 1989–90.[37] In the view of the urban reformers of the 1990s, ever–worsening educational and social problems in the cities meant their students must have the same educational opportunity as those in the lighthouse districts. That opportunity was properly measured in "inputs"—or dollars.

Although their arguments did not enjoy much political currency during the 1980s, urban advocates were counting on the New Jersey Supreme Court to make their case. Even before Kean became governor, and while Fred Burke was still education commissioner, a challenge to *Robinson v. Cahill*, brought by the Education Law Center, began its trip through the courts in February 1981.

This new case, *Abbott v. Burke*, claimed the *Robinson* remedy did not ensure urban students a "thorough and efficient" education. It reiterated that Chapter 212 violated the state constitution's equal protection and antidiscrimination clauses. When the case reached the supreme court in 1985, the justices remanded it to an administrative law proceeding. After nine months of hearings, Administrative Law Judge Steven Lefelt rendered a 607 page decision in August 1988.

Lefelt ruled for the plaintiffs. "I find," he wrote, "the pervasive nature of the political intrusion into Jersey City's school system shocking and harmful to the schoolchildren and qualitatively and quantitatively different from the pressures present in most other property–poor districts." He continued, "The expenditure differences are in some cases greater now than before Chapter 212 was enacted. I have concluded that the funding law contains systemic defects which contribute to the continued inequity."

Lefelt also addressed the controversy over "input" vs. "outcome" measures, noting "a pattern where children in high wealth communities enjoy high levels of expenditures and other educational inputs and children in low–wealth communities receive low levels of school expenditures and inputs." He went on, "The Constitution does not require that the desired output be measurable on standardized tests. An opportunity for every student to achieve this outcome is all that the political system must provide."[38]

Unsurprisingly, Commissioner Cooperman rejected Lefelt's reasoning in his own 234 page response on February 3, 1989: "No one has ever determined there is a minimum amount of funding necessary to provide a thorough and efficient education. Rather, the opposite is true. If a district is found to meet the criteria established by the State for T&E, then its spending is, by legal definition, adequate."[39]

Thus, Cooperman reiterated, T&E should be measured by whether a district met the minimum requirements of the 1975 T&E law, which the supreme court had accepted as part of the *Robinson* remedy. "Inputs" like computers or elementary school guidance counselors might be desirable, but the constitution did not mandate them. Cooperman also called unwillingness to meet the average district tax effort a "clear moral failure."[40]

The Kean administration suggested palliatives that did not alter the basic funding system or the emphasis on "outcomes." These included state aid to property–poor districts on a current rather than prior–year basis, "preferential treatment" for the same districts when the legislature did not fully fund the school aid formula, and a referendum to bond for new school facilities. The State Board of Education upheld Cooperman but also recommended that in years of funding shortfalls, minimum aid to the wealthiest districts should be eliminated before cutting equalization aid.[41]

The plaintiffs rejected these proposals and with administrative procedures exhausted, the supreme court reheard *Abbott* on September 25, 1989—less than two months before the November gubernatorial election. Although expected some months earlier, the court did not issue its 156 page decision until June 5, 1990.

Written by Chief Justice Robert Wilentz, the decision, like the first ruling in *Robinson* by seven different justices 17 years earlier, was unanimous. It found that Raymond Abbott, like Kenneth Robinson before him, had been denied a thorough and efficient education. Abbott, who was a 12–year–old student in East Orange when the suit was filed in 1981, had dropped out of school in eleventh grade. He received the news in the Camden County Jail, where he was serving time for violating parole after a previous conviction for burglary.

The justices agreed with the defendants that Chapter 212 did not violate the constitution's equal protection clause or state antidiscrimination laws, nor was there evidence of a general failure to provide a "thorough and efficient" education. However, they saw "absolutely no question that we are failing to provide the students in the poorer urban districts with the kind of education that anyone could call thorough and efficient." Acknowledging pervasive mismanagement in some urban districts, the justices ruled that their students must receive more resources anyway: "they are entitled to pass or fail with at least the same amount of money as their competitors."

The court went on to define which students were, in terms of dollar "inputs," being denied a "thorough and efficient" education. They relied on data from the Department of Education dividing school districts into eight economic District Factor Groups, labeled A (with lowest per–pupil spending) through J (with highest per–pupil spending).

The court required that in groups A and B, "the assured funding per pupil should be substantially equivalent to that spent in those districts providing the kind of education these students need, funding that approximates the average net current expense budgets of school districts in district factor groups I and J." They calculated this would add $440 million in current dollars to the existing $3.5 billion in state aid.

The justices also found the "minimum aid" distributed to the wealthiest districts unconstitutional. However, they rejected the plaintiffs' request to forbid any district from spending more than 5 percent above or below the state average per pupil: "The record convinces us of a failure of a thorough and efficient education only in the poorer urban districts. We have no right to extend the remedy any further...because of considerations of fairness unrelated to the constitutional command."

The legislature was given a year to "devise any remedy...as long as it achieves a thorough and efficient education as defined herein for poorer urban districts." The program could be phased in over five years. New Jersey's supreme court thus became the first to define educational equity for students in poor districts as the level of effort on behalf of students in the wealthiest districts.

In concluding their landmark opinion, the justices noted that with New Jersey's minority student population approaching a third of all students—highly concentrated in urban districts—"it is not just that their future depends on the state, the state's future depends on them....After all the analyses are completed, we are still left with these students and their lives. They are not being educated. Our constitution says they must be."

In first remanding *Abbott* to the administrative law process, the court had hoped the governor and legislature could shape a constitutionally acceptable program, but that had not worked. The Cooperman–Kean proposals had tried to anticipate the likely ruling but were unacceptable to the plaintiffs. Those following the case assumed the new governor and legislature would use the *Abbott* decision, when it came, as political "cover" for whatever tax increases were needed—as they had during the 1970s with *Robinson*. This did not turn out to be the case.

Governor Florio and the Quality Education Act

While the state awaited the court's decision, Democrat Jim Florio easily won the governor's contest in November 1989. Neither candidate made education a campaign theme but when asked directly about *Abbott*, the Democratic standard–bearer predicted that the court would throw out the existing school aid formula. However, Florio said, he "would stand by his no–new–taxes pledge even if that happens and would not seek to raise taxes." He said a full–scale state audit "would root out millions of dollars in waste and inefficiency" and produce the money for school aid and property tax relief.[42]

In March 1990, the governor declared urban education his highest priority. Pointing to the state's deep cleavages, Florio asserted, "We want to have one New Jersey as opposed to multiple New Jerseys....We don't have one New

Jersey in terms of its education system." Florio also advocated more equalized "inputs," saying uniform outcomes could not be required without uniform resources. He suspended the school monitoring system, ordered it redesigned, and spoke critically of "teaching to the test." Acknowledging urban–suburban hostilities, the governor said, "The political task that I have is to go out and sell all the people that it is not 'us and them'–it is us."[43]

However, as detailed in chapter 14, Governor Florio did not "sell" a plan for a "One New Jersey" educational policy, nor did he wait for an audit to find new revenues. Rather, he proposed $1.4 billion in increased income taxes dedicated to education aid and property tax relief as part of a $2.8 billion tax package. Without waiting for the *Abbott* decision, Florio revealed his vehicle for educational reform—the Quality Education Act (QEA). The complex QEA was pushed through the legislature in 22 days and passed in June 1990 with no Republican support. With the new income tax revenue, the state could provide about half of all education dollars and lower some individuals' property taxes.

Implemented over four years, almost half the new aid would go to 30 urban districts with low "educational inputs"—decaying school buildings, inexperienced teachers, outdated curricula, and inadequate equipment. The other half would go to "middle class districts," mostly in the southern half of the state where property values were lower. About a quarter of all districts, with a fifth of the students, would gradually lose all state equalization aid over four years. The number of districts affected and the plan's cost went far beyond the mandate of *Abbott v. Burke*. Dissatisfaction with QEA would thus be directed not at the court, but at the Democratic governor and legislature.

As school boards, teachers, and citizens grasped QEA's impact on individual communities, there was a crescendo of outrage—some of it from unlikely quarters. Wealthy, middle class, and even poor urban districts all had loud objections to the new revenue raising and allocation schemes.

Chapter 212—the existing system—was, as we have described, a capacity equalizing formula. Within this formula, many districts—particularly in older cities and suburbs—set relatively low school taxes because of the high cost of other municipal services—a problem called "municipal overburden." Others did not tax near capacity because residents voted down school budgets—the only portion of the local property tax that could be lowered by a public referendum.[44] Still others had low tax collection rates. Differences in school spending thus arose based on how much of their tax capacity local districts chose to tap or school boards and voters would approve.

In contrast, QEA was a foundation formula, which guarantees equal support of all students regardless of local tax effort. Districts must raise a local "fair share," based on aggregate property values and income levels, which when added to state aid, achieves the foundation amounts. By specifying each district's "fair share," the state virtually sets school tax rates, eliminating most local discretion. "Local leeway" provisions specify how much revenue above the foundation level districts are permitted to raise (i.e., how much "discrepancy" is permissible).

QEA required all districts to spend at a specified foundation level within five years, unless they could demonstrate a "thorough and efficient" education was provided for less. State aid was indexed at 1 percent above the average state increase in per–capita income (PCI). To comply with *Abbott*, 30 "special needs" districts were granted 5 percent more foundation aid than the rest of the state. The special needs districts were also permitted to increase their own spending annually at twice the PCI increase, while the wealthiest districts were held to the PCI increase.

Pension funding and compensatory education formulas were other important elements of QEA. The state had paid the full cost of teacher retirement plans since 1955. By 1990, this amounted to $900 million, or a quarter of all state aid. QEA specified that henceforth, individual school districts would assume these costs. Florio believed this would exert discipline on salary negotiations, since local districts could no longer negotiate pension costs with the state's money. Additionally, the definition of "at–risk" students eligible for compensatory aid was changed from those with failing test scores to those eligible for free school lunches.

Various QEA provisions were unpopular in almost every district in the state. Wealthy districts saw a triple whammy—loss of minimum aid, all pension aid, and thus inevitably higher local property taxes. Superintendents in these lighthouse districts also asserted that educational "leveling down" would inevitably occur when residents rejected huge property tax increases: "Average education throughout the state is not wise public policy. Nor is it required by *Abbott v. Burke*."[45]

"Middle income" districts discovered much of their "increased aid" would be swallowed up by pension costs and remedial programs for students who did not qualify for free lunches. The cap on annual state aid increases at 1 percent above PCI was well below recent growth, especially for teacher salaries and pensions.[46] NJEA claimed that with the pension money removed, QEA provided only $200 million in new money at a full funding level—almost all of it to the 30 special needs districts. It called the middle income aid "smoke and mirrors" to subsidize 30 districts.[47]

Even many special needs districts were unhappy with QEA. Some had to raise property taxes to meet their "fair share." Irvington calculated it would have to increase property taxes by $6.1 million to receive $5.8 million in new state aid. Trenton learned the $3 million increase needed to reach its "fair share" would require a 13 percent property tax increase in the first year of QEA.[48]

Some urban advocates argued QEA was not enough. Marilyn Morheuser, lead attorney for the *Abbott* plaintiffs, testified to the Assembly Education Committee that forcing poor districts to raise taxes defied the court's decree that funding in poor urban districts cannot depend on the budgeting and taxing decisions of local school boards. Further, QEA did not guarantee per–pupil spending parity between the poorest and wealthiest districts and was still based on prior–year funding.

Underlying the controversies were historic animosities of region, race, and class. In wealthy Bergen County in the north, many would see their income taxes double to pay for QEA, but 71 of Bergen's 78 school districts would lose all equalization aid. Conversely, three–quarters of the new aid, disproportionately financed by Bergen residents, would be flowing to special needs districts and five counties in the south with low average incomes and property values.

The GOP's senate minority leader, John Dorsey of Morris (another hard–hit wealthy northern county), enraged many but said what others thought when he declared QEA and *Abbott* required "working class people in middle class communities who drive around in Fords to buy Mercedes for people in the poorest cities because they don't have cars."[49] A Monmouth County Democratic assemblyman called the cuts to his wealthy district the act of "almost a socialist state" and proclaimed, "This is New Jersey, this is not Moscow in 1950."[50]

Such comments led Education Commissioner John Ellis and some urban legislators to call the opposition racist. Race was also an unspoken issue when Ellis and Florio urged districts to consolidate for economic reasons and became more overt when Public Advocate Wilfredo Caraballo announced his office was analyzing which de facto segregated districts could be integrated by suits seeking regionalization as a remedy.[51] School consolidation schemes in New Jersey have been as unpopular as tax increases. They often result in more rather than fewer districts, as residents refuse to include local elementary schools in newly regionalized high school districts.[52]

Genesis of the Quality Education Act

Given the predictable public protest, how did QEA come about? Three major forces shaped the Florio plan.

First was the governor's personal style. Whereas his predecessor, Tom Kean, was reluctant to take political risks or act decisively until the last possible moment, Florio put "good policy" above "good politics." His fifteen–year congressional career showed a preference for comprehensive rather than incremental solutions. He developed a reputation for disdain for those who did not agree with him and a willingness to lose control of issues rather than negotiate or compromise. Introducing "correct" policies gradually was anathema to Florio. Second, Florio and his advisors had embraced a political theory advocated by an unlikely coalition of Democratic and Republican political strategists and policy analysts–progressive populism. Popularized in Kevin Phillips's best–selling book *The Politics of Rich and Poor*, it held that Reagan–era "greed" and tax cuts aimed at the wealthy had antagonized a hard–pressed middle class, which was ready to join in a rebellion against the rich. Those who could forge and lead this majority would win both political and policy battles. Florio campaign manager and state Treasurer Douglas Berman said, "If Kevin Phillips is right, then Jim Florio is right."[53] Education policy was a crucial test of the theory. Educational opportunity was perhaps the most universally held American value. Wealthy school districts in New Jersey spent more on their schools but taxed at a lower rate than did poor and middle class districts.

Third, political factors permitted the governor to take dramatic action. Florio's style led him to exercise his constitutional powers more fully than had his more pragmatic predecessors. A one–time high school dropout and representative of the city of Camden, he understood the resentment of city dwellers and South Jerseyans toward wealthy, northern suburbanites. A landslide victory and the "honeymoon period" new executives enjoy helped him wield his powers.

Also, for the first time in a decade, urban Democrats led both houses of the legislature. The Florio money machine described in chapter 5 fueled Democratic campaigns. It made legislators pause before antagonizing the governor. Narrow majorities in both houses also inspired more partisan coherence than larger ones would have. Thus, despite severe qualms about constituents' reactions, almost all suburban Democrats swallowed their trepidations and voted for the tax package and the QEA.

THE FUTURE OF NEW JERSEY EDUCATION POLICY

Public protest from every quarter and massive Democratic defeats in 1990's state and local elections spelled doom for the QEA before it went into effect. In January 1991, Senate President John Lynch and Majority Leader Daniel Dalton introduced legislation to divert almost 40 percent of new QEA money directly to municipalities for property tax relief. Dalton, a Florio protegé from Camden County, had been the QEA's senate sponsor. He now said he had not understood all its implications.[54] Lynch traveled the state extolling the new property tax relief and criticizing teachers' wage and benefit demands, particularly during a recession.[55]

After weeks of bicameral negotiation with the governor on the sidelines, the legislature in mid–March passed a package of major amendments, known as "QEA 2," by the minimum necessary vote in both houses.[56] The bills again passed with almost unanimous Democratic support and with all Republicans opposed or abstaining. The legislature moved $360 million of new school aid into a statewide property tax relief fund and guaranteed state funding of teacher pensions for at least two years. Of the QEA's remaining $830 million, another $229 million also went to property tax reduction because of new education spending caps contained in the amendments.

Depending on districts' current spending levels, the amendments capped annual spending increases at between 7.5 and 9 percent for all but the 30 special needs districts. These urban districts could increase spending at a rate between 9.7 and 22 percent to achieve parity with the wealthiest districts within five years.

In many districts, even the poorest, the caps meant the remaining new money covered little more than contractual salary increases and higher insurance costs. In Camden, often cited as the state's educational worst case, the caps and diversion of funds to property tax relief cut municipal property taxes by 60 percent but reduced new school aid from $50 million to $24.8 million.[57]

The net effect, according to the director of school finance in the Education Department, was "an outflow of aid from the urban districts...to the middle and upper–wealth districts," as compared with the QEA's original provisions.[58] The plaintiffs in *Abbott* agreed and in June 1991 returned to the supreme court. Lead attorney Marilyn Morheuser asked the court to "assure prompt vindication of plaintiffs' constitutional rights....the court must set in motion a remedial process which will vindicate these rights, even if the Legislature fails to act in a constitutionally sufficient manner."[59] The justices' split decision to remand the case to a trial court in Mercer County removed the high tribunal from the education spotlight for a time and once again gave the political process time to work its will.

In November 1991, upon winning huge majorities in both houses of the legislature, Republican legislators proclaimed their intent to revise the school funding plan. Some advocated a constitutional amendment to remove the phrase "thorough and efficient" and specify the minimum level of state aid to poor districts, precluding interpretation by the state supreme court. The next chapter in New Jersey's educational policy debate had begun.

CHAPTER SIXTEEN

Quality of Life Issues

Everybody wants me to pick up his garbage, but nobody wants to let me put it down.

—New Jersey trash contractor[1]

While we expected that planning would teach us how to grow, we are discovering, instead, that it is growth that is teaching us how to plan.
—Bergen County Department of Planning and Economic Development[2]

Some years ago, Newark Mayor Kenneth Gibson predicted that wherever American cities were going, Newark would get there first. His thought applies more broadly to the quality of life issues that now preoccupy many states. America's most densely populated state may be the test of whether a desirable quality of life in urban and suburban America can be preserved. Northern New Jersey is among the nation's most expensive housing markets. Its waterways were among the first declared impure, and air pollution problems were evident by the 1950s. Traffic congestion also arrived early for New Jersey has the most roads per square mile of any state and two cars for every three people. However, New Jersey has also led the way in developing remedies for environmental problems, overdevelopment, and congestion.

The state's approach is shaped by the interplay of its home rule tradition with the powers the 1947 constitution granted the governor and supreme court. The governor is the representative and champion of the state interest. The legislature is dominated by former—and sometimes current—local officials. When clashing state and local interests produce gridlock, the supreme court has not hesitated to shape policy. These patterns are clearly seen in three related policy domains: environmental policy, transportation policy, and land use and zoning.

ENVIRONMENTAL POLICY

For many years, the public has identified environmental degradation as one of the most important problems facing New Jersey. Industry's diminishing role in the economy has helped change public thinking about environmental issues.

Table 21: Public Attitudes toward Antipollution Laws, 1977-1988

	Maintain anti-pollution laws	Relax laws to create jobs	Other/ Don't Know
1977	46	46	8
1982	56	34	10
1988	69	24	7

Source: Eagleton Poll, dates as shown.

Note: Table entries are percentages of all respondents choosing each option. Rows add to 100% except for rounding error.

Since 1977, the Eagleton Poll has regularly asked whether New Jerseyans prefer maintaining antipollution laws or relaxing them to create jobs. Table 21 shows the results over time.

In 1977, when New Jersey's economic transformation was beginning, public opinion was evenly split. By the end of the 1980s, when economic growth came overwhelmingly from the service sector, more than two–thirds of state residents saw environmental protection as more important than creating jobs that could harm the environment. Only the declining number of urban dwellers did not muster a majority for this position. For most New Jerseyans, a healthy environment has become linked to their own physical and economic health.

On the first Earth Day in 1970, Governor William Cahill signed a bill establishing the state Department of Environmental Protection. Significant environmental action, however, dates back to the nation's first state air pollution law in 1954. Although initially ineffective, it contained several pioneering principles. It recognized air pollution as a public policy problem, as a menace rather than a nuisance, and as requiring regional control and enforcement.[3]

Air and Water Pollution

The environment first became a political issue in 1961 when Democratic gubernatorial candidate Richard Hughes pledged reform of the 1954 Air Pollution Control Act. A 1962 revision still did not give the statute real teeth, and in Hughes's second term, lawmakers held hearings throughout the state. A stronger 1967 law required all new emission sources to have state–of–the–art pollution controls, regulated the sulfur content of fuels, and transferred rulemaking authority from a weak commission to a cabinet agency.

The federal Clean Air Act later established national emissions standards, and tough state laws enabled New Jersey to meet four of the six air standards on time. When the Clean Air Act amendments of 1990 were passed, northern New Jersey still flunked the carbon dioxide standard, and most of the state did not meet the ozone standard. Motor vehicle emissions are largely responsible. The 1990 Clean Air Act gives New Jersey and a few other areas until 2007 to achieve compliance.

Progress against water pollution has been slower. In 1972, 21 percent of New Jersey waters met "swimmable, fishable" standards, and only 30 percent do now.[4] Cleanup technologies have developed slowly, and bottom sediment endures a long time.

Much water pollution comes from more than 120 obsolete municipal sewage systems that do not meet federal standards. Modern regional wastewater systems are expensive and increasingly difficult to finance. New Jerseyans approved the first of many clean water bond issues in 1969. The state could then match federal grants for sewage treatment facilities, but federal funds dried up early in the Reagan administration.

In 1988, a malfunctioning sewage treatment plant in Asbury Park forced beach closings at the Jersey shore—decimating the tourist industry and bringing the kind of publicity state officials had labored to overcome. The unpleasant problems at the shore set the legislature to work on a two–year effort to produce a meaningful Clean Water Enforcement Act, which the legislature passed unanimously and Governor Florio signed in May 1990.

This act mandates fines for wastewater violations and also fines and jail terms for discharging wastewater without a permit. Penalties can be negotiated with the Department of Environmental Protection if municipalities agree to cleanups, and a portion of the fines is set aside to help finance them. Although hailed as one of the toughest state clean water statutes, the law focuses on direct discharges. It is still difficult to deal with the estimated 65 percent of water effluents from "nonpoint" sources, such as stormwater runoff and sewer overflows.

Toxic Waste

Strong state laws also address toxic waste hazards. New Jersey's Spill Compensation Control and Environmental Cleanup Responsibility Acts served as models for the federal Superfund law—principally authored by then–U.S. Representative Jim Florio— and for other states' legislation. Both "make the polluters pay."

The spill compensation measure, passed in 1976, created a cleanup fund financed by a transfer tax on petroleum and hazardous substances moved from one facility to another. The state can compel violators to clean up spills. If they refuse, the state commences cleanup activities and sues to recover costs. In 1979, the law was extended to cover abandoned hazardous waste sites.

ECRA—the Environmental Responsibility Cleanup Act of 1983—deals with potential problems before they become disasters. To be sold, transferred, or shut down, an industrial site must be free of toxic contamination, or the owners must pay for a cleanup acceptable to the state and the purchaser. By 1991, almost 300 cleanups had been completed at a cost of $106 million, and 475 more were in progress. Some involved minor infractions, but others were major efforts. For example, it cost the Ford Motor Company $4 million to clean up groundwater contamination before it could sell an assembly plant to an office park developer.[5] ECRA applies only to sites transferred since 1983. In 1991, however, the state supreme court ruled that companies that knowingly sold pollution–contaminated property before 1983 may also be "forever liable" for damages and cleanup.[6]

ECRA has spawned some concern about its effects on urban revitalization. Prohibitive cleanup costs leave land unused in old industrial cities that could be redeveloped to produce jobs. In 1991, an appellate court panel ruled the Department of Environmental Protection cannot order cleanups at times of minor corporate changes (such as sale of a partner's share), nor are owners responsible for cleaning up pollution leaking beyond a contaminated site. The court, however, firmly rejected an argument that ECRA was an unconstitutional infringement on the rights of business.

New Jersey has also aggressively sought federal money to clean up toxic wastes. When the first roster of Superfund sites came out in 1982, New Jersey led the nation with 418 entries—ten times more than Michigan, its nearest competitor. Funds were actually allocated for 109 sites—also the most in the nation. The Lipari Landfill in Gloucester County headed the list as the worst toxic waste site in the country.

Explaining these dubious "distinctions," Environmental Protection Commissioner Robert Hughey observed at the time, "We aggressively tried to be number one. We wanted to be number one. We worked hard for it....Other states may be worse. We're just two or three years ahead of them in identifying our sites."[7] Governor Kean also contended that the state's long–term health required some short–term embarrassment. New Jersey got so much Superfund money (about half of all allocations between 1980 and 1988) that when the program briefly lapsed in 1986, Trenton was able to loan the federal EPA funds to keep it going until it was reauthorized.[8]

New Jersey has been more successful in finding money to pay for cleanups than in completing them. Ten years after the establishment of the Superfund, only one site had actually completed cleanup, although many were in progress. DEP Commissioner Christopher Daggett blamed slow action on inadequate technology, bureaucratic quagmires, shortages of engineers, lack of uniform standards, and delays in reauthorizing the program.[9] The dilatory progress has led environmentalists to shift attention to areas where gains might be faster, such as air pollution and ocean dumping.

The state has done better in cleaning up less daunting sites that did not make the national Superfund list. A 1989 General Accounting Office study found that of 28,000 such sites nationally, only 1,736 had been cleaned, and 43 percent were in New Jersey. New Jersey had cleaned up about a quarter of the 3,000 such sites it had identified.[10]

Disposal plans for new toxic waste have also moved in slow motion. New Jersey industries produce 8 percent of all the hazardous waste in the nation.[11] Although a Hazardous Waste Siting Commission was established during the 1970s, it took almost 20 years to select an abandoned chemical manufacturing site in Union County, across the Arthur Kill from the New York City borough of Staten Island, as the location of a hazardous waste incinerator. Local residents, joined by New York State and New York City, immediately sued to prevent construction. Should New Jersey prevail, a facility is unlikely to be operational before 1995. Other states now accepting low–level radiation waste have threatened to bar shipments from New Jersey if it does not move faster in siting an in–state disposal facility.

These delays are examples of NIMBYism—not in my backyard. Municipalities welcome state and federal help in cleaning up the detritus of an industrial past. However, they throw up defenses when businesses and government go looking for new toxic dump sites.

Solid Waste

Similar problems plague more prosaic solid waste disposal—of garbage. The most densely populated state is running out of places to put it. Local politics in New Jersey has become, to a substantial extent, the politics of garbage. The solid waste crisis is where NIMBYism and home rule are most rampant.

Before 1970, each municipality simply sent trash to the closest cheap dump. That year, the Solid Waste Management Act required landfills to register with the Department of Environmental Protection and authorized the Board of Public Utilities to regulate trash haulers. Neither action addressed the problem of where to put the ever–growing mounds of garbage, so a County and Municipal Government Study Commission ("the Musto Commission") recommended in

1972 that county governments be given solid waste planning authority.

Home rule advocates greeted this proposal coolly, and it took three years for the legislature to pass amendments setting up county solid waste planning districts. Counties were directed to submit plans to the state DEP, which could accept, reject, or modify them. Regional plans were encouraged.

In 1976, the federal Resource Conservation and Recovery Act (RCRA) required phaseout of open dumps, complicating the problem. To comply, New Jersey shut down numerous dumps and rerouted most garbage to a dozen major landfills. As they filled up and the counties dallied in devising plans, the DEP sued eight of them and threatened as many others. The state also tried economic incentives. Statutory amendments in 1983 encouraged county incinerator construction. Dumping fee surcharges were to subsidize burner construction and provide handsome payments to "host communities."

Although this finally compelled counties to develop plans—and even produced some municipal competition for the incinerator subsidies—problems continued. After the first incinerators opened in Warren, Gloucester, and Essex counties, it became apparent that many of the planned burners were not needed. Fierce battles arose about where to locate transfer stations and dump incinerator ash. Siting and building the transfer stations and incinerators—and deciding where the reduced number would be—took time.

As an interim solution, New Jersey became a leader among the 30 states that export garbage. After years of accepting waste from New York City and Philadelphia, in 1991 New Jersey was sending about 4 million tons of trash a year out of state. Three-quarters went to Pennsylvania, with smaller amounts traveling as far as Ohio, Indiana, Kentucky, and Michigan.

Shipping garbage elsewhere solved the disposal problem, but surcharges and transportation costs greatly increased trash removal bills. They contributed to the upsurge in local property taxes in the late 1980s. In 1985, trash removal cost a typical household from $39 to $175. By 1989, this had soared to a range of $123 to $1,151.[12]

Recipients of the expensive garbage also rebelled. Pennsylvania Governor Robert Casey issued an executive order limiting out-of-state waste. Indiana Senator Dan Coates sponsored federal legislation allowing states to ban out-of-state garbage or charge very high fees. Coates declared that "Indiana and many other midwestern states are tired of being the dumping ground for New Jersey's solid waste." New Jersey Senator Frank Lautenberg responded that Indiana sent his state acid rain and threatened "retribution."[13]

The Coates amendment passed the U.S. Senate 68 to 31 in 1990 but was stripped from the legislation in conference committee. Coates called it a victory for the "East Coast trash caucus."[14] The Indiana senator, up for reelection that fall, had probably achieved his real objective. One of his political commercials featured a cigar–smoking, pot bellied man standing on an Indiana doorstep and clutching a bag of garbage as a "gift," while announcing himself as a visitor from New Jersey. A year later, Indiana Governor Evan Bayh and Governor Florio agreed on a pact cracking down on illegal dumpers—the apparent source of New Jersey trash arriving in the Hoosier State.

Beset by high costs for residents, external hostility, and environmentalists' crusades against incinerator–generated pollution, New Jersey stepped up recycling efforts. In 1987, the legislature replaced a voluntary program enacted in 1981 with the nation's first Mandatory Recycling Act. It requires all households to recycle at least three materials—generally glass, aluminum, and paper—as well as leaves.

By 1986, voluntary plans in 434 of the 567 municipalities had produced a 9 percent municipal recycling rate, the highest in the country. Mandatory recycling doubled that rate the following year. Within four years, the state was approaching its 25 percent goal for municipal recycling, and total recycling— including construction debris and scrap metal—reached 48 percent. Governor Florio announced ambitious new plans—freezing 12 county incinerator projects and setting a goal of 60 percent total trash recycling by 1995. The preferred strategy for dealing with solid waste has clearly shifted from incinerators to recycling.

Thus, although it will take many years to erase the fallout of an industrial past, and some problems still defy solution, its determined efforts to deal with environmental challenges place New Jersey in the forefront of the states.[15]

TRANSPORTATION POLICY

State transportation policy has followed a different pattern. Once a national leader, in the 1980s New Jersey was more reactive than proactive, and problems became worse rather than better. Unlike environmental concerns, transportation issues are often local or regional rather than statewide, and home rule forces are more dominant.

Highway Policy

During the 1920s, the country's first traffic circle and first cloverleaf interchange appeared in New Jersey. They were followed in the 1930s by the first divided highway. After World War II, the corridor state began choking on increased auto traffic.

In his 1947 inaugural address, Governor Alfred Driscoll called for construction of the New Jersey Turnpike. Quiet conversations about the patronage possibilities inherent in $250 million worth of equipment contracts, construction jobs, and a small army of toll collectors helped Driscoll win legislative assent for a Turnpike Authority in 1948. The turnpike undertaking also had the virtues of earlier transportation projects like railroads and canals. Authority bonds financed the project and left local taxpayers unscathed, and toll revenues came mostly from out–of–state travelers.

The 118–mile superhighway stretching from the Delaware to the Hudson opened in 1951.[16] It was followed by other toll roads offering access to the shore from New York and Philadelphia–the Garden State Parkway in 1955 and the Atlantic City Expressway in 1964. Although toll roads only comprise about 1 percent of route miles in the state, they carry about 14 percent of the annual traffic.[17]

Seasoned toll–road travelers expect construction delays as a standard part of the trip, as toll proceeds are used to expand the roads (the northern half of the turnpike is now twelve lanes wide, with separate roadways for cars and commercial vehicles, and more lanes are being added). In contrast, state and county roads are increasingly congested and in worse repair. Comprising about a quarter of route miles, they carry almost three–quarters of the annual traffic.[18]

Before the advent of the 1947 state constitution, the Highway Department was state government's largest and best–financed operation. All proceeds from the state gasoline tax were dedicated to the department responsible for keeping interstate as well as intrastate travel moving. After the new constitution banned dedicated funds and toll roads appeared, the department still prospered because state government had few other responsibilities. In 1961, it still claimed 28 percent of the entire state budget.

As Trenton took on new responsibilities, a sharp relative decline in transportation spending set in. By 1981, barely 5 percent of state funds went for transportation, and half the money generated by the gasoline tax was used for other purposes. After the Highway Department was reorganized as the Department of Transportation in 1966, its funds also supported mass transit, which demanded increasing subsidies.

As funding for state roads declined, their traffic load increased. Along with rapid population growth in the 1950s and 1960s, the average household eventually contained more cars than children, and more workers commuted to suburban jobs. As traffic congestion got worse, voters rejected four transportation bond issues during the economically turbulent 1970s. A successful $475 million initiative in 1979 was only a drop in the bucket.

Statistics give life to the problems facing the most intensively used roads in the country. Since 1974, road miles have increased by 3 percent, but vehicle miles are up 15 percent. In 1985, the average travel per mile on New Jersey roadways was 4,500, compared to 1,000 nationally, 2,000 in New York State, and 2,750 in Connecticut. The Department of Transportation rated a third of state roads as having "undesirable ride quality" and a similar proportion of bridges as "obsolete or structurally deficient."[19]

Commuters experience these problems only too personally. In a 1988 survey, 49 percent of state residents called reducing traffic congestion one of the "most critical" state problems of the next 5 to 10 years—outpaced only by the related issues of high auto insurance rates and environmental protection. Over a third said traffic congestion was a "very serious" problem in their own areas. Almost half the residents of the fastest—growing central area of the state gave this response.

More than 40 percent also said congestion had become worse in the past few years, that their commuting time had grown longer, and that they had changed travel times to avoid the worst traffic. Again, these figures were even higher in central New Jersey.[20] In 1988, New Jerseyans faced the longest average commute in the country—52 minutes.[21]

Worsening traffic problems and a healthy economy during the 1980s finally persuaded the legislature and the voters to ensure the Transportation Department a more stable and generous source of funding. In a 1984 referendum, voters approved a Transportation Trust Fund Authority. It is supported by state bonds to be repaid by a dedicated portion of the revenues from car registration fees, toll receipts, and the gasoline tax.

Mass Transit

Road congestion would decline if some of the 85 percent of workers who commute by car switched to mass transit. About 325,000 daily commuters use 7 railroad lines and 180 bus routes operated by New Jersey Transit, the nation's only statewide mass transit agency. However, this oft–proposed panacea can probably do little to solve New Jersey's transportation dilemmas. Over two–thirds of commuters report that mass transit routes to their jobs are not available. The rail lines, which have few connections to each other, run mostly to New York, Philadelphia, and New Jersey cities. Most commuting trips are from suburb to suburb, and most work destinations are far from the train stations.[22]

Bus travel, which commuters see as less attractive, has little potential for expansion either. Frequent bus service with reasonable fares and subsidies requires about 10,000 residents per square mile. Even in the most heavily populated county of Bergen, where 60 percent of the residents work within the county, the density is only 3,500 per square mile.[23]

State government, major employers, and some municipalities promote carpooling, vanpooling, and "flextime," but New Jerseyans seem to regard private car travel as a constitutional right. Flextime's principal effect has been to extend the "rush hour" to much of the day. Parochialism also works against expansion of mass transit. Rural dwellers in the south and west of the state have little enthusiasm for contributing tax dollars to mass transit schemes that do not benefit them. Consequently, New Jersey Transit riders pay 54 percent of the agency's operating costs, about 10 percent higher than the national average. Frequent fare hikes erase economic advantages of mass transit commuting, and each increase makes more potential riders take to their cars.

Regional Coordination

Home rule has contributed to the suburban sprawl that puts office parks and leisure–time destinations out of the reach of mass transit and along congested local roads. In the ceaseless search for tax ratables, these "clean industries" are the kind municipalities prize most. Yet they often produce negative spillovers for neighbors. To reach East Brunswick's miles of shopping malls, Parsippany's plethora of office parks, or the myriad research facilities surrounding Princeton, travelers must clog the roads of surrounding towns.

By the mid–1980s, the legislature was compelled to address the mounting complaints about traffic congestion, at least gingerly. The immediate impetus was a 1986 study of the infamous "Route 1 corridor," running from New Brunswick to Trenton through several municipalities and three counties and centered on Princeton's environs. In the space of a few years, the farms and woodland in the corridor were transformed into wall–to–wall office campuses, hotels, and malls. Princeton's mayor and Mercer County's county executive had lost a joint court battle seeking a construction moratorium in four towns. Proposals to establish a regional planning board and master plan had failed.

The study showed that municipal master plans projected nine times as many jobs as housing units in the corridor and office space equal to that of Dallas, New Orleans, or Seattle.[24] It was the genesis of "Transplan," a three–bill legislative package. Introduced in October 1986, it was intended to regulate municipal growth affecting surrounding areas and roadways.

Although significantly watered down, two of the Transplan bills finally gained passage in 1989. The first permitted the transportation commissioner to restrict access from new developments to limited–access highways and to revoke existing access permits if alternate access was available. After protests by a coalition of roadside businesses, the Transportation Department revised its new highway access code in 1991, diminishing the required distances between new driveways and "grandfathering" existing ones. State Planning Commission Chairman James Gilbert called the code a sellout to the "purveyors of gridlock and neon schlock." A lawyer representing business interests retorted that even the revised code would have a negative economic impact by "limiting development and lowering the value of highway property."[25]

The second Transplan measure permitted counties to establish Transportation Development Districts (TDDs) in rapidly growing areas. Such areas were defined as having 10 percent annual population and job growth and traffic increases of over 50 percent within a five–year period. If these stiff requirements were met, developers could be assessed a "fair share" of the costs of new roadways to carry development–generated traffic. Thus, new road construction still heavily depended on public financing.

When Governor Kean signed Transplan II, he urged rapid approval of the third bill in the package, likening it to the front wheel of a tricycle. This initiative mandates county approval of all new developments of "regional significance"— defined as more than 250 housing units or 100,000 square feet of nonresidential space. Strongly opposed by the League of Municipalities, Transplan III still languishes in committee.

LAND USE AND ZONING

The Transplan saga brings us to the arena where state and local interests clash most sharply: how land may be used, and who makes those decisions. When New Jersey municipalities received the power to zone in 1927, land use joined education as a linchpin of home rule.

It seems surprising that in a state with such a fabled affinity for local control, about 40 percent of New Jersey's land area came under the management of regional and state agencies during the 1970s. Recent governors and the state supreme court have tried to extend that control even further. Like education policy, land use has become one of the most contentious public issues New Jersey faces.

Precursors: Open Space and Farmland

Trenton's first two ventures into land use policy gave little hint of the conflict to come. Both dealt with preservation of the state's fast–disappearing open space. A 1961 Green Acres bond issue—the first in the United States for public land acquisition—passed easily, as have many subsequent referenda.

Between 1950 and 1960, 10,000 of the 27,000 active farms in the "Garden State" disappeared. Agricultural land went from 37 to 30 percent of total space in the state. In response, the legislature passed the Farmland Assessment Act in 1963, giving such land preferential tax status.[26] Although New Jersey still ranks among the largest producers of cranberries, peaches, and tomatoes, farmland continues to disappear rapidly.

By 1980, there was a third less agricultural land than there had been in 1960, and the decline between 1985 and 1986 was as large as the drop in the previous five years. The million farm acres of 1980 fell to 800,000 by 1990. Despite generous tax breaks, the value of farmland is the highest in the nation, and property taxes per acre are the second highest.[27] This combination makes enticing offers from developers difficult to resist. An entrepreneurial lot who receive little federal subsidy, New Jersey farmers have no interest in schemes that might lower eventual land–sale profits.

Like other Americans, New Jerseyans are sentimental about family farms, but it is the four out of five nonagricultural acres in the state that command their attention. As with so many things in the state, their status began to change around 1970. Within ten years, use of almost half of New Jersey's land area passed out of the control of owners and local municipalities—and under the control of the Hackensack Meadows Development Commission, the state Department of Environmental Protection, and the Pinelands Development Commission.

The Hackensack Meadowlands Development Commission

The first, geographically smallest, and most far–reaching assertion of state authority came in the Hackensack Meadowlands. This area comprises 31 square miles of wetlands in 14 municipalities and 2 counties. Located on the Hackensack River estuary across the bay from Manhattan, they were potentially "some of the most valuable real estate in the country."[28]

Before the 1960s, most people called such land "swamp" and treated it accordingly. More than a tenth of the Meadowlands was zoned as open dumps. They accepted 35 percent of the state's solid waste, from 121 municipalities, with "the additional aroma of hog farms adding to the ambience."[29] Outsiders were familiar with the area mainly through the reputation of Henry Krajewski, an eccentric Secaucus pig farmer who was a perennial third–party presidential candidate, or as the place to close car windows when traveling the New Jersey Turnpike.

Governor Richard Hughes, his commissioner of community affairs, Paul Ylvisaker, and State Senator Fairleigh Dickinson, whose Becton–Dickinson Pharmaceutical Company overlooked the Meadowlands, were among the first to grasp the potential benefits of proper development.[30] In a major legislative battle, they won establishment of the Hackensack Meadowlands Development Commission in 1968.

Ironically, it was the existing dumps that helped make the victory possible. In return for the votes of their legislators, towns using the landfills were granted the right to dump in the Meadowlands "in perpetuity"—"the rest of North Jersey preserved its home rule by obliterating that of 14 other North Jersey towns."[31] Another important factor was increasing reliance on federal flood control in the low–lying Meadowlands. The U.S. Army Corps of Engineers demanded a regional land–use plan to show the benefits—"Put simply, Congress was not about to spend hundreds of millions of dollars to protect garbage dumps and junkyards from flooding."[32]

The commission, consisting of an executive director and seven gubernatorial appointees, has extraordinary power to plan, zone, and grant variances in the Meadowlands portions of the 14 municipalities. Each mile of the district has an assigned use, and development projects must accord with the district's 1972 master plan to receive approval. A crucial element in making the whole scheme work is that all 14 municipalities must pool 50 percent of their tax revenues from Meadowlands ratables, which are then redistributed to them by formula. Affected towns still complain about the allocation formulas. However, protests are far more muted than they were during the battle to establish the commission, which featured posters "showing the hand of the State squeezing blood out of the crumpled body of Secaucus."[33]

Hughes's vision for the Meadowlands was carried forward by his successors. Today, the district boasts 170,000 jobs and a nationally preeminent entertainment and sports complex. Residential development has been slower, but the long–gone pig farms are gradually being replaced by elaborate hotels and condominiums, many developed by the Hartz Mountain Corporation. The 150 acres still zoned for landfills have had to grow up rather than out. Thanks to improving technology, only the ever–present seagulls alert the Turnpike traveler, passing by Giants Stadium and the Meadowlands Hilton, that the green hills they see are manmade.

The Meadowlands project was conceived primarily as an economic development initiative. In contrast, two other regional plans gained passage after being promoted as environmental protection measures. They affect much larger land areas—each covering about 20 percent of the state.

CAFRA—The Coastal Area Facilities Review Act

The Coastal Area Facilities Review Act of 1973 (CAFRA) regulates development in a 1,376–mile district along the shore. It includes 124 municipalities and parts of 6 counties. CAFRA designates the Department of Environmental Protection as the district's regional planning agency and requires DEP approval of all subdivisions, building standards, and zoning ordinances. The intent is to protect the shore and regulate its development.

CAFRA has been much less successful in regulating growth and development than has the Hackensack Meadowlands Development Commission. Local municipalities that do not gain the economic advantages the HMDC provides are antagonistic, and a major loophole in the law has permitted about half the development in the district to escape regulation. It exempts residential projects of fewer than 25 units from CAFRA requirements. The effect has been "an explosion of 24 unit condominium projects," many connected by roads or walkways that make them "separate development fictions." At least 190 developments of 24 units were built in Atlantic, Cape May, and Ocean counties just between 1986 and 1989.[34]

Increasing threats to the shore's environment led Governor Kean in 1987 to propose a Coastal Commission to serve as a regional development agency. It was to devise a master plan and tap user fees and state bonds to pay for sewers, open space purchases, and shore protection. A strong environmentalist and moving force behind CAFRA's passage while a legislator, Kean's failure to win passage of the Coastal Commission was one of his bigger disappointments.[35] None of the involved parties liked it. Municipalities rejected further regulation. The legislature thought it would be too expensive. Even the DEP opposed it because of the powers it would lose.

Unable to gain legislative approval, Kean issued a 1988 executive order requiring special approvals for coastal zone development. The executive order, based on a 1914 statute regulating piers and docks, covered new development within 1,000 feet of the coast or facing the coast without an existing building in front of it. Some such sites were more than a mile inland.

In 1989, a state appeals court unanimously overturned the executive order, saying there was "nothing in the Waterfront Development Act or in its legislative history to support... assertion of regulatory jurisdiction over broad expanses of land so far distant from any waterway."[36] Even though the order was modified to affect only structures within 1,000 feet of the water, the state supreme court upheld the appeals court, reiterating that existing law applied only to development directly affecting navigable waterways.[37]

When Governor Florio assumed office in 1990, he issued stopgap regulations affecting all structures within 500 feet of the waterline, which he hoped would comply with the supreme court's ruling. Florio did not believe a Coastal Commission was necessary but shared Kean's desire to protect the shore. An appeals court once again nullified his orders, asserting that failure to prove harm to navigable waterways remained "a fundamental defect."[38] It became clear that only new statutes could address the issue, and such bills began making their way through the legislature. Meanwhile, the coalition of developers and municipal home rule advocates had prevailed.

The Pinelands Commission

Along with the difference in size, the two greatest contrasts between the Meadowlands and coastal zone initiatives were the level of existing development and the costs and benefits to those regulated. The Meadowlands had little manmade development (except for garbage dumps), while CAFRA affected built–up areas. Despite initial objections, Meadowlands municipalities found the commission brought huge economic benefits. On the shore, the public good of environmental protection clashed with the private goods of landowners and developers and the hunger of municipalities for ratables.

When Governor Byrne moved to protect the Pinelands in the mid–1970s, it was largely undeveloped and lightly populated. The experience with CAFRA led Byrne and the legislature to seek a balance between property rights and environmental protection. The state successfully met this dual challenge.

John McPhee's sensitive book about the Pine Barrens, where fewer than 300,000 people live in 52 municipalities in seven counties covering almost a million acres of South Jersey, first brought this vast, wild area to public attention.[39] Named for its stands of dwarf pines, the Pinelands is also home to blueberry fields; cranberry bogs; a huge, fragile aquifer of pure water; taciturn natives who call themselves "Pineys," and the legendary Jersey Devil.

The Pinelands slumbered on through the 1960s, when the Port Authority began searching for a site for a fourth jetport for "the New York area." Environmentalists deterred a scheme to build it in the Great Swamp, a much smaller area in Morris County, by buying the land and presenting it to the federal government as a wildlife refuge. Burlington County officials then proposed the Pinelands as an alternative, accompanied by plans for a "new city" of 250,000 people.

In 1972, as environmentalists mobilized to fight the airport, the Pinelands

Environmental Commission, dominated by local officials and developers, was created to design uses for 320,000 acres in Burlington and Ocean counties. Environmental Commissioner David Bardin characterized their 1975 plan as a "developer's dream."[40] About the same time, the U.S. Interior Department proposed making the Pinelands a National Ecological Reserve. This designation would have banned federal grants for projects damaging to the environment. New Jersey Senators Clifford Case and Harrison Williams introduced the appropriate legislation, and in 1978, the entire Pinelands became the first National Reserve.

These actions had only limited effects on development, however, and the Pinelands might well have gone the way of suburban sprawl if Governor Byrne had not counted John McPhee among his tennis partners. McPhee pressed the case to Byrne. He responded with an executive order imposing a building moratorium and led the fight for the Pinelands Development Act, enacted in 1979. Byrne—who achieved passage of a state income tax, public financing of gubernatorial elections, legalized casino gambling in Atlantic City, and construction of the Meadowlands Sports Complex—considered saving the Pinelands his greatest accomplishment. He explained, "I'm convinced that if I hadn't done it, nobody would have done it. The Pinelands would be well on the way to extinction, as John McPhee had predicted....it was not a life–and–death issue with anybody....the legislators from Ocean County might admit that Pinelands preservation was a good idea but their campaigns were financed by developers....it was an economic political survival issue for them."[41]

The legislation set up a 15–member Pinelands Commission (composed of representatives from seven affected counties, seven gubernatorial appointees, and a member appointed by the U.S. secretary of the interior). It produced a district master plan intended to maintain large, contiguous areas in a natural state; safeguard essential environmental characteristics; protect water quality; and promote compatible agricultural, recreational, and development uses. The National Conference of State Legislators called the commission's work a model for the nation.[42]

The Pinelands Master Plan was implemented in 1981 and must be reviewed every three years. It requires all municipalities in the planning region to bring their zoning ordinances and local master plans into conformity with the comprehensive plan. The region is divided into a core preservation area where no development is permitted and buffer protection areas with limited development. An innovative Development Bank buys transfer development rights or credits from landowners in the preservation areas and sells them to developers who may then build at a somewhat higher density in the buffer areas than would otherwise be permitted.[43]

New Jersey's successful efforts at regional planning in the Hackensack Meadowlands and the Pinelands shared a number of characteristics that contributed to their success. These included strong gubernatorial leadership, economic "sweeteners" for those affected, no compromise on the authority of regional master plans, quick start–up, and controlled but meaningful local participation in planning.[44] Most of these were absent in the less successful planning effort at the shore.

Exclusionary Zoning and Affordable Housing

The Meadowlands and Pinelands initiatives address a goal New Jerseyans strongly approve—balancing economic development and environmental protection.[45] Another land use issue of recent years—zoning to permit affordable housing—has been far more conflictful and far less successful. Since the 1970s, the state supreme court's *Mount Laurel* decisions have been the force behind an effort to open the suburbs to affordable housing. Unlike regional planning, *Mount Laurel*–related developments affect home rule and land use decisions in every municipality in the state.

Trenton first took up affordable housing in 1972, after exclusionary zoning suits were filed against a number of suburbs. Republican Senator Albert Merck of Morris County introduced legislation, supported by Governor Cahill, that allowed the state to set "fair share goals" for municipalities and required state approval of their housing plans. It was roundly defeated, and Merck's loss of his "safe" seat in 1973 was widely attributed to his sponsorship of the bill.

In 1975, the state supreme court ruled unanimously for the plaintiffs in a zoning case brought against the township of Mount Laurel. The chief justice, former Governor Richard Hughes, wrote for the court, "Mount Laurel must, by its land use regulations, make realistically possible the opportunity for an appropriate variety and choice of housing for all categories of people who may desire to live there, of course including those of low and moderate income."[46]

The court directed municipalities to provide a "fair share" of affordable housing in their "region" but left the definition of those terms and the appropriate remedy unclear. Within six months of the *Mount Laurel* decision, 65 municipalities were in court over zoning challenges. In 1978, Essex County Democratic Senator Martin Greenberg, with the support of the League of Municipalities, introduced legislation similar to the 1972 Merck bill, and it was approved by the upper chamber. However, the League later withdrew its support and the bill failed in the assembly. To the court's embarrassment, *Mount Laurel* seemed unenforceable.[47]

The *Mount Laurel* plaintiffs resumed legal action. When *Mount Laurel II* reached the supreme court in 1983, many of those who rendered the earlier decision had been replaced by more activist judges, led by the new chief justice, Robert Wilentz. Writing for an again unanimous court, Wilentz reiterated that zoning regulations "that do not provide the requisite opportunity for a fair share of the region's need for low and moderate income housing conflict with the general welfare and violate the state constitutional requirement of substantive due process and equal protection."[48]

Noting that "We may not build houses, but we do enforce the constitution," the court set up an elaborate plan for determining municipal housing obligations to be monitored by judges in the three regions of the state (north, central, and south). A "builder's remedy" allowed developers who included affordable housing units to build at higher densities than local zoning ordinances permitted. Within two years of the decision, more than 100 "builder's remedy" suits had been filed.

Mount Laurel II's assault on home rule produced howls of outrage from the suburbs. Governor Kean called the decision "communistic," and others described the builder's remedy as "judicial terrorism."[49] Kean asserted he would not act on the court decision until the legislature produced an appropriate statute. Within a year, Essex County Democratic Senator Wynona Lipman's Fair Housing bill garnered the support of the League of Municipalities, the public advocate, and the Homebuilders Association.

Lipman's bill, released from committee in 1984, provided for a Council on Affordable Housing in the state Department of Community Affairs to determine and adjudicate municipal housing obligations. It was blended with a bill sponsored by Middlesex County Senator John Lynch, permitting municipalities to "buy out" of half their obligations by subsidizing affordable housing units in other municipalities willing to enter into such negotiations.

The Lipman–Lynch bill was endorsed by the senate in January 1985 and passed the assembly after being further watered down. However, Governor Kean, still hostile to judicial "social engineering," conditionally vetoed it in April. Observers believed his intent was "to push down the *Mount Laurel* numbers as far as possible, stopping just short of flatly seeking to reverse the decision through legislative action."[50]

The Fair Housing Act that Kean finally signed later in 1985 did greatly reduce the number of mandated affordable housing units. It also moved many of them out of the suburbs and back into the cities, made those that were built more available to "middle–income" than "low–income" New Jerseyans, and limited the number of purchasers and renters from "out of town." However, it did produce some units that would not have otherwise been built, converted suburban outrage to grudging acceptance, and returned the court to an adjudicatory rather than policy–implementing role. In a third *Mount Laurel* decision in 1986, the supreme court called the act the "kind of responsible remedy" it had "always wanted and sought" and transferred all its pending cases to the Council on Affordable Housing (COAH).[51]

Under the Fair Housing Act, COAH determines the number of units municipalities must provide. A town's "fair share" is based on regional growth, aggregate per capita income, and the rate of change in employment. Towns may meet their obligations with new or rehabilitated units or make regional contribution agreements subsidizing units in other towns for up to half their quotas. Half the local units may be restricted to current residents, and a quarter may be set aside for senior citizens. Half must be affordable for "low–income" residents (defined as half the county median income), and if the municipal quota is over 125, a fifth must be rental units.

Municipalities are not required to submit affordable housing plans to COAH, but doing so renders them immune from "builder's remedy" suits for six years. About 10 percent of the 567 municipalities still have not petitioned COAH for certification, and almost half of them have been sued since 1986.[52]

COAH has required many fewer units than *Mount Laurel II* originally mandated. A typical example is Warren Township in Somerset County, which saw its quota drop from 964 units to 367. The original COAH assessment for Middletown in Monmouth County was 1,800 units, but until a 1990 appeals court decision overturned it in a suit brought by a developer, COAH had capped the number of units any town would have to provide at 1,000.[53]

Regional contribution agreements also hold down the number of units constructed. Poorer urban towns bidding against each other for the housing funds the agreements provide have driven the price accepted per unit to about a quarter of the real cost of new units or half the price of rehabilitated units, although the suburbs get full credit against their quotas. The state public advocate has contended that regional contribution agreements perpetuate "a destructive pattern of economic segregation" and that reserving half the housing for local residents reduces the number of minorities occupying low–income units. The appellate division of state superior court rejected both arguments in March 1991.[54]

As with the "redistributive" schemes for school financing described in chapter 15, there are racial undertones to the affordable housing debate. Most regional contribution agreements are between heavily minority urban areas and heavily white suburbs. COAH has argued that if regional contribution agreements do perpetuate housing segregation, the problem is not with them, but the legislature and the courts. *Mount Laurel III* and the 1991 appellate court decision upheld both regional contribution agreements and the Fair Housing Act.[55]

When COAH was established in 1986, it projected the number of affordable housing units needed by 1993 at 145,000. By 1991, only about 8,000 units had actually been built, and economic recession had brought housing construction to a temporary halt. COAH estimated that 52,000 units were in the pipeline, while affordable housing activists put the number at only 23,500. New Jersey's approach to affordable housing can thus be seen as demonstrating that the state "remains hostile to the notion that the needs of poor people supersede the tradition of home rule," or alternatively, as "a compromise between radical idealism and reactionary preservationism."[56]

In any case, the influx of "poor people" many suburbs feared has not materialized, even in the relatively small number of units built. Over 80 percent of *Mount Laurel* units have been sold as condominiums, with stiff mortgage and down payment requirements and high closing costs. Their owners are mostly senior citizens, "pink and blue collar," and single parents. Although more than half have children, almost all units have only one or two bedrooms, precluding large families.[57]

The State Development and Redevelopment Plan

Mount Laurel II "plucked out of bureaucratic obscurity" a little–known document called the State Development Guide Plan. Prepared by the Department of Community Affairs' Division of State and Regional Planning during the 1970s to identify predicted growth zones but never officially adopted, it was used as a guide for courts hearing land use cases. The supreme court relied on it to construct its *Mount Laurel II* guidelines and ordered it be periodically revised.[58]

Overtly hostile to statewide planning, Governor Kean's response was to abolish the State and Regional Planning Division in 1983, saying *Mount Laurel II* had rendered it moot. Based on the work of an ad hoc, broad–based committee, Democratic Senator Gerald Stockman in 1984 introduced a bill for a state plan that would meet the court's requirements.

After much negotiation, Kean signed the legislature's State Planning Act in January 1986.[59] It specified a plan be drawn up in 18 months—by July 1987. The act set the following guidelines for the plan:

1. Protecting the natural resources and quality of the state

2. Promoting development consistent with sound planning and taking account of existing infrastructure

3. Identifying areas targeted for growth, limited growth, agriculture, and open space

4. Establishing state planning goals and objectives, and coordinating related activities

5. Integrating concerns of the poor, minorities, and the Mount Laurel decisions

6. Balancing development and conservation

A compromise accepted by the governor, the legislature, the League of Municipalities, the New Jersey Builders Association, and the state's leading newspapers, the act established a "cross–acceptance" process unique to New Jersey. Under cross–acceptance, in 18 months, the commission was to produce a plan, county planning boards were to gather comments from all municipalities about their role in the plan, the commission was to negotiate differences, and finally, the commission was to submit a revised plan to the governor for approval.[60]

Governor Kean did not name an executive director for the State Planning Commission until September 1986—eight months after the clock had started running—and the commission was not fully staffed until the end of the year. A draft plan, "Communities of Place: The State Development and Redevelopment Plan," was not released until December 1988, and the cross–acceptance process then began.

"Communities of Place" is intended to guide population, employment, and development trends through the year 2010.[61] Omitting the Hackensack Meadowlands, CAFRA, and the Pinelands area, it mapped the rest of the state into square–mile quadrants, each placed in one of seven "tiers:" Tier 1—redeveloping cities and suburbs; Tier 2—stable cities and suburbs; Tier 3—suburban and rural towns; Tier 4—suburbanizing areas; Tier 5—future suburbanizing areas; Tier 6—agricultural areas; and Tier 7— environmentally sensitive areas.

Each tier had specified development strategies, policies and standards, such as permissible population density, with development "unconstrained" in Tier I and progressively more constrained in each succeeding tier. The basic idea was to redirect growth to already developed cities and suburbs, discourage sprawl, and restrict development in agricultural and environmentally sensitive areas.[62] County and municipal master plans were to be brought into voluntary conformity with the state plan.

When the cross–acceptance process was finally completed in late 1990, local governments had rejected much of the "tiering" approach, and the planning commission changed "imposed" zoning requirements to "guidelines." The seven former tiers were now called "planning areas" and more loosely categorized as metropolitan, suburban, fringe, rural, and environmentally sensitive. The plan identified five types of "centers"—urban, town, regional, village, and hamlet, and each had its own development guidelines.

The process moved to an end as state planners commissioned an economic impact assessment of the revised interim plan and organized extensive public hearings.[63] In 1991, Governor Florio endorsed the plan's proposal to direct state capital construction funds to cities and already developed areas. Florio noted this policy would improve and expand "the infrastructure and transportation systems most utilized so we don't develop new ones in the middle of nowhere." Alluding to the "ratables chase" in less developed areas, he observed, "Not a lot is going to happen without access to capital and infrastructure improvements."[64]

After farmers received assurances they would be compensated for land that could not be developed, the state plan was finally approved in June 1992, some five years behind schedule. Its future remains a question mark. The State Planning Commission cannot compel state and local agencies to make their decisions conform with its own.[65] Whether they will, as Governor Florio proposed, adjust regulations and resource allocations to conform with the plan over its lifetime, will depend on political pressures and the will of future governors.

STATE AUTHORITY, HOME RULE, AND QUALITY OF LIFE ISSUES IN NEW JERSEY

The most complex American state plan ever developed symbolizes the complexities and continuities of contemporary policy–making in New Jersey. Cross–acceptance embodies an intricate balance between the old localist culture and emerging state identity and authority. The plan is another effort to make New Jersey's cities a vibrant part of a profoundly suburban state and to balance economic growth and environmental protection. In their increasingly demanding quest for a healthy and attractive environment, workable transportation networks, and appealing and affordable housing, state residents see themselves as "New Jerseyans" more than they ever have. But as this chapter shows, they remain also citizens of 567 municipalities.

CHAPTER SEVENTEEN

Epilogue

If you look at the way people live in this country, the land of opportunity is
New Jersey.

—Joel Garreau, 1991[1]

Four developments will help shape the United States of the twenty–first century.
First, fewer Americans will live in either cities or rural areas. The 1990 census
found that almost half of all Americans now live in suburbs. The United States
is becoming "a suburban nation with an urban fringe and a rural fringe."[2] There
will be further development of "edge cities." An edge city is not a suburb as
usually defined. It is a place where people do not simply sleep, but work, create,
and spend their leisure time.[3] Peter Rowe calls such suburbs "middle land-
scapes" between city and country.[4]

Second, the American economy will be based increasingly on the work of
brain rather than brawn and production of services rather than goods. An
educated work force will become ever more important. Those without the
requisite skills will become increasingly marginalized.

Third, politics and government will become at once more distant and more
intimate. More decisions will be made in capitols than town halls. The
technology–based direct democracy of public opinion polls, referenda, and
"electronic town meetings" will claim a place alongside organized interest
groups and political parties. Officeholders will communicate with more of their
constituents on television and through computer–generated mailing lists than
they do in speeches, appearances, and individual conversations.

Finally, adjusting to new cultural diversity will become a growing American
preoccupation. In significant measure, American political debate has always
been a dialogue about how best to assimilate newly arriving ethnic, religious, and
racial groups who demand a place in the political universe. Older groups have
always harbored fears of newer ones. As the turn of the century approaches, a
new wave of political petitioners promises to shape American political dialogue
as dramatically as a previous wave did at the turn of the last century.

To know what much of America will be like some decades hence, one may study New Jersey now, for all these trends are already manifest there. They have combined to shape a new suburban politics—postindustrial, posturban, and postparty. As William Schneider has written, the United States's first century was dominated by the agrarian myth of the self–sufficient Jeffersonian farmer. Its second century was dominated by the urban myth of the city as engine of prosperity. Its third century will be the century of the suburbs.[5]

THE RISE OF SUBURBAN POLITICS

Suburban politics is distinct in style and substance from the urban politics that preceded it. Urban politics was party–centered; suburban politics is candidate–centered. Urban politics attracted adherents by providing the necessities of life; suburban politics promises quality of life. Urban politics was organized around culturally homogeneous geographic precincts accessible by shoe leather; suburban politics is organized around "issue precincts" accessible through targeted media. Urban politics was activist and in the forefront of people's lives. Suburban politics is less intrusive and protects private space, both physical and psychological. Political corruption was a by–product of urban politics' individualist political culture; suburban politics has a strong moralist strain.

The particular qualities of suburban politics grow from these characteristics, and they are writ large in New Jersey. A candidate–rather than party–centered politics calls on officeholders to appeal to voters one by one. It is volatile and unpredictable. What appears to be strong partisan competition is often individual competition. New Jersey now often elects governors of one party and legislative majorities of the other because of the powerful appeal or affront individual candidates convey. New Jersey's suburban voters judge political aspirants less by their policy positions than their personal characteristics. They prefer candidates who seem be like them and share their particular values.

For suburban voters, quality of life is paramount. They seek above all physical security, clean air and water, easy access to amenities, attractive and affordable housing. Economic security is important to them because it makes a desirable quality of life possible. Candidates promoting an economy that nurtures individual achievement are the ones who win their votes. New Jersey elections revolve around the issues related to quality of life as suburban residents understand it: environmental protection, steadfastness against crime, good local schools that will help their children achieve even more than they.

Only in the worst economic times are New Jerseyans deflected from these quality of life concerns, and when they are, they see government spending as villain rather than savior. "The middle class is who lives in the suburbs. The word that best describes the middle class is 'taxpayers.'" For suburban voters, a government program "that helps the few and taxes the many is an outrage. A program that helps the many and taxes the few seems eminently fair."[6]

Old urban neighborhoods were ethnically and religiously cohesive. Suburban homeowners are linked less by these ascriptive categories and their accompanying institutions than they are by the more impersonal interests they share. Politicians reach New Jersey's suburbanites by thinking of them as motorists, environmentalists, hunters, members of professions, or senior citizens. Their campaigns depend not on armies of precinct workers but on checks from groups of developers, lawyers, auto dealers, teachers, union members, or health–care professionals. "To move to the suburbs is to express a preference for the private over the public"— for backyards rather than public parks, for private cars over mass transit, for the security of the enclosed shopping mall rather than the potential dangers and insecurity of downtown. "Suburban voters buy 'private' government— good schools and safe streets for the people who live there."[7]

New Jersey's suburban dwellers have fled the congestion, disorder, and dangers of cities for more than 100 years. They have been both "pushed" and "pulled" to the suburbs—"pushed" by the congestion and tensions of urban life and "pulled" by the lure of homes of their own at a reasonable price, which become their most fiercely prized possessions. [8]

Urban "dangers" have always been linked to the arrival in cities of alien "others." In an earlier time, "other" was defined by religion and ethnicity. Protestant, Anglo–Saxon suburbs built walls to keep out Catholics, Jews, Eastern and Southern Europeans. The new arrivals were seen as bringing crime and political corruption. Suburban politicians crusaded then against alcohol, gambling, and aid to parochial schools, and sent urban mobsters and mayors to jail.

Now, "other" is defined by race. "White ethnics," themselves newly middle class, emptied out of New Jersey cities after the Newark and Plainfield riots of the 1960s. Their new suburban representatives crusaded against drugs, school busing, and regionalization to achieve integration and filled the jails with drug dealers. Suburban hostility is directed, as ever, less at particular groups per se than at the groups who happen to dominate the cities.

Through the 1960s, New Jersey was less a state or state of mind than a collection of antagonistic communities—urban, suburban, rural. City and country owned New Jersey state government. After World War II when their great migration began, suburbanites became numerous enough to elect the weak governor, but a coalition of urban Democrats and rural Republicans ruled the powerful, malapportioned legislature and collaborated to protect their own fiefdoms.

During the 1970s, a political shock wave hit New Jersey. The U.S. Supreme Court's "one person–one vote" decisions ended county–based representation in Trenton. The New Jersey Supreme Court laid siege to the locally based fiscal system when it decreed that the funding of public education could no longer rely so heavily on local property taxes. The virtually inescapable remedy for the court's decision was broad–based state taxes, which New Jersey had resisted longer than almost every other state.

New Jersey's traditional political system lay in ruins. Its suburban voters— their numbers now inflated by the flight from cities within the state and on its borders—suddenly found themselves at the center of state politics. The most suburban state in America was compelled to devise a politics suitable to its residents. Because so many New Jersey suburbs now melted seamlessly into one another both geographically and culturally, and their residents were so numerically dominant, it was possible to have a genuine state politics that was impossible before.

For the first two decades of New Jersey's suburban era (roughly 1970 to 1990), the central political symbol of the state was its governor, the only statewide elected official. Before 1970, New Jersey governors were still constrained by the traditional county politicians who dominated the legislature, the absence of fiscal resources the state could command, and the limited channels through which they could reach their constituents.

Their successors gradually surmounted these obstacles. The courts dispatched the county politicians. Commerce followed the new suburbanites to their homes. Sprawling shopping malls generated revenue for a new state sales tax. As more of the region's trained and educated work force moved to the New Jersey suburbs, more of the corporations that employed them followed them there. Media patterns were the slowest to change, but the governor was Trenton's focal point and dominated what communication channels there were.

Thus, all the changes that were occurring in New Jersey reinforced each other. Growing middle–class suburbs made a postindustrial economy possible. A postindustrial economy made a real state government possible. State government increasingly served the political and economic interests of the new suburban majority. The old rural–urban political coalition had given little attention to the suburbs. The new suburban regime gave little attention to the cities. The governor directed Trenton's activities. Those gubernatorial aspirants who understood the psychology of suburban voters were elected and rewarded. Those who rejected or misunderstood them were punished.

THE GOVERNORS OF THE SUBURBAN ERA

Four governors—two Democrats and two Republicans—have led the state since the suburban era reached full flower in the 1970s. Governors have so dominated state politics for the past two decades that each one's tenure has been an expression of their personalities, philosophies, and political skills. Thus, their personal qualities can override, or at least shape, the effects of the particular temporal environment in which they operate. By their own measures and those of the public, two of these governors succeeded in putting the mark they desired on the state, and two failed. Success and failure are always relative terms, but a chasm yawns between these two pairs.

Of the two who succeeded, one was a Democrat and one a Republican. One generally enjoyed partisan majorities in the legislature and among the public, and one did not. One served primarily in good economic times; the other faced economic difficulties. The same comparisons are largely true of the two who failed. What distinguishes the successes from the failures is the extent to which they understood the new suburban politics, in both its style and substance.

The successful suburban politician's style is, first of all, moralistic, in a "good–government" sense. Nothing repels New Jersey's suburban voters more rapidly than the urban politics of cronyism and petty corruption. It was uncompromising rectitude that gave Democrat Brendan Byrne in 1973 what was then the greatest victory in any New Jersey gubernatorial election. A superior court judge who had never before run for office, his standing in the race improved dramatically when a local mobster was heard to say in a tapped telephone conversation that Judge Byrne was "a man who couldn't be bought."

An honest, tax–aversive jurist from West Orange who had never held political office was irresistible to New Jersey's suburban voters, especially in the year of Watergate. His appeal was heightened further by the contrast with his predecessor, Republican William Cahill. While Cahill had great personal integrity, he insisted on remaining loyal to political comrades he appointed to office, too many of whom had a propensity for being indicted for official corruption. Among Byrne's first actions in office were what he called "the integrity package"—the nation's first public financing law for gubernatorial elections, the first cabinet–level public advocate to serve as the public's legal representative in complaints against state government, and strict financial disclosure laws for all high–ranking administration officials.

A second component of the suburban political style is the ability to make personal contact with one's constituents. When they number in the millions, that contact is largely through television. Byrne's successor, Republican Tom Kean, was New Jersey's master of political television.

The most personally popular governor of the suburban age, Kean's critical insight was that governing a suburban state had many of the same requirements as campaigning. Moving legislators no longer tied to party organizations required strong public support, especially from the suburbs, and that could be gained with effective use of television.

Because of New Jersey's secondary status in the New York and Philadelphia media markets, Kean probably had the least official access to television of any governor in the country. He solved this problem the way candidates do—he bought television time, and the state paid for it. During the Kean years, the state's television budget increased from $1 million to $8 million, and virtually every dollar of advertising, whether boosting state tourism or touting the state lottery, starred Tom Kean.

Walking along the shore or joking with Brooke Shields and Bill Cosby, the governor told viewers, "New Jersey and You—Perfect Together." As Kean has written, the phrase became "a mantra."[9] The not–very–subtle subliminal message was that Tom Kean was also perfect for New Jersey. And large numbers of his constituents, warmed by the attractive portrayals of the state its governor came to symbolize and basking in a healthy economy, agreed.

Kean was not only a master of the suburban style but also the suburban policy agenda. Critics charged him with reluctance to spend his enormous political capital on difficult urban problems. His thematic priorities—the environment and education—had few "downside risks." They were also the issues that engaged New Jerseyans' attention when most—especially the suburban majority—were enjoying good economic times, and issues of taxing and spending seemed less pressing.

Kean was adroit at wrapping urban programs in a suburban mantle. When he decried suspected dioxin contamination in Newark's Ironbound neighborhood along with his quest for clean beaches at the shore, all New Jerseyans could appreciate the governor's commitment to the environment. Taking over decaying urban school systems was an act of courage those in both cities and suburbs could applaud. Sponsoring a state arts center in Newark and a state aquarium in Camden could help revitalize cities with amenities suburban patrons would enjoy. Mandatory sentences for drug–related crimes were a widely applauded policy. Like the opera singers he admired, Kean had perfect political pitch.

Kean's administration was not altogether "perfect" for either New Jersey's urban minority or its suburban majority. Residential and educational segregation increased, affordable housing became harder to find, property taxes rose sharply, and highways became increasingly congested. In one view, Kean chose not to risk his popularity—instead "artfully distancing himself from problems that could test his reputation."[10] In another view, Kean was only willing to lead the state in directions he thought its suburban majority was willing to go. He left office after his second term almost as personally popular as when that term had begun.

If Tom Kean sometimes seemed to float above difficult choices, reigning rather than ruling, Brendan Byrne was willing to take on the state's tougher problems—to a point. After pleasing a suburban constituency by running on a platform of no new taxes "in the foreseeable future," he strongly displeased them by finding the future was just a few months after his election and proposing a new and sharply progressive state income tax.

His tax proposal responded to the decree of the New Jersey Supreme Court in *Robinson v. Cahill* that some equitable funding mechanism must be found to support a "thorough and efficient" public school education everywhere in the state. Education was least "thorough and efficient" in New Jersey's increasingly beleaguered urban areas. Suburban voters were disinclined to provide support for the urban schools many of them had recently fled and skeptical that money was the thing they needed first or most to improve. In five months, Byrne's approval rating dropped more than 20 points, to barely a third of the electorate.

Rather than pressing the case for a progressive tax, Byrne withdrew and let the suburban–dominated legislature figure out how to satisfy the court's demands. After two years, the lawmakers, prodded by the court, devised a bipartisan agreement on a more modest and less redistributive income tax package that provided new state aid to all suburbs as well as cities and also presented all homeowners with an annual rebate on local property taxes.

The governor's personal standing in the suburbs never recovered from his betrayal on the income tax, but his political fortunes did. In the first year of the tax, as Byrne stood for reelection, suburban homeowners found that property taxes did indeed go down substantially. Byrne made then–unprecedented use of television to reach these voters, remind them of what the court demanded be done, and how he had done it in a way that benefited all New Jerseyans.

For the first time in New Jersey history, a majority of gubernatorial campaign spending went for the expenses of broadcast media. Television gave Byrne the direct communication link between candidate and voters that suburban political campaigns require. Between April and November of 1977, a million television viewers changed their minds about the tax and Brendan Byrne.

Disproportionately suburban independents, they were no fonder personally of the income tax or the governor than they had been three years earlier, but the years of public discussion and the governor's televised explanations eventually grudgingly persuaded them of the merits of his case. In the voting booth, perhaps they recalled that the Byrne administration had also brought them the professional football teams at the Meadowlands stadium and the nightclubs and casinos in Atlantic City, all of which one could enter directly from secure parking lots or garages. No longer would they have to venture onto city streets for entertainment.

Byrne's accomplishments in his second term—a state public transit agency that saved failing suburban commuter lines; extension of public financing to gubernatorial primaries; and an inventive plan to protect the pure drinking water and recreational uses of the Pinelands without taxpayer expense, while compensating property owners and developers—also sat well with the suburban majority. Byrne left office feeling that his failure to provide more help to the cities was the major unfinished item on his agenda but one that might have been impossible to accomplish in any case.[11]

The suburban agendas of Byrne and Kean may be contrasted with those of Byrne's predecessor, Bill Cahill, and Kean's successor, Jim Florio. When Cahill was elected in 1969, New Jersey was on the cusp of the new suburban era. Suburban areas had grown apace in the previous decade, and the legislature was in the process of conversion from county–based representation. Like Kean, Cahill attempted to integrate New Jersey's cities and suburbs in a way that would make them interdependent and part of a recognizable state rather than a collection of 567 municipalities. Like Byrne, he sought to accomplish these ends through tax reform that would make the fiscal system centered on broad–based state taxes rather than the local property tax, educational policies that would rescue failing urban schools, and housing policies that would open the suburbs to those city residents who could not afford them. All were dismal failures.

The income tax Cahill proposed was a sharply graduated and complex scheme that would have taken 55 separate pieces of legislation and three constitutional amendments to accomplish. His educational policies involved state–enforced busing and integration plans and regionalization of urban and suburban schools. He also proposed for the first time that suburbs be required to meet "quotas" of affordable housing. Each of these policies was anathema to the suburbs. Each asked suburban residents for sacrifices to save the cities they had recently abandoned. None offered the suburbs any benefits that they could see.

Cahill had neither the temperament nor the channels to explain these policies to suburbanites in any kind of persuasive way. Abandoned by suburban independents and attacked by his party's leaders, Cahill suffered the ignominy of losing his renomination contest in the 1973 Republican gubernatorial primary and became the first governor since the 1947 constitution permitted immediate reelection to the governorship not to win two consecutive terms. Cahill failed at both challenges of suburban politics: he did not offer a policy agenda the suburban majority could appreciate, and he could not personally connect to these voters or show that he respected their concerns.

If Tom Kean could be accused of not seeing the difference between campaigning and governing, his successor Jim Florio could be charged with failing to see their connection. Florio succeeded Kean by running a masterful TV–oriented political campaign and then proceeded to govern as if public support and approbation no longer mattered.

Florio had run against Kean in 1981. He carried the traditional Democratic urban base but fell short in the suburbs. Kean won by fewer than 2,000 votes, the closest gubernatorial election in state history. When Florio ran again after Kean's 1989 retirement, he had learned some lessons about suburban campaigning. He engaged the best national Democratic media consultants, "sucked up information on modern media campaigns like a sponge," and "boiled his policies down to simple phrases, such as 'clean water,' 'lower auto insurance rates', and 'opportunity.'" Promises of pristine beaches and cheaper auto insurance appealed to the suburban voters who had supported Tom Kean.

The austere candidate who frightened many voters in 1981 was now "radiating warmth" as he held hands with his attractive new wife and "chirped on about his new grandson," while anonymous announcers in his television advertisements conducted a highly negative campaign against his opponent.[12] Assisted by an inept Republican campaign, Florio this time made strong showings in the suburbs.

Once in office, however, the candidate who had repeatedly told suburban voters New Jersey had "an expenditure problem, not a revenue problem" immediately imposed a huge and redistributive tax increase that took from the suburbs and gave to the cities. Unlike Brendan Byrne, he waited for neither the "political cover" another court decision on school finance would shortly have given him, nor did he seek the bipartisan legislative support both Kean and Byrne effectively utilized to make tough issues "nonpartisan." Instead, he rode roughshod over Democratic legislators whose campaigns he had just financed and pronounced the Republican minority "irrelevant."

Florio's imperious style and apparent signal that some campaign promises were just convenient means to a "greater end" enraged many New Jerseyans and offended others. If Kean can be charged with refusing to spend his political capital, Florio can be accused of spending political capital he had not yet earned. The governor's program was perceived as calling on suburban voters to pay for programs designed to cure urban ills. Florio was seen as doing much that his campaign had assured voters he would not do.

Suburban voters sent their own strong message back to the governor in public opinion polls and 1990's election results. Once that message was sent, Democrats in the legislature fell over themselves to restore what the suburbs had lost, and the governor soon tried to follow them.[13] So deep was suburban voters' anger, however, that almost every assembly Democrat representing a suburban constituency was defeated in 1991, and the Republicans gained veto–proof majorities in both houses. Whether Florio could still run successfully for reelection in 1993, as Brendan Byrne had in 1977, would depend on whether he learned how to frame issues in a way his predominantly suburban constituency could appreciate and support.

The 1991 elections and their aftermath were harbingers of other significant trends in New Jersey's suburban politics. All of them revolved around a growing sense of New Jersey as a state—but a particular kind of suburban state. These trends could be seen in the political communication channels, the nature of the legislative campaigns, the campaign's issues, and subsequent legislative action.

Gradually but inexorably, New Jersey is developing the statewide communication channels that have been the last barrier to forging a state identity. The tax revolt of the 1990s began on an virtually statewide "talk–radio" station based in Trenton that identifies itself as "New Jersey 101.5—not New York, not Philadelphia, but New Jersey!" As they had when the income tax was first passed in 1976, thousands traveled to Trenton in 1991 to take part in tax protests, but hundreds of thousands listened to New Jersey 101.5. As the national TV network audiences declined, more New Jerseyans—especially in the suburbs—turned to cable stations where legislative candidates could tailor highly targeted, reasonably priced messages to their constituents alone.

It would probably not be long before they were distributing their messages on videocassettes, as candidates for higher offices (and even one state legislator) had done in the 1989 and 1990 primary elections.

The 1991 legislative campaigns were also the first that could be seen as state–based contests for ostensibly local offices. Each individual race became a referendum on a statewide issue—the redistributive Florio tax increases of 1990. Secondary issues were founded in demographic rather than geographic constituencies. Voters were mobilized as hunters seeking loosening of a recent ban on "assault weapons," as environmentalists seeking to save the shore, as senior citizens whose property tax rebates might be threatened. These issues all spoke to "the prevailing imperative of suburban life...security both economic and physical," as did proposed constitutional amendments the following year to tighten the death penalty and prevent state government from regionaliz-ing school districts against their will.[14]

Demographically targeted mail and phone calls replaced the local appeals of the past. They were increasingly orchestrated and paid for by state party organizations created by the legislative caucuses. The renewed call for the state initiative and referendum represented a kind of "home rule" and direct democ-racy at the state level. Proposals to elect statewide officials in addition to the governor—a state auditor, for example—were another attempt to link residents to state government in a meaningful way.

An assertive legislature, its leadership's more visible public profile, and the proposals for "I and R" have challenged the governor's supremacy and made the public and its representatives increasingly important players in state politics. These developments were doubtless stimulated by Governor Florio's unusually activist agenda and style, but they are likely to survive him. The legislature's 1992 proposal to amend the constitution to provide for a legislative veto received bipartisan support. Although the legislature will always represent substate interests, it is evolving into a body that also, like the governor, has a statewide perspective.

When Woodrow Wilson was elected governor of New Jersey, reporters asked him how he could win political reforms from legislators loyal to their county party organizations. He replied, "I can talk, can't I?"[15] New Jersey's political leaders must still rely on persuasive talk to win their policy priorities, but now the conversation takes place not only in the governor's office and the legislative caucus rooms but on television and in public opinion polls, and the conversants number in the millions.

New Jersey is today, as it has always been, well–endowed with people, resources, location. Whether it can provide the quality of life for all its citizens—

social, economic, and political—to which its overwhelmingly suburban voters now aspire, depends more than ever on the quality of its political leadership. New Jersey is now more than the sum of its parts. The state that was once defined by the places it was near is now a place unto itself. New Jersey was once a republican state, and now it is a democratic state. Those labels have nothing to do with its political parties and everything to do with its politics.

An Annotated Bibliography

GENERAL REFERENCE WORKS AND PRIMARY SOURCES

The best one–volume reference work on New Jersey politics and government is the annual *New Jersey Legislative Manual*. The manual is privately published but printed "by authority of the legislature." Because its thousand pages provide such a range of material, it is useful to describe its contents in some detail:

— Key documents, including the state constitution, the text of the governor's annual message, and the inaugural message.

— Historical data about the legislature, including chronologies of members and officers, and current data, including biographies of current members and officers, committee assignments, composition of legislative districts, and names and addresses of registered lobbyists and their clients.

— A chronology of New Jersey's governors since colonial times, statewide gubernatorial election returns since 1844, biographies of the current governor and high–ranking administrative officials.

— The organization of the court system, a list of judges appointed since 1948, current assignment judges, and biographies of current supreme court justices and court administrators.

— The organization of cabinet departments, lists of commissions and boards and their members and staff, summary data on department budgets and work force.

— State fiscal data, including receipts and disbursements by department, a summary of bonded debt and trust fund cash balances, descriptions of state taxes, and the revenue each has generated in the past five years.

— Annual statewide voter registration and turnout figures since 1920; annual election results by county and municipality; public question results since 1947; historical presidential voting; primary election data for recent presidential, gubernatorial, and U.S. Senate elections.

— Lists and descriptions of colleges and universities, special schools, hospitals, prisons, and state parks and forests.

— County and municipal data, including information on officers, government types and forms, dates of creation, and population.

— Lists of newspapers, television and radio stations, and their correspondents.
— Current members of the Democratic and Republican state committees and county committee chairs.

The manual has been published since 1872, and back issues are available in most major libraries.

For statistical data, the best overall source is the annual *Legislative District Data Book*, published since 1977 by Rutgers University's Bureau of Government Research in New Brunswick. It includes data on population, property tax rates, fiscal resources and expenditures, election returns, and school enrollment in each of New Jersey's legislative districts and the municipalities within them.

The State Archives Bureau, a division of the State Library, maintains the permanent records of the state. These include a collection of all laws since 1710, governors' papers since 1878, and detailed election returns since 1912. There is no complete catalog of its holdings.

The State Library publishes bimonthly a detailed *New Jersey Bibliography*, a checklist of official state documents with a cumulative annual index, and the narrower *Selected New Jersey Documents*. The library compiles a variety of special bibliographies. In 1989, it published the first complete directory of state agency and departmental libraries.

The State Library distributes state documents to more than 60 depository libraries at major public and private universities, law schools, and some county colleges; county libraries; and designated public "area reference libraries" in the larger municipalities. Out–of–state depositories include the Library of Congress, the California and New York State libraries, the Center for Research Libraries in Chicago, the main branches of the New York and Philadelphia public libraries, and the Council of State Governments in Lexington, Kentucky.

The State Library's special collections include a legal reference section, state and local histories, and New Jersey genealogies. State officials and members of the bar and press may borrow books directly. Others may request them through interlibrary loan.

The New Jersey Historical Society published a general *Guide to the Manuscript Collections of the New Jersey Historical Society*, compiled by D.C. Skinner and R.C. Morris in 1979, and an annotated bibliography of its collections on the *Politics and Government of New Jersey 1900–1980*, compiled by Benjamin R. Beede and Anne Brugh, in 1989.

The State Library and the Historical Society have the largest collections of New Jersey materials. Other major collections are the Rutgers University New Jersey Collection in the Alexander Library in New Brunswick, and the collection of the Princeton University Library System. The Alexander Library collection is a particularly useful source of doctoral dissertations on New Jersey subjects.

Regular publications of state agencies offer detailed statistical data. Illustratively, these include the Treasury Department's *Appropriation Handbook* and its Division of Taxation's *Annual Report*; the *Annual Reports* of the commissioner of education, the Administrative Office of the Courts, and the Department of Community Affairs' Division of Local Government Services; and the Department of Labor's monthly report on *New Jersey Economic Indicators*.

The *Journal of the Senate* and the *Minutes of the General Assembly* record official actions and the results of all roll call votes. The *New Jersey Legislative Index*, published by the private Legislative Index Company, issues, on all session days, synopses of introduced bills, their current status, and chronologies of legislative actions. Copies of enacted bills appear in annual volumes of the *Laws of New Jersey* and West Publishing Company's *New Jersey Statutes Annotated*.

Single copies of bills, resolutions, committee statements, and fiscal notes are available while the supply lasts from the statehouse bill room, and the Office of Public Information operates a telephone hotline for the status of bills and the legislative calendar. Committee votes have been recorded since 1972 and may be inspected in the offices of the senate and assembly clerks. Legislative debate is not recorded or transcribed. The Office of Legislative Services published a guide to *Sources of New Jersey Legislative Information* in 1985.

The governor's proposed budget for the next fiscal year is issued by the governor's office annually, usually in late January. It includes appropriation recommendations for every agency and program, actual expenditures for the previous fiscal year, and approved appropriations for the current year. It usually also contains a number of graphs, charts, longitudinal spending summaries, and the like, which focus on areas the governor wishes to emphasize that year.

Commissions often issue special reports on government policies and programs. The County and Municipal Government Study Commission, established by the legislature in 1967, has issued a large number on Jersey local government, embracing such topics as charter reform, regionalization of services, and urban revitalization.

Most recent governors have established commissions to review operations and organization of state government. Their published reports are usually included among the documents sent to state depository libraries. These include the reports of Governor Cahill's Governor's Management Commission, Governor Kean's Governor's Management Improvement Plan, and Governor Florio's Governor's Management Review Commission. Periodically, commissions are established to study the state fiscal system. Most recently, the State and Local Revenue and Expenditure Policy Commission issued several detailed background reports during the mid–1980s.

New Jersey Supreme Court decisions are printed and bound in *New Jersey Reports* and those of the superior court and its appellate division in *New Jersey Superior Court Reports*. They are indexed in West's *New Jersey Digest* and Shepherd's *New Jersey Law Locator*.

Since 1972, the Eagleton Poll, sponsored by the Eagleton Institute of Rutgers University in New Brunswick, has conducted regular surveys of public opinion in New Jersey. The Eagleton Poll is the preeminent source of survey data on public opinion about candidates, public officials, and major state issues. It has conducted polls on these topics at least quarterly since its inception. In 1983, the *Star–Ledger* newspaper assumed some of the costs of the surveys, and they became known as the *Star–Ledger*/Eagleton Poll. Major findings are published in the *Newark Star–Ledger* and most New Jersey newspapers regularly; all are available from the Eagleton Institute on request.

Eagleton also conducts commissioned surveys on policies and programs for state agencies and other public or quasi–public entities, with the proviso that all results may be released no later than a year after the surveys are conducted.

Other state polls sponsored by media outlets have come and gone. The longest–lasting is the *Record* poll, sponsored by the *Record of Hackensack* newspaper and conducted at irregular intervals since 1980. It focuses on current elections and issues.

New Jersey Network, the state's public television agency, produces a nightly news program, several regularly scheduled public affairs programs, and political documentaries. It also offers extensive election coverage and broadcasts significant legislative sessions. Videocassettes of its offerings are available for purchase.

SECONDARY SOURCES

Newspapers

There is no statewide New Jersey newspaper. Until it ceased publication in 1972, the *Newark Evening News* was the best source of state news. Since then, by far the most complete source has been the *Star–Ledger*, also headquartered in Newark. Other New Jersey papers providing extensive state news coverage are the *Times* of Trenton, the *Record of Hackensack*, the *Asbury Park Press*, and the *Press* of Atlantic City. Major New Jersey political events are reported by the *New York Times* and the *Philadelphia Inquirer*, but coverage is sporadic and concentrated on statehouse action.

All of these newspapers are available on microfilm at major state libraries. No New Jersey newspaper has an easily available index. The Newark Public Library has compiled an index of the *Star–Ledger* since 1970 and the *Newark*

Evening News from 1914 to 1972, which may be used at the library. The New Jersey Historical Commission published a *Directory of New Jersey Newspapers, 1765–1970*, edited by William C. Wright and Paul Stellhorn, in 1977, which includes the New Jersey newspaper holdings of major in–state and out–of–state libraries. The State Library maintains a clipping file on state policy. The Office of Public Information of the Legislative Services Library maintains a clipping file of articles related to the New Jersey state legislature.

Periodicals

Several periodicals regularly publish useful analyses of New Jersey politics and government. The nonpartisan Center for Analysis of Public Issues in Princeton, supported by New Jersey foundations and major corporations, has published, at various intervals and under various titles, "a journal of public issues" since 1971. For about the last decade, it has been called the *New Jersey Reporter* and is currently published bimonthly. The *New Jersey Reporter* is the best journalistic source of state policy analysis and also publishes frequent articles on state politics.

State issues that come before the courts are analyzed in the journals of New Jersey's law schools: the *Rutgers Law Review* (Newark), the *Rutgers Law Journal* (Camden), and the *Seton Hall Legislative Journal*. Articles on politics, state political figures, and major policy questions also appear in *New Jersey Monthly*, although this mass–audience magazine devotes more of its attention to subjects like day trips and restaurants.

Several groups issue periodicals directed primarily to members, which carry useful articles on specialized topics. These include *New Jersey History*, published by the New Jersey Historical Society; the League of Municipalities' *New Jersey Municipalities*; the New Jersey Education Association's *NJEA Review*; the Business and Industry Association's *New Jersey Business;* and *New Jersey Bell Journal*.

The chapter footnotes in this volume cite the rich monographic literature on New Jersey subjects.

In compiling this bibliography, we were much assisted by a similar effort by Richard Lehne: "New Jersey: A Reference Guide and Course Syllabus," published by the American Political Science Association in *News for Teachers of Political Science* (Spring 1982): 10–11. This chapter updates and expands on many of the topics Lehne explored.

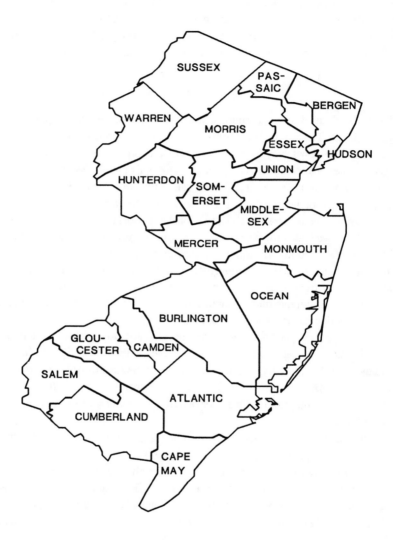

Map of New Jersey

Endnotes

CHAPTER 1

1 Paul Simon, "America."

2 Edmund Wilson, Jr., "New Jersey: The Slave of Two Cities," in *These United States: A Symposium*, ed. Ernest Gruening (New York: Boni and Liveright, 1923; reprint, Freeport, N.Y.: Books for Libraries Press, 1971), 56–7.

3 Ibid., iii.

4 Ibid., 61, 65.

5 Although everyone who lives there calls it Toms River, and there is a Toms River parkway exit and post office and school district, typical of New Jersey, Toms River is really a "place," not a municipality. Toms River technically composes most of Dover Township.

6 Joe McGinniss, *Blind Faith* (New York: G.P. Putnam's Sons, 1989), 43.

7 Ibid., 45.

8 Michael Danielson, quoted in John J. Farmer, "Crucial Cities: Rebound is vital to state's future," *Newark Star–Ledger*, April 8, 1991, p. 20.

9 John J. Farmer, "The *N–E–W* New Jersey: Era of a quiet revolution transforms the state," *Newark Star–Ledger*, April 7, 1991, p. 1.

CHAPTER 2

1 Lincoln Steffens, "New Jersey: A Traitor State," in *The Struggle for Self–Government*, (New York: McClure, Phillips and Co., 1906), 212.

2 Edmund Wilson, Jr., "New Jersey: The Slave of Two Cities," in *These United States*: A Symposium, ed. Ernest Gruening (New York: Boni and Liveright, 1923; reprint, Freeport, N.Y.: Books for Libraries Press, 1971), 56.

3 In a speech to the Newark Board of Trade and reported by the *Newark Evening News*, January 26, 1911. Quoted in Federal Writers' Project, Works Progress Administration, *New Jersey: A Guide to its Present and its Past* (New York: Hastings House, 1939), 35.

4 Susan Vankoski, "If at first you don't secede...," *New Jersey Reporter* (November 1983): 16–20.

5 Frederick Hermann notes that most other antebellum state governments played at least as active a role as their local governments in taxing and spending. Frederick Hermann, "Stress and Structure: Political Change in Antebellum New Jersey", (Ph.D. diss., Rutgers University, 1976), 341n.

6 Thomas Fleming, *New Jersey: A History* (New York: Norton, 1984), 65.

7 Francis Bazeley Lee, *New Jersey as a Colony and as a State* (New York: Publishing Society of New Jersey, 1902), 4:28.

8 Bernard Bailyn, *Voyagers to the West: A Passage in the Peopling of America on the Eve of the Revolution* (New York: Alfred A. Knopf, 1986), 246–51.

9 Fleming, 98.

10 Gibbons v. Ogden, 22 U.S. (9 Wheat.) 1 (1824). Gibbons's country estate in Bottle Hill (now Madison) was later purchased by Daniel Drew and became the site of Drew University.

11 From the charter granted by the legislature, as quoted in Wheaton J. Lane, *From Indian Trail to Iron Horse* (Princeton, N.J.: Princeton University Press, 1939), 325.

12 Fleming, 103

13 Floyd W. Parsons, New Jersey: Life, Industries and Resources of a Great State (Newark: New Jersey Chamber of Commerce, 1928), 41–44; Duane Lockard, *The New Jersey Governor: A Study in Political Power* (Princeton, N.J.: D. Van Nostrand, 1964), 61.

14 Lockard, 57.

15 Richard P. McCormick, *A History of Voting in New Jersey*,

16 J. R. Pole, "The Suffrage in New Jersey, 1790–1807," *Proceedings of the New Jersey Historical Society* 71 (January 1953): 39–61. Women were granted the right to vote in school board elections in 1887, "which seemed wholly in keeping with their motherly duties." John F. Reynolds, *Testing Democracy* (Chapel Hill, N.C.: University of North Carolina Press, 1988), 30.(New Brunswick, N.J.: Rutgers University Press, 1953), 115.

17 John Bebout, "The Making of the New Jersey Constitution," Introduction to the *Proceedings of the New Jersey State Constitutional Convention of 1844* (Trenton: MacCrellish and Quigley, 1945), lxxxiv.

18 Lee, 3:387.

19 McCormick, 124.

20 Steffens, 214. See also William Edgar Sackett, *Modern Battles of Trenton*, vol. 1, (Trenton: J. R. Murphy, 1895), 17–18.

21 Hermann, 306–10; A. Q. Keasbey, "Slavery in New Jersey," *Proceedings of the New Jersey Historical Society*, 3d ser., 5 (1906–1907): 15–18.

22 Route 1 entered New Jersey in Camden and ran through Bordentown, Princeton, New Brunswick, and Perth Amboy to Staten Island or Jersey City. Route 2 entered Salem and Cumberland counties from Delaware, running through Woodbury, Camden, Mount Holly, and Bordentown to Princeton. It was especially favored for its large number of forested areas and friendly Quaker communities. Route 3 crossed the width rather than the length of the state, from Phillipsburg to Somerville to Elizabeth. Routes were designated with numbers; "station stops" by letters.

23 For a fascinating picture of the life of these southern students and their political concerns as the war loomed, see Robert Manson Myers, *A Georgian at Princeton* (New York: Harcourt Brace Jovanovich, 1976).

24 John T. Cunningham, *New Jersey: America's Main Road* (Garden City, N.Y.: Doubleday, 1966), 184. This section also draws on Elizabeth H. Salmore, "A Jersey View: An Inside Look at the Civil War, 1864–65," (Highland Park, N.J., 1989, (privately printed).

25 Cunningham, 194.

26 Hermann K. Platt, "Jersey City and the United Railroad Companies, 1868: A Case Study of Municipal Weakness," *New Jersey History* 91 (Winter 1973): 252.

27 Fleming, 148.

28 William Edgar Sackett, *Modern Battles of Trenton*, vol 2, (New York: Neal, 1914), 144.

29 Hermann, 347.

30 Fleming, 128.

31 Steffens, 209

32 See the discussion of New Jersey Democrats' discomfort with "Bryanism" in John F. Reynolds, *Testing Democracy* (Chapel Hill, N.C.: University of North Carolina Press, 1988), 80–96.

33 Jerrold G. Rusk, "The Effect of the Australian Ballot on Split–Ticket Voting, 1876–1908," *American Political Science Review* 64 (December 1970): 1221.

34 McCormick, 156–61; quote at 161.

35 Lockard, 85–88.

36 Walter E. Edge, *A Jerseyman's Journal* (Princeton, N.J.: Princeton University Press, 1948), 60–63.

37 Ibid., 57.

38 Steffens, 281.

39 Elazar's arguments, briefly presented here, are developed fully in Daniel J. Elazar, *American Federalism: A View from the States* (New York: Thomas Y. Crowell, 1966), especially chapter 4.

40 Ibid., 89.

41 Ibid., 103. Although Elazar does not mention it, the third type of political culture he identifies, traditionalistic (marked by hierarchy and deference to elites and found primarily in the American Deep South) characterized portions of South Jersey, with its truck farms and pockets of black poverty. We are indebted to John Kincaid for this point.

42 Gerald Pomper has noted the long–standing practice in which New Jersey politicians made their entire living from multiple political offices, such as state legislator and a county patronage job. Gerald Pomper, "New Jersey County Chairmen," *Western Political Quarterly* 18 (March 1965): 186–97.

CHAPTER 3

1 This chapter title is drawn from the book of this title by George C. Rapport, *The Statesman and the Boss: A Study of American Political Leadership Exemplified by Woodrow Wilson and Frank Hague* (New York: Vantage Press, 1961).

2 This comment was made to Joseph Tumulty, who reports it in his *Woodrow Wilson as I Knew Him* (Garden City, N.Y.: Doubleday, Page and Co., 1921), 15.

3 Thomas Fleming, *New Jersey: A History* (New York: Norton, 1984), 180.

4 The New York–area counties were Hudson, Essex, Passaic, Bergen, Union, and Middlesex; the other was Camden. See Floyd W. Parsons, *New Jersey: Life, Industries and Resources of a Great State* (Newark: New Jersey Chamber of Commerce, 1928), 74–75; John T. Cunningham, *New Jersey: America's Main Road* (Garden City, N.Y.: Doubleday, 1966), 239–40.

5 Edmund Wilson, Jr., "New Jersey: The Slave of Two Cities," in *These United States: A Symposium*, ed. Ernest Gruening (New York: Boni and Liveright, 1923; reprint, Freeport, N.Y.: Books for Libraries Press, 1971), 57.

6 Parsons, 74–5.

7 Richard J. Connors, *A Cycle of Power* (Metuchen, N.J.: Scarecrow Press, 1971), 9–12. The Hudsonites who trekked to Monmouth led to its being called "Jersey City South."

8 Arthur S. Link, *Wilson: The Road to the White House* (Princeton, N.J.: Princeton University Press, 1947), 135. Two overviews of the Progressive movement in New Jersey are Ransom E. Noble, *New Jersey Progressivism before Wilson* (Princeton, N.J.: Princeton University Press, 1946) and John F. Reynolds, *Testing Democracy: Electoral Behavior and Progressive Reform in New Jersey, 1880–1920* (Chapel Hill, N.C.: University of North Carolina Press, 1988).

9 Tumulty, 24.

10 This limited form of primary was legislated in 1903.

11 Richard P. McCormick, *The History of Voting in New Jersey* (Princeton, N.J.: Princeton University Press, 1953), 188–95.

12 Lincoln Steffens, "New Jersey: A Traitor State," in *The Struggle for Self-Government*, (New York: McClure, Phillips and Co., 1906), 289–90.

13 From an article by Edmund Wilson, Jr. in the *Atlantic Monthly*, (November 1907); as quoted in Fleming, 153.

14 Link, 120.

15 Ibid., 133.

16 For an account of Harvey's career, see Francis Russell, *The President Makers* (Boston: Little, Brown, 1976), ch. 4.

17 Tumulty, 12.

18 Ibid., 14–15.

19 David Hirst, *Woodrow Wilson, Reform Governor* (Princeton, N.J.: Van Nostrand, 1965), 24–26. A detailed account of the dinner by an eyewitness appears in William O. Inglis, "Helping to Make a President," *Collier's Weekly* 58 (October 7, 1916): 37–39.

20 Hirst, 14–15.

21 Link, 156, 158.

22 Inglis, *Collier's Weekly*, 58 (October 14, 1916), 12–14.

23 Tumulty, 22. Wilson's acceptance speech is reprinted in Hirst, 53–59.

24 Wilson's answers were published in many newspapers on October 26, 1910. They are reprinted in Hirst, 100–106.

25 Link, 195.

26 Tumulty, 46.

27 Hirst, 137–38.

28 Ibid., 129–30.

29 Ibid., 161.

30 Link, 280.

31 Ibid., 281.

32 Hirst, 242.

33 There are interesting portraits of Hague's early life in Fleming and Connors.

34 Reynolds traces New Jersey party organizations' use of reform measures, especially in chapter 7.

35 Connors, 19.

36 Ibid., 60.

37 Although five of the six governors elected between 1949 and 1985, after the 1947 constitution permitted two consecutive four year terms, won twice, none has yet won a third nonconsecutive term. Robert Meyner, elected in 1953 and 1957, tried and failed in 1969.

38 Dayton David McKean, *The Boss: The Hague Machine in Action* (New York: Russell and Russell, 1940), 69.

39 George Crystal, T*his Republican Hoffman: The Life Story of Harold G. Hoffman, a Modern Fighter* (Hoboken: Terminal Printing and Publishing Co., 1934), 54.

40 For Roosevelt's relations with Hague, see James A. Farley, *Behind the Ballots* (Harcourt, Brace and Co., 1938), 115, 150, 158; John Kincaid, "Frank Hague and Franklin Roosevelt: The Hudson Dictator and the Country Democrat," in *FDR: The Man, the Myth, the Era 1882–1945*, ed. Herbert D. Rosenbaum and Elizabeth Bartelme (New York: Greenwood Press, 1987), 13–38.

41 Fleming, 185.

42 McKean, 127.

43 Kincaid, 34.

44 Bennett Rich, *The Government and Politics of New Jersey* (New York: Crowell, 1957), 21.

45 Walter E. Edge, *A Jerseyman's Journal* (Princeton, N.J.: Princeton University Press, 1948), 281–84. In other races, Roosevelt won by about 25,000 votes and the Republican senate candidate by about 30,000. The constitutional referendum, with many fewer votes cast, went down by 126,000.

46 *Newark Evening News*, October 21, 1947, p. 9.

47 Connors, 155.

48 Edge, 257.

49 When "reformer" John Kenny took over City Hall in 1949, he discovered 210 unfiled indictments in the county prosecutor's office, kept ready to insure the political loyalty of those named. See John J. Farmer, "When bossism ruled in Jersey," *Newark Star–Ledger*, May 21, 1989, sec. 3, p. 1.

50 Thomas F. X. Smith, *The Poweriticians* (Secaucus, N.J.: Lyle Stewart, 1982), 75–76.

51 The father of one of the present authors often told tales of working his way through medical school by recording betting transactions in a Hudson City "wire room" in the late 1920s.

52 The CIO's successful challenge of a Jersey City ordinance requiring a permit to speak on public property, which Hague refused to grant, was one of a series of important U.S. Supreme Court cases defining the rights and limits of free speech on public property. See *Hague v. CIO*, 307 U.S. 496 (1939).

53 The definitive catalogue of Hague machine scandals, from which many of these examples are taken, is McKean, *The Boss*.

54 Incorporating women into the Hague organization after they received the vote in 1920 served to close off another possible avenue of opposition to Hague.

55 Connors, 76.

56 Kincaid, 19.

57 Fleming, 136.

58 Farmer, 1.

59 Meyner carried only three counties besides his native Warren: Hudson, Mercer, and Camden. Hudson was then controlled by Hague archenemy John Kenney. See Alvin S. Felzenberg, "The Impact of Gubernatorial Style on Policy Outcomes" (Ph.D. diss., Princeton University, 1978), ch. 2; Duane Lockard, *The New Jersey Governor: A Study in Political Power* (Princeton, N.J.: D. Van Nostrand, 1964), 123–24.

60 Lockard, 125.

61 Thomas J. Anton, "The Legislature, Politics and Public Policy: 1959," *Rutgers Law Review* 14 (Winter 1960): 275.

62 Jeffrey Kanige, "Brendan Byrne on Brendan Byrne," *New Jersey Reporter* (June 1988): 8.

63 "Editorial Comment," *National Municipal Review* 39 (March 1950): 120. Eleven votes were required until 1952. The caucus reduced the number to nine partly as a result of the Meyner victory in 1949. Meyner had made caucus control a major campaign issue. See Belle Zeller, ed., *American State Legislatures* (New York: Thomas Y. Crowell, 1954), 206–7.

64 Edge, 295.

65 Anton, 276n.

66 Hughes's proposal for an income tax passed the assembly but was defeated in the senate when the Essex County Democratic leader withdrew his support at the last minute. With Republican support, Hughes did achieve passage of the first broad-based state levy-a sales tax. On the Hughes tax initiatives see, Richard C. Leone, "The Politics of Gubernatioral Leadership: Tax and Education Reform in New Jersey" (Ph.D. diss., Princeton University, 1969), ch 2. On the Cahill initiatives, see Felzenberg, ch 5.

67 Richard P. McCormick, "An Historical Overview," in *Politics in New Jersey*, rev. ed., Richard Lehne and Alan Rosenthal ed. (New Brunswick, N.J.: Eagleton Institute of Politics, Rutgers University, 1979), 20; Stephen A. Salmore, "Voting, Elections and Campaigns," in *The Political State of New Jersey*, ed. Pomper, (New Brunswick, N.J.: Rutgers University Press, 1986), 76.

68 In 1984, one of the independent television stations in New York City, WOR, was required to move its license to New Jersey. However, it did not have a studio in the state until 1986, does not maintain a full–time correspondent in Trenton, and still has one of the smallest audiences among the seven VHF stations in the New York metropolitan area.

69 Stephen A. Salmore, "Public Opinion," in *Politics in New Jersey*, ed. Alan Rosenthal and John Blydenburgh (New Brunswick, N.J.: Eagleton Institute of Politics, Rutgers University 1975), 74.

70 Reynolds v. Sims, 377 U. S. 533 (1964). These decisions were successive rulings in the case of *Jackman v. Bodine* between 1964 and 1970 and *Scrimminger v. Sherwin* in 1972. See the discussion in Stanley H. Friedelbaum, "Constitutional Law and Judicial Policy Making," in Lehne and Rosenthal, *Politics in New Jersey* 212; Arthur J. Sills and Alan B. Handler, "The Imbroglio of Constitutional Revision–Another By–Product of Reapportionment," *Rutgers Law Review* 20 (1965): 1ff.

71 In the case of the Democrats, the county organizations were dealt a severe blow when they were able to engineer the nomination of former Governor Meyner in 1969 but were unable to secure his election.

72 An additional blow to the already reeling county organizations was a 1978 law that prohibited local candidates from running on the same ballot line with statewide candidates in party primary elections. This further disconnected state and local campaigns and candidates.

73 Data demonstrating the major effect of the candidates' positions on the state income tax appears in Salmore, "Public Opinion," 70–79.

74 The fullest account of his career in his own Thomas H. Kean, *The Politics of Inclusion* (New York: Free Press, 1988).

CHAPTER 4

1 Thomas H. Kean, *The Politics of Inclusion* (New York: Free Press, 1988), 144.

2 On the liberal reformers New Jersey never had, see James Q. Wilson, *The Amateur Democrat: Club Politics in Three Cities* (Chicago: University of Chicago Press, 1962); on the short, unhappy life of the New Jersey New Democratic Coalition, see Vicki Granet Semel, *At the Grass Roots in the Garden State: Reform and Regular Democrats in New Jersey* (Cranbury, N.J.: Associated University Presses, 1978).

3 Among the other ethnic groups whose New Jersey experiences are included in Barbara Cunningham, The *New Jersey Ethnic Experience* (Union City N.J.: William H. Wise, 1977) are Syrians, Egyptians, Palestinians, Armenians, Belorussians, Circassians, Copts, Croatians, Czechs, Estonians, Filipinos, Greeks, Serbs, Swedes, Turkistans, and Ukrainians.

4 Demographic data in this chapter are from the *Statistical Abstract of the United States* (Washington, D.C.: U.S. Department of Commerce, 1989) and *American Diversity* American Demographics Desk Reference Series, no. 1, July 1991.

5 Rob Gurwitt, "Back to the Melting Pot," *Governing* (June 1992): 32.

6 Robert Cohen, "Census finds more diverse, affluent New Jersey," *Newark Star–Ledger*, April 17, 1992, pp. 1ff.

7 Correlation of the Republican base with ethnic self–identification: English and German, both .46; Irish, .22; Italian, –.11; Polish, –.14; Black, –.57. Correlation of

the Democratic base with ethnic self–identification: German, –.51; English, –.40; Irish, –.35, Italian, –.04, Polish, –01.

8 "Population and Labor Force Projections for New Jersey: 1990–2030," (Trenton: New Jersey Department of Labor, February 1989), 1:19.

9 Peter Bearse, "What's to be Done With an Old Industrial State?" *New Jersey Magazine*, February 1977, 42.

10 Donald Warshaw, "Region loses 300,000 jobs in deepest downturn," *Newark Star–Ledger*, December 20, 1991, p. 1; Cohen, p. 1.

11 Sternlieb and Hughes, "Demographic and Economic Dynamics," 37, 39.

12 Joel Garreau, *Edge Cities* (New York: Doubleday, 1991). New Jersey's Edge Cities are Fort Lee/Edgewater, Paramus/Montvale, Mahwah and the Meadowlands in Bergen County; Whippany/Parsippany/Troy Hills in Morris County; the Bridgewater Mall area in Somerset County; the Woodbridge Mall and Metropark areas in Middlesex County; the Route 1 corridor from New Brunswick to Princeton in Middlesex and Mercer counties; and Cherry Hill in Camden County. Emerging edge cities center around Morristown and the Hudson County waterfront.

13 David Mayhew, *Congress: The Electoral Connection* (New Haven, Conn.: Yale University Press, 1974); Gary C. Jacobson and Samuel Kernell, *Strategy and Choice in Congressional Elections* (New Haven, Conn: Yale University Press, 1981); Bruce Cain, John Ferejohn, and Morris P. Fiorina, *The Personal Vote* (Cambridge, Mass.: Harvard University Press, 1987).

14 The three retiring members were Bernard Dwyer (elected in 1980), Frank Guarini (elected in 1978), and Robert Roe (elected in a special election in 1969).

15 Recognition levels of gubernatorial candidates are discussed in more detail in chapter 5.

16 The exception is Governor William Cahill (1969–73), who was defeated in the 1973 Republican primary when county leaders abandoned him. Governor Jim Florio was elected in 1989 and is eligible to run for reelection in 1993.

17 On gubernatorial recruitment generally, see Joseph A. Schlesinger, *Ambition and Politics* (Chicago: Rand McNally, 1966); Larry J. Sabato, *Goodbye to Good–Time Charlie: The American Governorship Transformed* (Washington, D.C.: CQ Press, 1983).

18 It was widely assumed that Senate President John Russo withdrew partly as a result of the unflattering and barely disguised portrayal of him as "Ray DiOrio" in Joe McGinniss's best–selling book *Blind Faith*, about a murder case in Russo's hometown of Toms River. McGinnis offered no evidence for his charges that "DiOrio" acted improperly to suppress evidence in the case, and the state political establishment was unanimous in its condemnation of McGinnis. Russo briefly considered a libel suit but eventually neither sued nor ran. See Gordon MacInnes, "Blind Man's Bluff," *New Jersey Reporter* (March 1989): 26–27.

19 For one such analysis, see Bob Narus, "Paradise Lost," *New Jersey Reporter* (September 1985): 8–13. Narus describes recent voting patterns in Middlesex County, noting that its average Democratic vote for governor between 1973–81 dropped 11 percent from the average in 1949–69.

20 The relationship was also somewhat attenuated in 1981, when Governor Kean's narrow margin should have produced three more assembly seats, and the Republicans only gained one. See Stephen A. Salmore, "Sizing Up the Vote," *New Jersey Reporter* (March 1986): 45–47.

21 Neal R. Peirce, "New Jersey: In the Shadows of Megalopolis," in *The Megastates of America: People, Politics and Power in the Ten Great States*, New York: W.W. Norton, 1972), 199.

CHAPTER 5

1 Lloyd Grove, "How Experts Fueled a Race with Vitriol," *Washington Post*, January 18, 1989, sec. A p. 1.

2 Background memo, Star-Ledger/Eagleton Poll, release 25-1, October 1, 1989.

3 In response to a Democratic complaint, the state Election Law Enforcement Commission (ELEC) ruled this expenditure did not count against Kean's 1985 spending limits and was permissible because he was leader of the state Republican party.

4 Barbara G. Salmore and Stephen A. Salmore, *Candidates, Parties, and Campaigns*, 2d ed. (Washington, D.C.: CQ Press, 1989), 71, 210-211.

5 Ibid., ch. 6.

6 Background memo, Star-Ledger/Eagleton Poll, release 26-2, October 26, 1989. Florio was cited for his better understanding of issues by a margin of 46-20 percent. On their positions on the insurance issue, 68 percent said they did not know or were not sure of Courter's position, and 65 percent said the same of Florio. Although voters correctly chose Florio over Courter as the more pro-choice of the two candidates by 37-7 percent, 3 percent responded both or neither, and 54 percent said they weren't sure or didn't know. After auto insurance, the issue cited most frequently as the most critical to voters was the environment. Abortion and taxes were tied for third place.

7 Channel 2 News/New York Times 1989 Election Day Poll, November 8, 1989. "Honesty" was cited by 41 percent of respondents, followed by "competence," chosen by 27 percent.

8 All data on New Jersey in this section, unless otherwise noted, are drawn from Center for Public Interest Polling, "Images III: A Report on the Quality of Life in New Jersey" and based on data generated by the Eagleton Poll. Data for the seven other states are reported in Cliff Zukin, "Political Culture and Public Opinion," in *The*

Political State of New Jersey, ed. Gerald Pomper (New Brunswick, N.J.: Rutgers University Press, 1986), 3-26.

9 During the 1940s and 1950s when television was much less widespread, Channel 13, an independent commercial station, was licensed to Newark. When Channel 13 became the "New York area" Public Broadcasting System outlet in 1961 (although still technically licensed to Newark), its local public affairs coverage became "regionalized." Channel 13's programming now consists primarily of the usual PBS fare. When the New Jersey Public Broadcasting Authority, transmitting on four UHF stations, began producing the only nightly New Jersey news program in the 1970s, Channel 13 was pressured to pick it up. For an analysis and history, see Eric Sauter, "Double Exposure," *New Jersey Magazine*, May 1977, 33-40.

10 Jeremy Gerard, "A Channel Innovates and Moves Up: WWOR further erodes the barriers between news and entertainment," *New York Times*, September 16, 1989, p. 50.

11 The news program is also broadcast on the New York City UHF public television station, which is technically licensed to Newark, and the Philadelphia UHF public television station.

12 Center for Public Interest Polling, 88.

13 Allen Wolper, "Dateline: Nowhere," *New Jersey Reporter* (October 1984): 32.

14 David Sachsman and Warren Sloat, "The *Star-Ledger*: Does Bigger Mean Better?" *New Jersey Reporter* (February 1983); Michael Aron, "The Media," *New Jersey Reporter* (January/February 1991): 34.

15 Donald Linky, "The Governor," ed. Pomper, 112.

16 An additional 6 percent named radio, 8 percent said "other people," 1 percent each said magazines or "don't know," and 7 percent mentioned other combinations. When asked whether TV news or TV ads were more informative, 66 percent picked TV news, and 17 percent picked TV ads. The remainder said they were the same or that they did not watch any TV. Background memo, *Star-Ledger*/Eagleton Poll, release 26-1, October 22, 1989.

17 For a still accurate analysis of print and TV coverage of gubernatorial elections in New Jersey, see Mary Churchill, "The Media and Their Messages," *New Jersey Magazine*, November-December 1977, 10-17.

18 Stephen A.Salmore, "Public Opinion," in *Politics in New Jersey*, rev. ed., ed. Richard Lehne and Alan Rosenthal (New Brunswick, N.J.: Rutgers University, Eagleton Institute of Politics, 1979), 73; Zukin, 23; *Star-Ledger*/Eagleton Poll, release 28-3, April 15, 1990.

19 See the comparative data presented in S. Salmore, "Public Opinion," 74.

20 S. A. Paolantonio, "Countdown: New Jersey's independent voters have proven volatile and potent," *Philadelphia Inquirer*, October 30, 1988, p. 1.

21 Channel 2 News/*New York Times* 1989 Election Day Poll, November 8, 1989.

22 Gary Jacobson and Samuel Kernell, in *Strategy and Choice in Congressional Elections* (New Haven, Conn.: Yale University Press, 1982); Gary Jacobson, *The Electoral Origins of Divided Government* (Boulder, Colo.: Westview Press, 1990).

23 Channel 2 News/New York Times 1989 Election Day Poll, November 8, 1989.

24 S. A. Paolantonio, "Bill Bradley's Season of Discontent: Catching up with a Campaign Debacle," *New Jersey Reporter* (January-February 1991): 23.

25 A thorough summary is Frank Sorauf, *Money in American Politics* (Glenview, Ill.: Scott-Foresman/Little, Brown, 1988).

26 The combined spending for an open seat in the Third District was $2.6 million. In 1984, the Eleventh District race, producing a rare incumbent defeat, saw combined spending of $1.14 million.

27 Data from the New Jersey Election Law Enforcement Commission.

28 For some comparative figures, see Barbara G. Salmore and Stephen A. Salmore, "The Transformation of State Electoral Politics," in *The State of the States*, ed. Carl Van Horn (Washington, D.C.: CQ Press, 1989), 195-99; Sorauf, 264, 280.

29 For a thorough discussion of the state's experience with public financing, see Robert A. Cropf, "Public Campaign Financing in New Jersey," *Comparative State Politics* 13 (April 1992): 1-11.

30 For a summary, see "Kean signs updated campaign finance law," *Newark-Star Ledger*, January 24, 1989, p. 19. The law was a compromise between Republican Assembly Speaker. Chuck Hardwick, who saw lower primary limits and higher general election limits to his advantage, and Democratic Senate President John Russo, who saw higher primary limits and lower general election limits as advantaging him. Russo withdrew from the Democratic contest shortly thereafter; Hardwick came in third in the Republican primary.

31 Bob Fitzpatrick, "Soft Money on a Hard Roll," *New Jersey Reporter* (February 1990): 14-18.

32 Jerry Hagstrom and Robert Guskind, "Shopping for Airtime," *National Journal* (February 20, 1988): 462-467.

33 Robert Guskind and Jerry Hagstrom, "In the Gutter," *National Journal* (November 5, 1988): 2787-88.

34 *Congressional Quarterly Weekly Report*, December 7, 1985, 2561.

35 Some examples: voters reacted disapprovingly to Pete Dawkins's charges that self-made millionaire Frank Lautenberg went to the Senate to cast votes that would allow him to make more money. They also rejected Jim Courter's accusation that it was improper for Jim Florio's law firm to defend "drug dealers." Similar examples in other states are cited in John Nugent, "Positively Negative," *Campaigns and Elections* 7 (March-April 1987), 47-49.

36 See the analysis in B. Salmore and S. Salmore, *Candidates, Parties and*

Campaigns, 161-63.

37 James A. Barnes, "Legislative Races Counted, Too," National Journal (November 11, 1989): 2760. The "leading edge" nature of New Jersey legislative tactics generated a second article; see also James A. Barnes, "Campaign Letter Bombs," *National Journal* (November 25, 1989): 2881-87.

38 Conference on the 1991 Legislative Elections, Eagleton Institute, Rutgers University, New Brunswick, N.J., December 11, 1991.

39 Alan Ehrenhalt, *The United States of Ambition* (New York: Times Books, 1991).

40 Cornelius Cotter et al., *Party Organizations in American Politics* (New York: Praeger, 1984).

41 The first political scientists to call attention to this phenomenon were Malcolm Jewell and David Olson, *Political Parties and Elections in the American States*, 3rd ed. (Chicago: Dorsey Press, 1988), 217-22. The data Jewell and Olson present already seriously underestimate the amount of this activity. For a somewhat more up-to-date assessment, see B. Salmore and S. Salmore, "The Transformation of State Electoral Politics," especially 188-204.

As far as we can determine, legislative leadership fund-raising and campaign direction began in New Jersey after the 1973 elections, when the Republicans were reduced to 14 members in the assembly. Assembly Minority Leader Thomas Kean raised about $70,000 purely for 1975 assembly races and spent it on generic newspaper advertising and targeted radio ads.

42 New Jersey Election Law Enforcement Commission (ELEC), *ELEC White Paper, Trends in Legislative Campaign Financing: 1977-1987, No. 2* (Trenton: May 1989).

43 David Wald, "Republican State Committee completes the year $844,000 in the Red," *Newark Star-Ledger*, January 20, 1988, p. 29. (Of the $844,000 debt, $500,000 was an outstanding loan from the Governor's Club; the rest was owed to vendors of campaign services).

44 Jean Dykstra, "Feeding at the Campaign Trough," *New Jersey Reporter* (February 1990): 10.

45 Wald, "Republican State Committee," 29. A full account of the Russo PACs' activities appears in Joel Bradshaw and Elizabeth Sullivan, "The Case for Cooperation," *Campaigns and Elections* (March-April 1988): 57-62.

46 See Dykstra, 11; Chris Conway, "Democrats' coffers hit New Jersey record," *Philadelphia Inquirer*, October 31, 1989, sec. A, p. 1; Dan Weissman, "Florio coat tails bolster state Democratic fund raising," *Newark Star-Ledger*, October 15, 1989, p. 30; "Democratic coffers overflowing in quest to win Assembly seats," *Trenton Times*, October 31, 1989, sec. A, p. 4.

47 Schwaneberg, "Election Tab;" McCoy, "Call to rein in costly N.J. Assembly races."

48 The Democrats hired ten different consultants, including two mail consultants and

three phone bank consultants.

49 David Wald, "State Democrats ended 1990 with $1.5 million despite Florio's troubles," *Newark Star-Ledger*, February 6, 1991, p. 24.

50 The lively debate in the political science community on this topic can be sampled in Cotter, Advisory Commission on Intergovernmental Affairs (ACIR), *The Transformation of American Politics: Implications for Federalism* (Washington, D.C.: ACIR, 1986); the articles by Patterson and B. Salmore and S. Salmore in Van Horn; ed., and Jewell and Olson.

51 This argument is further developed in B. Salmore and S. Salmore, *Candidates, Parties and Campaigns*, ch. 11.

CHAPTER 6

1 Dayton David McKean, "A State Legislature and Group Pressure," *Annals* 179 (May 1935), 127.

2 Joseph Gonzales, executive director of the New Jersey Business and Industry Association, as quoted in Dan Weissman, "Fourth Branch of Government: Lobbyists Play Pivotal Role in Legislative Action," *Newark Star–Ledger*, March 22, 1987, p. 1ff

3 State Senator Lawrence Weiss and lobbyist Frank Capece, both quoted in Weissman, "Fourth Branch of Government: Lobbyists Play Pivotal Role in Legislative Action," *Newark Star–Ledger*, March 22, 1987.

4 McKean, "A State Legislature," 129; McKean, *Pressures on the Legislature of New Jersey* (New York: Columbia University Press, 1938), 223.

5 For a discussion of changing interest group politics in the states, see Clive S. Thomas and Ronald J. Hrebenar, "Interest Groups in the States," in *Politics and the American States*, ed. Virginia Gray, Herbert Jacob, and Robert Albritton (Glenview, Ill.: Scott, Foresman/Little, Brown, 1990), ch. 4.

6 Much of this chapter is a revised version of Stephen A. Salmore and Barbara G. Salmore, "New Jersey: From the Hacks to the Political Action Committees," in *Interest Groups in the Northeastern States*, ed. Ronald J. Hrebenar and Clive S. Thomas, forthcoming.

7 This count is based on our analysis of the registered interests listed in the 1991 *Manual of the Legislature of New Jersey*.

8 McKean, *Pressures*, 52–120.

9 Wording from the questionnaire in John Wahlke et al., *The Legislative System* (New York: Wiley, 1962), 498–500.

10 Ibid., p. 315.

11 Philip H. Burch, Jr., "Interest Groups," in ed. Richard Lehne and Alan Rosenthal, Politics in New Jersey, rev. ed. (New Brunswick, N.J.: Rutgers University, Eagleton

Institute of Politics, 1979, 111.

12 The Gallup Study's internal evidence, and our conversations with Gallup, lead us to speculate that the clients were probably the state's largest corporations and the state Chamber of Commerce, which they dominate. The chamber is the only often–discussed major lobby not rated in the publicly released material. Other questions center on legislators' views of PACs and contract lobbyists. The chamber did not establish a PAC until 1987, and these corporations have also not much utilized the burgeoning contract lobbyists, discussed below. We cannot confirm these speculations, however.

13 Gallup Organization, *The 1987 Gallup Survey of the New Jersey State Legislature* *Princeton*, 1987), 5.

14 This finding may relate to an overrepresentation of Republicans in the Gallup sample. Although both groups give financial support to both parties, NJBIA is usually more "bipartisan," relatively, in its giving.

15 Gallup Organization, 6.

16 Thomas Fleming, *New Jersey: A History* (New York: Norton, 1984), 162.

17 For discussions of the political role of labor in New Jersey, see Leo Troy, *Organized Labor in New Jersey* (Princeton, N.J.: Van Nostrand, 1964); Bob Narus, "The Marciante Mystique," *New Jersey Reporter* (April 1984): 22–27; Joel R. Jacobson, "Guilty Until Proven Innocent," *New Jersey Reporter* (March 1988): 15ff.; Donald Warshaw, "State AF of L chief urges labor to develop bipartisan political strategy," *Newark Star–Ledger*, February 19, 1989, p. 42; Donald Warshaw, "IUC pledges major push for Florio," *Newark Star–Ledger*, August 6, 1989, p. 19.

18 Jacobson died in 1989, after service as the state's first commissioner of energy and on the Casino Control Commission.

19 Donald Warshaw, "Labor federations split their Assembly ticket," *Newark Star–Ledger*, October 22, 1989, p. 45.

20 Donald Warshaw, "State labor urged to sit out Assembly elections," *Newark Star–Ledger*, September 24, 1989, sec. 1 p. 53.

21 A 1953 law gives the chief justice of the state supreme court power to name the six public members of Prudential's 24– member board. It applies only to Prudential, which is the only insurance company with 10 million or more policyholders, headquartered in the state (the requirement of the law), and is unique in the nation. Public members serve six–year terms; the other members, selected by policyholders, serve four–year terms.

22 Alice Chasan Edelman, "Church and State Street," *New Jersey Reporter* (November 1985).

23 Richard Sullivan, "Environmental Policy," in *The Political State of New Jersey* , ed. Gerald Pomper, (New Brunswick, N.J.: Rutgers University Press, 1986), 224.

24 Bill Glovin, "The Quintessential Art of Lobbying," *New Jersey Business* (July 1987): 62.

25 Nancy H. Becker, *Lobbying in New Jersey* (New Brunswick, N.J.: Center for the American Woman in Politics, Eagleton Institute, Rutgers University, 1978).

26 Ibid., 53.

27 Data from *Legislative Manual* of New Jersey of relevant years; see also Brian O'Reilly, "Lobbying: A Survey," *New Jersey Magazine*, February 1978, 9–47; Neil Upmeyer, "The Sunshine Boys," *New Jersey Reporter* (June 1983): 12–19.

28 Rick Linsk, "Millions spent on lobbying legislature," *Asbury Park Press*, February 24, 1991, sec. A, p. 1.

29 Calculated by the authors from data in the *1987 Gallup Survey*, p. 7.

30 For a full account of the battle, see; Becker, and Dan Weissman, "Just one little word in lobbyist law makes big difference on disclosure," *Newark Star–Ledger*, March 24, 1987.

31 Weissman, "Fourth Branch".

32 Upmeyer, 18.

33 Robert Schwaneberg, "Hired guns report collecting fees of $6.6 million for Trenton lobbying," *Newark Star–Ledger*, February 21, 1990, p. 19.

34 Bob McHugh, "Tougher ethics rules cleared by assembly," *Newark Star–Ledger*, June 18, 1991, p. 1.

35 In addition to the total veto and the line–item veto, New Jersey's governors may exercise conditional vetoes, which permit them to send a bill back to the legislature with suggestions for changing in wording.

36 McKean, *Pressures*, 204, estimated that two–thirds of all bills in the 1930s were written by lobbyists.

37 Dan Weissman, "Legislators have become too dependent on PAC money to let go easily," *Newark Star–Ledger*, May 8, 1988, sec. 3, p. 3. The Gallup Survey found that more than 50% of legislators found the provision of such information "very useful." Legislators were much less likely to appreciate lobbyists' organization of constituent support or opposition (18%) or working with party leadership (16%) as "very useful." Gallup Organization, p. 17. Just about half said they relied on lobbyists "very" or "somewhat" frequently for information, and only 11% said "not frequently at all." Senior legislators were only slightly less likely to say they relied on lobbyists with some regularity. Ibid., 14.

38 Quoted in Weissman, *Newark Star–Ledger*, March 22, 1987.

39 Banks, insurance companies, railroads, casinos, and utilities are not permitted to contribute directly to campaigns. However, the state attorney general ruled in 1979 that their employees could set up PACs to accept voluntary contributions. Most financial institutions did so immediately; most utilities followed suit in the late 1980s. Frederick Hermann, director of the Election Law Enforcement Commission,

points out that the 1911 law applied to those enterprises then regulated by the state, but "All companies today are highly regulated by the state." See Ted Sherman, "PACs formed by utility managers stir concern on undue influence," *Newark Star–Ledger*, March 4, 1990, p. 46.

A 1990 blue ribbon commission recommended limiting PAC contributions to $5,000 per candidate. See "Findings and Recommendations of the Ad Hoc Commission on Legislative Ethics and Campaign Finance: A Report to the President of the Senate, the Speaker of the Assembly and Members of the New Jersey Legislature," (Trenton: October 22, 1990).

40 Michael Specter, "Assault With a Deadly PAC: The NRA lets loose against a New Jersey legislator," *Washington Post National Weekly Edition*, August 12–18, 1991, p. 14. In 1992, the Republican legislative majority sought to weaken the law.

41 Charles Jacobs, "PACs Attract Funds And New Attention," *New York Times*, April 21, 1991, sec. 12, p. 1. The restaurant owners increased their activities in 1991 as a result of new state excise taxes on liquor and a pending bill for a new payroll tax to underwrite a health care fund for the poor and uninsured.

42 ELEC news release, December 9, 1987. In 1992, the legislature again considered reforms that limited PAC contributions to $5,000 and required PACs to file registration statements describing their political interests.

43 Thomas and Hrebenar, "Interest Groups in the States."

44 *Bergen Record*, "Quotas and Blackjacks; how the system works," October 13, 1987, p. 1.

45 1987 Gallup Organization, 9–10.

46 Dan Weissman, "Political Hardball: PACs Fill Void as Party Influence Wanes." *Newark Star–Ledger*, March 23, 1987, p. 1.

47 Stephen Adubato, "GOP takes the lead on finance reforms," *Asbury Park Press*, May 5, 1991, p. 1.

48 Weissman, "Political Hardball," p. 1.

49 Kanige, "Money and Power: A Dangerous Brew," *New Jersey Reporter* (February 1988): 8ff.

50 Gallup Organization, 13. Senior legislators (serving more than five years) with more experience with the "incumbency advantage" were more likely (70%) to favor restrictions than were their more junior colleagues (56% favoring restrictions).

51 Some of the more common "end–runs" around public financing or campaign contribution limits include in–kind rather than cash contributions, increased independent expenditures, and "individual" contributions by employees rather than corporate or trade association PAC contributions. See Kanige, 12; Barbara G. Salmore and Stephen A. Salmore, "The Transformation of State Politics," in *State of the States*, ed. Carl Van Horn (Washington, D.C.: CQ Press, 1992), 77–78n.

52 Linsk, p. 1.

53 For examples of the use of these techniques, see Becker, 40–52; Keith Hoffman, "No More Mr. Nice Guy: PIRG Turns Pugnacious," *New Jersey Reporter* (July–August 1989): 20–22.

54 Advisory referenda on nonstate issues are permitted, however. In 1982, voters endorsed a "verifiable" U.S.–Soviet nuclear weapons freeze by a margin of two to one.

55 Lisa R. Kruse, "Initiative, referendum a black hole for GOP," *Asbury Park Press*, July 18, 1991, sec. A, p. 1.

56 After numerous failed attempts to secure direct legislative approval, the physicians' assistants did manage to get the legislature to transfer the decision to the State Board of Medical Examiners. In 1990, the board authorized P.A.s to practice in the state, with many restrictions, for a two–year trial period.

57 O'Reilly, 16.

CHAPTER 7

1 Julian M. Boyd, "Introduction," in *Fundamental Laws and Constitutions of New Jersey, 1664–1964*, ed. Julian M. Boyd (Princeton, N.J.: D. Van Nostrand, 1964), 8.

2 Daniel J. Elazar, "The Principles and Traditions Underlying State Constitutions," *Publius* 12 (Winter 1982): 11–25.

3 Richard N. Baisden, *Charter for New Jersey: The New Jersey Constitutional Convention of 1947* (Trenton: New Jersey State Library, 1952), 109

4 Principal authorship is usually attributed to Jonathan Dickinson Sergeant, a New Jersey delegate to the Continental Congress. See Charles Erdman, *The Constitution of 1776* (Princeton, N.J.: Princeton University Press, 1929), 32–37. Lucius Q. C. Elmer, in *The Constitution and Government of the Province and State of New Jersey* (Newark: Martin R. Dennis and Co., 1872) is the leading proponent of those who attribute chief authorship to John Witherspoon, president of the College of New Jersey at Princeton.

5 Erdman, 39.

6 John Bebout, "The Making of the New Jersey Constitution," in *Proceedings of the New Jersey State Constitutional Convention of 1844*, ed. Bebout (Trenton: McCrellish and Quigley, 1945), xix.

7 William Griffith [Eumenes, pseud.], Collection of Papers Written For the Purpose of Exhibiting Some of the More Prominent Errors and Omissions of the Constitution of New Jersey and to Prove the Necessity of Calling a Convention for Revision and Amendment (Trenton: G. Craft, 1799). The papers started appearing in the *New Jersey Gazette* in 1798, and were published as a book the following year.

8 These problems characterized many of the early state constitutions. See Albert L. Sturm,

"The Development of American State Constitutions," *Publius* (Winter 1982), 62–63.

9 The legislature statutorily abolished the right to trial by jury at least 50 times between 1790 and 1800.

10 *State v. Parkhurst*, 9 N.J.L. (4 Halsted) 427, 433 (1802). Erdman, 78–80, discusses the case in detail. The earlier 1780 case, *Holmes v. Walton*, is described in Austin Scott, ["*Holmes v. Walton*: the New Jersey Precedent,",] *American Historical Review*, 4 (1898–99), 463.

11 Francis Bazely Lee, *New Jersey as a Colony and as a State* (New York: Publication Society of New Jersey, 1902), 3:268, 267.

12 There were occasions when local election officers disregarded the law, holding it to be unconstitutional and void, and permitted aliens, women, and nonwhites to vote. See Elmer, 49.

13 James Madison [Publius, pseud.], *Centinel of Freedom*, Newark, January 23, 1816; quoted in Bebout, "Making of the New Jersey Constitution," xliii.

14 Erdman, 46, 47, 99.

15 For example, the major reason the legislature adjusted the representation of Hunterdon, Sussex, Cumberland, and Cape May counties in 1797 was a desire to reduce Quaker influence and insure the defeat of a bill to abolish slavery. Lee, 272.

16 James Madison [Publius, pseud.], *The Federalist Papers*, No. 47. Mentor edition, with an introduction, table of contents, and index of ideas by Clinton Rossiter (New York: New American Library, 1961), 301, 305

17 Bebout, "Making of the New Jersey Constitution," xx, lvi.

18 H. McD. Clokie, "New Jersey and the Confederation," in *New Jersey: A History*, ed. Irving S. Kull, ed., *4 vols.* (New York: American Historical Society, 1930–32) 2:563.

19 New Jersey *Minutes of the Assembly*, 1842, 18.

20 Richard J. Connors, *The Process of Constitutional Revision in New Jersey*, State Constitutional Convention Studies, no. 4 (New York: National Municipal League, 1970).

21 Sturm, 63–64.

22 Biographies of the delegates were compiled by the New Jersey Federal Writers' Project of the WPA; the data are reported in Bebout, "Making of the New Jersey Constitution," lxi–lxxiii.

23 The one dissenting delegate objected to the provision giving each county equal representation in the senate. This stipulation, which would have momentous consequences, was not perceived as very significant. Every county but Monmouth observed a bipartisan agreement to apportion delegates evenly, resulting in a convention of 30 Democrats and 28 Whigs.

24 Bebout, "Making of the New Jersey Constitution," lxix.

25 Ibid.

26 Although the New Jersey bill of rights borrowed heavily from the federal Constitution, the local Quaker influence was evident in the strict subordination of the militia to civil authorities and the omission of a stated right to keep or bear arms.

27 "Report of the Committee of Council, on the Proposed Alteration of the Constitution," in *Journal of Council*, 1844; quoted in Frederick M. Hermann, "The Constitution of 1844 and Political Change in Antebellum New Jersey," *New Jersey History* 101 (Spring and Summer 1983): 32.

28 *Trenton State Gazette*, February 26, 1844, quoted in Bebout, "Making of the New Jersey Constitution," lxiv.

29 Boyd, 36.

30 *Bebout,* "Making of the New Jersey Constitution," ciii.

31 Federal Writers' Project, *New Jersey: A Guide to Its Present and Past* (New York: Hastings House, 1939), 56.

32 Elazar, 19. For an argument that the 1844 constitution took some small steps in that direction, see Frederick Hermann, 29–51.

33 William E. Sackett, *Modern Battles of Trenton*, II, (New York: Neale, 1914) 380.

34 Connors, 17.

35 Bebout, *"Making of the New Jersey Constitution,"* lviii.

36 For the details of these many failed efforts, see ibid., civ–cvii; Bebout, "New Task for a Legislature," *National Municipal Review* 33 (1944): 18; notes by Bebout in *National Municipal Review* 33 (1944): 88, 200; Erdman, 31–36. The most frequent topics were court reform, longer terms for officeholders, biennial legislative sessions, single member assembly districts, and a simpler amending process. Altogether, there were seven constitutional commissions during the life of the 1844 charter, and the legislature passed amendments five other times.

37 The sectarian aspects of the 1875 election are described in William E. Sackett, *Modern Battles of Trenton* (Trenton: J. L. Murphy, 1895), 94–97.

38 Boyd, 38.

39 Bebout, "Making of the New Jersey Constitution," cvi.

40 Voorhees E. Dunn, Jr., *Chief Justice Arthur T. Vanderbilt and the Judicial Revolution in New Jersey,* (Ph.D. diss., Rutgers University, May 1987.)

41 For accounts of Edison's battles with Hague throughout his term, see John D. Venable, *Out of the Shadow: The Story of Charles Edison* (East Orange, N.J.: Charles Edison Fund, 1978); Jack Alexander, "Ungovernable Governor—Charles Edison, First New Jersey Executive Since Wilson, has Hague and his Hessians groggy in the Second Battle of Trenton," *Saturday Evening Post*, January 23, 1943, 9ff.

42 Letter from Arthur T. Vanderbilt to James P. Alexander, chief justice of the Texas Supreme Court, December 20, 1943, Vanderbilt Papers, Wesleyan University, Box 147; quoted in Dunn, 74.

43 The report of the commission is reprinted in *Record of the Proceedings Before the Joint Committee of the New Jersey Legislature to Ascertain the Sentiment of the People as to Change in the New Jersey Constitution* 1942, 909–58.

44 Letter from Arthur T. Vanderbilt to Herbert Harley, July 17, 1942, Vanderbilt Papers, Box 147, quoted in Dunn, 81; Bennett M. Rich, "Convention or Commission?" *National Municipal Review* 37 (1948): 133–39.

45 *In re Hague*, 123 N.J. Eq. 475, 150 A 323 (1930).

46 Hague had predicted that Hendrickson and Vanderbilt would use the commission "for the purpose of revising the constitution to suit themselves and the interests they represent: the railroads and other malefactors of great wealth." *Jersey Journal*, November 25, 1941, quoted in Arthur T. Vanderbilt II, *Changing Law: A Biography of Arthur T. Vanderbilt* (New Brunswick, N.J.: Rutgers University Press, 1976), 125.

47 *Record of the Joint Legislative Committee*, 869.

48 Connors, 65.

49 *New Jersey Legislative Manual*, 1943, 632.

50 Vanderbilt II, *Changing Law*: 147.

51 The only major differences from the Hendrickson product were the removal of the nine specifically named cabinet departments and dropping a proposal for limited, biennial legislative sessions—both concessions to the legislature.

52 See Connors, 99; Alexander, 173; Venable, 170–81. The state supreme court ruled the tax debt cancellation unconstitutional in July 1943, and the court of errors and appeals, in a 10–4 ruling, upheld the supreme court in June 1944. See Dunn, 82–83. However, this was a Pyrrhic victory, as the court of errors and appeals upheld the new tax formula in 1946. See Baisden, 88.

53 *Newark Sunday Call*, April 23, 1944, quoted in Connors, 90.

54 The opponents' plurality was 126,000. The constitution lost by 87,000 votes in Hudson County and by 53,000 votes in Camden County. Connors, 108.

55 See the summary assessments in Connors, 110–12; Dunn, 96–99.

56 *New Jersey Legislative Manual*, 1947, 705.

57 Vanderbilt II, *Changing Law*, 150.

58 Speech to the Headquarter's Committee of the Clean Government Republican Committee, April 11, 1947, Vanderbilt Papers, Box 174, quoted in Dunn, 125, 129.

59 Baisden, 8. Connors, 128–29, writes that there were 31 legislators or ex–legislators.

60 This did not prevent interest groups from deluging the delegates with written special pleadings, mailed to them both at their homes and at the convention site. See the examples cited by Hudson County delegate Frank G. Schlosser, *Dry Revolution: Diary of a Constitutional Convention*, (Newton, N.J.: Onnabrite Press, 1960), 15, 32, 47.

61 Connors, 145.

62 In a referendum of state bar association members, there were 583 votes to retain the

equity courts and 549 opposed. Of the 16 associations that took positions, seven favored retention, three were opposed, and six so divided they could not make a recommendation (including the two largest—the state and Essex County associations). See Baisden, 47.

63 Connors, 156.

64 Ibid., 165.

65 Schlosser, 39.

66 Ibid., 176.

67 Albert Sturm called it "probably the most noteworthy accomplishment" of all constitutional action on state judiciaries in the period 1900 to 1950. Sturm, 71.

68 Baisden, 100; Connors, 181.

69 Sturm, 74. The average length is about 26,000 words.

70 Of the 34 constitutional amendments from 1947 to 1993, 6 relate to gambling, 12 to taxation (of which 7 deal with veterans' and senior citizens' exemptions), 3 to the executive branch, 3 to the judicial branch, 2 to the legislature, and 5 to other subjects (state purchase of school bonds, debt refinancing, publication requirements for public questions, changes in required length of residence for presidential voting, and extensive powers for the legislature in the event the state should fall under attack by an external enemy).

71 Connors, 203, 198.

CHAPTER 8

1 Alexis De Tocqueville, *Democracy in America* (New York: Vintage Books, 1954), 1:86.

2 Thomas H. Kean, *The Politics of Inclusion* (New York: Free Press, 1988), 63.

3 N.J. Const. of 1776 art. VII.

4 Francis Bazely Lee, *New Jersey as a Colony and as a State* (New York: Publishing Society of New Jersey, 1902), 3:272.

5 Julian P. Boyd, "Introduction," in *Fundamental Laws and Constitutions of New Jersey, 1664–1964*, ed. Julian P. Boyd (Princeton, N.J.: D. Van Nostrand, 1964), 29. See Duane Lockard on the "patrician governors," *The New Jersey Governor: A Study in Political Power*, (Princeton, N.J.: D. Van Nostrand, 1964), 36–56; and Walter R. Fee, *The Transition from Aristocracy to Democracy in New Jersey* (Somerville, N.J.: Somerset Press, 1933).

6 Speech of delegate Peter Clark, *Proceedings of the New Jersey State Constitutional Convention of 1844*, 185. Clark's fears were well founded. Governors of the second half of the nineteenth century were primarily business figures. See Lockard, *The New Jersey Governor*, ch. 4.

7 N.J. Const. of 1844 art. V, sec. 6. Ransone makes this point in *The American Governorship* (Westport, Conn.: Greenwood Press, 1982), 123. New Jersey's governors apparently began issuing substantive messages to the legislature as early as 1830. See Lockard, *The New Jersey Governor*, 50.

8 The classic discussion of informal presidential power is Richard Neustadt, *Presidential Power* (New York: John Wiley & Sons, 1960). Duane Lockard applies the concept to the governorship in *The Politics of State and Local Government* (New York: Macmillan, 1963), 363–64, and specifically to New Jersey's governors in *The New Jersey Governor*, 130. See also Alan Rosenthal, *Governors and Legislators: Contending Powers*, (Washington, D.C.: CQ Press, 1990), ch 4.

A survey of state senators found that in states where governors had strong formal powers, legislators saw them as most important; where governors were constitutionally weak, informal powers were seen as more important. E. Lee Bernick, "Gubernatorial Tools: Formal vs. Informal," *Journal of Politics* 41 (1979): 103–9.

9 See the rankings in Thad L. Beyle, "Governors," in *Politics in the American States*, 4th ed., ed. Virginia Gray, Herbert Jacob, and Kenneth Vines (Boston: Little, Brown, 1983), 458–9.

10 New Jersey presently has 19 cabinet officials. Of these, the governor may freely appoint (with the consent of the state senate) and remove 15. The secretary of state and the attorney general are appointed in the same way but may not be involuntarily removed during a gubernatorial term except for cause. The chancellor of higher education serves a five year term and is technically appointed by the State Board of Higher Education but must be approved by the governor and by tradition resigns at the governor's request. The agriculture secretary–an increasingly insignificant official–is selected by the self–perpetuating State Board of Agriculture and approved by the governor.

11 Kean, 63. This list of gubernatorial powers is outlined in Rosenthal, ch. 2. A final item on Rosenthal's list is the power of experience–their own service in the legislature, bringing friendships and understanding. All but one of New Jersey's seven postwar governors has also had this advantage.

12 Data to 1963 from Lockard, The *New Jersey Governor*; later data from *New Jersey Legislative Manual*, 1964–90. Nationally, 37.5 percent of the states had divided governments between 1930 and 1950, 46.8% between 1952 and 66, and 51.8% from 1970 to 74. Ransone, 18.

13 Bennett Rich, *The Government and Administration of New Jersey* (New York: Thomas Y. Crowell, 1957), 100.

14 Comparative data in this section are drawn from Larry J. Sabato, *Good–bye to Good Time Charlie: The American Governorship Transformed*, 2nd ed. (Washington, D.C.: CQ Press, 1983), ch. 2. The New Jersey data are from Duane Lockard, *The New*

Jersey Governor appendix; and *the New Jersey Legislative Manual*, 1965–90.

15 The four Catholic governors are Richard Hughes, William Cahill, Brendan Byrne, and James Florio. Governor Robert Meyner, elected in the 1950s, was raised a Catholic but later described himself as unaffiliated with a denomination. Although Florio is often called "the first Italian governor," his maternal ancestry is Irish. The first Catholic to be nominated for governor was Democrat Vincent J. Murphy of Hudson County, in 1943.

16 The effects of such powers are addressed in Terry Sanford, *Storm over the States* (New York: McGraw–Hill, 1967); Carl W. Stenberg, "States under the Spotlight: An Intergovernmental View," *Public Administration Review* 45 (March/April 1985): 321; Advisory Commission on Intergovernmental Relations, *The Question of State Government Capability* (Washington, D.C.: Advisory Commission on Intergovernmental Relations, 1985), 129; Thad L. Beyle, "From Governor to Governors," in *The State of the States*, ed. Carl Van Horn (Washington, D.C.: CQ Press, 1989), 34–48.

17 Donald Linky, "The Governor," in *The Political State of New Jersey*, ed. Gerald Pomper (New Brunswick, N.J.: Rutgers University Press, 1986), 93.

18 Sarah McCalley Morehouse, "The State Political Party and the Policy–Making Process, *"American Political Science Review* 67 (March 1973): 60; Alan S. Wyner, Gubernatorial Relations with Legislators and Administrators," *State Government* 41 (Summer 1968): 199–203; Lee Sigelman and Nelson C. Dometrious, "Governors as Chief Administrators: The Linkage Between Formal Powers and Informal Influence," *American Politics Quarterly* 16 (April 1988): 157–70.

19 Personal communication, May 1989.

20 For an analysis of gubernatorial styles, see Alvin S. Felzenberg, "The Impact of Gubernatorial Style on Policy Outcomes: An In Depth Study of Three New Jersey Governors" (Ph.D. diss., Princeton University, October 1978).

21 Linky, 98; Virginia D. Sederis, "Mr. Hughes Remembers," *New Jersey Reporter* (April 1985): 15.

22 Kanige, "Brendan Byrne," *New Jersey Reporter* (June 1988): 12.

23 Ibid., 16.

24 Personal communication, April 1989.

25 George Rapport, *The Statesman and the Boss* (New York: Vantage Press, 1961), 150–56.

26 Jim Goodman, "The Governor," *New Jersey Reporter* (October 1987): 7; Thomas H. Kean, interview with authors, September 29, 1989.

27 Alan Rosenthal, "The Governor and the Legislature," in *Politics in New Jersey*, rev. ed. ed. Alan Rosenthal and Richard Lehne (New Brunswick, N.J.: Eagleton Institute, Rutgers University, 1979), 143–44

28 "Three Decades in the Governor's Office: A Panel Discussion," (Trenton: New Jersey Historical Commission, 1983), 20.

29 Linky, 100.

30 Maureen Moakley, "New Jersey," in *The Politics of the American States*, ed. Alan Rosenthal and Maureen Moakley, (New York: Praeger, 1984), 233.

31 Walter E. Edge, *A Jerseyman's Journal*, (Princeton, N.J.: Princeton University Press, 1948), 340.

32 Federal Writers' Project, Works Progress Administration, *New Jersey* (New York: Hastings House, 1939), 58.

33 "Three Decades in the Governor's Office," 19–20.

34 Kanige, 18; Felzenberg, 391.

35 Kean describes these experiences in his informal autobiography, *The Politics of Inclusion*, ch. 1.

36 Thomas H. Kean, interview with authors, September 29, 1989.

37 Harvey Fisher, "The Governor: Something for Everyone," *New Jersey Reporter* (March 1984): 46.

38 Thomas H. Kean, interview with authors, September 29, 1989. Kean had a regular, hour–long, monthly call–in program on a New York City radio station that was also carried on an eight–station New Jersey radio network.

39 Wayne King, "Florio to Talk Directly to Citizens on Tax Increases," *New York Times*, August 9, 1990, sec. B, p. 2; "460,000 tune in to Florio's 'chat,'" *Trenton Times*, August 17, 1990, sec. A, p. 8.

40 Wayne King, "Florio Going to the People in Drive to Improve Image," *New York Times*, November 20, 1991, sec. B, p. 6.

41 Among these concessions were reinstatement of the popular homestead rebate, cancellation of a proposed tax on cable television, an adjustment in proposed marginal income tax rates, several million dollars in additional school aid for populous and politically competitive Bergen County, and passage of a law that had the effect of dramatically increasing the eventual pension of one key senator.

42 Peter Kerr, "Florio Shifting Style to Let Legislators Set the Agenda," *New York Times*, March 28, 1991, sec. B, p. 1. The legislature's activities are addressed at length in chapters 14 and 15. Dalton joined the Florio administration as secretary of state in 1992.

43 When Governor Byrne began his second term in 1977, there were about 60 people in the governor's office. In 1979, according to the National Governors' Association, the average number of such employees nationally was 34, with a range from 6 to 262. Thad L. Beyle, "Governors' Offices: Variations on Common Themes," in *Being Governor: The View from the Office*, (Durham, N.C.: Duke University Press, 1983), 158–73. The number of New Jersey staffers increased moderately in Byrne's second term but grew most sharply during the Kean administration.

44 Thomas O'Neill, "Viewpoint: The Governor," *New Jersey Magazine*, January 1978,

14–15. For a description of the second–term reorganization from the point of view of Robert Mulcahey, Byrne's first chief of staff, see Don Di Maio, "The Mulcahey Formula: Loyalty and Long Hours," *New Jersey Magazine*, May 1978, 21–24.

45 The consequences of such fragmentation are described in George C. Edwards, *Implementing Public Policy* (Washington, D.C.: CQ Press, 1980), 134–40.

46 Personal communication, May 1989.

47 Thomas H. Kean, interview with authors, September 29, 1989.

48 Personal communication, May 1989.

49 See the comparative discussion in Thad L. Beyle, "The Governor as Innovator in the Federal System," *Publius* 18 (Summer 1988): 133–54.

50 Christine Walton, "On top of Florio's mail," *Trenton Times*, July 23, 1990, sec. A, p. 4; Vincent R. Zarate, "Mounds of mail–Florio flooded with record gripes," *Newark Star–Ledger*, September 12, 1990, p. 1.

51 Personal communication, May 1989.

52 Thomas H. Kean, interview with authors, September 29, 1989.

53 Dan Weissman, "Selective entry into the Governor's inner office," *Newark Star–Ledger*, May 19, 1991, sec. 3, p. 1.

54 Ibid.

55 Matthew Reilly, "Cabinet officers called too 'green' to present budgets to legislators," *Newark Star–Ledger*, April 4, 1990, p. 25.

56 The Florio management strategy was first outlined during the gubernatorial transition period by his first chief of staff, Stephen Perskie. See Dan Weissman, "Florio team maps 'inner circle' to end overlapping operations," *Newark Star–Ledger*, December 17, 1989, p. 1; Dan Weissman, "High–level staffers are named by Florio," Newark Star–Ledger, January 9, 1990, p. 1.

57 Lockard saw this pattern emerging in New Jersey as early as the 1960s. See his discussion of "the modern governor," in *The New Jersey Governor*, 9. Ransone also notes the increasing need for governors continually to build new coalitions in the face of divided government or faction–ridden majority parties. See 146, 168–70.

58 Personal communication, March 1989.

CHAPTER 9

1 Passaic County Assemblyman Emil Olszowy, during the debate over the income tax.

2 Duane Lockard, "The Strong Governorship: Status and Problems—New Jersey," *Public Administration Review* 36 (January–February 1976): 96.

3 Alan Rosenthal, "The Legislature," in *The Political State of New Jersey*, ed. Gerald Pomper (New Brunswick, N.J.: Rutgers University Press, 1986), 136.

4 John Wahlke, *The Legislative System: Explorations in Legislative Behavior* (New

York: Wiley, 1962), 44–62.

5 Bennett M. Rich, *The Government and Administration of New Jersey* (New York: Thomas Y. Crowell, 1957), 55.

6 Rich, 53. The other states were Idaho, Montana, Nevada, New Mexico, and South Carolina.

7 Dayton David McKean, *Pressures on the Legislature of New Jersey* (New York: Columbia University Press, 1938), 44; Eagleton Institute of Politics, Rutgers University, *The New Jersey Legislature* (New Brunswick, NJ, November 15, 1963), 5.

8 Senators may have to run after two years as a result of the decennial census and subsequent legislative reapportionment. For example, the last several elections for the senate occurred in 1977, 1981, 1983 (as a result of reapportionment), 1987, and 1991, and will next be held in 1993 (as a result of reapportionment) and 1997. This peculiar schedule results in alternating periods when the senate is frequently elected at the same time as the governor (e.g., 1973, 1977, 1981, 1993, 1997) and periods when it is elected mostly in the gubernatorial midterm (e.g., 1983, 1987). The 1980s' election schedule meant the senate's Democratic majority did not have to run in the 1985 Republican landslide gubernatorial election, which saw the assembly go Republican for the first time in 14 years.

9 For a description of the 1980 process and the differing interests of party organizations and their incumbents, see Bob Narus, "A Rubik's Cube for Pols," *New Jersey Reporter* (May 1981): 3–15. For the 1990 process, see Peter Kerr, "New Jersey Redistricting Sets Off Debate on Shift in Minority Voters," *New York Times*, March 29, 1991, p. 1; David Wald, "New legislative map clears in bitter vote," *Newark Star–Ledger*, March 29, 1991, p. 1.

10 Richard A. Zimmer, "Less Could Be More," *New Jersey Reporter* (June 1984): 16–17.

11 The New Jersey data in this section are drawn from the *New Jersey Legislative Manual*, 1992, Alan Rosenthal, "Better Than It Used To Be," in *The Development of the New Jersey Legislature*, ed. William C. Wright, (Trenton: New Jersey Historical Society, 1976); Alan Rosenthal, *Legislative Life* (New York: Harper & Row, 1981).

12 In 1992, 40 states had a greater percentage of women legislators than New Jersey did. Whereas all nine black and Hispanic members of the 204th Legislature were Democrats, three of the 14 minority members in the 205th were Republicans (the current or former mayors of Mount Holly, Asbury Park, and Willingboro).

13 New Jersey data from Rich, 59; U.S. data from Belle Zeller, ed., *American State Legislatures* (New York: Crowell, 1954), 71.

14 For citation, see Table 9–2.

15 Eagleton Institute, 79.

16 Thomas H. Kean, interview with authors, September 29, 1989.

17 Rich, 61.

18 For development of the legislative staff, see Alan Rosenthal, *Legislative Performance in the States*; (New York: Free Press, 1974); Rosenthal, "Better Than It Used To Be"; Alice Chasan, "The Brains Behind the Bills," *New Jersey Reporter* (April 1989): 18–25; Virginia D. Sederis, "Empty offices, padded payrolls," *New Jersey Reporter* (June 1984): 6–11.

19 See 1930s' Assemblyman Dayton McKean's, McKean's description, 127. With no bill drafting office and no law degree, McKean had to go for assistance to the attorney general's office or to lobbyists. The attorney general was so busy that a legislator was "almost compelled to use the bills handed to him by a group."

20 Thomas H. Kean, interview with authors, September 29, 1989.

21 Chasan, 21.

22 Peter Kerr, "Spying by Computer: Is It a Trentongate?" *New York Times*, September 25, 1990, sec. B. p. 1.

23 Robert Schwaneberg, "Jury finds aides played politics on state time," *Newark Star–Ledger*, February 8, 1991, p. 1. A second investigation by the state Division of Criminal Justice also "produced no evidence which warranted a continued investigation." Quoted in Robert Schwaneberg, "State probe of Legislature reveals no basis for shakedown allegations," *Newark Star–Ledger*, July 21, 1991, p. 1.

24 Sederis, 6–11.

25 Data compiled by the National Conference of State Legislators, reported in Rosenthal, *Legislative Life*, 211; Chasan, 20.

26 Eagleton Institute, 22.

27 Ibid., 18

28 Neal R. Peirce, *The Megastates of America* (New York: Norton, 1972), 202; Zeller, 206–7.

29 Rosenthal, *Legislative Performance in the States*, 27, 37, 57, 113. In 1971, 13 percent of all bills and a quarter of those dealing with the governor's legislative program were still bypassing committees under "emergency procedures."

30 Rosenthal, "Better Than It Used To Be," 102. The New Jersey senate was also one of five ranking "very high" in discontinuity of senate chairmanships dealing with tax and revenue. The assembly ranked in the third quintile on a similar measure before the seventies. Rosenthal, *Legislative Performance in the States*, 178.

31 Calculated from the data in McKean, 45; Jay Romano, "State Office Kept Busy Preparing Legislation," *New York Times*, December 31, 1989, sec. 12, p. 4; Vincent R. Zarate, "'Recycle Fever' quickly gluts legislative hopper," *Newark Star–Ledger*, January 2, 1990.

32 Rosenthal, "The Legislature," 119.

33 Chris McGuire, "Recording Sessions," *New Jersey Reporter* (May 1988): 26–29.

34 Citizen's Conference on State Legislatures, *The Sometimes Governments* (New York: Bantam, 1971), 52–53.

35 Eighty–five percent called their constituency service activities "excellent or good," 49% gave this rating to their role in policy and program formulation, and only 32 percent awarded it to their role in policy and program control. The 1967 to 1971 survey, in addition to New Jersey, included Arkansas, Connecticut, Florida, Maryland, Mississippi, and Wisconsin. See Rosenthal, *Legislative Performance in the States*, 12.

36 Chasan, 21. David Kehler of the Public Research Institute has suggested that the bill glut also results from the legislature's "perpetual" sessions, rather than the limited ones characterizing most other states. See Dave Neese, "Jersey pols pen bill after bill," *The Trentonian*, July 19, 1991, p. 3.

37 Chasan, 25. Both of these former partisan staffers are principals in major lobbying firms and thus well placed to assess the changes.

38 Thomas H. Kean, interview with authors, September 29, 1989.

39 Jim Goodman, "Sound Over Substance," *New Jersey Reporter* (January 1985): 31.

40 Richard Sinding, "Fixing Up the Legislature," *New Jersey Reporter* (March 1984): 10.

41 Personal communication, March, 1989.

42 Personal communication, March 1989.

43 Alan Rosenthal, in "The Legislative Institution—Tranformed and at Risk," *State of the States*, ed. Carl Van Horn (Washington, D.C.: CQ Press, 1989), 69–98.

44 Ibid., 96, 97–98.

45 Sinding, 9.

46 Bruce Cain, John Ferejohn, and Morris Fiorina, *The Personal Vote: Constituency Service and Electoral Independence* (Cambridge, Mass.: Harvard University Press, 1987), 229.

CHAPTER 10

1 Donald Linky, "The Governor," in *The Political State of New Jersey*, ed. Gerald Pomper (New Brunswick N.J.: Rutgers University Press, 1986), 110.

2 Personal communication, April 1989.

3 Lynn Muchmore, "The Governor as Manager," in *Being Governor: The View from the Office*, ed. Thad L. Beyle and Lynn R. Muchmore (Durham, N.C.: Duke University Press, 1983), 83.

4 N.J. Const. art. V, sec. 4.

5 William Edgar Sackett, *Modern Battles of Trenton* (New York: Neale, 1914), volume 2, 143–44.

6 National Institute of Public Administration, *Survey of the Organization and Administration of the State Government of New Jersey: A Report to the Governor and the*

State Audit and Finance Commission of New Jersey, as quoted in the 1932 Inaugural Address of Governor T. Harry Moore, *New Jersey Legislative Manual*. 1932, 667–8.

7 Neutral competence had replaced the ideal of representativeness. See Herbert Kaufman, "Emerging Conflicts in the Doctrines of Public Administration," *American Political Science Review* 50 (1956): 1057.

8 The senate's rejection of Governor Cahill's reappointment of Education Commissioner Carl Marburger in 1972 was the first and last such event in modern memory.

9 For use of these resources, see Hugh Heclo, *A Government of Strangers: Executive Politics in Washington* (Washington, D.C.: Brookings Institution, 1977), 170–80; and John W. Kingdon, *Agendas, Alternatives and Public Policies* (Boston: Little, Brown, 1984), 32–37.

10 On the pros and cons of rigorous monitoring versus persuasion and incentives, see Herbert Kaufman, *The Administrative Behavior of Federal Bureau Chiefs* (Washington: Brookings Institution, 1981), 190–92.

11 These figures are derived from data found in Charles Jacob, "The Governor, the Bureaucracy and State Policy–Making," in *Politics in New Jersey*, ed. Richard Lehne and Alan Rosenthal (New Brunswick, N.J.: Eagleton Institute of Politics, Rutgers University, 1979), 170; Eleanor R. Laudicina, "The Bureaucracy," in *The Political State of New Jersey*, ed. Gerald M. Pomper (New Brunswick, N.J.: Rutgers University Press, 1986), 143; Harold M. Klein and Ernest C. Reock, Jr., *Patterns of Public Employment: New Jersey, 1957–67* (New Brunswick, N.J.: Rutgers University Bureau of Government Research and University Extension Division, February 1971); and figures provided to us by the New Jersey Office of Management and the Budget, November 1989.

12 Current data from Council of State Governments, *The Book of the States, 1988–89*, (Lexington, Ky.: Council of State Governments, 1988), 275–313; 1967 data from Klein and Reock, 5.

13 See Heclo's discussion of the different perceptions and roles of "program bureaucrats" and "staff bureaucrats," in 148–49.

14 Laudicina, 143.

15 David Osborne, *Laboratories of Democracy* (Cambridge, Mass.: Harvard Business School Press, 1989); Peter Eisinger, *The Rise of the Entrepreneurial State* (Madison, Wis.: University of Wisconsin Press, 1990).

16 Richard P. Nathan, Fred C. Doolittle, and associates, *Reagan and the States* (Princeton, N.J.: Princeton University Press, 1987), 19; Richard W. Roper, John R. Lago, Nancy C. Beer, and Martin A. Bierbaum, *Federal Aid Cuts in New Jersey, 1981 to 1984*, Council on New Jersey Affairs Working Paper no. 9 (Princeton, N.J.: Princeton Urban and Regional Research Center, March 1986).

17 In 1992, the Republican majority in the legislature cut the budgets of all but the public

defender's office so severely that the other divisions were at least temporarily effectively eliminated.

18 See the discussion of uses of reorganization in Harold Seidman, *Politics, Position and Power: The Dynamics of Federal Organization*, 3d ed. (New York: Oxford University Press, 1980), ch. 1.

19 "Governor's Management Improvement Program: What We Have Accomplished With Your Help," issued by the governor's office in October 1989; Matthew Kauffman, "Tackling the Bureaucratic Machine," *New Jersey Reporter* (May 1983): 6ff; Kauffman, "From the top to the bottom line," *New Jersey Reporter* (April 1984): 6–11.

20 Kauffman, "From the top to the bottom line"; Harvey Fisher, "The Governor," *New Jersey Reporter* (May 1983): 30.

21 Kauffman, "From the Top to the Bottom Line," 11.

22 Tom Johnson, "DEP beset by controversy, morale problems," *Newark Star–Ledger*, August 12, 1990, p. 35; Jim Goodman, "Putting one boss at the helm," *Trenton Times*, August 26, 1990, sec. A, p. 1.

23 Alice Chasan, "O Tempora! O Moore," *New Jersey Reporter* (June 1989): 8–15; quote at 14–15. Estimates of Moore's overspending range as high as $32 million.

24 Donna Leusner, "Departing Commissioner looks back at trying to solve the unsolvable," *Newark Star–Ledger*, August 20, 1989, p. 47. Codey's experiences at Marlboro State Hospital are described in Jeffrey Kanige, "The Marlboro Man: Codey in the Cuckoo's Nest," *New Jersey Reporter* (April 1987): 15–18. Both convicts in question were deceased.

25 See discussion of cabinet appointments in chapter 8.

26 Dan Weissman, "Haberle is moving to a staff post in shakeup of Florio's inner circle," *Newark Star–Ledger*, January 10, 1992, p. 30.

27 For the colorful history of the DMV, see Matthew Kauffman, "Division of Spoils," *New Jersey Reporter* (June 1985): 6–12; Jeffrey Hoff, "The High Price of Happy Motoring," *New Jersey Reporter* (April 1989): 14–17. The quotation is from Kauffman, "Division of Spoils," 8.

28 Lynn, Managing Public Policy, 216.

29 Symposium on the Transition, Princeton University, Princeton, N.J., November 20, 1989, transcribed remarks.

30 Rick Sinding, "Saving DCA: A Community Affair," *New Jersey Magazine*, June 1977, 31–38.

31 Personal communication, April 1989.

32 Sederis, "Interview: Ken Biederman," 12.

33 Jim McQueeney, "Changing of the Guard," *New Jersey Reporter* (February 1982): 13.

34 Symposium on the Transition.

35 Brian O'Reilly, "Power Politics," *New Jersey Magazine*, Summer 1978, 5.

36 Warren Craig, "Lights Out for Energy," *New Jersey Reporter* (April 1986): 10.

37 Ibid., 11.

38 As we have noted, many observers also thought the proposal to abolish DCA was a last attempt to get rid of its defiant commissioner, who refused the governor's request that she resign.

39 Sinding, 34.

40 Kenneth J. Meier, *Politics and the Bureaucracy*, 2nd ed. (Monterey, Calif.: Brooks–Cole, 1987), 58–61. See also Glenn Abney and Thomas P. Lauth, *The Politics of State and City Administration* (Albany, N.Y.: State University of New York Press, 1986), 84–105.

41 This figure is an understatement. As the authors of the *New Jersey Legislative Manual* note annually when they compile lists of authorities and commissions, there are several others that are listed with the departments of which they are a part. In 1989, Governor Kean's chief of staff estimated that there were 45 authorities over which the governor had appointment power and 32 over which he had veto power.

42 In 1990, the state's autonomous authorities had $15 billion in combined outstanding debt, an amount five times greater than the state's outstanding bonds.

43 Alice Chasan, "Exacting Change on the Parkway," *New Jersey Reporter* (March 1988): 11.

44 Ibid.

45 Associated Press, "Kean Accused of 'Conspiracy' in a Toll Increase," *New York Times*, October 11, 1989, sec. B, p. 2.; P. L. Wyckoff, "Conspiracy–Report Accuses Kean in Parkway Toll Furor," *Newark Star–Ledger*, October 11, 1989, pp. 1ff.

46 Kean quotations from Wyckoff, "Conspiracy," 1; quotation from Transportation Commissioner Hazel Gluck from Chasan, "Exacting Change," 14. In 1991, Robinson threatened to file suit against the new Florio appointees at the authority, charging there was a "continuing pattern of discrimination." P. L. Wyckoff, "Official mulls Parkway bias suit," *Newark Star–Ledger*, July 25, 1991, p. 6.

47 Dan Weissman, "Independent authorities face tighter control: Florio stresses accountability," *Newark Star–Ledger*, March 4, 1990, p. 1.

48 Annmarie Walsh, *The Public's Business* (New York: Twentieth Century Fund), 164–65.

49 For descriptions of such past problems at the Highway Authority and the Turnpike Authority, see ibid., 228–29; Angus Gillespie and Michael Rockland, *Looking for America on the New Jersey Turnpike* (New Brunswick, N.J.: Rutgers University Press, 1989), ch. 4.

50 Personal communication, April 1989.

51 Laudicina, 150. For a defense of the system by Charles P. Messick, director of the

New Jersey Department of Personnel Management from the 1920s to 1949, see his chapter on "The New Jersey Proving Ground," in Messick, *The Passing Scene: A Commentary on Public Affairs*, (Newark, Del.: University of Delaware, 1976), ch. 9.

52 Institute of Public Administration, "Review of Civil Service Reform in New Jersey: A Report to the New Jersey Department of Personnel," (New York: Institute of Public Administration, November 1989, photocopy), 5. This includes job titles in the 20 counties and 192 municipal governments that have chosen to participate in the state personnel system. In state government alone, there were 6,500 titles in 1986, second only to New York State's 7,300. See Council of State Governments, 289.

53 Laudicina, 150. Governor Harold Hoffman (1935–1938) apparently decided that if he couldn't beat them, he would join them. A "government efficiency" team appointed by Governor Meyner in the early 1950s investigated why the Division of Employment Security, which Hoffman headed, was taking as long as a year to issue unemployment checks. Hoffman was found dead in a New York City hotel room during the course of the investigation. In a letter discovered posthumously, he confessed to having embezzled $300,000. See Meyner's recounting in "Three Decades of the Governor's Office: A Panel Discussion," (Trenton: New Jersey Historical Commission, 1983) 18–19; Lockard, *The New Jersey Governor: A Study in Political Power*, (Princeton, N.J.: D. Van Nostrand, 1964), 96.

54 Institute of Public Administration, 4.

55 Don J. DiMaio, "When It Comes to Pensions, Public Is Better than Private," *New Jersey Magazine*, August 1976, 11–13.

56 Institute of Public Administration, 3. Unless otherwise noted, the assessment of the act's success that follows is based on this source.

57 "New Jersey Senior Executive Service (SES)" (Trenton: Department of Personnel, no date).

58 Ibid. A related initiative was the Certified Public Manager program, established in 1983. Of 22 similar state programs, New Jersey's is the largest. By 1989, over 1,500 state employees, including more than half the members of the SES, had completed all six levels of courses. Another 5,000 had been nominated for some of the levels. CPM holders were seen as prime candidates for the SES.

59 Eugene J. McCaffrey, Sr., "Senior Executive Service, 1988" Trenton: Department of Personnel, April 12, 1988, photocopy.

60 Institute of Public Administration, 11. Political appointees had a different view of the mobility provisions. One departing Kean commissioner observed privately, "I'm dying to see if anybody has the courage to do what the SES will allow them to do, and that is to transfer some of these ridiculous people someplace else, because [their positions] are in the Senior Executive Service; and start to scare the hell out of some of [the bureaucrats] who want to control the whole mechanism. I want to see

if in a year or two some of that takes place." Personal communication, April 1989.

61 Vincent R. Zarate, "CWA details proposal for cutting 'fat not muscle' from state budget," *Newark Star–Ledger*, December 6, 1990, p. 40.

62 Governor's Management Review Commission, "Operational Review of the Senior Executive Service" (Trenton: Governor's Management Review Commission, September 14, 1990), 14, 23.

63 Calculated from data presented in ibid., 44.

64 The Florio administration raised some eyebrows in 1991 when–apparently to protect his state pension rights–it appointed the executive director of the Democratic State Committee to a $14,500 per year position on the Merit Systems Board, which approves SES nominations and hears civil servants' complaints about political interference.

65 Thomas H. Kean, interview with authors, September 29, 1989. The anecdote, which Kean recalled with considerable accuracy, is reported in Richard Neustadt, *Presidential Power* (New York: John Wiley and Sons, 1962), 9. Truman said, "He'll sit here and he'll say, 'Do this! Do that!' *And nothing will happen.* Poor Ike—it won't be a bit like the Army." Original italics.

CHAPTER 11

1 D. W. Brogan, *The American People, Impressions and Observations* (New York: Knopf, 1943), 108.

2 Sheldon D. Elliott, *Improving Our Courts* (New York: Oceana, 1959), 25.

3 Robert Hendrickson, quoted in Bennett Rich, *The Government and Politics of New Jersey* (New York: Crowell, 1957), 173.

4 Letter from Arthur T. Vanderbuilt to Robert Caldwell, April 7, 1951, Vanderbilt Papers, Wesleyan University, Box 194. Quoted in Voorhees E. Dunn, Jr., "Chief Justice Arthur T. Vanderbilt" (Ph.D. diss., Rutgers University, 1987), 289.

5 Rich, 173.

6 For example, in a comparison of New Jersey with five other states (California, Kentucky, Michigan, Nebraska, and Arizona), the New Jersey Supreme Court issued the fewest opinions. Susan Fino, *The Role of State Supreme Courts in the New Judicial Federalism* (Westport, Conn.: Greenwood Press, 1987), 66. The total in 1988 to 1989 was 139.

7 Data from New Jersey Judiciary, Administrative Office of the Courts, "1988–1989 Annual Report," (Trenton, 1989), 6–7, 23–24. Between 1986 and 1989, the percentage of prisoners incarcerated for drug–related offenses rose from 11 to 25.

8 1987 N.J. Laws ch. 67.

9 The tax court replaced the Treasury Department's Division of Tax Appeals, which

was staffed by eight part–time judges and which had a backlog of 26,000 cases, in 1978. See Tony DePalma, "Appealing for Change in Tax Appeals," *New Jersey Magazine*, April 1978, 17–24. In 1988 to 1989, the tax court received 4,481 complaints.

10 Most other states did not have such an office until the 1970s. See Council of State Governments, *The Book of the States, 1986–87* (Lexington, Ky.: Council of State Governments, 1987), 174. The AOC collects and publishes relevant statistics, assists the chief justice in assigning judges, oversees court clerks, investigates complaints, and publishes and distributes opinions.

11 Letter from Arthur T. Vanderbilt to the Honorable Milton Feller, September 1953, Vanderbilt Papers, Box 200; quoted in Dunn, 194.

12 Eugene Gerhart, *Arthur Vanderbilt: The Compleat Counsellor* (Albany, N.Y.: Q Corp., 1980), 231.

13 See the data in Arthur T. Vanderbilt, "Our New Judicial Establishment: The Record of the First Year," *Rutgers Law Review*, 4 (1950): 353–65.

14 Kathy Barrett Carter, "Zeal for the job sustains Wilentz after heated decade as chief justice." *Newark Star–Ledger*, August 27, 1989, p. 1.

15 The legislature can veto judicial rulemaking in about half the states. See Henry R. Glick, "Supreme Courts in State Judicial Administration," in *State Supreme Courts: Policymakers in the Federal System*, ed. Mary Cornelia Aldis Porter and G. Alan Tarr (Westport, Cpnn.: Greenwood Press, 1982), 114.

16 N.J. Const. of 1947 art. VI, sec. 2.

17 Dunn, 313.

18 Ibid., 323–24.

19 Note, "Evidence Revision: A Legislative Achievement," *New Jersey Law Journal* 83 (1960): 284.

20 Dunn, 221, 369.

21 Glick, "Supreme Courts in State Judicial Administration," 122–23. Bernard Schwartz rates Vanderbilt the "most effective judicial administrator in American history" in "The Judicial Ten: America's Greatest Judges," *Southern Illinois University Law Journal* (1979): 405, 432.

22 Alan G. Tarr and Mary Cornelia Aldis Porter, eds., *State Supreme Courts in State and Nation* (New Haven, Conn.: Yale University Press, 1988), 247.

23 *The Book of the States*, 1986–87, 130–32.

24 Richard J. Connors and William J. Dunham, *The Government of New Jersey* (Lanham, Md.: University Press of America), 163.

25 Henry Robert Glick, *Supreme Courts in State Politics* (New York: Basic Books, 1971), 62, 105, 127.

26 Kathy Barrett Carter, "Two judges reprimanded for attending Florio ball," *Newark Star–Ledger*, January 30, 1990, p. 1.

27 Herb Jaffe, "Jersey means what it says on disbarment," *Newark Star–Ledger*, August 28, 1990, p. 11.

28 Joseph F. Sullivan, "In Search of Respect for Judiciary," *New York Times*, May 23, 1990, sec. B, p. 1.

29 Editorial, "Senatorial Courtesy: A Public Outrage," *New Jersey Law Journal* 113 (September 22, 1983). 1.

30 Thomas H. Kean, *The Politics of Inclusion* (New York: Free Press, 1988), 196. Kean discusses the Wilentz confirmation battle in detail, at 191-98.

31 Peter Buchsbaum, "The Courts," *New Jersey Reporter* (June 1988) 33–34.

32 Fino, 52–53. Recently, other states have named more politically experienced judges. See the observations by Justice John Dooley of Vermont, in Lawrence Baum and David Frohnmayer, *The Courts: Sharing and Separating Powers: Eagleton's 1988 Symposium on the State of the States* (New Brunswick, N.J.: Eagleton Institute of Politics, Rutgers University, 1989), 20.

33 The New Jersey Supreme Court has some of the institutional features—particularly an appointive rather than elective selection process—that have been found to promote consensual decisions in state supreme courts. See Paul Brace and Melinda Gann Hall, "Neo–Institutionalism and Dissent in State Supreme Courts," *Journal of Politics* 52 (February 1990): 54–70.

34 *Schipper v. Levitt and Sons*, 207 A.2d 314, 325 (N. J. 1965).

35 *State v. Johnson*, 346 A.2d 66, 68n.2 (N. J. 1975).

36 Tarr and Porter, *State Supreme Courts in State and Nation*, 209.

37 Michael Booth, "Judges refuse to let cops nose into N.J. trash," *Trenton Times, July* 18, 1990, p. 1; Dennis Hevesi, "Trash Searches Illegal, Jersey Court Finds," *New York Times*, July 19, 1990, sec. B, p. 1. Compare Sue Davis and Taunya Lovell Banks, "State Constitutions, Freedom of Expression and Search and Seizure: Prospects for State Court Reincarnation," *Publius* 17 (Winter 1987): 13–31.

38 Porter and Tarr, *State Supreme Courts*, xvi–xviii.

39 *In re Quinlan*, 70 N.J. 10, 355 A.2d 647 (1976.) For a discussion of the privacy right and *Quinlan*, see Stanley H. Friedelbaum, "Independent State Grounds: Contemporary Invitations to Judicial Activism," in *State Supreme Courts*, ed. Tarr and Porter, 45–46.

40 Porter, "State Supreme Courts and the Legacy of the Warren Court," in ibid., 16.

41 U.S. Supreme Court Justice William J. Brennan, a justice of the New Jersey Supreme Court when he was elevated to the federal high court, urged this strategy on state courts. William J. Brennan, "State Constitutions and the Protection of Individual Rights," *Harvard Law Review* 90 (1977): 489–504.

42 G. Alan Tarr and Mary Cornelia Porter, "Introduction: State Constitutionalism and State Law," *Publius* 17 (Winter 1987): 1–12.

43 Tarr and Porter, *State Supreme Courts*, 233.

44 Lawrence Baum and Bradley C. Canon, "State Supreme Courts as Activists: New Doctrines in the Law of Torts," in *State Supreme Courts*, 98.

45 Ibid, 99. The case is *Henningsen v. Bloomfield Motors*, 161 A.2d 69 (N. J. 1960). Another novel liability decision favoring the plaintiff is *Kelly v. Gwinnel*, 476 A.2d 1219 (N. J. 1984), which makes "social hosts" liable for serving alcohol to guests who are intoxicated and will be driving. The legislature later limited liability in such instances.

46 Tarr and Porter, *State Supreme Courts*, 197–204; Dominick A. Mazzagetti, "Chief Justice Joseph Weintraub: The New Jersey Supreme Court 1957–1973," *Cornell Law Review* 59 (1974): 197–220.

47 See Bradley C. Canon, "Organizational Contumacy in the Transmission of Judicial Policies: The Mapp, Escobedo, Miranda and Gault Cases," *Villanova Law Review* 20 (1974): 50–79; Note, "The New Jersey Supreme Court's Interpretation and Application of the State Constitution," *Rutgers Law Review* 15 (1984): 508–9.

48 Joe McGinniss, *Blind Faith* (New York: G. P. Putnam's Sons), 1989.

49 In 1992, directly as a result of the "Bonfire" dispute, the legislature passed a bill giving the counties control over the use of county courtrooms for non–judicial uses after business hours. Tom Johnson, "Assembly votes to give counties 'final cut' on courthouse use," *Newark Star Ledger*, June 30, 1992, p. 25.

50 Council of State Governments, 174.

51 Tarr and Porter, *State Supreme Courts*, 210.

52 *In re Karcher* 97 N.J. 483, 479, A.2d 403 (1984). The line–item veto case is *General Assembly of New Jersey v. Byrne*, 90 N.J. 376, 448, A.2d 438 (1982). Public employee bargaining rights are confined to wages, hours, and fringe benefits. Repeated efforts by teachers, in particular, to gain bargaining rights on issues such as class size and teacher transfer have been turned back by the court. See chapter 15.

53 Alan Shank, *New Jersey Reapportionment Politics* (Cranbury, N.J.: Associated University Presses, 1969), 168–84.

54 Richard Lehne, *The Quest for Justice* (New York: Longman), 139, 136–37.

55 Ibid., 159.

56 Russell S. Harrison, "State Court Activism in Exclusionary Zoning Cases," in *State Supreme Courts*, ed. Porter and Tarr, 58.

57 Between 1969 and 1979, New Jersey ranked first in LEXIS citations of notable cases involving exclusionary zoning. *Ibid.*, 64–65.

58 *South Burlington County NAACP v. Township of Mount Laurel*, 92 N.J. 158, 456 A.2d 390 (1983). ("*Mount Laurel II*").

59 Kean, 194.

60 Ibid.

61 Fair Housing Act, N. J. Stat. Ann. 52:27D–301 *et seq.* (1985).

62 *Hills Development Co. v. Township of Bernards* ("*Mount Laurel III*").

63 John Kolesar, "The Supreme Court Isn't Always the Last Resort," *New Jersey Magazine*, August 1976, 9–11.

64 Alan Mallach, "Blueprint for Delay," *New Jersey Reporter* (October 1985): 20–27; Jerome Rose, "Caving In to the Court," *New Jersey Reporter* (October 1985): 28–33.

65 Tarr and Porter, *State Supreme Courts*, 185.

CHAPTER 12

1 Thomas M. O'Neill, "LULUs, NIMBY and the Three Paradoxes of Home Rule," *New Jersey Bell Journal* (Special Issue, 1987): 2.

2 Rick Sinding, "The Ringing of Bells, the Crying of Goods," *New Jersey Reporter* (September 1984): 6–20.

3 Joseph F. Zimmerman, "Measuring Local Discretionary Authority," publication M–131 (Washington, D.C.: Advisory Commission on Intergovernmental Relations, 1981), cited in Deil S. Wright, *Understanding Intergovernmental Relations* (Pacific Grove, Calif.: Brooks/Cole, 1988), 323–25; Sinding, 7, 8.

4 The argument in this paragraph is made by O'Neill, 6–10.

5 New Jersey County and Municipal Government Study Commission, "Forms of Municipal Government in New Jersey," 17th report (Trenton: January 1979), 16.

6 For an elaboration of the themes and data of this section, see John E. Bebout and Roland J. Grele, *Where Cities Meet: The Urbanization of New Jersey* (Princeton, N.J.: D. Van Nostrand, 1964), 3–26; Joel Schwartz and Daniel Prosser, eds., *Cities of the Garden State: Essays in the Urban and Suburban History of New Jersey* (Dubuque, Iowa: Kendall/Hunt Publishing Co., 1977); John F. Reynolds, *Testing Democracy* (Chapel Hill, N.C.: University of North Carolina Press, 1988).

7 Joel Schwartz, "Suburban Progressivism in the 1890s: The Policy of Containment in Orange, East Orange, and Montclair," in *Cities of the Garden State*, ed., Schwartz and Prosser, 54.

8 Ibid., 54–67.

9 Bebout and Grele, 45.

10 Ibid., 27. See also Stanley H. Friedelbaum, "Origins of New Jersey Municipal Government," in *Governing New Jersey Municipalities*, ed. Julius J. Mastro and J. Albert Mastro (New Brunswick, N.J.: Bureau of Government Research, Rutgers University, 1979), 56–64.

11 Ernest C. Reock, Jr., "What are New Jersey's Local Governments?" Public Policy Forum on New Jersey Local Government, *Proceedings* (New Brunswick: Bureau of Government Research, 1967), 3–4.

12 Schwartz and Prosser, "Editor's Introduction," in *Cities of the Garden State*, ed.

Schwartz and Prosser, x.

13 Michael A. Pane, "Functional Fragmentation and the Traditional Form of Municipal Government in New Jersey," (Trenton: County and Municipal Government Study Commission, November 1985).

14 A constitutional amendment in 1875 and further legislation in 1896 ended special laws permitting unique charters for single municipalities.

15 For more examples of "micromunicipalities," see Sinding, 12–15. For the clearest explanation of the bewildering issue of "type" and "form," see New Jersey County and Municipal Government Study Commission, "Forms of Municipal Government," 33–35.

16 In 1950, there were 61 municipalities employing the commission form, including most of the largest, and only eight using the municipal manager.

17 Richard J. Connors and William J. Dunham, *The Government of New Jersey* (Lanham Md.: University Press of America, 1984), 210.

18 The Walsh and Municipal Manager acts provided for the recall, but it was never used. Indeed, the recall provision of Faulkner Act plans was not employed until 1964, when Belleville recalled two council members.

19 For extensive discussion of municipal governance and the Faulkner Act and its effects, see New Jersey County and Municipal Government Study Commission, "Forms of Municipal Government," and Julius J. Mastro and J. Albert Mastro, eds., *Governing New Jersey Municipalities*, 5th rev. ed. (New Brunswick, N.J.: Bureau of Government Research, Rutgers University, 1984).

20 Clifford Goldman, "The Hackensack Meadowlands: The Politics of Regional Planning and Development in the Metropolis" (Ph.D. diss., Princeton University, 1975), 58.

21 Robert C. Wood, *Suburbia: Its People and Their Politics* (Boston: Houghton, 1958), 198.

22 *Significant Features of Fiscal Federalism, 1989*, (Washington, D.C.: U.S. Advisory Commission on Intergovernmental Relations), 2:79. In 1947, the legislature gave a limited number of communities along the shore the power to levy a local retail sales tax; of the eight eligible, only Atlantic City took advantage of this provision. A 1970 statute limited to Newark permitted it to impose taxes on alcoholic beverages, parking, gasoline, and employee payrolls; it adopted only some of these. Aside from state aid therefore, the reliance on the local property tax is almost total.

23 Sinding, 8. An 1894 school consolidation law reduced the number of school districts from 1,408 to 374, but as new municipalities arrived, the number once again crept upward, in contrast to the marked downward trend across the country. Of 593 districts in 1967, only one–third operated K–through–12 systems, and 54% operated only elementary schools. *Proceedings*, of the public policy forum on New Jersey local government, 3–4, 34.

24 Elisabeth Ryan Sullivan, "As state grapples with its budget, local bodies let their

deadlines loom," *Philadelphia Inquirer*, March 9, 1989, sec. J, p. 3; Wisam Ali, "State threatens to set budget if South Amboy officials don't," *Central New Jersey Home News*, May 11, 1990, sec. B, p. 2. For a brief history of the state role in municipal budgeting, see Robert M. Gordon et al., "Governing New Jersey: The Toughest Management and Policy–Making Jobs In Trenton," (New Brunswick, N.J.: Partnership for New Jersey, 1989), 22–24.

25 These local governments may retain the traditional fiscal year by adopting a resolution then approved by the Division of Local Government Services.

26 Gordon, 19; Thomas P. Murphy and John Rehfuss, *Urban Politics in the Suburban Era* (Homewood, Ill.: Dorsey Press, 1976), 174–75.

27 Peter Yerkes, "Wheel of Misfortune," *New Jersey Reporter* (October 1986): 14–19. A study of municipal corruption in the early 1970s and U.S. Attorney Herbert Stern who prosecuted "8 mayors, 2 secretaries of state, 2 state treasurers, 2 powerful political bosses, 1 U.S. congressman and 64 other public officials," is Paul Hoffman, *Tiger in the Court* (Chicago: Playboy Press, 1973). In January 1992, Jersey City Mayor Gerald McCann was convicted of crimes in which he engaged while out of office.

28 Joseph F. Sullivan, "Multimillion Fraud Shakes New Jersey Haven for Aged," *New York Times*, September 3, 1990, p. 23.

29 Jeffrey Hoff, "Who Ya Gonna Call?" *New Jersey Reporter* (September 1988): 26–30; George James, "Jersey Murder Trial is Bias Issue for Indians," *New York Times*, March 4, 1989, sec. B, p. 1.

30 Bebout and Grele, 28.

31 Harris I. Effross, *County Governing Bodies in New Jersey* (New Brunswick, N.J.: Rutgers University Press, 1975) is an exhaustive history of the governmental development of the counties. See also Friedelbaum, 56–64; Matthew Kauffman, "Counting on Counties," *New Jersey Reporter* (September 1984): 25–30; and for a social history of the counties, John T. Cunningham, *This is New Jersey*, 3d ed. (New Brunswick, N.J.: Rutgers University Press, 1978).

32 Before 1972, certain counties such as Essex and Hudson had an elected county supervisor who appeared to fill an executive role. However, they were essentially powerless offices, merely providing another patronage job.

33 New Jersey County and Municipal Government Study Commission, "The Structure of County Government: Current Status and Needs," (Trenton: New Jersey County and Municipal Government Study Commission, July 1986), 51.

34 Camden and Middlesex rejected the county manager plan; Passaic rejected the board president plan.

35 Until fiscal year 1992, counties contributed substantially to AFDC costs and to county hospital budgets. That year, the state government assumed those costs as part

of Governor Florio's tax reform package. The estimate is that this will lower the amount of property taxes dedicated to the counties by 20 percent.

36 See the discussion of county government and services in Thomas H. Reed, *Twenty Years of Government in Essex County, New Jersey* (New York: D. Appleton–Century Co., 1938).

37 Lucy Mackenzie, "Can Management Replace Politics?" *New Jersey Magazine*, May 1977, 41–46; quote at 46.

38 Lucy MacKenzie, "Charter Change Goes the Distance," *New Jersey Magazine*, November–December 1977, 19; see also Don Di Maio, "The Donnybrook in Essex," *New Jersey Magazine*, June 1978, 4ff.

39 Stephen Barr, "You Say You Want an Evolution," *New Jersey Reporter* (June 1989): 27ff.

40 *City of Clinton v. Cedar Rapids and Missouri R.R. Co.*, 24 Iowa 455 (1868).

41 *People of Michigan ex rel LeRoy v. Hurlbut*, 24 Mich. 44 (1871).

42 An argument made by Daniel J. Elazar, "State–Local Relations: Reviving Old Theory for New Practice," in *Partnership Within the States: Local Self-Government in the Federal System*, ed. Stephanie Cole (Champaign–Urbana: University of Illinois Institute of Government and Public Affairs and the Center for the Study of Federalism, 1976), 29–42.

43 N.J. Const. of 1844 art. XI, sec. 7.

CHAPTER 13

1 "The Social Statistics of Cities," 1880 U.S. Census Report, quoted in John E. Bebout and Roland J. Grele, *Where Cities Meet: The Urbanization of New Jersey* (Princeton, N.J.: D. Van Nostrand, 1964), 91–92.

2 Thomas H. Kean, The *Politics of Inclusion* (New York: Free Press, 1988), 111.

3 Recent examples are Senator Harrison Williams and Representative Frank Thompson, both indicted and convicted in the 1980 FBI sting operation known as Abscam.

4 A point developed by William M. Lunch in *The Nationalization of American Politics* (Berkeley, Calif.: University of California Press, 1987), ch. 1.

5 Charles Dickens, *American Notes*, (New York: Penguin Books, 1972), 144.

6 *Garcia v. San Antonio Metropolitan Transit Authority*, 105 S. Ct. 1005 (1985). For discussion of the implication of Garcia, see the articles by John Kincaid, Stephen L. Schechter, and A. E. Dick Howard in *Publius* 16 (Summer 1986).

7 Daniel J. Elazar, *The American Partnership* (Chicago: University of Chicago Press, 1962), 204.

8 Richard Nathan and Fred C. Doolittle, *Reagan and the States* (Princeton, N.J.: Princeton University Press, 1987), 19.

9 George E. Peterson, "Federalism and the States: An Experiment in Decentraliza-

tion," in *The Reagan Record*, ed. John L. Palmer and Isabel V. Sawhill (Cambridge, Mass.: Ballinger, 1984), 247–52.

10 Thomas H. Kean, interview with authors, June 26, 1990.

11 Jay Romano, "More Enterprise Zones Sought," *New York Times*, October 28, 1990, sec. 12, p. 1.

For a detailed analysis of New Jersey's response to Reagan–era intergovernmentalism, on which this section draws heavily, see Richard W. Roper, John R. Lago, Nancy G. Beer, and Martin A. Bierbaum, "Federal Aid in New Jersey, 1981–84," Working Paper no. 9 (Princeton, N.J.: Program for New Jersey Affairs, Princeton Urban and Regional Research Center, Woodrow Wilson School of Public and International Affairs, Princeton University, 1986).

12 Thomas H. Kean, interview with authors, June 26, 1990.

13 Data from a regional study by the Northeast–Midwest Congressional Coalition released March 22, 1990, and reported in Robert Cohen, "Dead Last: Jersey gets back the least in tax dollars," *Newark Star–Ledger*, March 23, 1990, p. 1.

14 Douglas W. Simon, "New Jersey and United States National Security," learning module of the "New Jersey in the World, the World in New Jersey Project," funded by the International Education Grant program of the New Jersey Department of Higher Education (Union, N.J.: Global Learning, Inc.: 1989). Data presented here are drawn from this study.

15 Office of Legislative Services, New Jersey Legislature, "Analysis of the New Jersey Fiscal Year 1989–90 Budget for the Department of Environmental Protection" (Trenton: Office of Legislative Services, 1989). These data cast strong doubt on the assertion that New Jersey remains a state with high state commitment and low federal dependence for environmental programs, as noted in James P. Lester, "New Federalism and Environmental Policy," *Publius* (Winter 1986): 157–58.

16 David Marziale, "Washington," *New Jersey Reporter* (March 1988): 32–33.

17 Thomas H. Kean, interview with authors, June 26, 1990.

18 Carl Van Horn, interview with authors, May 6, 1990.

19 Richard H. Leach, "War on the Port Authority," in *Cooperation and Conflict: Readings in American Federalism*, ed. Daniel J. Elazar et al, (Itasca, Ill.: F. E. Peacock, 1969), 405; Jeffrey Kanige, "Bridging the Troubled Waters," *New Jersey Reporter* (February 1986): 23.

20 Kanige, 23; Alan Finder with Jacques Steinberg, "In Eye of Economic Storm, the Port Authority Battens Down," *New York Times*, November 22, 1991, sec. B, p. 1; Annmarie Hauck Walsh, *The Public's Business: The Politics and Practices of Government Corporations* (Cambridge, Mass.: MIT Press, 1978), 89.

21 Walter E. Edge, *A Jerseyman's Journal* (Princeton, N.J.: Princeton University Press,

1948), 96.

22 In 1977, the U.S. Supreme Court, in a four–to–three decision, reversed a New Jersey Supreme Court decision and ruled that repeal of the bonds' covenants would violate the contract clause of the U.S. Constitution.

23 Guy T. Baehr, "New chairman says Port Authority should follow governors' agendas," *Newark Star–Ledger*, April 16, 1990, p. 1.

24 Guy T. Baehr, "Transportation chief wants to tap authority funds for overall goals," *Newark Star–Ledger*, May 4, 1990, p. 19.

25 The port district handles 45 percent of ocean–borne cargo in the North Atlantic, and the New Jersey ports handle over 70 percent of all the cargo in the district. See James T. Prior, "International Trade: Reverse Investment," *New Jersey Business*, September 1986, 51.

26 Finder with Steinberg, B1.

27 Thomas H. Kean, interview with authors, June 26, 1990.

28 Martin Bierbaum, "Living in New York's Shadow," *New Jersey Reporter* (February 1986): 32.

29 Ibid., 33.

30 For a discussion of the tax and the court case (Salorio v. Glaser, decided June 8, 1983), see Peter Buchsbaum, "The Courts," *New Jersey Reporter* (July 1983): 41; Bebout and Grele, 76.

31 Thomas H. Kean, interview with authors, June 26, 1990.

32 Barbara Sturken, "Businesses' Enthusiasm for the State Said to Drop," *New York Times*, February 10, 1991, sec. 12, p. 1.

33 Bob Narus, "Battle for the Bucks," *New Jersey Reporter* (February 1986): 8–11. See also Alice Chasan Edelman, "The New York State of Mind," *New Jersey Reporter*, (February 1986): 12–16.

34 Edelman, 12–16.

35 See Ingrid W. Reed, "The Life and Death of UDAG: An Assessment Based on Eight Projects in Five New Jersey Cities," *Publius* 19 (Summer 1989): 93–109.

36 Between 1985 and 1989, state arts funding quadrupled, from about $5 million to $21 million. By 1992, the Florio administration, facing budget crises, had reduced state aid to about $10 million.

37 For the "sports wars," see Warren Craig, "Playing for Keeps," *New Jersey Reporter* (February 1986): 17–22ff. Although still unsuccessful in attracting a baseball franchise (negotiations with the New York Yankees came close but failed when New York City agreed to renovate Yankee Stadium after the football Giants left the Bronx facility), if it does, the state will have the advantage of a provision of the 1986 federal tax reform act, which makes New Jersey the only government in the nation still permitted to issue tax exempt bonds to finance a stadium.

38 *City of Philadelphia v. New Jersey*, 437 U.S. 617 (1978).

39 Gordon Bishop, "New York letting dirty water flow into North Jersey," *Newark Star–Ledger*, March 18, 1990, p. 19.

40 Guy T. Baehr, "Five year plan looks to boost tri–state region," *Newark Star–Ledger*, March 29, 1990, p. 26.

41 Jack L. Walker, "The Diffusion of Innovations among the American States," *American Political Science Review* 63 (1969): 883, 891.

42 Virginia Gray, "Innovation in the States: A Diffusion Study," *American Political Science Review* 67 (December 1973): 1184; James M. Lutz, "Regional Leadership Patterns in the Diffusion of Public Policies," *American Political Quarterly* 15 (July 1987): 391–95.

43 Kean, *Politics of Inclusion*, 89.

44 Ibid., 89, 209, 222; Alan M. Cartter, "The Shaping of the Compact for Education," in *Cooperation and Conflict*, ed. Elazar et al., 400.

45 John Kincaid, "The American Governors in International Affairs," *Publius* 14 (Fall 1984): 101.

46 Kean's trips also eventually came under press scrutiny. See, e.g., Chris Mondics, "Kean's trips: high cost, low return," *Bergen Record*, July 24, 1988, sec. A, p. 1.

47 Comparative data from Massachusetts Institute for Social and Economic Research, University of Massachusetts–Amherst; reported in Penelope Lemov, "Europe and the States," *Governing* (January 1991): 50. Of New Jersey's $8.6 billion in worldwide exports, 33% went to the European Community.

48 Kean, *Politics of Inclusion*, 125–26; Kincaid, 96.

49 Kean, *Politics of Inclusion*, 198–203.

50 Bebout and Grele, 101.

CHAPTER 14

1 Princeton University, School of Public and International Affairs, *Report on a Survey of Administration and Expenditures of the State Government of New Jersey* (Princeton, N. J.: December 1932), 11. This survey was commissioned by Governor A. Harry Moore.

2 Ibid., 10, 11.

3 New Jersey Office of Legislative Services, "Questions and Answers: A Legislator's Guide to the State Budget," (Trenton, March 1989), 12.

4 Ibid., 2.

5 Robert M. Gordon, "Governing New Jersey: The Toughest Management and Policy—Making Jobs in Trenton" (New Brunswick: The Partnership for New Jersey, 1989), 283–85; State of New Jersey Budget, General Information, Fiscal

Year 1989–90; New Jersey State and Local Expenditure and Revenue Policy Commission, "State and Local Finances 1974 to 1984: A Background Report," (Trenton: April 1987).

6 New Jersey Committee, Regional Plan Association, "New Jersey Tax Facts," (Newark: Regional Plan Association, December 1983), 7.

7 Estimate by Treasurer Douglas Berman cited in Vincent R. Zarate, "Florio orders spending cut $200 million for '92," *Newark Star–Ledger*, September 10, 1990, 1.

8 Data from a study by David Kehler, executive director of the Public Affairs Research Institute (successor to the New Jersey Taxpayers Association); reported in Vincent R. Zarate, "Jersey's Spending Up Sharply," *Newark Star–Ledger*, May 15, 1990, 26.

9 Data from a report by the Public Affairs Research Institute, as reported in John Froonjian, "Report: Property tax bad for New Jersey," *Atlantic City Press*, April 29, 1991.

10 Alvin S. Felzenberg, "The Impact of Gubernatorial Style on Policy Outcomes" (Ph.D diss., Princeton University, 1978), 67.

11 Paul J. Strayer, *New Jersey's Financial Problem* (New Brunswick: Rutgers University Press, 1960), 6.

12 Morris Beck, "Government Finance in New Jersey," *The Economy of New Jersey: A Report Prepared for the Department of Conservation and Economic Development of the State of New Jersey*, ed. Solomon J. Flink et al (New Brunswick, N.J.: Rutgers University Press, 1958), 560.

13 Ibid., 3, 17. For the position of the tax commission, see, e.g., State of New Jersey, 6th Report of the Commission on State Tax Policy, "The General Property Tax in New Jersey: A Century of Inequities," (Trenton, February, 1953).

14 Beck, 565. Beck provides a detailed comparison of New Jersey's general expenditures by function compared to all states at 566–67.

15 State of New Jersey, Commission on State Tax Policy, xxvi.

16 Clifford A. Goldman, "Tax Disparities," in Council on New Jersey Affairs, New Jersey Issues: Papers from the Council on New Jersey Affairs, Princeton, N.J.: Princeton University Urban and Regional Research Center, Woodrow Wilson School of Public and International Affairs, Program for New Jersey Affairs, March 1988.

17 Richard Lehne, "Revenue and Expenditure Policies," *Politics in New Jersey*, (New Brunswick, N.J.: Eagleton Institute of Politics, Rutgers University, 1975), ed. John Blydenburgh and Alan Rosenthal, 249.

18 Beck, 578. See also Tri–State Regional Planning Commission, "Financing Public Education: A Study of Property Taxation and Legislative Reform in New Jersey," Interim Technical Report S–887 (New York: Tri–State Planning Commission, September 1978).

19 Our summary of tax proposals from 1966 to 1976 draws on Richard Lehne, "Revenue and Expenditure Policies," *Politics in New Jersey*, rev. ed., ed. Richard

Lehne and Alan Rosenthal, (New Brunswick, N.J.: Eagleton Institute of Politics, Rutgers University, 1979), 229–247.

20 For analysis of the Hughes tax initiatives, see Felzenberg, ch. 4.

21 Felzenberg notes that lottery revenues, like the earlier moral obligation bonds, state bond issues, and the railroad tax were all "promoted as revenue devices most New Jerseyans could escape through abstinence," Ibid., 62.

22 After the tax issue ended William Cahill's gubernatorial career, Byrne's strategy was to minimize political risk, paint himself as a "passive broker who sought to fulfill his legal responsibilities," and "rely on judicial pressure" to get the income tax passed. (Ibid., 429). Although Byrne lost control of the process, and the "final product was more a legislative creation, passed under judicial pressure, than an executive one," the public saw the governor as primarily responsible for the tax. (Ibid., 451).

23 Richard F. Keevey, "Fiscal Resources and Public Programs," *The Outlook on New Jersey*, ed. Silvio R. Laccetti, (Union City, N.J: William S. Wise, 1979), 158.

24 Casino legalization passed on its second try, after a referendum that would have permitted casinos anywhere in the state failed.

25 Known as the "Ford bill" for its sponsor, Democratic Assemblywoman Marlene Lynch Ford of Ocean County, it was intended to help Ford win a tough reelection battle in 1985. She lost narrowly anyway.

26 The account of SLERP's recommendations that follows draws on Susan Lederman, ed., "The SLERP Reforms and Their Impact on New Jersey Fiscal Policy," (Princeton, N.J.: Program for New Jersey Affairs, Woodrow Wilson School of Public and International Affairs, Princeton University, September 1989); Susan Lederman and Clifford Goldman, "Replenishing the Fiscal Well: Who Will Pay in the 21st Century," *New Jersey Reporter* (September 1989): 28–30; Warren Craig, "The Tax Commission: Progress or Procrastination?" *New Jersey Reporter* (June 1986): 8ff., and the several commission reports.

27 Henry J. Coleman, "State Revenues and Expenditures in the 1990s," in *Meeting the Challenges of the 1990s: Proceedings from the Eighth Annual State Data Center Conference* (Trenton: New Jersey Department of Labor, Division of Planning and Research, October 19, 1987), 33–39. Coleman was executive director of the SLERP Commission.

28 See, e.g., "Tax shock looming," *Trenton Times*, January 5, 1991, sec. A, p. 1.

29 John R. Baldwin, "Administrative Problems," in Council on New Jersey Affairs, 39.

30 Goldman, "Tax Disparities," in Council on New Jersey Affairs, 42.

31 Robert Ebel, "The New Jersey Property Tax: Searching for Fiscal Balance," in Council on New Jersey Affairs, 31, Joseph F. Sullivan, "In Newark, Downtown Glitter Battles Neighborhood Gloom," *New York Times*, August 13, 1991, sec. A, p. 1.

32 Lederman, "SLERP Reforms," 64–65.

33 John Baldwin, quoted in Ibid., 64.

34 New Jersey SLERP Commission, "Revenue Capacity and Fiscal Effort: A Background Report," (Trenton, January 1987), 30. Data are for 1985. These measures are based on property tax revenue capacity and effort, and average municipal incomes. This study also examined tax capacity and effort for the 567 individual municipalities, using the same measures. It found that 14.6 percent exhibited high capacity and low effort, 39.9 percent had low capacity and low effort, 45.3 percent had low capacity and high effort, and only 1 (.2 percent) had high capacity and high effort.

35 New Jersey SLERP Commission, "State and Local Finances 1974 to 1984: A Background Report," (Trenton: April 1987), 11; Peter Kerr, "As Realty Taxes Go Up, Up, Dreams Die in New Jersey," *New York Times*, February 1, 1991, sec. B, p. 1.

36 *Star–Ledger*/Eagleton Poll, July 1990.

37 Dan Weissman, "Florio rethinks policy after election rebuke," *Newark Star–Ledger*, November 8, 1990, p. 1.

38 *The (Bergen) Record* Poll, April 6–10, 1991; as reported in David Blomquist, "Poll says GOP has new fans," *The News Tribune*, April 21, 1991, sec. A, p. 1.

39 *The Record* Poll, reported in David Blomquist, "Most don't understand tax plan," *Sunday Record*, October 7, 1990, p. 1.

40 Ibid., *Star–Ledger*/Eagleton Poll, July 1990.

41 This was a lesson Byrne had learned from the failure of the Cahill proposal in 1972, which involved 55 different bills and 3 constitutional amendments. "The very complexity of Cahill's proposals made them difficult to explain in public." Felzenberg, 333).

42 Lederman, *SLERP Reforms*, 43.

43 Citizens for Tax Justice 1991 Study, as reported in Larry McDonnell, "Split Decision on Taxes," *Asbury Park Press*, April 24, 1991, sec. A, p. 1.

CHAPTER 15

1 Federal Writers' Project, Works Progress Administration, *New Jersey: A Guide to its Past and Present* (New York: Hastings House, 1939), 139; Floyd W. Parsons, *New Jersey: Life, Industries and Resources of a Great State* (Newark: New Jersey Chamber of Commerce, 1928), 93.

2 Leonard B. Irwin, *New Jersey: The State and its Government* (New York: Oxford Book Co., 1942), 57. Like the funds for most state programs, education aid came from a complex set of dedicated funds distributed according to different criteria—including state taxes on railroad and canal property; a small portion of the income from state riparian rights; and a state property tax collected by municipalities and counties, a minuscule portion of which was not returned to the municipalities

collecting it but retained for an "equalizing fund" for districts' "special needs."

3 Stephen K. Bailey, *Schoolmen and Politics* (Syracuse, N.Y.: Syracuse University Press, 1972); Michael D. Usdan et al., *Education and State Politics* (New York: Teachers College Press, 1969); James Conant, *Shaping Education Policy* (New York: McGraw–Hill, 1964), 27–38.

4 Robert W. Noonan, "A Study of Factors Influencing the Establishment of the Minimum Basic Skills Tests in New Jersey," (Ed.D diss., Rutgers University, May 1984).

5 Kenneth David Pack, "The New Jersey Department of Education: The Marburger Years" (Ph.D. diss., Rutgers University, 1974), 196.

6 Richard Leone, "The Politics of Gubernatorial Leadership: Tax and Education Reform in New Jersey" (Ph.D. diss., Princeton University, 1969), ch. 3.

7 Rutgers, a colonial college founded by the Dutch Reformed church, became the "state university" when it beat out Princeton for designation as New Jersey's Morrill Act land–grant institution. However, it retained affiliation with the Dutch Reformed church and an independent, self–perpetuating board of trustees and received only a small portion of its budget from the state. It was not officially designated "the state university" until 1945, and the state actually assumed control of the university's governing body in 1956.

8 Donald E. Langlois, "The Politics of Education in New Jersey: A Study of Legislator Behavior and Four Major Interest Groups," (Ph.D. diss., Columbia University, 1972), 8.

9 Paul Feldman, "Those Who Can, Lobby" (*New Jersey Reporter*, April 1983): 25.

10 For an analysis of changes in the NJEA and other educational interest groups, see Carole Webb Holden, "The Effects of Environmental Change on New Jersey's Educational Interest Groups," (Ph.D. diss., Rutgers University, October 1980).

11 Ibid., 221–22; Albert Burstein, "Education Policy," in *The Political State of New Jersey*, ed. Gerald M. Pomper, (New Brunswick, N.J.: Rutgers University Press, 199–213.

12 The bill eventually passed provided substantially less total money and less adjustment for AFDC students than a commission chaired by Bateman had recommended. It was also accompanied by a controversial law providing aid for parochial schools for the first time. See Langlois, 91–119; Pack, 124.

13 The 19–19 vote was on ideological rather than partisan lines, with almost equal numbers of Democrats and Republicans on each side. Pack, 185.

14 The case is *Chappell v. Commissioner of Education of New Jersey*, NJ 343 A 22d 811 (1975).

15 The others are Connecticut, New Hampshire, and New York.

16 John Froonjian, "Report: Property tax bad for New Jersey," *Atlantic City Press*, April 29, 1991, p. 1.

17 118 N.J. 223.

18 *Robinson v. Cahill* I, 303 A.2d 273 (N.J. 1973).

19 For a discussion of these different approaches to school funding, see Kenneth K. Wong, "State Reform in Education Finance: Territorial and Social Strategies," *Publius* 21 (Summer 1991): 125–42.

20 Richard Lehne, The *Quest for Justice* (New York: Longman, 1978), 165–73.

21 The effects of such legislative discretion are described in Theodore Lowi's classic work, The *End of Liberalism* (New York: Norton, 1964).

22 Eagleton Institute of Politics, Rutgers University, "The Goal Setting Process under T&E in New Jersey." (New Brunswick, N.J.: Eagleton Institute, Rutgers University, 1978).

23 For a detailed analysis, see Raymond L. Schwartz, "The Relationship Between the NJEA Endorsement of State Legislative Candidates and Their Key Votes, 1973–1985" (Ed.D. diss., Rutgers University Graduate School of Education, January 1989). Schwartz assigned all bills to the categories (not mutually exclusive) of "innovative" or "maintaining" educational policy measures and "professional" measures such as pension or bargaining rights bills. Approximately half of all NJEA–sponsored bills were "professional."

24 The court decision rejecting the expansion of bargaining rights to include, e.g., class size and involuntary transfer, was *Ridgefield Park Education Association v. Ridgefield Park Board of Education*, 78 N.J. 144, 393 A.2d 278 (1978).

25 He used this expression as the title of chapter 8 of his informal autobiography, Thomas H. Kean, The *Politics of Inclusion* (New York: Free Press, 1988).

26 John Kingdon, *Agendas, Alternatives and Public Policies* (Boston: Little, Brown, 1984).

27 Peter Marks, "The Blackboard Jungle," *New Jersey Reporter* (February 1984): 22–26.

28 Pack, 157.

29 Stephen Barr, "Turning Toward Success," *New Jersey Reporter* (July–August 1988): 20–26, quote at 20.

30 The full state takeover of the Jersey City system appeared to be a historical first for both state and nation. Takeover laws in Kentucky and South Carolina, dating from 1984, had not been used in either state to that point. In New Jersey, the only precedent was a more modest state intervention in Trenton in 1982, which took three years to accomplish. See Robert J. Braun, "State poised to move in on Jersey City schools," *Newark Star–Ledger*, October 1, 1989, p. 14.

31 See the data in Annelise Wamsley, "The New Route to Teaching," *New Jersey Reporter* (March 1987): 15ff; Robert J. Braun, "'Alternate route' to teaching gets good marks," *Newark Star–Ledger*, June 30, 1990, p. 6; Patricia Cappon, "Rookie Teachers," *Newark Star–Ledger*, August 29, 1990, p. 1. Because of NJEA objections and the costs of required courses and mentoring for alternate route teachers, only a third of the state's districts were using the alternate route when Kean

left office in 1990.

32 Kean, 232.

33 Thomas B. Corcoran and Herbert T. Green, "Educating New Jersey," New Jersey *Reporter* (October 1989): 32–37.

After leaving office, Kean continued his crusade for outcomes testing when he and his education commissioner, Saul Cooperman, launched Educate America, an advocacy group formed to push for a mandatory national achievement test for all high school seniors.

34 Jeffrey Kanige, "Showdown Over the Schools," *New Jersey Reporter* (February 1987): 24.

35 For example, the results of the state's College Basic Skills Placement Test, administered to all entering students in state colleges, showed no improvement between 1978 and 1989 despite the much higher pass rates on the HSPT. There was also evidence of very high absentee rates on test days in urban schools where scores were apparently "improving," as compared with little change in those schools where attendance was high. A year after Kean left office, SAT scores once again were on the decline. Corcoran and Green, 34; Robert J. Braun, "'No–shows' skew rise in scores on skills test," *Newark Star–Ledger*, December 10, 1989, p. 1.

36 From the plaintiff's brief in *Abbott v. Burke*, quoted in Kathy Barrett Carter, "Legal brief brands school funding formula racially, economically biased," *Newark Star–Ledger*, June 25, 1989, p. 34.

37 Jean Dykstra, "A New Path for School Funding," *New Jersey Reporter* (June–July 1990): 10.

38 Lefelt decision, quoted in Matthew Reilly, "School funding formula ruled inequitable and unworkable," *Newark Star–Ledger*, August 26, 1988, p. 1; Robert J. Braun, "Governor leaning toward equalized school spending," *Newark Star–Ledger*, March 18, 1990. p. 1.

39 Margaret E. Goertz, "Financing New Jersey's Public Schools," paper for the Eagleton Institute of Politics Workshop on School Finance, October 17, 1989, 8–9.

40 Joan Verdon, "Commissioner backs school finance law," *Bergen Record*, February 24, 1989, sec. A, p. 1.

41 After 1976, the legislature fully funded the aid formula only in fiscal year 1981 and fiscal year 1985 (both gubernatorial election years).

42 Sherry Conohan and Rick Linsk, "School funding called possible without tax rise," *Asbury Park Press*, September 28, 1989, p. 1.

43 Robert J. Braun, "Governor aims at policy shift on education," *Newark Star–Ledger*, March 4, 1990, p. 1.

44 The rate at which budgets pass is closely connected to the state's economic health and the status of tax debates. In 1976, while the legislature was still grappling with

the new funding formula, only 44 percent of all school budgets passed. Similarly, only 52 percent passed in 1990 and 56 percent in 1991 while the state was enmeshed in the QEA debate. In contrast, after the income tax actually brought property taxes down in 1977, 80 percent passed. In the boom year of 1985—one of the three since the advent of Chapter 212 that Trenton fully funded the school aid formula—a record 87 percent of budgets passed. See Scott Bittle, "Educators brace as voters put budgets to the test," *Atlantic City Press*, April 30, 1991, p. 1.

45 Robert J. Braun, "School chiefs say funding law threatens the best," *Newark Star–Ledger*, October 26, 1990, p. 1.

46 New Jersey teachers' salaries doubled in the 1980s, averaging $38,411 in 1991, fifth highest in the country. In 1989–90, New Jersey's per pupil expenditure of $8,439 was the nation's highest, according to the National Education Association. Wayne King, "Anger Increases at Teachers' Raises in New Jersey," *New York Times*, May 27, 1991, p. 21.

47 Patrick Jenkins, "NJEA seeks cost switch," *Newark Star–Ledger*, November 9, 1990, p. 1.

48 Robert Hanley, "School Officials Vent Anger on New Jersey Financing Law," *New York Times*, November 1, 1990, sec. B, p. 1; Joseph Dee, "Trenton officials fret about strings tied to school aid," *Trenton Times*, October 9, 1990, p. 1.

49 Kathy Barrett Carter, "Amorphous school funding decision shouldn't be used as a divisive ploy," *Newark Star–Ledger*, August 26, 1990, sec. 3, p. 3.

50 Assemblyman Daniel Jacobson, D–Monmouth, quoted in Bittle, p.1.

51 Associated Press, "Breaking racial barriers: Public advocate wants to regionalize schools," *Trenton Times*, August 12, 1991, section A, p. 4. Caraballo's comments came in the context of a long–running court case to compel regionalization of the Englewood, Englewood Cliffs and Tenafly school districts in Bergen County for reasons of racial balance. When an appellate panel suggested in May 1992 that regionalization be considered as a solution, Republican legislators introduced a constitutional amendment preventing any branch of state government from forcing school systems to join regional districts.

52 When the Cahill administration gave tax breaks to municipalities forming regional school districts for example, 49 new regional high school districts were formed in addition to the old districts that retained their elementary schools. There are only 17 consolidated K through 12 districts in the state. Vera Titunik, "The great school idea nobody wants to hear," *Bergen Record*, July 21, 1991, sec. A, p. 1.

53 John B. Judis, "A Taxing Governor," *New Republic*, October 15, 1990, 26.

54 Peter Kerr, "Democrats Urge Big Shift In Florio Plan," *New York Times*, January 8, 1991, sec. B, p. 1; Matthew Reilly, "Dems ask 'skimming' school aid," *Newark Star–Ledger*, January 8, 1991, p. 1.

55 The NJEA retaliated a few months later when it announced its 1991 legislative endorsements of 46 Republicans and only 3 Democrats—a reverse of its customary partisan ratio (it took a neutral stance in the remaining 71 races).

56 For details of the revised legislation, see Matthew Reilly, "Assembly votes QEA revise providing property tax relief," *Newark Star–Ledger*, March 12, 1991, p. 1.

57 Joseph N. DiStefano, "Insurance to devour school aid; Little change seen in Camden," *Philadelphia Inquirer*, March 26, 1991, sec. B, p. 1. Camden's 1991–92 school budget included $132.7 million in state aid and $17.9 million raised through the local property tax.

58 Lisa R. Kruse, "Suburbs gain in new act," *Asbury Park Press*, March 17, 1991, A1. See also Scott Bittle, "Everything you want to know about the QEA—so far," *Atlantic City Press*, March 24, 1991, p. 1; Audrey Kelly and Raymond Fazzi, "Schools declare QEA plan DOA," *Home News*, March 24, 1991, sec. A, p. 1.

59 From a brief submitted to the New Jersey Supreme court June 12, 1991, quoted in the *Newark Star–Ledger*, June 13, 1991, p. 1.

CHAPTER 16

1 Quoted in Richard J. Sullivan, "Environmental Policy," in *The Political State of New Jersey*, ed. Gerald M. Pomper (New Brunswick, N.J.: Rutgers University Press, 1987), 226.

2 Bergen County Department of Planning and Economic Development, "Bergen County's Cross–Acceptance Report to the State Planning Commission," Executive Summary, September 1989, 2.

3 Sullivan, "Environmental Policy," in Pomper, 215.

4 Bruce Ransom, "Environmental Issues and Public Policy," in *New Jersey: Profiles in Public Policy*, ed. Silvio R. Laccetti, (Palisades Park, N.J.: Commonwealth Books, 1990), 322–23.

5 Thomas H. Kean, The *Politics of Inclusion*, (New York: Free Press, 1988), 104.

6 The ruling (in T&E Industries v. Safety Light, on March 27, 1991) applied to Safety Light Corporation, which dumped radium–tainted waste at an Orange industrial site from 1917 to 1926, and sold the site in 1943. When state and federal environmental officials discovered the contamination in 1979, the site had already been resold four times. Yet the court unanimously found Safety Light (formerly the U.S. Radium Corporation) liable. See Kathy Barrett Carter, "Sellers of toxic land ruled 'forever' liable," *Newark Star–Ledger*, March 28, 1991, p. 1.

7 Robert Hanley, "Toxic Waste Rank Wanted by New Jersey," *New York Times*, December 22, 1982, sec. B, p. 1.

8 Kean, 103.

9 Robert Hanley, "Superfund Sites Lose New Jersey Priority," *New York Times*, November 7, 1989, sec. B, p. 1.

10 Robert Cohen, "Congressional study finds New Jersey toxic clean–up effort far outpaces U.S." *Newark Star–Ledger*, November 8, 1989, p. 21.

11 Karen West, ed., *New Jersey: Spotlight on Government*, 5th ed. (New Brunswick, N.J.: Rutgers University Press, 1985).

12 Tom Johnson, "Fuel to the fire," *Newark Star–Ledger*, May 15, 1989, p. 1.

13 Robert Cohen, "Midwest lawmakers act to block New Jersey trash," *Newark Star–Ledger*, September 15, 1990, p. 5; J. Scott Orr, "Jersey rips senate vote to let states bar garbage," *Newark Star–Ledger*, September 19, 1990, p. 1.

14 Robert Cohen, "Congress kills trash ban in a victory for Jersey," *Newark Star–Ledger*, October 13, 1990, p. 1

15 For an overview, see Barry Rabe, "Environmental Regulation in New Jersey: Innovations and Limitations," *Publius* 21 (Winter 1991): 83–103.

16 The logistics and politics of the turnpike's construction are entertainingly described in Angus Kress Gillespie and Michael Aaron Rockland, *Looking for America on the New Jersey Turnpike* (New Brunswick, N.J.: Rutgers University Press, 1989), chs. 2 and 3. A more sober account is Arthur Warren Meixner, "The New Jersey Turnpike Authority: A Study of a Public Authority as a Technique of Government," unpublished Ph.D dissertation, New York University, 1978).

17 Harf and Zupan, "Transportation Issues," 291.

18 Ibid.

19 Ransom, 318.

20 Data from a study by the Center for Public Interest Polling, Eagleton Institute of Politics, Rutgers University, "The Crowded Road: A Survey of New Jerseyans' Opinions about Transportation, Growth and Development," (New Brunswick, N.J.: Eagleton Institute of Politics, March 1, 1988). Even in the least developed southern portion of the state, about a third of residents gave these kinds of responses.

21 Robert Schwaneberg and Richard S. Remington, "Developers 'enlisted' in the war against traffic," *Newark Star–Ledger*, June 27, 1989, p. 1.

22 Almost 60 percent of New Jerseyans report they work in suburbs or rural areas. One long–sought improvement may finally be realized in the late 1990s—the "Kearny Connection," linking the major east–west rail lines that presently terminate in Hoboken with the north–south lines that go directly to midtown Manhattan.

23 Bergen County Department of Planning and Economic Development.

24 Rick Cohen and David S. Surrey, "Development Patterns in New Jersey: Inclusion for Some and Exclusion for Others," in Laccetti, ed., 255–57.

25 Both quoted in Steve Chambers, "'Neon schlock' vs. economic prosperity," *Asbury Park Press*, July 10, 1991, sec A, p. 1.

26 To qualify for farmland assessment, a property must be no less than five acres, actively devoted to agricultural or horticultural use for at least two years, and have produced at least $500 worth of farm products for sale annually. Approximately half of this land is owned by persons or firms who do not farm for a living.

27 Susan V. Lenz, "Keeping the Garden State Green," (Princeton, N.J.: Woodrow Wilson School, Princeton Urban and Regional Planning Center, Program for New Jersey Affairs, October 1985); John Kolesar, "Battle for the Boondocks," *New Jersey Reporter* (May–June 1992): 25–31.

28 Sullivan, 223.

29 West, 275.

30 Clifford Goldman, "The Hackensack Meadowlands: the politics of regional planning and development in the metropolis" (Ph.D diss., Princeton University, 1975).

31 Jon Kimmel, "The Regional Approach," *New Jersey Reporter* (September 1984): 32. South Jersey legislators thought their votes were a trade for a riparian rights referendum they wanted, but Hughes was later able to force repeal of the referendum.

32 Goldman, 10.

33 Ibid., 186. For a review of recent local grievances, see the New Jersey Senate Hackensack Meadowlands Development Task Force, Public Hearing, Rutherford Borough Hall, March 30, 1988 (Trenton: Office of Legislative Services, 1988).

34 Rick Cohen and Surrey, 274; Rick Linsk, "Builders fight bill to broaden coast oversight," *Asbury Park Press*, May 13, 1991, sec. A p. 1. New Jerseyans quip that archeologists hundreds of years from now will try to determine the religious significance of the number "24" in twentieth century New Jersey.

35 Kean did win passage of the Freshwater Wetlands Protection Act, restricting uses of 300,000 acres (6 percent of the state's total land area) of inland wetlands in 15 of the 21 counties. The state DEP replaced the U.S. Army Corps of Engineers as the areas' permitting agency.

36 Tom Johnson, "Kean dealt setback on Shore curbs," *Newark Star–Ledger*, April 8, 1989, p. 1.

37 Michael Booth and Thomas Fitzgerald, "Developers Cheer," *Trenton Times*, June 21, 1990, p. 1.

38 Thomas Fitzgerald, "New Jersey court tosses out Shore building limits," *Trenton Times*, December 22, 1990, sec. A, p 1.

39 John A. McPhee, *The Pine Barrens* (New York: Farrar, Straus and Giroux, 1968).

40 Russell Wilkinson, "Bureaucracy Makes Plans to Save the Pinelands," *New Jersey Magazine*, September 1976, 12.

41 Jeffrey Kanige, "Brendan Byrne on Brendan Byrne," (*New Jersey Reporter* June 1988): 18.

42 West, 269.

43 Kimmel, 31–6; Michael Catania, "The Pinelands Plan At Ten," *New Jersey Reporter* (January–February, 1991): 18–21.

44 Keith Wheelock, "New Jersey Growth Management," (Skillman, N.J.: Managing Growth in New Jersey, Inc., 1989).

45 The desire for balance was demonstrated graphically in a 1992 poll of state residents, in which 88 percent of respondents affirmed that continued growth and development were very or somewhat important for New Jersey, while at the same time, 84 percent also said that growth controls should be somewhat or very strict. See Iver Peterson, "Poll Says Home Rule Could Bend to Ward Off Sprawling Growth," *New York Times*, March 18, 1992, sec. B, p. 5; Tom Johnson, "Survey finds most Jerseyans favor growth with careful management," *Newark Star–Ledger*, March 18, 1992, p. 20.

46 *South Burlington County NAACP v. Township of Mount Laurel*, 67 N.J. 151, 336 A.2d 713 (1975).

47 Patricia F. Fingerhood, "Viewpoint: The Courts—Mount Laurel Three Years Later," *New Jersey Magazine*, March 1978, 23–24; Alan Mallach, "Blueprint for Delay," *New Jersey Reporter* (October 1985): 21–27.

48 *South Burlington NAACP v. Township of Mount Laurel*, 92 N.J. 158, 456 A.2d 390 (1983). The decision echoed a dissent by Justice Frederick Hall in the 1962 case of *Vickers v. Township of Gloucester*, which upheld the town's right to zone out trailer parks: "The general welfare transcends the artificial limits of political subdivisions and cannot embrace merely local desires." Quoted in Goldman, 66.

49 Josh Goldfein, "The Legacy of Mount Laurel," *New Jersey Reporter* (November 1988): 20; Jerome Rose, "Caving in to the Court," *New Jersey Reporter* (October 1985): 28.

50 Mallach, 25.

51 Goldfein, 20; *Hills Development Co. v. Township of Bernards*, 510 A.2d 621 (N.J. 1986).

52 Mary Jo Patterson, "Affordable housing taking hold," *Newark Star–Ledger*, January 28, 1990, p. 1.

53 Middletown was one of 23 municipalities affected by the ruling. See Alan S. Oser, "Reshaping New Jersey Housing Patterns," *New York Times*, April 2, 1989, sec. 12, p. 9; Richard S. Remington, "Mount Laurel quota cap overturned; 23 municipalities could face hike," *Newark Star–Ledger*, November 20, 1990, p. 1.

54 Richard S. Remington, "Court clears transfers of Mt. Laurel housing," *Newark Star–Ledger*, March 27, 1991, p. 1.

55 Stuart McKeel, "Regional housing deals popular," *Morristown Daily Record*, August 27, 1990, p. 1.

56 Goldfein, 18, 17.

57 Rick Cohen and Surrey, "Development Patterns in New Jersey: Inclusion for Some

and Exclusion for Others," 275–76; Goldfein, 18–19.

58 Dan Jones, "The sounds of silence," *New Jersey Reporter* (May 1983): 16–21, quote at 16.

59 Kean's counsel (and second term attorney general) Cary Edwards, who did most of the negotiating, had led the fight in the assembly to defeat the 1972 affordable–housing bill supported by his fellow Republican governor.

60 In 1987, Governor Kean vetoed a bill giving the legislature the right to review, revise, or reject the state plan. A similar bill introduced in 1992 failed to receive a majority.

61 New Jersey State Planning Commission, "Communities of Place: the New Jersey preliminary state development plan," (Trenton: State Planning Commission, 1988–89).

62 See Chris Conway, "Roadblocks in planning development," *Philadelphia Inquirer*, July 17, 1989, sec. B, p. 1.

63 The impact assessment's project manager found that "the economic impact on the state will be neutral and that environmentally frail and agricultural lands will be saved." Norman J. Glickman, "State Plan Will Benefit Most Jersey Residents," *CUPReport*, New Brunswick, N.J.: Rutgers University Center for Urban Policy Research, Spring 1992), 3. See also Center for Urban Policy Research, "Impact Assessment of the New Jersey Interim State Development and Redevelopment Plan, Executive Summary," February 28, 1992.

64 Dan Weissman, "Florio endorses plan for directing state's development toward cities," *Newark Star–Ledger*, March 27, 1991, p. 23. See also Clyde Lieb, "N.J. shifts plan for growth," *Trenton Times*, July 13, 1991, sec. A, p. 1.

65 Catania, 21.

CHAPTER 17

1 Joel Garreau, *Edge City: Life on the New Frontier* (New York: Doubleday, 1991), 23.

2 William Schneider, "The Suburban Century Begins," *The Atlantic*, July 1992, 33.

3 Garreau, Edge City.

4 Peter G. Rowe, *Making a Middle Landscape* (Cambridge, Mass.: MIT Press, 1991).

5 Schneider, 33.

6 Ibid., 38.

7 Ibid., 37.

8 Kenneth T. Jackson, *The Crabgrass Frontier* (New York: Oxford University Press, 1985).

9 Thomas H. Kean, *The Politics of Inclusion* (New York: Free Press, 1988), 115).

10 Peter Kerr, "Jersey After Kean: Problems to Persist," *New York Times*, December 15, 1988, sec. B, p. 1.

11 Jeffrey Kanige, "Brendan Byrne on Brendan Byrne," *New Jersey Reporter* (June 1988): 8ff.

12 Peter Kerr, "Read His Lips: More Taxes," *New York Times Magazine*, May 20, 1990, 56.

13 See the analysis in John B. Judis, "A Taxing Governor," *The New Republic*, October 15, 1990; Peter Kerr, "Florio Shifting Style to Let Legislators Set the Agenda," *New York Times*, March 28, 1991, sec. B, p. 1.

14 Schneider, 34.

15 John Milton Cooper, Jr., *The Warrior and the Priest* (Cambridge, Mass., Harvard University Press, 1983), 173.

Index